The Wall Between

The Wall Between

Anne Braden

WITH A NEW EPILOGUE

Foreword by Julian Bond

The University of Tennessee Press / Knoxville

The paper used in this book meets the minimum requirements of ANSI/
NISO Z39.48-1992 (R 1997) (Permanence of Paper). The binding mate-
rials have been chosen for strength and durability. Printed on recycled
paper.

Library of Congress Cataloging-in-Publication Data

Braden, Anne, 1924–
    The wall between: with a new epilogue / Anne Braden; foreword
by Julian Bond. —2nd ed.
    p.   cm.
ISBN 1-57233-060-0 (cl.: alk. paper)
ISBN 1-57233-061-9 (pbk.: alk. paper)
1. Afro-Americans—Segregation—Kentucky—Louisville.
2. Afro-Americans—Kentucky—Louisville.
3. Louisville (Ky.)—Race relations. I. Title.
F459.L89 N43 1999
305.896'073076944–dc21
                                        99-6193

For my children,
Jimmy and Anita,
and all the other white children
in the South, who today
may have the opportunity
my generation never had —
to grow up without the
blight of segregation on
their souls

Contents

Illustrations

Foreword

Julian Bond

First published in 1958, *The Wall Between* was a nonfiction finalist that year for the National Book Awards. Its republication gives it the earmarks of a classic.

In 1954, Anne and Carl Braden bought a house in an all-white neighborhood in Louisville, Kentucky, for a black couple, Andrew and Charlotte Wade. *The Wall Between* is Anne Braden's account of what this act of friendship precipitated—mob violence against the Wades, the bombing of the house, and a prison term for sedition for Carl Braden.

Anne Braden, unlike Carl, was an unlikely actor in the drama that unfolded in May 1954. Born into a middle-class family and raised in Anniston, Alabama, she acknowledges that she "might well have been on either side of the conflict."

As a young girl, she absorbed the benign paternalism of her society toward poor whites and all Blacks. In Anne's polite world, they were objects of pity—lesser beings with lesser rights than whites from her social strata.

Deeply felt religious beliefs first penetrated the barrier erected between the larger world and Anne Gambrell's world, prompting her initial reactions against the white supremacist ethic. Her family had accepted without question the privileges segregation guaranteed them. Church, school, and community reinforced racial conformity in young Anne's world, but her descriptions of her growing unease and eventual repudiation of her youthful attitudes are compelling.

She first saw racism's evil in the damage done to its primary victims, and then to its designers and defenders. Segregation had made

Blacks an invisible people, both childlike and animalistic in whites' eyes, but whites were stunted, too.

Her literal acceptance of the message of Christian love became the basis for her departure from the orthodoxy of her times.

Attending college during the war fought to make the world safe for democracy, she found herself among other doubters and skeptics, and then a chance social encounter with a young black woman taught her that "there was no race problem at all! There are only people who have not realized it yet."

Her instant realization did not immediately propel her into a lifetime of activism; it would take the trauma of 1954 to accomplish that. After graduation, career advancement and the desire to escape complicity in the horrors of the segregated deep South took her to Louisville, where she met Carl Braden.

Carl was born to social activism. His mother's devout Catholicism insisted on the brotherhood of man; his father's socialism and trade-union activism taught that brotherhood, too.

By 1954, Carl was a copyeditor at the *Louisville Courier-Journal,* one of the South's premier liberal newspapers. Anne had left work to raise their family. Together they energetically participated in a range of organizations and activities which fostered their vision of an integrated world.

Andrew and Charlotte Wade were a peripheral part of the Bradens' world, casual acquaintances until their friendship was cemented—and then nearly blown apart by the purchase of a house.

Andrew Wade was a Navy veteran of World War II, and like so many others, white and black, he made friends across the color line for the first time in the service.

Wade pursued the failed promise of the war years in the few organizations of Louisville's left wing, such as the Progressive Party, for which the Bradens also worked.

The Bradens bought the small stone house for the Wades on May 10, 1954. One week later, the Supreme Court ended segregation's legal sanction when it outlawed segregated schools in *Brown v. Board of Education.* Anne Braden mentions the court decision only in passing. Few realized in the middle-1950s that the resistant white South, anticipating the ruling years before, had prepared for it so well.

Demagogues in every southern state had loudly predicted racial

Armageddon if the Court ruled against segregation, and when it did, the architects of interposition and more aggressive resistance were ready. It was this climate which enveloped Louisville and Rone Court, where the Wades' new house stood. Anne Braden has some sympathy for the stone-throwers and bombers, the "trapped men," victims themselves of myths which had become their truths—a black presence on a white block lowers property values, Blacks are not as good as we are, we are justified in any action to protect our values.

Anne Braden has no sympathy for those who resorted to Red-baiting. Four years earlier, Senator Joseph McCarthy had embarked upon his anti-Communist crusade, and while McCarthy did not invent witch-hunting and Red-baiting, he raised it to an art. Racists had long known that integrationist efforts could be discredited by tying them to Marxism. The link helped explain as well why supposedly satisfied Blacks were insistent on an improvement of their condition.

Louisville's paranoia about Communist conspiracies may seem quaint as the Evil Empire collapses in economic ruin, or joins with us to oppose aggression in the Persian Gulf. Today's readers may find it hard to credit the fear which gripped and paralyzed otherwise rational women and men in the middle 1950s, but the fear of losing job and reputation if suspected of any association with Communism was real.

Segregationists knew then how effective the smear could be and did not hesitate to employ it with a broad brush. The taint frightened the unsophisticated; those who knew better were cowered just as easily, scared into silence and into non-participation in the struggle to build a democratic world.

Thus in Louisville's eyes, Andrew Wade was the innocent subverted by the Bradens. This poison nearly sundered the relationship between the families as it separated Carl and Anne Braden from the support they had expected from Louisville's liberals.

The liberal community caved in, as it would do time and again in community after community across the South. To call the liberals' behavior cowardly is to give it praise.

Some few whites and a few more Blacks leapt to defend the Bradens and the Wades, but most Louisvilleans accepted the formula that the victims had been responsible for the crime. It fit the South's description of the origins of racial trouble—outside agitators and Communists preying on the simple minds of unsuspecting southern Blacks.

So right was the structure of segregation in their eyes that only alien, un-American forces could oppose it.

The Wall Between is a chilling depiction of a pattern repeated over and over again across the South as brave Blacks and whites tried to breach the barrier between the races. Anne Braden's book is valuable in other ways as well. It is one of only a few first-person accounts from civil rights movement activists. Because a minority of these activists were white, it is even rarer. And because Anne Braden herself is unique, her story is rarer still.

These few first-person accounts give an insider's view of movement history in which no distance separates readers from the picket line or protest march, or, as in the Bradens' case, the two years of torture that followed their act of friendship. The partnership between the Wades and Bradens nearly does come apart; its existence at all in Louisville in 1954 is a central part of the story.

Forty-five years later, federal law passed at a great price requires a more integrated life than either couple had a right to expect then. Few today, however, find or seek the bridges between races that both the Wades and the Bradens sought and found in 1954.

The Wades and Bradens believed that an integrated world was possible to achieve, that through perseverance and organizing like-minded others, they could break down the walls of race, caste, and class. Such optimism should give encouragement to potential activists of today, dismayed as they may be by the seeming difficulty of their task. Another lesson they might learn is to set their sights on some achievable goal. The Bradens understood that what transpired on a dead-end dirt road called Rone Court in Louisville's Shively suburb could shape events in the larger world.

What's missing today isn't Wades who want a home, but Bradens who will help them fight for one. Ending racism is largely the segregated concern today of Blacks alone; Anne and Carl Braden made it clear through word and deed that integrated groups fight best for an integrated world.

The Bradens were active in the Louisville NAACP, in the Negro Labor Council, and in separate committees to end segregation in schools, hospitals, and public accommodations. Today this effort is left largely to civil rights professionals rather than committed private citizens. No wonder the Wades would find segregated housing nearly as prevalent now as it was more than four decades ago when their ordeal began. No wonder their presence in many neighborhoods still would invite a bomb and a mob.

Stronger legal sanctions against racism exist today, in part because of struggles like that waged in Louisville in 1954 and 1955. But laws alone cannot guarantee an end to privilege based on skin color; that requires the constant testing only an organized citizenry can provide. Today's civil rights movement is carried out through rallies and press statements, much like our politics, and both are mere imitations of the discourse an effective democracy requires.

Anne and Carl Braden belong to a small band of modern abolitionists willing to brave danger in pursuit of the unfinished American racial revolution. Their contributions to freedom cannot be overvalued. Committed souls like Carl and Anne Braden faced the ostracism of their own community, and were often special targets, because they dared to break ranks with the rigid conformity required to enforce the color line.

Compare the Bradens' actions with those of Carl's employer, the *Louisville Courier-Journal,* the "liberal" paper in the city. From the first, the paper blamed the trouble on the Bradens for buying the house—not on the bombers who destroyed it, on the neighbors who formed a mob, on the grand jury which indicted them on sedition charges, or on the prosecutor who sent Carl to jail. And when the court verdict was rendered, the paper announced that Carl was fired.

The Bradens' two years of tragedy began on the eve of the modern civil rights movement—one week before *Brown v. Board of Education,* a year before Emmett Till was lynched, and a year and a half before Rosa Parks refused to give up her seat on a Montgomery, Alabama, bus.

The *Brown* decision drove a wedge in the legality of the segregated system; the Till murder exposed its horrors; and the Montgomery Bus Boycott showed a way to fight it that did not lower the oppressed to the oppressor's level. Anne and Carl Braden were present at the movement's creation and remained lifetime participants in it. (Carl died in 1975.)

They became advisors to the new Student Nonviolent Coordinating Committee (SNCC) in 1960 and helped SNCC hire its first white field secretary. They heightened SNCC's appreciation for civil liberties and its hatred of political tests. Through the newspaper they edited, the Southern Conference Education Fund's *Southern Patriot,* they became interpreters of the civil rights movement to a nationwide audience. Anne today continues as an organizer of a broad-based coalition against racism and economic injustice, work she had begun when Andrew Wade asked if Carl and she would help him buy a house.

This lifetime of service is described in *The Wall Between* with honesty and humility. The notion of a low-paying career aimed at helping others fight for civil and political rights is attractive to too few of us today. This book makes such a life's work perfectly understandable. And noble. We need to know Anne Braden's story, perhaps even more in 1999 than when she wrote it in 1957.

Author's Note

This book was written in 1956 and 1957. I recently reread it for the first time in almost four decades. The issue it deals with is, unfortunately, as current as yesterday's newspaper. Some of the language, however, seems archaic.

I had expected to be jolted, as I reread it, by the use of the term "Negro" throughout. Long ago, we abandoned that term for "Black," and now "African American" somehow sounds more "right."

I had not remembered, though, the sexist nature of the terminology of the 1950s. So it was jolting also when I noted how in this story I constantly used such words as "mankind," when I meant "humankind"—and "man" and "men," when I was referring to people.

We all live and learn in struggle. And the struggles of the last forty years have most certainly changed our language, if not always the substance of our lives.

It was a temptation to change all these outdated terms for the reprinting of the book. But I decided against it. If I changed one thing, I'd have to change many and end up practically rewriting the book. It appears here just as I wrote it so long ago, with my apologies to the reader for its many shortcomings. An epilogue provides some sequel and some of the conclusions l have reached more recently.

I want to express my profound gratitude to Julian Bond, who took time from his many responsibilities, surely more important than this book, to write the foreword for the new edition. I also would like to add to the list of acknowledgments in the original preface the name of the man who gave the book its title, the superb writer and my very good friend, the late Harvey O'Connor. He was omitted from the original acknowledgments because he named the book after the text was already on the press.

I also want to thank several people who read the epilogue in draft form and gave me encouragement and some helpful suggestions: Dr. Blaine Hudson, chair, Pan African Studies Department, University of

Louisville; Dr. Arlene Avakian, associate professor of women's studies, University of Massachusetts; and these friends—writers, sharp critics, and good editors all, Ilene Carver, Carol Ferry, Catherine Fosl, and Yvonne Pappenheim. Some of their suggestions I incorporated into what I had written, some I did not. So the usual disclaimer applies: the final product is my responsibility alone.

And finally, I want to add to the names of my children, to whom the original book was dedicated, that of the child who came later, Beth, and her two children, Alice and Henry. It seems now that it will be their generation that must in the twenty-first century take up the task we of the twentieth have failed to complete—meeting the challenge Dr. W. E. B. DuBois posed almost one hundred years ago, when he said the problem of the twentieth century would be the problem of the color line.

Preface to the 1958 Edition

In Louisville, Kentucky, on Monday, August 6, 1855, mobs of men entered the sections of town occupied by German and Irish immigrants, set fire to scores of houses and, when their occupants tried to escape, opened up with gunfire and killed them. Even women with babies in their arms were shot as they fled from burning houses. The mobs were urged on by the shouting of staid housewives and their daughters, wishing that "every German, every Irishman and all their descendants were killed."

It became known as "Bloody Monday," and it developed at the incitement of the Know-Nothing Party, the "America for Americans" movement of that day. Louisville does not like to remember it now, and little is known of the people who made up those mobs. It seems reasonable to assume, however, that most of them were God-fearing, law-abiding citizens — average people, who, so far as was ordinarily visible to the observer, were civilized men and women in a civilized community. They doubtless went back to their jobs the next day, did their day's work as decent men do, and went home at night to kiss their children, putter around the house and dream pleasant dreams of a better future for themselves and their families. The men in high places who helped inspire the mob, if they were not a part of it, went back to their desks in respectable business establishments, talked with their fellow businessmen about civic improvement for their community, and — if they wrote or talked of the horrifying events of Bloody Monday at all — consoled themselves by believing and saying that the trouble had all been started by the "foreigners." Some of these men, elected to the City Council that year, went down to City Hall and salved the conscience of a community by passing a resolution assessing property damages of the riot against the surviving victims. More thoughtful people who had no part in the massacre, either active or passive, sat quietly by, deploring the fact that such a thing could happen and sadly concluding there was nothing they could do about it.

The wounds of Bloody Monday are all healed now. Descendants of the German and Irish immigrants who survived and of the others who came later are completely integrated into the life of Louisville. In a real sense, they have been the leaders of the city in more recent years and have contributed richly to making Louisville the growing, thriving community it has become. It would be hard to find even a remnant of the old prejudice left now, and any sociologist studying the development of the city would tell you that Louisville would have been a poorer place — economically, culturally, and spiritually — had it not been for the infusion of new blood and talents in the wave of German-Irish immigration in the mid-nineteenth century.

Human society, with its tremendous creative capacity, in this case resolved the conflicts and tensions of its growing pains and rose to a new level, and two groups whose interests had been in apparent conflict learned to live together and to benefit from what each had to give the other. People in Louisville would tell you that what happened on Bloody Monday could never happen again and that the decent people of this city would never again become like mad dogs and turn savagely on a group in their midst and attempt to destroy it.

And yet, a hundred years later, in the spring of 1954, some God-fearing, law-abiding men went to the home of a new resident in a Louisville suburb and hurled a rock with a threatening message through his window. In the darkness, someone fired rifle shots into his house, and a group of men burned a cross in the adjoining field; finally, someone set a charge of dynamite under the house at night and half destroyed it. Like the Bloody Monday mobsters of old, the men who did these things were urged on by decent God-fearing wives, who loved their children and were generally good to their neighbors. And they went back to their jobs the next day, and decent people in Louisville told themselves there was nothing they could do about such horrifying events and that it was the man whose house had been destroyed, he and his friends, who had been responsible for the trouble. Several months later, when one of these friends was on trial in a Louisville court, kind old men and gentle women were saying in the streets that he should be lynched.

The incident of 1954 did not reach the proportions of Bloody Monday, and by the hand of some merciful fate no one was killed. But the seeds were there. And the conflict which gave rise to this new outburst has not yet been resolved by the creative forces of our society. For the man who bought and moved into that house in a Louisville suburb was a Negro — and the neighborhood into which he had moved considered itself "all white."

The problem goes deeper than the one presented in the Irish-German immigration of the last century. Behind it is the ugly and inescapable heritage of a slave society. Superimposed on it is the barrier of color, making the differences harder to forget and the wounds harder to heal.

And yet, essentially, the core of the problem is perhaps the same. In a sense, all of history has been a story of man's efforts to learn to live with other men — resolving first his individual conflicts with other men in order to form societies for the common good, and then resolving or trying to resolve the conflicts of one society or group of men with another. Always there have been those groups which were the oppressed; always there have been those others who felt their security and way of life threatened by the group struggling for its place in the sun. Where the creative forces needed to resolve the conflict have failed, groups of human beings have turned on others — and have destroyed themselves as well as sometimes their opponents. Where the conflicts have been resolved, society has reached a new level and groups that once feared and hated each other have enriched each other's lives. Sometimes such conflicts smolder uneasily for generations, and then there comes a moment of climax when they boil to the surface and when society must finally summon up the creative capacity to resolve them or face disaster.

The Louisville incident, developing in the wake of the 1954 Supreme Court decision which declared racial segregation in the schools illegal, came at a moment when our nation was reaching this stage of climax in Negro-white relations. Simultaneously similar passions were flaring in communities all over the South and in some, as if by contagion, in the North. The forms varied, but the content was the same. The Louisville episode is by no means the most important of these incidents but like each of the others it presents in miniature the essence of them all. Because I think a detailed study of a single incident may illuminate this vast problem as no generalities can, I have written the story down.

My husband and I are protagonists in this story because we are the white people who sold the house in the Louisville suburb to the Negro and we became the recipients of much of the fury that was unleashed. But I do not tell the story to plead our side of the case. There are no heroes in this story as we see it, and no villains; there are only people, the product of their environment, urged on by forces of history that they often did not understand. My husband and I did what we did because we felt we had to do it, impelled by forces that begin far back in past generations and culminate in the conflicts of our times and of our lives. We may not have done the wise thing; we may not have done the best thing. But we had to do it. And if it had not been us, it would have been someone else. The people who opposed us, they too did what they thought they had to do — driven on by forces that grow out of the distant and half-forgotten past.

At best, there are disadvantages when a story is told by one of its principals. Some degree of bias, no matter how hard one seeks to avoid it, is probably inevitable. But there may also be advantages. Today, when so many "objective" observers are attempting to analyze the sources of racial conflict, some additional insights may be gained if the story of one of these incidents is told from the inside — by one who was deeply involved and by one who might well have been on either side of the conflict.

In this book, I make some suggestions as to how what happened in Louisville can be prevented from happening again. But I do not attempt to give any final answer to the problems of segregation and desegregation. I am convinced that there are no easy answers. But I am also convinced that the answers can be found — by many minds working together on the problem. They will not be found by simply standing in one spot and deploring the fact that man finds himself in conflict with his fellow man. They will only be found by meeting the problem head-on, by taking hold of its most terrifying aspects and weaving them into the solution. I hope that this book will contribute to an understanding of some of these more terrifying aspects. When we solve or seem to solve a problem by burying part of it, the buried part rises up to destroy the solution. But it is the essence of the creative ability of man that he can take hold of forces that appear to be destructive and turn them into something fertile and constructive. It is this kind of creative effort that is needed in the years that lie immediately ahead as we Americans face this tremendous challenge in human relations. I think the effort will be forthcoming.

I am indebted to a number of people who have read this book in manuscript and have made many helpful suggestions. If I were to thank here some of these people who live in the Deep South — implying that they approve, even in part, my views on the questions discussed in the book — it might cause them loss of jobs and even more serious difficulties. Since in the atmosphere of today I cannot name all the people whose criticism has been of assistance, it seems better not to name any. But I hope that all these people, North and South, are aware of the gratitude I feel. In addition, I want to thank Dan Gillmor, whose advice was a stimulus and guide in the original writing; John M. Pickering, who gave generously of his time and his interest in working on the first draft; and, finally, John Rackliffe, whose editorial sympathy, understanding and skill have been of incalculable value throughout the preparation of the final draft for the press. My chief debt, of course, is to the people who appear in the book — all of them without exception — and especially to Carl Braden.

A. B.

Louisville, Kentucky
February 17, 1958

1

A House to Live In

It was on a beautiful spring day in 1954 that this story begins —
one of those days in early March when the earth throbs with the
promise of new life and it is hard to believe that all is not right
with the world.

I had been to town and my husband, Carl, had stayed home to
take care of our two children, Jimmy, two and a half, and Anita,
a year old, and to wait for a friend, Andrew Wade, who had called
the day before to say he was coming by to see us.

When I came in, Carl followed me into the kitchen where I was
putting groceries away.

"Darling," he said cheerfully, "we're going to buy a house."

I stopped dead in my tracks. We had bought the house we were
living in only two years before and had paid no more than a few
hundred dollars on the $6,500 mortgage. Carl's salary as a news-
paperman was adequate for our needs, but we rarely had any
money left after living expenses were paid, and our savings were
practically nil. A new house at this point was utterly fantastic.

"Buy a house?" I exclaimed. "Oh, Carl!"

"Sure," he insisted. "Don't you want to?"

"What are you talking about, Carl?" I asked. "We can't buy
another house, and anyway I like this house." The house we lived
in was a small four-room cottage, and it had been a little crowded
since Anita's arrival over a year before. In addition to our own
children our family included Sonia, Carl's sixteen-year-old daughter by a previous marriage. But at that very moment we were in the
process of converting the unfinished attic into two more rooms.
It seemed to me this would make the house quite sufficient for our

1

family and even for the new baby we were hoping would soon be on the way.

"But this house will be in the country," Carl went on, his eyes twinkling. "Wouldn't you like that?"

I looked at him in confusion, and he evidently realized he had joked long enough. His face suddenly became serious.

"No," he explained. "Andrew Wade wants us to buy a house and transfer it to him. He'll put up the money for the down payment of course."

Immediately I understood. Andrew Wade was a Negro. We were white. Louisville was a segregated town — a town of unspoken restrictive covenants long after restrictive covenants had been declared non-enforceable by the Supreme Court of the United States.

"What's the problem?" I asked. I knew the answer. The question was almost rhetorical.

"He's been looking for a house for months," Carl said. "He's got a little girl two years old — just Jimmy's age — and his wife is pregnant. They've been renting a little apartment and they're crowded up. He's looked all over the Jim Crow sections and there just aren't any new houses for sale. They haven't built any new houses for Negroes here to amount to anything since the war. He could get an old house, but that's not what he wants. And anyway the down payment on those old houses is too much, and he doesn't have much money saved. His wife has her heart set on a new little ranch-type house out in a suburb. There are hundreds of them going up in all directions from town, you know. He's tried to buy several of them, but every time when they find out it's a Negro negotiating for the house, the deal gets squashed. He's got a real problem. He wants us to help him." Carl's face was quite serious now.

"What did you tell him?" I asked.

"I told him of course we would," Carl replied. "But he said for me to talk it over with you and he'd come back tomorrow to get a final answer. He didn't believe me when I told him I could speak for you too because I knew what your answer would be. But I did know."

I smiled. Of course Carl knew what my answer would be. We

had been married six years, and there was no doubt in the mind of either of us as to where the other stood on this question. Never had either of us refused to act when someone asked us to help in any effort to break down segregation. These were things that were understood between us. They needed no discussion.

"Of course you knew," I said. "He didn't need to come back for an answer."

That was all. The decision was made. It was as simple and natural as breathing, for any other answer would have been unthinkable. I went back to my chores — putting groceries away, preparing supper, thinking of other things — little knowing that Carl and I had just made one of the major decisions of our lives.

Only twice after that did I ever hesitate or express any doubt about our decision. Once was several weeks later when Andrew was having difficulty settling on the particular house he wanted to buy and in which suburb. I suggested that perhaps he would like to buy in our neighborhood. It was not in the country, and the houses were not ranch-type, but they were relatively new little frame houses — sparkling white with red, green, or blue roofs and shutters. There were already Negroes living in the next block and in several other blocks close by, for this was the old section of town into which Negroes had been moving for a number of years; he might perhaps have bought a house in our block himself. I did not analyze my doubts, but I had some vague feeling that the atmosphere in our block would be more congenial for him and, if any of the neighbors did object to his presence, we would be there to try to influence people to be friendly. I will never forget his dignity as he turned down my proposal.

"No," he said, "we want to get out of town where the children will have more room to play. And my wife has her heart set on a stone ranch-type house. We're not looking for an easy way out. Some of the people where we move may be hostile, but we can take a few hurts and rebuffs. In time they'll come around to being friendly."

I realized that he neither needed nor wanted my maternalistic efforts to protect him and his family. I never mentioned my proposal again.

The other time I expressed a passing doubt about the project on which we were embarking was on that same afternoon when Carl first presented it to me. Carl had gone into the living room to play with the children. I was busy with supper. Carl's job at the newspaper was a night one, and there were therefore only two evenings a week when he could be at home. Supper on his off-nights was always something of an occasion, and I usually tried to prepare something he especially liked. That night I was frying chicken, taking great care to see that each piece was cooked just right. Suddenly as I was turning the chicken in the skillet — and almost like a premonition of things to come — I felt a shadow of a cold chill pass over me. I went into the living room.

Carl and the children were sitting on the floor, all three of their heads bent over a blockhouse Carl was helping them build on the rug. The children's blond heads made a sharp contrast to Carl's. His hair — although it was already streaked with some gray, and would be much grayer before the next two years had passed — was still predominantly black.

"Carl," I said, "this is legal, isn't it?"

Carl stopped work on the blockhouse and looked up at me. He appeared baffled. He had obviously dismissed the subject of Andrew Wade and a house from his mind, as he always dismisses a matter once a decision is made; he did not realize immediately what I was talking about.

"Is what legal?" he asked.

"This buying a house for Andrew. I mean we can't get into any trouble, can we?"

"Oh, sure not," he replied confidently. "There'll be some people who won't like it of course, but it's completely legal. You've got a right to sell property to anybody you want to."

His tone was contagious. I nodded and went back to my cooking. The cold chill had passed now, and I never felt it again.

I doubt that it was a premonition. Nothing in my experience has ever indicated that I have any psychic powers. It is more likely that I was sensing some way the magnitude of the thing we were about to do.

I did not see it consciously. Neither Carl nor I nor Andrew ever considered for an instant the possibility that what did happen later might happen. Louisville's race relations, such as they were, had always been quiet. There had been no open clashes. One man wanted a house. We were helping him get it. It seemed a small thing. And yet, in that step, three powerful worlds were coming into contact. There was the world of Andrew Wade. There was the world of Carl and me. And there was the world of segregated Louisville — complacent, self-satisfied, locked in a fancied security. It was strange we did not see it; it was strange we did not sense it except for that shadowy chill that passed over me in our kitchen that night; for it is easy to see now that when these three worlds met in a decisive course of action, there were bound to be far-reaching repercussions.

2

The World of Andrew Wade

Andrew Wade, IV, is important to this story, as Carl and I are, not as an individual, but because he like us represents a whole group in our society. The problems he faced are the problems of a people. The answers he found are the answers of many.

Andrew was a young electrician in his late twenties when we first met him. That was four or five years before he came to us and asked us to buy him a house. We met when he came to do some electrical work at a union hall where we were employed as public relations workers. Subsequently, we saw him on occasion at some of the few public gatherings in Louisville where white and Negro people mingled. We sometimes saw his parents at social gatherings in the homes of some of our friends — interracial events that had always been a part of the pattern of Carl's and my lives, if not of the life of Louisville generally.

Our acquaintance with Andrew, however, was only casual on that day when he asked us to buy the house. We considered him a highly intelligent young man, apparently a militant one — we had heard him on a number of occasions express his determination to stand up for what he felt were his rights. And when he talked of the principles he believed in he had a way of choosing his words carefully, an almost formal manner of speech that from someone else might have sounded like oratory. Yet this seemed somehow perfectly natural with Andrew — probably because you sensed that this was not any artificial rhetoric, that he felt deeply every word he was saying. Other than what we could gather from these brief snatches of conversation, we knew little about him in that early spring of 1954.

But as time went on, we came to know him rather well. We

saw him under stress and strain, as he did us. Perhaps it is impossible for any white person ever to know a Negro completely. Not in our generation. History and society still maintain a chasm that separates our worlds and experiences. But in the events that followed our purchase of the house for the Wades, some of the protections that go with white skin in our society fell from Carl and me. To an extent, at least, we were thrown into the world of abuse where Negroes always live. This tended to bridge the chasm — not completely, as the story will show, but partly.

Andrew had grown up in Louisville. His father had moved here from Nashville and set up an electrical contracting business and achieved a degree of success. The Wades came to be among Louisville's more prosperous Negroes — not wealthy but comfortable — leaders in their church and in the civic organizations of the city's Negro community.

They reared their children, Andrew and a daughter who died before we knew them, as relatively prosperous Louisville Negroes rear their children. Andrew lived in a comfortable house — in Louisville's Negro section. He had the advantages of an education, college after high school — in the South's segregated schools. As a child, he had his share of a child's normal recreation — in segregated parks and segregated movies. As a teen-ager he had his share of normal social life — in the segregated world in which he lived.

Awareness of the nature of this segregated world comes early to the Negro child. Andrew tells of the time when it first came to him. It must have been one of the traumatic experiences of his life, for he has told the story often, as if it burns in his memory and must find constant release.

He and his parents and his sister were riding in their car. Andrew was only five or six years old. They passed Louisville's one big amusement park, Fontaine Ferry. An amusement park is a tempting fascination to a child — the Ferris wheel turning, the music from the merry-go-round, the laughter of those within. Andrew and his sister asked to stop and go in.

"No, not today. Maybe sometime. Not today," Andrew says his father replied.

This happened several times, whenever they rode that way.

There was always an excuse, always the promise of maybe some-day. The park took on even more fascination because it was out of reach. Finally one day, evidently realizing he could no longer make excuses, Andrew's father told him the truth.

"Son, I can't take you there," he said. Andrew recalls that his father seemed to be chagrined, almost guilty as he spoke. "That park is for white people. We're colored people. There are some places colored people are not allowed to go."

Andrew was stunned. A door had slammed in his face, the first of many slamming doors that he and every Negro child en-counters. Forbidden parks, forbidden buildings, forbidden movies, forbidden restaurants — white folks' schools — white folks' places — white world — your world — you are colored — you can't go there — you are colored — that's for white people: the endless chant steady and unceasing, down the years of a Negro child's life — watch out — be careful — watch what you say — watch where you go — a hemmed-in world — a wall around your life.

Every Negro child knows it. It becomes a part of his life, this wall. There are only three ways to cope with it. Either you build a little life for yourself within the wall, you shut away part of your-self and say this is the way it must be. Or you beat your head against it, lashing out blindly, destroying yourself but not the wall. For it can't be crashed through — not from your side alone. Or, the third alternative, you find gates through the wall. You find that it is not a vast gateless expanse. You find there are ways through it and people on the other side willing to meet you there — people who will work with you to take it down, brick by brick.

Andrew, like many of his generation, took the third course. He found there were gates in the wall.

During World War II, he went into the Navy. There, like many Southern Negroes of his day, for the first time in his life he came to know friendly white faces. White faces that looked you straight in the eye when they talked. White voices that called you man instead of "boy." White hands that clasped yours in a grip of friendship. White men who stood by your side as equals instead of standing before you as sentinels on the wall. A white world no longer the hostile unknown, a white world no longer a formidable and undifferentiated mass — a white world filled with white human beings, some of them good and some of them bad, but all of them people, individual people, people not very different from yourself.

Service in the armed forces during World War II opened up new vistas for many young men from the South, both white and Negro. It did for Andrew. It was only an illusion, of course, that the wall had fallen; and he came back to Louisville, as servicemen returned to their home communities all over the South, to find the old ways of life relatively unchanged. But somewhere the walls had crumbled in his mind, as they had in the minds of so many others; the body was still shut in, but the spirit for the first time had the room to grow. He like others would never be quite the same again.

Knowing now that there were in the white world real human beings that one could know and like, he began to look for gates in the wall in Louisville. Louisville had them, for those who looked. In the general atmosphere of liberalism that had grown up during the war and spilled over into the postwar years, there were more than before. Especially among the young people, there were places where one could meet and know members of the other group. There were the beginnings of organized campaigns to pull down the wall — agitation for peacetime Fair Employment Practices legislation, the stirrings of efforts to end segregation in the schools, in the city's parks.

Andrew gravitated toward these movements. As always, such efforts often centered in the more radical political organizations. Like a magnet, such drives seem to attract the people who are in a hurry to get things done, who do not know the meaning of moderation or planning for slow and long-range action, who often in their impatience move much faster than the great majority of people whom they vaguely hope to influence are willing to go. This was attractive to Andrew, because he was impatient. He belonged for a short time to the Progressive Party in its early stages. This was later used by his opponents to hint that he had Communist leanings. I am sure that he did not. Regardless of what influence Communists and Communist sympathizers may have had in some parts of the Progressive Party, I don't think it ever meant anything to Andrew except a place where a gate seemed to have been built in the wall. At Progressive Party headquarters, Negro and white young people met together as equals and planned to change the world. As Andrew himself later explained it:

"Outside on the street I was an outcast. When I went in there, I was a human being — a man."

The *esprit de corps* of groups like this often gives to their followers the illusion that the progress they are making is more real than it actually is. Fired by the zeal of their own mutual visions, they easily forget — because it is pleasant to forget — that outside their circle the mass of people in their community are living their lives complacently in the old circumscribed way, untouched by any change. The Progressive Party disintegrated in Louisville, as it did everywhere; many of its younger followers whom Andrew had known, growing older and more weighted down with the normal responsibilities of life, went back to their old patterns of living, the years closing over their brief flirtation with social change as finally and completely as the waters of the sea closing over a ship that has sunk. Louisville was not much changed.

The white people Andrew had known in the Navy and in the postwar Progressive Party could forget their youthful glimpses of a world without walls — if they wanted to and if their consciences let them. But Andrew, like other Negroes, could not forget. Segregation to him was a hard fact of life, a fact that made his life in ways impossible.

He too had his growing responsibilities with the years — a family to house, a child to provide for. But for him these things, rather than making it more difficult to work for social change, made it imperative that he do so. It was a fact, what he told us when he asked us to buy the house: that if he was to obtain a house that met his needs and fell within his income he had no choice but to challenge segregation. There were no houses that met his requirements within the limits the white man had set around his segregated world. He had looked not only all over Louisville but also in two suburban communities across the Ohio River in southern Indiana; here too he had found, as in Louisville and its Kentucky suburbs, that the new houses were not for sale to Negroes.

Andrew said later that when he decided to buy a house in a neighborhood where no Negroes had lived before, he had no thought of launching a crusade, that he just desperately needed a house and this was the only way to get one. I think that is probably true — at least in his conscious mind. And it is true basically, too, for almost invariably it is a fact that concrete steps toward social change are made by the person or the group with the hard material need. Even the most crusading of us have a tendency to vacillate and hesitate, to try to live as long as possible with the status quo, if there is nothing but abstract principle pushing us on.

And yet, intertwined with Andrew's material need, was a spiritual need that went back to that time at the amusement park in his childhood when the first door slammed in his face — a need to break through the wall. If he was looking for a home where his children would have a chance to stretch their young bodies in the open air and sunshine, he was also looking for a world where he and his family would have the opportunity to stretch the muscles of their spirit in a world that was free, a world that was not hemmed in. A man needs a sense of dignity just as he needs food and shelter — maybe not more than he needs these material things, but just as much. The colonial people of the world, struggling today to improve their conditions, undoubtedly are primarily urged on by the hunger and material need that have resulted from years of exploitation by the white world. But they are also prodded by a need for dignity — an end to humiliation from a white civilization that considers them second-class people.

This burning desire for dignity that gripped Andrew and grips the Negro people all over America and the colored people all over the world was perhaps best articulated by an elderly and crippled Negro woman participating in the bus protest that united the Negroes of Montgomery, Alabama, a year and a half after Andrew bought his house in Louisville. Urged by her fellow boycotters to go ahead and ride the bus because of her crippled condition, the old woman steadfastly refused, saying:

"All of my life I've been able to rest my feet, but my soul has been tired. Now my feet may be tired, but my soul is rested."

The thing that Andrew Wade had that most of the Negroes of his father's and grandfather's generations did not have was the knowledge that the wall was not gateless — that it was possible to find a way through. His experiences in the Navy and in postwar years in Louisville had indicated that to him. His wife, Charlotte, had never yet found any real openings in the wall — but Andrew knew the wall was not inviolate.

And yet, as always, it could not be stormed from his side alone. He had to find the gate and the people from the other side to meet him there. He found this in Carl and me. On the day he came to ask us to buy the house, he knew no more about us than we knew about him. But he knew we had been active in various movements to end segregation in the schools, in hospitals, in public places. He knew we had a reputation for opposing segregation. He later told us that before he came to us he approached three other white couples whom he knew better than he knew us with the same request but that each, for one reason or another, refused. So he came to us on the chance and with the hope that we meant the things we said.

3

Carl's World and Mine

The world of a white child has its walls too. Carl's did, and so did mine. Carl's were economic; mine were of the spirit.

Carl grew up in the part of Louisville known as Portland, where his mother still lives. If Louisville were a town arranged that way, Portland would be on the "wrong" side of the tracks. Its streets were and are lined with tiny white cottages, L-shaped houses, neat and clean but sparsely and cheaply furnished. The tiny yards are usually well kept and often filled with flowers, but provide little space for children to play without spilling over into the narrow streets. The people there were always poor, even in the "prosperous" 1920s when Carl grew up.

Carl's father worked in the big Louisville & Nashville Railroad shops. In 1922, when Carl was eight years old, the shopmen went on strike for higher pay. The strike lasted several months and was finally lost. Carl's father lost his job as a result of the dispute. Later he worked on the assembly line in Ford's Louisville plant. Carl's chief memory of those years is of his father coming home at night and falling into bed, too tired to eat supper. The elder Braden later left the Ford plant and worked in various other industries. He died in 1935.

If we think in terms of traumatic experiences of childhood, that 1922 railroad shopmen's strike was probably the dominant one in Carl's life. The Bradens had little money to tide them over the months without work, and during the latter part of the strike there was never much on the table but beans — beans for breakfast, beans for lunch, beans for supper. Carl remembers that he and his brothers and sister were often hungry.

I have never been hungry — hungry with the knowledge that

13

there is nowhere I can get food to satisfy my hunger. Despite the fact that probably a majority of the people in the world have at some time in their life been hungry and that some of them in some parts of the world live out their lives in an almost constant state of hunger, it is also a fact that many people like myself have never in their lives known this experience. It forms a great dividing line. I think that those of us who have not known hunger can never quite understand or imagine how it feels. Those who have once been hungry never again see the world quite as we do.

Certainly for Carl life was never the same again. The carefree years of childhood ended early for him. He became acutely aware before he was old enough to understand his own emotions that there were haves and have-nots in the world and that he was one of the have-nots. He became acutely aware of injustice in the world.

He also became aware of certain ideals. These came into his life from two directions, two channels that converged in an unusual sort of merger in his childhood. Carl's mother was a devout Catholic, and he was reared close to the church; his father attended no church, was something of an agnostic, and was an ardent socialist, a follower of Eugene V. Debs. And Debs, along with the saints of the church, became something of a hero to Carl as he was growing up. The strange thing is that Carl does not recall that he ever as a child felt any sense of conflict about what he heard from his mother and the church and what he heard from his father. He had no feeling of being pulled in two opposite directions. He could never see much difference between the human brotherhood his father told him the socialists believed in and the brotherhood of man in God as he heard it taught in the church. Both sides of the family were large, and the Braden home was often the center of family gatherings. Aunts and uncles and cousins would come and spend the evening sitting around the big table in the Braden kitchen talking about the world and life. Carl, being a thoughtful child, often sat in on the discussions, and he remembers that many times the talk turned to religion. His father, the unchurched, always refused to argue with people about their religious beliefs, maintaining these were their own business. At the end of the discussion, however, he would often comment:

"Well, it seems to me that Jesus Christ was a socialist, so what is all the argument about?"

For him, that settled the matter. It settled it for Carl too.

Life in Portland was rough in those days, and the children traveled in gangs. Carl early learned to hold his own in a fight, and for many years when he was small he was the leader of the gang on his block, which often had to defend itself against attacks from boys from surrounding neighborhoods. But he was endowed with an above-average intellect, and when he was not out with the gang he was reading books. He became, and still is, a voracious reader. Neither his mother nor his father had ever completed elementary school, but they were eager for their children to acquire an education and encouraged their intellectual interests. Carl made an outstanding record in the Catholic parochial school he attended, and the nuns who taught him began to suggest that he had an obligation to use the intellect with which he had been blessed to serve God and man by entering the priesthood. The idea appealed to Carl — to the embryonic sense of social responsibility he was already developing. It was also, in his eyes and those of his family, something of an honor for a member of a poor family like the Bradens to be picked for such a calling. At the age of thirteen, Carl entered the proseminary to begin his preparatory work for study for the priesthood.

By the time he was sixteen, he had decided against being a priest. He left the proseminary, and at the same time for all practical purposes he left the church. However, the interesting thing to me has always been that Carl, unlike so many ex-Catholics, never became anti-Catholic. I often think that the bitterness many people feel toward the Catholic Church after they leave it springs from the fact that they are still fighting with themselves over the beliefs of the church they are trying to repudiate. I don't think Carl repudiated any beliefs he ever really held. As far as I have been able to determine by his own latter-day analysis of his thinking at sixteen, Carl's break with the church had little to do with basic beliefs one way or the other. It was part of an adolescent revolt against all authority — church, school, and family. The teachings of the church which had really registered with him — the unity of all mankind and the social responsibility of each man to the whole —

continued to influence his life. When the adolescent revolt was finally over and he matured, his basic beliefs were not much different from those he had held when as a child he entered the Catholic proseminary. They were still not very different twenty years later when, after we were married, Carl — a confirmed socialist — joined the Episcopal Church with me. The theologians of both the Catholic Church and the Episcopal Church might cringe at the suggestion that their teachings amounted to the same thing and that they both had much in common with Eugene V. Debs. They might argue for a million words over the theological points of difference between them. But it is also true that "by their fruits ye shall know them," and it is a fact that Carl and I found many years later that the effect of the Catholic Church and Eugene Debs in his life and that of the Episcopal Church, in which I had been reared, in mine had been very similar.

Carl never went back to school after he left the proseminary at sixteen. But, because of his intellectual interests, it was natural that he gravitated to a semi-intellectual field of endeavor — the newspaper business, instead of the field of manual labor where his father had worked. He became a reporter first on Louisville papers and later on papers in Cincinnati. Finally he became editor of the Kentucky edition of the *Cincinnati Enquirer,* at the age of twenty-five — after having worked as their labor reporter during the big CIO organizing drive.

But despite the fact that he had seemingly solved life's economic problems for himself, Carl never got over a sense of identification with the underdog. Perhaps it was the memory of hunger when he was eight years old. Or perhaps it was the almost unconscious memory of the teaching of the church in his childhood — that "of everyone to whom much has been given, much will be required": the teaching that meshed so well with one of the cardinal principles of Eugene V. Debs as Carl had learned it from his father — that one born into the working class has a moral responsibility to remain in the working class and to rise *with* his class and not *from* it. Or maybe it was just that Carl had an idealized image of himself. But most of us do. It is another way of breaking through the walls life builds around us — the striving of every human soul to conquer its loneliness by reaching out and identifying itself with other human beings.

In any event and no matter what the reason, Carl continued to feel pangs of personal hurt whenever he encountered injustice against any human being, and a compulsion to do something about it. This drive, often derided by the more cynical, is still a vital force in the lives of many people — the people who in every society and in every age of our civilization have turned into reformers.

Carl himself attributes some of his zeal to reform the world to his early experiences as a police reporter. A reporter working around police stations and the courts sees at close hand the dregs of society. They cannot be mere numbers to him, because he is close enough to see them as human beings. He comes to like many of them as human beings and to sense what kind of people they might have been. He sees that those whose lives have been wrecked are basically much like people whose lives have been, so far as is visible to the naked eye, successful. Only a twist of fate, somewhere in the past, has made the difference. If society had been different somewhere along the line, the potential reformer believes, these people would have been different. The waste of human talent seems appalling; the sensitive person becomes oppressed with the thought of it.

"A police reporter," Carl often says, "has to become one of three things — a drunk, a cynic, or a reformer." He did his share of drinking in his early days as a police reporter. For several years in his late teens he was much more interested in proving himself tough enough to be a companion to the older and more worldly reporters in their various escapades than he was in the problems of the world and society. But the problems of those he saw get raw deals in the courts could not be pushed into the background. Despite his drinking he was sober during working hours, and he often worked long and hard to bring to light information that would help correct injustices to defendants. And finally he came to the conclusion that social injustice could not be basically corrected by action in individual cases alone. By this time he had matured enough to organize himself. He knew that alcohol was no answer; he finally quit drinking entirely; I don't think he ever even threatened to become a cynic; and he took the third possible course: he became an active social reformer.

A person with a zeal to reform can channel his energies in any of several directions. Probably because of his memory of his father's trade union activities, Carl began to channel his into the organized labor movement. When he was twenty-two, he was active in the organization of the American Newspaper Guild in Cincinnati. By the time I met him in 1947, when he was thirty-three, he had given up his job in Cincinnati to come back to Louisville to work on the *Louisville Times* for less pay. One reason he left, he always said, was that he had risen to a semi-executive position on the paper there and he "didn't like being a boss." When I met him, he was working as a labor reporter and was identifying himself ever more closely with the trade-union movement in Louisville. In his spare time after work, he was writing radio scripts and other literature for various unions — both AFL and CIO. This was the postwar period when efforts were just beginning to replace the old Wagner Act with what later became the Taft-Hartley Act. Carl saw this as an effort to make it more difficult for working men to organize, an effort to turn the clock back to the days when he and his brothers and sister almost starved while their father's strike was broken at the Louisville & Nashville shops. He spoke out against it — and against other things he thought were unjust.

People who know both Carl and me, some of those who think they are our enemies as well as those who are our friends, have often speculated as to whether it was I who got Carl into trouble or whether it was he who influenced me. It is a question that we cannot answer too certainly ourselves. Probably we influenced each other. In Carl I found, in contrast to most of the socially conscious people I had known up to that time, a person who did not hesitate to take decisive action in the face of injustice. But undoubtedly I influenced him too. He was destined to be a rebel in any event. As long as there is wrong in the world, and probably there always will be, the world will produce its rebels; they will constantly get into trouble, because in every society yet produced on this earth some forces seek to silence the rebel instead of accepting his energies as a healthy force in the body politic. Carl would very likely have got himself into some sort of trouble somewhere down the road. Without me, it might have been that this trouble would not have been in the field of segregation. The emotional push on that question came from me.

Carl grew up in segregated Louisville, but he never knew the bitterest fruits of racial prejudice. The children in the Braden home were always taught that all people were equal and to be treated with respect. All of them remember sharp rebukes from their parents at an early age if anyone chanced to make some derogatory remark about another person because of his race or religion. Partly this was the influence of their father's socialist thinking; partly Carl says it may have been the fact that his father was reared in one of the rural areas of Kentucky where there had been a certain amount of amity and mutual respect between poor white people and Negroes, and this pattern had not been completely lost in the rigidly segregated pattern of city life. To be sure, the Braden children like all white children in Louisville at that time had little opportunity to know Negroes as equals. But there was never any doubt that they were equal.

It was different with me. I too was born in Louisville — in 1924, ten years after Carl — but I grew up in Alabama and Mississippi. My first memories are of Jackson, Mississippi, where my family moved when I was a baby, and of Columbus, Mississippi, where I started to school. When I was seven, I moved to Anniston, Alabama, and it was there that I grew to adulthood. My family descended from the earliest settlers of Kentucky and considered itself one of the first families of the South. My own parents were never wealthy although they were always extremely comfortable — my father being a salesman and a rather successful one. But it is a unique characteristic of Southern society that a place in the upper social brackets is more often accorded by family background than by great wealth. My family moved with the "elite" of society; they lived in the "better" sections of town. All people were of course human beings, but I learned early — one of the things a child learns by osmosis without anyone ever putting it into words — that I was one of the "better" human beings, more privileged because my people came of a "superior" stock. The other people in the world — the less privileged, the ones who lived on the other side of the tracks in the cotton-mill town where I was reared — could not be ignored. One must attempt to feed them when they were hungry and house them when they were shelterless, insofar as one could without entailing any sacrifice, because the Bible said this must be done. But one need not be disturbed by the sight of plenty side by side with need — by tramps, for example, who came to our door begging for food during the Depression — for obviously God had intended it that way since He had made some people superior to others.

Most especially, He had made the white people superior to Negroes. It was most regrettable that the Negroes had ever been brought to this country in the first place, and slavery had certainly been wrong. The presence of the Negroes in the South today was probably our punishment for the sins of our forefathers in bringing them here as slaves — although actually the greater sin was that of the New England slave traders; in any event, the only thing to do now was to make the best of it. Negroes were really not bad creatures and certainly they had their uses, as they were available as domestic servants so white women could be freed of the burden of housework. Negro men were useful to work in the yard and in some dirty occupations that no white man, not even those inferior ones on the other side of the tracks, wanted to be bothered with. The point was to treat them kindly, not only because this was of course right according to Biblical teaching but also because if you treat a Negro with kindness he is also good to you — somewhat in the way a pet dog is good to the master who is good to him. And of course the Negro people are happy in this relationship, there is no reason to feel sorry for them — goodness, they are more carefree and happier than most white people and there's nothing they like better than having some white folks who will take care of them. Negroes in your kitchen and the kitchens of your friends you can become very fond of, although of course you would never sit down to eat with them, but you must be careful of strange Negro men on the street because it is a fact that most Negro men have an unconscious urge to hurt white women; in the more domesticated Negroes this urge is under proper control, but you never know when the savage instincts will come to the surface with Negroes you don't know. Things like that do happen sometimes — and then there is violence. One hears now and then some rumor of a lynching. Of course people we know don't do things like that; they are the work of the crude whites who live across the tracks; it is most deplorable, and the best way to avoid such events is to stay away from places where you might come in contact with Negroes except the ones who work for you or your friends and who know their place. Most of these things, it is true, were never said in words. They were impressed on the mind of the white child of the South's privileged class almost before he could talk by the actions that speak louder than words — in a world where Negroes were always in the kitchen and white people were always in the living room. Sometimes, the commandments became explicit. For example, I could not have been more than four or five years old when one day I happened to say something to my mother about a "colored lady."

"You never call colored people ladies, Anne Gambrell," I can hear her voice now. "You say colored woman and white lady — never a colored lady."

It was like the chant of "Don't go there — white folks' places — not your place" that beats constantly in the ears of the Negro child. The white child hears the chant too: Don't call colored women ladies, don't call colored men Mister — we sit in the downstairs of the theater, Negroes sit upstairs in the balcony — you drink from this fountain, Negroes use that fountain — we eat in the dining room, Negroes eat in the kitchen — colored town, our streets — white schools, colored schools — be careful of Negro men on the streets — watch out — be careful — don't go near colored town after dark — you sit in the front of the bus, they sit in the back — your place, their place — your world, their world. But the voices chanting these firm commandments of Southern society never used the word "Negro." Today in the South many of the most die-hard segregationists have learned to say, albeit with some effort, "Nigra." That was not so when I was a child. No matter what the level of a person's education, in the circles in which I grew up the word was "nigger" — although of course one always said "colored" when talking to a Negro. I was well in my teens before I knew what the correct pronunciation was. For years after my social views on segregation were well established I still had an odd feeling of speaking in an affected way when I said the word "Negro."

I suppose there was a time when I accepted the commandments of the South unquestioningly. Looking back on it, it appears to me that there was never a time when I did not question — at least subconsciously. I was a deeply religious child. I loved the services of the Episcopal Church, and these services are rich with the words of brotherhood: "O God, the Creator and Preserver of all mankind . . . O God, who hast made of one blood all nations of men for to dwell on the face of the whole earth . . ." I can hear the voice of the minister of that church now as he intoned the prayers. And as he spoke, I would feel a sense of exaltation — a sense of being momentarily a part of a world that was large enough to include all mankind, a world that I felt vaguely even then was bigger than anything I had ever known. For even then I sensed a contrast between this bigger world and the one in which I lived. The Bible said all men were brothers, and the pictures on the Sunday School walls showed Jesus surrounded by children of all colors, the black and the yellow along with the white — all sitting in a circle together. Long before I could put it into words even in my own mind, I sensed that this did not square with the relations I saw practiced and which I practiced myself in the world around me.

I knew some Negro children. But we did not sit in a circle together. We did not sit anywhere together. They were the children of women who washed our clothes or who cleaned our house. I can remember when I was only in elementary school my feelings when I went with my mother to take our clothes to the Negro wash-woman who lived on the other side of town. I can remember how I felt when I looked at her little cabin, clean but so frightfully bare, cracks in the walls with newspapers over them. I can remember wondering even then as I looked at her children how I would feel if my mother had to spend her evenings washing other people's clothes and her days in other people's kitchens. And as time went on and I grew older, I began to wonder more and more how I would feel if I knew, as the Negro boys and girls my age knew every minute of their lives, that there were places I could not go, places I could not sit, doors I could not enter. I am not sure that deep down in my heart I ever really accepted the myth that Negroes were happy with things as they are.

But the thing that it took me much longer to articulate was the other side of the coin: the fact that I was not happy with things as they were either.

The passage from the Bible that impressed me the most deeply in my early religious training was the one from Christ's story of the Last Judgment: "For I was an hungered, and ye gave me no meat, I was thirsty, and ye gave me no drink; I was a stranger, and ye took me not in; naked, and ye clothed me not . . . Verily I say unto you, Inasmuch as ye did it not to one of the least of these, ye did it not to me." I thought about that passage a great deal; it worried me almost constantly. And it would have been hard not to worry about it in those days, for this was the 1930s and there was hunger everywhere. The people I knew tried, I think, according to their lights to practice what Christ taught. My family did. They fed many people who were hungry. Sometimes my mother, growing weary of it, would turn away one of the beggars who came to our door, and that would cause me a sleepless night worrying for fear she was going to hell; but most generally she fed them. Especially, she and my father made sure that the Negro family who worked for us from time to time were not hungry or shelterless or naked. If they were short of money to pay the rent, my father provided the money. The family was always clothed because they got our castoff clothes after they were too faded and old for us to want them any more. But something happened to me each time I looked at the Negro girl who always inherited my clothes. Sometimes she would come to our house with her mother, wearing one of the dresses I had discarded. The dresses never fitted her because she was fatter than I was. She would sit in a straight chair in our kitchen waiting for her mother, because of course she could not sit in one of our comfortable chairs in the living room. She would sit there looking uncomfortable, my old faded dress binding her at the waist and throat. And some way I knew that this was not what Jesus meant when he said to clothe the naked. I recalled that Jesus had also said, "Therefore all things whatsoever ye would that men should do to you, do ye even so to them." And I knew that if I were in her place, if I had no clothes, I would not want the old abandoned dresses of a person who would not even invite me to come into her living room to sit down. And I could not talk to her because I felt ashamed. And as I watched her, I would feel a binding sensation around my own throat. And I would feel to see if my own dress was too tight. But of course it was not. My clothes were always well cut and perfectly fitted. Instead there was a small straitjacket around my soul.

I did not analyze it then, and the eventual revelation did not come to me in any blinding flash of light, in any one moment I can place in time. But gradually through the years, like a picture slowly coming clear in the developing fluid, the truth appeared before my eyes. And by the time I was in my late teens I knew and with the knowledge came the key to all the paradoxes in my world: *Racial bars build a wall not only around the Negro people but around the white people as well, cramping their spirits and causing them to grow in distorted shapes.*

I saw it first in the people I loved best, my family and my friends. These were good people. Essentially they were kind people. Their philosophy and their religion taught them to help their fellow man, and they did so — insofar as the problems of their fellow men came within the view allowed by the blinders they wore from their birth unto the grave. But as regards one group of human beings, their way of life automatically forced them to renounce all they believed in. They renounced it so completely that they did not even realize they had done so. The conflicts that inevitably arose from this renunciation were pushed back into some dark recesses of their souls where they festered in darkness and where the sunshine never entered. The poison from this dark sore seeped out and contaminated their entire lives, without their ever knowing it, and occasionally it erupted into the conscious places of their minds.

For example, when I was in my teens, I had a memorable conversation with a Southern white man of a generation older than mine. He was one of the kindest men I had ever known. He would do anything for a friend. He was a leader in his church and in the community, and no man in need — friend or stranger, black or white — who ever went to him for help was turned away. But he believed in segregation. He believed in it with a violence that squared with nothing else in his personality. We were discussing the advisability of a federal anti-lynch law, which was at that time a live issue before the country. I was arguing in favor of such a law. My elder friend was infuriated that I, a Southern girl, supposedly "well bred," could express such treason. Suddenly in the heat of the argument, he said:

"We have to have a good lynching every once in a while to keep the nigger in his place."

I was speechless. I could not believe what I had heard. To the day I die, I think I will hear those words ringing in my ears. Words of murder from one of the gentlest people I ever knew. A moment later when he was calmer, he regretted what he had said. I still have doubts that this particular man under any circumstances would ever himself join a lynch mob. But in a very profound sense he meant exactly what he had said. His words had sprung out of the unconscious places of his soul, provoked to the surface by his fury that I should be expressing the views I was. They had been spoken because they were there, buried in his being. A gentle, apparently civilized man, he had already committed murder in his heart and mind. I thought to myself then and have often wondered since, *What could segregation ever do to the Negro as terrible as the thing it had done to this white man?*

In my horrified reactions to the effects of segregation in the South, I was not unlike many white young people of my generation. It is significant to me that very few Southerners, even among those who disagree with me, have in recent years asked me the question so many Northerners ask: where did I get my ideas on segregation? Southerners know. People who see the Southern white as a rigid stereotype do not realize that many, many white Southern children go through to some extent the same tortures of soul that I did. I was not an exceptional child. To all outward appearances, my childhood and youth were happy — filled with the normal, if somewhat superficial, pleasures of girlhood in a small Southern town. I knew that something was wrong, but for years I did not understand what it was. In the social stratum I knew in Alabama in that day — this is not true now, of course — segregation was not discussed; it was accepted. People sometimes talked about the "race problem" or the "nigger problem," the implication being that it was the Negroes who were the problem, but I did not know until I was in my teens that anyone even questioned segregation. By the time I was in college, however, World War II was in progress — a war that many people felt was being waged basically against the racist philosophy of Nazism — and I began to find that people *were* questioning. I found them, paradoxically perhaps, at the fashionable Virginia women's colleges I attended: a few among the teachers and more among the students, and practically all of them Southerners. For the first time in my life, segregation became a topic for conversation. Then it was that the developing fluid began to work. Now that the subject was open for discussion, I began to understand the things that had been bothering me so long. I don't think anyone gave me any new ideas; I discovered them buried in my own mind when the channels were opened through which they could flow. And I discovered too that many of my friends in Anniston were also beginning to discuss these things and that many of them had felt the same conflicts I had felt — they, too, unable to articulate them, unable to understand them because they had been bottled up in the netherland of the undiscussable.

And yet many of these contemporaries of mine, with whom I discussed my feelings years ago, have to all appearances adjusted their lives to the old patterns and have ceased to question very deeply. Sometimes their early reactions have become so deeply buried that they come out only in such distorted shapes as the expression of hate from the gentleman of an older generation with whom I discussed the anti-lynch law — their sense of guilt reduced to hatred of the victim. Where conscience cannot be stilled — and these cases are more numerous in my generation than in the previous one — it sometimes expresses itself in parlor talk and some lukewarm support of gradualist efforts to "improve things," in a paternalistic desire to "help" the Negro people. Under the soothing balm to conscience of these parlor conversations and gradualist efforts, the lives of these contemporaries of mine go on not too different from those of their parents: their white world still mostly inviolate, and the Negroes still in their kitchens or in the cabins on the other side of the railroad tracks. But there are others, like myself, who for one reason or another have clung to the conviction that they must do something to help change the situation, that they must challenge segregation at the roots. That my life took this latter course was due perhaps to the fact that I found some cracks in the wall — the wall of segregation and all the other protective enclosures that privileged-class white Southern society builds around its children.

Like most Southern white children, I grew up with never an

opportunity to meet and know a Negro as an equal or a superior. I was nineteen years old and in my third year at college before this pattern was broken.

At that time, a friend of mine from Virginia invited me to visit her in New York City, where she was then living. While I was there, she arranged for me to meet and have dinner with a friend of hers, a young Negro woman just about my age, who was playing a part in a Broadway play. I was going through a momentary phase of wanting to be an actress, and that was the reason for the introduction. I have today forgotten this young girl's name, but I will never forget her face or her personality or what she did for me.

I went to the meeting with some misgivings. Never in my life had I eaten with a Negro. I was intellectually pleased at the opportunity to break this lifelong pattern, but I was somewhat ill at ease in the face of a new experience. She of course was much more mature. She too was from the South, and I think looking back on it that she must have realized my feelings. She undoubtedly went out of her way to put me at ease. Soon we were talking — talking, talking — discussing all the things in which we were mutually interested. To me she was a wonder, for she was a success in a field that I at the moment aspired to. Suddenly, in the midst of the conversation, the realization swept over me that I had completely forgotten that there was a difference in our color. We were no longer white and Negro — we were just two young women talking about things we liked to talk about. Somewhere inside of me a voice seemed to say: "Why, there is no race problem at all! There are only the people who have not realized it yet."

It was a tremendous revelation. It may sound like a small thing when it is told, but it was a turning point in my life. All the cramping walls of a lifetime seemed to come tumbling down in that moment. Some heavy shackles seemed to have fallen from my feet. For the first time in my nineteen years on this earth, I felt I had room to stretch my arms and legs and lift my head high toward the sky. In more recent years, I have known many friendships across the race bar, more close and certainly more lasting than that one was; but never again was there the startling revelation of that first moment when the walls came tumbling down. Here, for a moment, I glimpsed a vision of the world as it should be: where people are people, and spirits have room to grow. I never got over it.

After I finished college, I went back to Alabama to work on newspapers — first in my home town and later in the larger city of Birmingham. I covered the police courts in the small town of Anniston and the courthouse in Birmingham. Here, inevitably, I had to step out of the walled-in world in which I had grown up. I had to take off the blinders that most people of my environment wear all of their lives. Although I was approaching it from a different direction, I was coming in contact with the same world that Carl knew as a police reporter — the world that makes one "a drunk, a cynic, or a reformer." People could no longer be put in pigeonholes and safely catalogued where they do not bother one's way of life; they could no longer be just "better" people and "inferior" people, people on this side of the tracks and on that side, the "unfortunate" people and the "select" ones. I had to look at them all as human beings — and I liked what I saw. The concepts of "inferior" and "superior" began to melt away; and all that remained was people — some of them disorganized, some of them unable to cope with their environment, some of them with lives temporarily wrecked, but all of them with the potential of great worth: a potential that if given a chance I felt could find its own way. The pillars of my old world had begun to crumble, and I began to sense that great changes were needed in the society in which I lived.

Especially I came to feel more strongly as each day passed that segregation was a curse and should be abolished. In covering the Birmingham courthouse, I soon learned that there were two kinds of justice, one for whites and one for Negroes. If a Negro killed a white man, that was a capital crime; if a white man killed a Negro, there were usually "extenuating circumstances" if not outright justification; if a Negro killed a Negro, that was "just a nigger murder" — worth at most a year or so in prison. If a white man took advantage of a Negro woman, it never reached the courts. If a Negro so much as looked at a white woman in a way she thought improper, that was "assault with intent to rape." I remember specifically the case of a young Negro man whom I saw get a prison sentence on a charge of assault with intent to rape. The

white woman testified that he had passed her on the opposite side
of a country road and looked at her in an "insulting" way. . . . Over
the door of the Birmingham courthouse, as on many courthouses,
are inscribed the words of Thomas Jefferson: "Equal and exact
justice to all men of whatever state or persuasion." I read it every
morning as I went to work until finally I began looking the other
way as I entered the building; I could no longer bear to read the
words. Eventually, an incident in the sheriff's office almost tipped
the scales of my sanity.

The sheriff's office prided itself on its record of crime solution.
I don't think it was as good as they said but they often boasted about
it. One day, while I was killing time talking to some of the deputies,
one of them said:

"You know there's been only one murder in this county in the
last two years that has never been solved."

"And what was that?" I asked.

"Come on, I'll show you," he said. He took me back into
another room, opened a cabinet and took out a skull.

"There it is," he said, setting the skull on a table. "And it never
will be solved — that man was a nigger and he was killed by a
white man."

I looked at the deputy. His eyes were twinkling — and they
were twinkling not because he was joking but because he was
talking of a conspiracy that pleased him, and of which he was a part,
and which he evidently expected would please me too. I looked at
the skull. It grew larger before my eyes. It filled the room and the
world. It became a symbol of the death that gripped the South.
I couldn't say anything. I left without comment, terror-stricken.

This was the end of the road where segregation led — death
and decay, death in the skull on the table, death in the heart and
soul of the gentle white man who had talked to me of lynching. I
felt that I must fight against it, but I did not know where to turn.
I know now that there were people in the South in those days
fighting against segregation; there were probably some in Birmingham, but I did not know them. There were probably organizations,
but I did not know them. I — like so many other Southern white
people then and now who feel as I felt — believed that I was alone.
I knew some people who talked among themselves against the

evils that ate at my soul, but all they did was talk and more was needed than talk. Much more was needed, but I did not know what it was. The forces of segregation seemed too strong — and what could one do?

I tried for a time to shut it all out of my mind. I would rise above it, I told myself. I would not let it touch me. I buried myself in my work as a newspaper reporter and in my personal social life. I kept myself at a high tension making deadlines, trying to beat the competition newspaper with each story — racing through each day so that I had no time or energy left to think. But these things did not work either. For finally I came to realize that no one can go untouched by segregation in the South. *No white person in the South, now as then, can be neutral on this question.* Either you find a way to oppose the evil, or the evil becomes a part of you and you are a part of it, and it winds itself about your soul like the arms of an octopus.

This realization came home to me one morning in a Birmingham cafeteria. In those days, it was my custom to get up quite early in the mornings and, before leaving home for work or immediately when I got downtown, to call the coroner's office and the sheriff's office to see if there had been any murders or other big news during the night. If there had been, I could then call the newspaper office before going to the courthouse and make our first edition with the story. If everything had been quiet during the night, I could take time for a leisurely breakfast before going to the courthouse to gather the routine day's news for the later editions. On this particular morning, I was meeting another reporter for breakfast at a downtown cafeteria. I was running a little late that morning, so I asked him to get my breakfast while I made my usual calls. When I had finished at the telephone, I met him at our table where a Negro waitress was taking our breakfast off the trays.

"Anything doing?" my friend asked.

I shook my head.

"No," I said. "Everything quiet. Nothing but a colored murder."

It was the newspaper reporter that I had become who was talking. Reporters soon learn to think in terms of news values rather than human values. It was a simple fact that in Birmingham the killing of one Negro by another was not big news. At most, it might rate a paragraph on an inside page of the paper. It was nothing that I had to rush around about, get the details on, nothing that I had to phone my paper about before the first edition. It was nothing to stop me from settling down and taking time for breakfast before going on to work. I might never have given a further thought to the remark I had made — except that, even as I spoke, I suddenly sensed the reaction of the Negro waitress who was pouring coffee into my friend's cup.

I sensed it before I looked at her. It was as if a sixth sense had flashed across the table. It was as if I had heard her speak, but of course she had not spoken. I forced myself to look up at her. Her body was stiff; and her hand on the coffee pot jerked. But her face was a stony mask, her eyes cast down.

My impulse was to rush over to her and take her hand. I wanted to say: "I'm sorry for what I said. I didn't mean it. It's just that I meant it wasn't news. It's not that I don't care if one of your people is killed. I don't feel that way. It's the newspaper; they say what the news is — I don't. I am not a part of this thing that says a Negro life does not matter. It isn't me."

But all of a sudden — like a shaft of morning sunlight over that breakfast table — the truth dawned on me. I *had* meant what I had said; I had meant it just as surely as the man who had talked to me about lynching had meant what he had said. He had said what he did because it was buried in his mind; if what I had said had not been in my mind, I would not have said it. I could not shift the blame to my newspaper; I was a part of this white world that considered a Negro life not worth bothering about. If I did not oppose it, I was a part of it — and I was responsible for its sins. There was no middle ground. Unless a person did something to change it, he was strengthening it — and the first thing he knew, its octopus arms were closing about his own soul, twisting it out of shape, hardening it, making it callous. They were twisting about me. I felt strangled, as I had so long ago when I looked at the little Negro girl sitting pinched and uncomfortable in my old dresses that didn't fit. I wanted air. I wanted freedom.

Soon after that, when an opportunity came to go to Louisville and work on the *Louisville Times,* I left Birmingham. I left feeling that I was running away and rationalizing my departure by telling myself the move was the best thing for my career but knowing in my heart that I was leaving because I had to get away, that I had to escape from the social decay and the death symbolized by that skull on the courthouse table and from the octopus that had reached out to enfold me.

I did not run far, of course, for Louisville was still the South, and I found things here were not too different, although segregation was perpetuated by somewhat more subtle means. The new thing that happened to me in Louisville was that I was thrown into experiences that finally seemed to cut my ties to the walled-in world of my childhood. Now I found some of the people on the other side of the wall, the ones who had not let society disorganize them, forging ahead in creative ways to build a new future.

I found them in the trade union movement, to which Carl introduced me. Carl and I met and were married while we were working together on the staff of the *Times*. Up until that time, the labor movement as far as I was concerned had been only a name. Now, as I began going with Carl to union gatherings and meeting his friends, I finally learned emotionally the thing I had long suspected intellectually — that the people who had been presented to me in childhood as the "underprivileged" people on the other side of the tracks were not inanimate objects to be "helped" by people like me. I learned that they were vigorous human beings who were changing their own world. I found the same thing in organizations of the Negro people: human beings who were shaping their own destiny, welcoming my cooperation if I cared to give it but not depending on people like me to be solicitous or to lift them up. It gave life a new dignity, this realization. Paradoxically, I felt freer than I ever had before.

It was all as if the world had been turned upside down, and my memory of these first years in Louisville is of some rapid floodwaters rushing over my soul, tugging at my entrails, pulling me up by the roots. I was falling in love with Carl and seeing the world from an entirely new vantage point, his vantage point, the vantage point of a different place in society. The roots weren't really washed away of course. They never are. No one ever completely breaks away from the earth that nourished him, and if he did or could his spirit would probably die. But when the floodwaters subsided, I knew that some of the old soil had been carried downstream: the old concept of *noblesse oblige,* the old belief in superiority conferred

by social class; and with it had gone some of the filth of race prejudice. Not all perhaps, and who can say that one of my environment
will ever lose it all. But some of it, at least, I knew was gone.

It was in this period too that I first came in contact with the
so-called political Left — the Progressive Party and all the other
organizations that sprang up in its wake in Louisville, as elsewhere,
and some of which got put on the Attorney General's list. I joined
practically all of them that were around because they all stood
steadfastly opposed to segregation — and this of course caused us
no end of trouble later. None of them was ever very large or important in Louisville, and looking back on it I have never been
sure that any of them were ever remarkably effective in the struggle
against segregation there, although they probably sometimes played
a gadfly role. And yet I have never regretted these affiliations,
because of what they did for my own growth. For in a place like
Louisville these organizations on the Left were just about the only
places that one could find Negroes willing to tell white people some
measure of what they really thought. In almost every other setting
— at least in the South — a Negro still tends, whether he really
wants to or not, to defer somewhat to the white people with whom
he associates. In these left-wing organizations, for some reason,
the Negroes were more frank — maybe not completely so, but more
so. Here and only here — for the first time since my experience
with the young Negro actress in New York — I found Negroes
who looked at me and other white people as equals, who looked
at me as a human being, who felt no necessity to defer to me and
call me "Ma'am," who had no inhibitions about setting me straight
on all the things they felt I was wrong about. I learned a great deal,
and for a person like me, saturated from childhood with the doctrines of white supremacy, it was an invaluable experience.

Carl and I later left the *Louisville Times* and worked for a while
handling public relations for a group of CIO unions — Farm
Equipment Workers, Transport Workers, Public Workers, and
Furniture Workers. Carl's desire to do this stemmed from his lifelong devotion to the trade union movement, dating back to the
Louisville & Nashville shopmen's strike so long ago. With me, the
great attraction was that here were white people who were willing
to take a stand against segregation. These union men called each

other "brother," and when they said that word "brother" they meant all other people who worked; they meant white brothers and black brothers, it didn't matter; they were uniting — or striving to — in their common aims. It was a new world to me; it was a wonderful world; it was a world for which I had long been seeking.

In my spare time, I worked in every way I could at the thing closest to my heart — the ending of segregation, in the community as well as the union. Gradually I probably influenced Carl to put his emphasis on these things too. In 1950, he went back to newspaper work as a copy editor on the *Courier-Journal,* and I quit work to have a baby. When my first child was born, I found I had more of a desire than ever to do something about segregation; I knew that within five years my son would be starting to school — starting to school, unless changes were made, in the segregated schools of the South — and that the whole vicious pattern would be beginning all over again in my life. To strike out against segregation became like a compulsion to me.

Carl and I were active in the National Association for the Advancement of Colored People; we worked on a committee to end discrimination in hospitals; we worked on a committee against segregation in the bus stations and other public places. I became a member of the diocesan Department of Christian Social Relations of the Episcopal Church and — in the eyes of the more conservative members — made a constant nuisance of myself by bringing up at almost every meeting some question related to segregation. When the Negro Labor Council organized a chapter in Louisville and began a campaign to end job discrimination against Negroes, we joined that. After our children were born, we worked hard on a committee against segregated schools in Kentucky.

Always I found myself among the people favoring the more radical course on this question. I could not see the argument of waiting and taking the more prudent way. If segregation in the parks was wrong, it should be ended now. And if segregation in the hospitals was wrong, it should be ended now. If segregated schools were wrong, they should be integrated now — before any more children grew up absorbing the poison I had absorbed. Whenever the opportunity arose to tug at the roots of segregation, I had to act and act now. Everything in my life, past and present, demanded it.

I have been told that the intensity of my feeling about segregation is neurotic. I have never denied that this may be so. I grew up in a sick society, and a sick society makes neurotics — of one kind or another, on one side or another. It makes people like those who could take pleasure in killing and mutilating Emmett Till, and it makes people like me. The United States Supreme Court in its historic decision against segregation in the schools outlined what segregation does to the Negro child. The justices might have added some discussion of what it does to the white child. There are many white "neurotics" like myself in my generation in the South — if that is what we are. The people who describe themselves as "saner" and more "practical" and more "moderate" tell us to wait, not to go too fast. But that is no answer. They may persuade some of us to take a slower course, but they can never convince us all. As long as segregation remains a fact in communities all over the South, there will be people like us who are compelled to act.

When Andrew Wade asked us to buy him a house, I did not conceive of it as a big project — not consciously. I foresaw nothing of the trouble that would follow. I have told people we did it to help a friend, and that is true. I have said that we could do nothing else because we had never refused to help when a Negro took a stand against segregation and asked our assistance, and that is true. I did not believe that I as a white person had a right to say to any Negro: "Now is not the time . . ." I had not refused when Negro friends had asked me to aid their efforts to end segregation in the hospitals and the schools; I could not refuse now on the question of a house. All this is true.

But who can ever say for sure what unconscious motives make him act? How can I say for sure that the purchase of the house did not also fulfill a need in me: a need to fling a dramatic challenge to a community I thought was moving too slowly, to a society too satisfied with its sins — to fling it like an answer back through the years of my own life, to the man who talked of lynching, to the man with the skull, to the throbbing of my own conscience as I felt the decadent white world closing around me — to fling it like a prophecy, impractical perhaps but hopeful, of a new world that could come, a world that I had seen through a glass darkly, a world without walls.

4

The World of Segregated Louisville

Louisville in 1954 was a segregated community. Not as viciously and inflexibly segregated as some communities in the Deep South. Not as completely segregated as it had been even seven years before, when I came here to work. But still segregated — in most of its physical manifestations and certainly in the pattern of its heart and mind.

When I came here in 1947 my first impression was that the atmosphere was quite different from what I had known in Birmingham. I felt this the first morning I rode downtown on a city bus to go to work. When the bus reached the central part of town, Negroes began to get on — and they sat down in any empty seat available, front or back. This was very different from Birmingham, where they not only had to ride in the back but at that time could not even walk through the front of the bus or streetcar to get there; even if it was pouring down rain, they had to pay the driver at the front and then walk around to the rear door to board.

I noticed the difference too as I began my work as a reporter for the *Louisville Times*. In addition to working outside the *Times* office gathering news about the school system, I was assigned part-time to the rewrite desk, where I took stories from other reporters over the telephone and wrote them for publication. Often these concerned political news. One day soon after I went to work a reporter was giving me a story about the prospects of various candidates expected to run for office that year. In referring to one possible candidate, he told me that I should mention in the story that this particular man could probably count on most of the Negro vote in Louisville. I think I almost dropped the telephone; I realized with a start that I was now living in a place where Negroes voted! At the time I left Alabama, some of the returning Negro war veterans were beginning to attempt to register, and during my last months there the people had been in turmoil over a state constitutional amendment to block this move.

Before I wrote the story, I asked another reporter in the office about it.

"Negroes vote in Louisville?" I said somewhat doubtfully.

"Oh yes," he replied. "Always have, I guess."

"And nobody tries to keep them from it?" I asked.

"None that I ever heard of — not in recent years anyway," he said. "So far as I know, they've voted around here for a long time. It's pretty much an accepted thing. In fact, the Negro vote in Louisville is often the balance of power. Negroes make up only fifteen percent of the population, but Louisville is so closely divided between the Democrats and Republicans that sometimes the Negroes can swing the vote either way. That can be important in state elections too, because sometimes the way Louisville goes decides whether the state goes Democrat or Republican."

That was a new concept to me too. It was my first experience in living with a two-party system.

Another thing that immediately struck me as different in Louisville was the fact that when predominantly Negro organizations such as the National Association for the Advancement of Colored People or the Urban League held important meetings or when their leaders made statements on some subject related to civil rights, it was newsworthy. I wrote some of these stories myself, and sometimes they made front-page news. This was quite different from Birmingham, where from reading the daily papers at that time — this is far from true today — one would have hardly known an NAACP existed in the city. Sometimes the Birmingham papers ran a separate page of news about colored people — such as innocuous items about social affairs — but statements by Negro leaders on civil rights were generally ignored, evidently on the theory that if the white world ignored these statements and organizations they would go away.

I found too in my early days in Louisville that I was thrown with a number of white people who openly and without qualification opposed segregation. These were mostly among the younger reporters on the newspapers and among the young people I met at the University of Louisville, where I enrolled for night courses. These men and women were quite outspoken in their views, and a few of them even attended meetings of the NAACP occasionally. It was the kind of thing I had never heard of in Birmingham; there I knew some white people who sat among themselves and brooded about the evils of racial discrimination, but they usually were quite careful, before they expressed an opinion, to make sure they were among people who agreed with them; and, in the constricted atmosphere of Alabama, they would never have considered doing such a revolutionary thing as attending an NAACP meeting. The differences I felt among some of the people I first met in Louisville led me for a time to think I was in a world that was quite different.

As time went on, however, I came to know the city better. I learned it first as a newspaper reporter, for it was my job to know it. I learned it later as the place where I had decided to settle down and rear a family. Because it had become my home, because it was where I had met Carl, I came to love it; and as I grew to love it I felt its faults as my own. Slowly and painfully, I learned that its differences from the Deep South did not go very deep. Before I had been here very long, I knew that white and Negro people in Louisville lived out their lives with a world between them; I met more and more white people who talked about "niggers" and, like most white people I had known in Alabama, had never in their lives sat down and talked with a Negro on an equal basis. I knew I was still in the South. . . . And yet, even today — after all the things that have happened to me here — I never approach the city as I return from a trip without feeling a thrill of home-coming as I cross the Clark Bridge and see Louisville on its curve of the Ohio River.

But I soon found that if you were a Negro in Louisville, you almost invariably had to live in one of two parts of town. One was the central section, bordering on the business district, mostly slums. If you were lucky, you might have a place in one of the public housing projects which were pleasant and attractive. Louisville had four such projects for Negroes, and apologists for Negro housing conditions often pointed out that over half of all the public housing units in the city were for non-whites. But it wasn't nearly enough to meet the needs; there were always long waiting lists, and if your income was that low it was much more likely that you would live in one of the old two- and three-story buildings abutting on the sidewalks. Maybe you and your five or six children all lived in one room. Maybe you shared a bath with nine or ten other families. Or maybe you lived on one of the back alleys in the downtown section. The United States Census for 1950 showed that 84.4 percent of the city's Negroes were living in dwellings rated as poor or very poor, and the Health Department reported that thousands were living in coal sheds and chicken coops.

The other section where you might live would be the West End. This is the old part of town, blocked to expansion by the Ohio River. It was formerly all-white, and many white people still live there — it is here that Carl and I live — but in recent years more and more of its homes have been occupied by Negroes, as the white people have moved to the suburbs to the south and east of town. If you were one of the city's few wealthy Negroes, you might live in a very handsome house in this section; if you were poor, you would probably live on one of the West End's rutted dirt streets — in a tumbledown cottage without indoor toilet facilities. If you were in the middle-income bracket, you might buy one of the older but fairly decent houses the white people were moving out of — if you wanted to and could afford to pay more than it was worth. Outside of the central and western sections there were a few pockets of Negro homes which had been there for many years; but these neighborhoods were not expanding, and the newer sections were all lily-white.

Many of my Negro friends who live under slum conditions have told me they could afford something better — if it were available. Not that they are wealthy. But if they were white they could get a new house for a very low down payment and for monthly payments lower than the rent they often have to pay where they are living. But between the end of World War II and 1954 only 300 new houses had been built for Negroes in the entire Louisville area. As for the rest of the residential property, when I came here it was almost all covered by restrictive covenants. When the Supreme Court ruled in 1948 that these could not be enforced in the courts, the situation did not change. It was common knowledge that the banks and real estate companies and builders had unwritten agreements that no one would sell or lend money on property in white sections to Negroes. The one exception was when the realtors agreed in advance to "break a block" — and breaking a "white" block by selling one house to a Negro family usually means that the real estate companies have decided to try to make the section all-Negro.

I soon learned too that if you were a Negro in Louisville most job opportunities were closed to you. If you could carve out a profession or a business for yourself in the city's Negro community, you might become quite prosperous. Otherwise when you went job hunting you found that in most industries — there were a few exceptions — the only jobs available were as janitors or in the foundries or in the lowest paid and dirtiest occupations. In the offices of large white business establishments, Negro faces were almost never seen; Negro clerks in downtown stores were virtually unheard of. I know Negro men of great talent working as waiters. I know Negro women with exceptional ability working in domestic service. I think of a Negro woman with whom I worked on a committee that was attempting to persuade officials of a big new General Electric plant in Louisville to hire Negroes on an equal basis. This woman saw the new plant as a golden opportunity.

"I have to work," I remember her telling me, "because my husband doesn't make enough. You know, garage mechanics don't. And I don't mind. I have my mother-in-law to look after the children. But I just don't like domestic work. Not that there's anything wrong with it — not if the pay is good enough and people treat you with some respect. Some people like it, and I say it's all right for those who do. But for me, I just don't like housework. I don't even like doing my own — and I hate it that just because I'm a Negro that's the only kind of job I can get. My mother always had to work so hard out in service, and I vowed when I was a little girl that I'd never do it. I took typing and shorthand in school hoping I could get an office job. But when I started looking, there wasn't anything. There just aren't enough jobs in Negro offices to go around. But I've kept on practicing my typing and shorthand so I wouldn't get rusty. I think I'm pretty good."

General Electric did later hire some Negroes on the production lines, but it never hired any for office work. Today that woman is still working in domestic service. And periodically Louisville employers complain that they have trouble finding competent secretaries.

I learned too that the schools in Louisville were segregated, from kindergarten through college, and that in fact Kentucky had a state law imposing criminal penalties for violation of school segregation. I quickly found out also that the city's outstanding park system was divided white and Negro with the more beautiful and spacious parks reserved for white people and the smaller ones for Negroes. It was not long after I came to Louisville that a young Negro man was arrested for trying to play tennis in one of the white parks; I interviewed him for the *Times,* and he told me the tennis courts in the one major park reserved for Negroes were in such bad repair that it was impossible to play on them. I found out that most of the city's private hospitals, although not the public hospital, refused to admit Negroes. And I learned that most public places in Louisville — restaurants, hotels, bus and train stations, theaters — were behind the color bar.

I think I never felt segregation quite so acutely as I did one summer day when I happened to meet a Negro woman, a friend of mine, on Louisville's main downtown street. We talked a few minutes and then she suggested that I go with her into a nearby store which had advertised a dress sale. I did, and in a little while she found a dress she thought she liked. She asked me what I thought about it. I was doubtful; it had a narrow skirt and she was rather thin; I felt she might look better in something with a full skirt.

"I'm not sure," I said. "If I were you, I'd try it on before I decided."

There was a flash of embarrassment on her face.

"I'm not sure they let Negroes try on dresses here, Anne," she said. "And I just don't feel like having a fight about it."

I bit my lip. Of course I had heard that some of the better Louisville stores refused to allow Negroes to try on clothes — a few of them consistently as a matter of management policy, others spasmodically at the whim of some of the clerks. I had heard that many Negro women, never knowing when they might be refused, just preferred not to ask. I knew too that most of the downtown stores refused their rest room facilities to Negroes and that because of the problems this presented some Negro women hesitated to take their children to town with them. But somehow these things had never really registered with me before because they were things I had never experienced myself.

I felt the full impact again after my friend and I left the store and were walking down the street together. It was quite hot, and I was very thirsty. I almost suggested to her, before I thought, that we stop in at a drugstore and get something cool to drink. I caught myself in time on that and saved her the embarrassment of having to remind me that no drugstore in that section would serve her. But I think I got some inkling that day walking along Louisville's main street — hot and thirsty and with no place I could quench my thirst — of what it meant every minute of the day, every hour of your life to be a Negro in a segregated society — even here in Louisville, a border city on the very edge of the Mason-Dixon Line.

And yet there was also some real basis for those early impressions I got when I first moved here — that Louisville was different from the Deep South. The fact that Negroes voted here was an important factor. It meant that no politician, no matter how anti-Negro he might be in private, could completely ignore the demands of the Negro people. This gave Negro leaders a certain prestige in the city's political life, and even in 1947 they were quite outspoken in their demands for equality and were making themselves felt.

The other things I had noticed early — the fact that demands of the Negro people were treated with respect in the press and also the fact that a number of white people I met in semi-intellectual circles frankly opposed segregation — were manifestations of another basic factor in the city's make-up too. There was, as I soon found, a considerable section of the white leadership in Louisville which was liberal in its view. I use the word "liberal" here, and throughout this book, as it applies to segregation; I am aware that the word can mean many things to many people in different places; but in the South it is almost always used to describe a person who is liberal on the race question — who opposes, although in varying degrees, the system of segregation. Of course the most feverish of the segregationists call all such people "Communists," but liberal is the word they use to describe themselves; it is also the label used to describe them by the more moderate segregationists. The people

I am describing as liberals might or might not be liberal on all subjects; they might be Democrats, Republicans, or political independents; but they agreed generally in their belief that racial discrimination is evil. Completely aside from the young radicals with whom Andrew Wade was thrown on his return from World War II, this liberalism had a great deal of influence in the intellectual centers of Louisville, and it also reached into high places in the community. Its leadership centered in the ownership and management of the *Louisville Courier-Journal,* the morning paper, and the *Louisville Times,* the afternoon paper. The owner of the two papers was Barry Bingham and their publisher was Mark Ethridge, who fought the Ku Klux Klan in Georgia in his youth and got himself well hated in parts of the South during World War II for his work with President Roosevelt's Fair Employment Practices Committee.

The *Courier* and *Times* had always worked against segregation, sometimes quietly and sometimes more outspokenly, but always on the side of progress toward complete equality for all — steadily and repeatedly through the years like the beat, beat, beat of a stream of water, eating away at the patterns that once seemed set as rock. This policy had made the newspapers objects of fury on the part of many powerful people in Louisville, as well as elsewhere in Kentucky. However, the policy had also won strong supporters among influential people in the community and had gradually recruited more. These people were generally gradualist in their approach and their methods, but some of them had been unbending in their adherence to the principle of desegregation as a fixed star in their heavens — sometimes a star far off and not soon to be reached but always there. Their opponents among the die-hard segregationists often charged snidely that they themselves lived in exclusive white subdivisions and sent their children to white private schools; and of course their critics among the small groups of impatient radicals that occasionally sprang up in the city charged them with moving too slowly. But when the Negro people pushed hard enough, these people often followed the voice of their consciences and moved to help change things. Under the combined impact of the actions of the vocal Negro leadership, the prodding of small radical groups, and the work of powerful white liberal forces, cracks appeared in the wall of Louisville segregation. I saw many of them develop between 1947 and 1954.

For example, the year after I went to work on the *Times,* a Negro high school teacher filed a suit to enter the graduate school of the University of Kentucky for summer courses. I interviewed him at the time, and it made a rather important news story because it was something few people had expected to happen in Kentucky for a long time to come. At that time school segregation was so settled in Louisville that many people who did not oppose the man's suit considered it a somewhat quixotic and futile move.

And yet the suit was won and soon the Kentucky legislature passed an amendment to the state's compulsory school segregation law to allow admission of Negroes to white colleges at the undergraduate as well as the graduate level, wherever a college's governing body voted to do so. Louisville's three Catholic colleges immediately announced that they would admit Negro students. The NAACP prepared to sue to force admission of Negroes at the University of Louisville, and before the suit was filed the board of the University agreed to their admission. By 1954, Negro students were enrolled at the city university in fairly large numbers. When the policy first changed, there were all sorts of dire predictions of the evils to follow, but none of them materialized. Even early critics of the program had to acknowledge it was working smoothly.

Before the beginning of the crack in segregation in the field of education, the board of the Louisville Free Public Library had voted to admit Negroes to its main branch. Now, when the University of Louisville opened its doors, the library agreed to also desegregate its smaller branches scattered throughout the city — because the library and the university often engaged in joint activities that involved use of library facilities. On any day in reading and reference rooms, one could see Negro men and women seated at tables beside white men and women, reading and studying without incident.

It was about this time too that the color bars began to crumble in Louisville hospitals. This process was speeded up — as such things unfortunately often have to be — by a tragedy. Three Negro men, injured in an automobile accident, were refused treatment at a hospital in a small Kentucky town about ninety miles from Louisville. One of them died. A public outcry followed, and a committee was formed to try to see to it that this kind of thing could not happen again. Carl and I worked long and hard on this committee; like many other white people we were shocked to learn what every Negro in Louisville of course knew — that most hospitals in our own city refused to admit Negroes. The committee was finally able to get the state legislature to pass a law providing that any hospital which refused emergency treatment to anyone because of race would be denied a state license. We were unable to get this legislation broadened to say that they must also admit patients regardless of race for all forms of treatment; but in the wake of publicity that followed the incident, some of the city's private hospitals voluntarily opened their doors to Negroes. Several hospitals also opened their facilities to young Negro women who wanted to train for nursing careers, and they began to minister to white patients as the white nurses did to Negro patients, often on unsegregated wards. Again there were predictions as to the trouble that would result — and there was no trouble.

The constant demand of Negro citizens and the work of an interracial committee finally brought an end to segregation in the city's bus and train stations. An NAACP suit in federal court ended segregation on the city's golf courses. The amphitheater in one of the city parks, where operettas were presented in the summertime, was opened to Negroes. That happened after the city and the University of Louisville jointly presented a pageant-play on the life of Abraham Lincoln at the amphitheater in 1953. Unable to ignore the incongruity of the presentation of a play about Lincoln before an all-white audience, officials agreed to admit Negroes for that production only. When the sky did not fall in on that occasion, demands for desegregation of the amphitheater for all productions were renewed by the NAACP and such groups as the Women's International League for Peace and Freedom; and, with people like Barry Bingham working behind the scenes, the board of the amphitheater had finally agreed in the spring of 1954 to let down the racial bars for that season. By the time a favorable decision came down on a suit that had been pending to force desegregation of the amphitheater, the question was moot.

The weakness of Louisville's advances toward desegregation, however, was that they affected only a few people — and didn't affect them much. There had been something of a tacit understanding, almost unconscious but nevertheless potent, between the segregationists and the white liberal leadership that things would not move too fast. This unspoken agreement undoubtedly sprang from a commendable desire not to upset so-called race relations or cause trouble. But the net result was that the pattern of life for the great majority of Louisville citizens, white and Negro, had been little affected by the changes, if at all. In 1954, one might see Negro and white students engaged in friendly conversation on the campus of the University of Louisville and studying together in the Louisville Free Public Library; one might see Negro and white golfing parties passing each other on the city's golf links. But the schools below the college level were still segregated; most white-owned restaurants, hotels, theaters and other public places were closed to Negroes; despite repeated NAACP court attacks, the city parks — except for the golf courses — remained tightly segregated. And in the vital areas of their lives — on their jobs and in their neighborhoods — the majority of Louisville citizens, white and Negro, were still behind their own walls, untouched by and hardly conscious of any change: the Negroes in the ghetto, the white people in their own white world, safely locked in their old and settled ways. To most of Louisville's people in 1954, segregation was a way of life that one did not question.

There were indications, though, that the pattern was not as unbreakable as it seemed. Limited experience in Louisville had shown that people of both groups could break down the barriers in a very short time if given the opportunity. Carl and I came into direct contact with one of these group experiences when we were employed as public relations workers for the United Farm Equipment Workers, which represented the production force at International Harvester Company's Louisville plant. (This union is now a part of the United Automobile Workers, which played a big part in the later struggle that developed around Wade's house.)

The Harvester plant had opened after World War II, and it was one of the few industries in the city that employed Negroes on a non-discriminatory basis. Both the company and the union claimed credit for this development, and it may have been some of both. At any rate, it had been that way from the beginning, and thus many Negroes had high seniority in the plant and were promoted to better and better jobs. By the time Carl and I went to work for the union in 1949, this policy was an accepted thing in the community. Negroes were integrated into the union as well as the shop; some of them held major offices in the local; and it was a usual thing to see Negro and white members sitting together in the union hall discussing their common problems, informally as well as in formal meetings. The new pattern spilled over outside the union hall, and many of these same white men visited in the Negro unionists' homes, and the Negroes went to the white members' homes.

It was revealing to consider the change that had come in the attitude of some of these white men in a very short period. Except for a few who had moved to Louisville from coal-mining areas, where there had constantly been some friendliness between the races, most of them had grown up accepting the segregated life of Louisville as unchallengeable. But once they were thrown with Negroes in a common work situation, something happened. As one of them put it to me:

"I always thought colored people were something to look down on. But when I went to work at Harvester I saw something different. The Negroes were some of the best leaders the union had; they were the ones you could depend on to stick up for you when you got into a fight with the company; they knew what to do and they weren't afraid. You can't help but respect them, and pretty soon you get to like them, and the first thing you know you almost forget they're colored and you think of them as just people like yourself." It was like that revelation that came to me with the young Negro actress in New York when I was nineteen: he too was beginning to glimpse a world without walls.

The company and the union also both claimed credit for convincing the white workers of the value of a non-discriminatory policy. Again it may have been some of both. I know the union carried on a constant campaign to convince the white workers that only by solidarity of Negro and white could the union be strong, and this undoubtedly had an effect. But probably the most effective thing of all was the hard pragmatic fact that under the conditions and circumstances that existed the workers did not need their prejudices any more.

The wage level at the Harvester plant was high; the union always claimed it was the highest in the South. Furthermore, many of the workers were young, recently returned war veterans, and they were supermilitant. They engaged in numerous spontaneous work stoppages over pay scales. These brought unlimited criticism from some sections of the community; the union leadership was called irresponsible because it could not — or did not — halt the continuous stoppages. The validity of these charges, the wisdom or lack of wisdom of the workers' supermilitancy, is not pertinent to the present discussion. The point is that no matter what the good or bad overall effects of such actions, they did give the workers at the time a sense of strength and dignity that the workers in most Louisville plants did not have. They made each man feel temporarily that he was strong enough to deal with his giant employer, and removed some of the helplessness and insignificance that a man often has working each day for a big company. The higher pay that apparently resulted from the militancy removed some of the constant worry of a pay check too small to cover the bills at home each week. For the white workers, this new sense of dignity and security meant they no longer needed the Negro as an object of scorn, no longer needed him for the inflation of their own egos and as an outlet for their frustration and worries; for the Negro workers it meant they could look at the white workers without bitterness. The results in terms of human relations were startling.

This is not to argue that frequent work stoppages are necessarily a good thing; and some of the leaders of this local considered the supermilitancy unwise and unsound. It may be that other avenues to the same result can be found. But the Harvester experience is a demonstration of the fact that the removal of inner feelings of insecurity and inferiority on the part of both white and Negro people is a long step toward reduction of group tensions. In our present society this kind of development most often occurs under the impact of some union struggle. I saw the same thing a few years later when the hotel workers in Louisville went on strike. Here some of the lowest-paid and probably most insecure workers in Louisville, the maids and waiters and waitresses and cooks of the large hotels, joined together in a show of strength against what was to them a powerful employer. The strike was finally lost, but in its early stages it seemed strong. A new dignity seemed to fall on the shoulders of all the strikers, both white and Negro; the world looked different to them, and they could look at their fellow men through different eyes. The group set apart from them previously by an artificial color bar, and thus an object for unreasoning hatred and unacknowledged aggressions, could be seen as human beings. The white workers saw the Negro workers as among their best strike leaders; the Negro workers saw the white workers as people like themselves with the same problems. Negro and white women walked the picket lines together, arm in arm; at the union dining room they sat down and ate together, talked together, made their plans together.

While I was working for the Harvester union, I had an opportunity to watch from very close range as racial prejudice melted away. The Harvester plant hires no women, and the experiences of integration learned by the men had rarely extended into the lives of the women who were their wives. Soon after Carl and I went to work there, it was decided to organize a women's auxiliary of the union, and I was asked to help with it. It was accepted, of course, that this auxiliary would be set up on a non-segregated basis, like the union. On the night of the first meeting about twenty women appeared, six or seven of them Negroes. As they gathered in one of the smaller rooms in the union hall, I could sense the tensions. The Negro women sat ill at ease. I noticed some of the white women start in surprise as they came to the door and saw the Negro women there. One of these same white women told me months later, "You know, I didn't know what to think when I walked in there that night and saw Negroes sitting there. I'd never been in the room with a colored person in my life. I almost turned around and walked out."

Why she didn't leave — why the others didn't — is hard to analyze. All of them felt a strong desire to be a part of the interesting things outside their homes that their husbands were part of, and perhaps this desire was stronger at that moment than all the prejudices of a lifetime. In any event, no one left. And they returned the next time a meeting was called. As time went on they began coming to the union hall between meetings to sit together, Negro and white, addressing envelopes, planning parties and other activities. To a certain extent, some of the white women were influenced by a new kind of social pressure which the atmosphere in the union hall created; outside, in the atmosphere of Louisville generally, they were accepted by their friends and acquaintances if they shunned Negroes, for that was the pattern; but inside the union hall they found that they were accepted by the others if they ignored race bars, because here the pattern was different. And in time deep friendships developed between some of the Negro and white women. The woman who told me she had started to leave on that first night, for example, came to consider a Negro woman as her closest friend. Each of them had four children, and they talked together of their problems with their children, of their dreams for them. They began to visit in each other's homes often, and their children played together.

"At first I held her off," the white woman told me later, speaking of the Negro woman, "but she kept on talking to me anyway. She wouldn't let me hurt her feelings. And then — you know — why, all of a sudden I found out she was just like me. I really forgot there was a difference in our color."

There was wonder in her voice as she spoke, and I could see that she too was experiencing almost exactly the same thing I had experienced with the Negro actress. I could see also that her Negro friend had that same beautiful maturity and understanding and patience that my actress friend had. She was willing to put up with the prejudiced attitude of the white woman, as the actress had been willing to put up with my stiff and uneasy behavior, because she had faith that underneath the veneer was a human being.

I have wondered sometimes where the Negro people get it: this maturity and this patience and this faith. How can they — some of them, for not all of them do, but even some of them — have this forgiving and outgoing attitude toward white people when people with white skin have abused them all of their lives? How many white people could do it if our positions were reversed? How many of us who are white and who are lucky enough to have glimpsed the vision of the world without walls owe our vision and our new-found freedom to the fact that some Negro person somewhere in the past was patient enough to put up with us until we could find our way! It should make us humble and appreciative; it should disabuse us forever of whatever remnants we may have of the feeling that our white skin has made us "superior."

The experience of my white friend at the union hall also verified for me a theory I had long held: that race prejudice being an emotional thing cannot be removed by intellectual arguments alone. There must be some real emotional experience, such as a deep friendship across the race bars. The impact of such an experience is perhaps the only thing that can shake the emotional patterns of a lifetime.

Something like this had happened in other instances in Louisville, especially where Negroes had moved into previously all-white neighborhoods in the city's West End. Usually when the real estate companies decided to "break a block" and the first Negro family moved in, the white people began moving out. Several houses on the block might be sold to Negroes very quickly. But almost always a few white families stayed. Those who stayed found, as my friends at the union hall found, that the old emotional patterns gave way under the impact of new ones. They found their new Negro neighbors were people very much like themselves; they found them good friends in trouble and good company in happiness. A small miracle in human relations occurred.

But these were scattered instances. Important as they had been in the lives of some people, they had not much affected the life of Louisville generally — no more than had the breaking down of segregation in the intellectual centers. Most white people in Louisville in 1954 had never known any emotional experience that could upset the old ways. And, in Louisville as elsewhere, the majority of people do not find it easy to think beyond the confines of their own personal experience. Social problems in broad terms are something beyond their ken, except insofar as they translate themselves into problems in their own personal lives. For most white people in Louisville in 1954, race relations was not a problem that had translated itself into personal terms. Segregation was an accepted part of their lives — unchanged, unchallenged, and unquestioned. Within its framework and hardly thinking of it, they pursued their personal drives and dreams and plans, giving their attention and their efforts to the things men and women live out their lives in doing — building for themselves a snug structure of security, dreaming of something better for their children. One of these people was James Rone.

5

"Everybody Out Here Is Blaming Me..."

James I. Rone was the builder and owner of the house which Andrew Wade finally selected as the one he wanted us to buy for him. Carl and I first met Rone on the day we went to the office of the real estate company for the completion of the transfer of the property from Rone to us. Our preliminary dealings had been entirely with representatives of the real estate company rather than with Rone; Carl had taken care of most of this, and I had paid little attention to the details.

That had been a busy spring for me; I had been fixing up the two new rooms in our attic, which had just been completed, and painting all the walls and woodwork in our downstairs — quite an ordeal, since I am a highly amateur painter. And, as always, I had taken on more than I could really manage in responsibilities away from home: I was serving as secretary of my women's auxiliary unit at the church; both Carl and I were working on a state-wide committee that was trying to get Kentucky's school segregation law repealed; I was a team captain in the annual membership drive of the Louisville NAACP, my task being to enlist more white members in the organization. As for Andrew Wade's house — although it appears fantastic in hindsight that this should have been so — it seemed at that time like a quite minor project in our lives. Andrew was consulting with Negro real estate men and insurance executives as to the best methods of procedure, and we were giving the whole matter little thought at all. Carl handled the necessary negotiations with the real estate company more or less with his left hand, usually on his way to work at the newspaper in the afternoon.

On the day that we were to close the deal on the house, I had rushed through my morning house-cleaning chores and hurried to get the daily load of diapers on the line so that we could have an early lunch, take our younger child Anita to Carl's mother's house and get to the real estate office for our 2 o'clock appointment. But Anita balked over eating her lunch, and we were ten minutes late arriving. When we got there, Rone was already on hand, seated beside the desk of Ben Hudson, president of the Hudson Realty Company. Our little boy Jimmy was with us, and Hudson gave him a paperweight to amuse himself with. One of Hudson's assistants, Mrs. Thomas, handed Carl the deed and second mortgage papers to look over. She and I talked a bit, and I sat and studied Rone.

He looked to be a man in his middle forties, ruddy-faced with rather pleasant smiling blue eyes, and hands that obviously knew the meaning of hard work. He wore an open-neck shirt and work trousers, for he had come to the real estate office directly from his job in a Louisville industrial plant where he had asked for the afternoon off to complete this real estate deal. Although it was not until later that I learned more details about him, it was not difficult to picture his life and world.

Rone was not a large-scale builder. A working man all of his life, he had been fortunate enough to acquire a small tract of land just outside an incorporated suburb of Louisville called Shively. An old-fashioned white frame house, where he and his wife lived, stood on one corner of the tract. Running back into his property from Crums Lane — a main road through this section of the county — was a short dead-end dirt road. Until a few years before, all of this part of the county had been farmland. Now, with the rapid expansion of residential Louisville, it was fast filling up with new houses. Rone, with a knack for building and some experience in construction work, had recently started a development of small ranch-type houses along the little dead-end road on his property.

The house selected by Andrew Wade for us to buy lay across the dirt road and down a bit from Rone's own frame house at the corner of his road and Crums Lane. It had just been completed when we started negotiations for it and was only the third house in Rone's project. Directly across the road from it was a similar house, already sold and occupied. Down the road a bit toward the dead end was another like it, already occupied by the brother-in-law of Rone's young married son. A much smaller house at the end of the road, looking something like a temporary dwelling, was the only other house on the same side of the road with the house we were buying. Mostly, the house Andrew had selected was surrounded by open fields. The only other neighbors were several hundred feet away in older houses that backed to his from a distance, houses facing on Crums Lane and on another road running parallel to Rone's road some distance away. One of these houses had a large barn near the rear end of Andrew's lot, indicating how recently this had been farming country.

On the lot just adjacent to the one Andrew was to buy was a foundation Rone had already laid for his next house. Rone could build only one house at a time because he did not have much capital. Having completed Andrew's house and negotiated with us to sell it for $11,300, he had gone to a bank, the South End Federal Savings & Loan Association, and borrowed $8,000 on it. We were to assume this mortgage and give Rone a second mortgage of $1,900 and a cash down payment of $1,400. With the cash he obtained from us and the money he borrowed from the bank, he planned to proceed with the building of the next house — and so on, until the entire road was built up. He was building in his spare time with the help of his son and a few other construction workers he could afford to hire. He could not work on it full time because it was not yet a self-supporting project, and this was why he retained his full-time job in the industrial plant.

He had named his short dirt road Rone Court for himself and his family. It was obviously the fulfillment of a dream, a dream which many an American worker has — of going into business for himself, of independence, security. He talked of it with pride as we sat there in the real estate office. He seemed pleased that we were buying the house.

"I think you'll like it out there," he told us. "It's not fixed up yet just like I want it, but it will be. I'm going to plant trees all along the road there on either side. In a few years, it'll be shady and pretty."

Ben Hudson joined cordially in the conversation and agreed that Rone Court would someday be one of the most pleasant

residential streets in that part of the county. Hudson too had a
pride in new small housing developments. He was a small business-
man too, just getting his start. His was not one of the city's larger
real estate firms. The office was small, and he did much of the
work himself. Started on a shoestring, the business was now booming because of the mushrooming of small developments like Rone
Court around the county.

Later when we went from the real estate company to the South
End Federal Savings & Loan Association to sign a card saying
we agreed to assume payments on Rone's mortgage, Rone continued his genial conversation as our new neighbor.

"Now, I want you all to let me know if anything is wrong with
the house," he said. "I'll be around out there all the time except
when I'm working because I'm building that house next door.
There's some defective tile in your bathroom that I'll fix right
away. Anything I can do to help you, let me know."

By that time Jimmy was letting off energy by running around
the bank and trying out the various chairs. Rone looked at him in-
dulgently.

"He'll like it in the country," he smiled. "I bet the first thing
he does when he gets out there is to get a pony. My little grandson's
not much bigger than that, and he's got a pony."

We were ready to go then. Rone had the deed in his hand.
When he left us he would be on his way to the courthouse to record
it. It was not binding until it was recorded. This was the last moment
when, if we had told him our reason for purchasing the house, he
could have canceled the transaction.

How many times afterward was I to relive that moment! How
many times I was to try to analyze — as the questions came from
all sides: Why? How? . . . How could you do it? . . . Didn't Rone
have rights too? . . . You deceived him. . . . It was subterfuge. . . .
Oh no, technically and legally he had no right to know your plans,
but what about morally? . . . Subterfuge. . . . No, you didn't *tell*
him you planned to live there, but a lie does not have to be spoken:
you let him think it. . . . You say you believe in the brotherhood of
man . . . wasn't Rone your brother too? . . . Why? . . . How?

From my earliest memory, I had been taught to revere honor.
When I was a small child, I learned it was right to tell the truth,

wrong to tell a lie. As I grew older I learned there was a deeper reason for honesty in human relations. I remember the words of one of my college teachers in Virginia:

"Honesty is what makes human relationships possible," she had said. "If a person is honest with me, I know where I stand: we can have a relationship. But if he is not honest, it's as if I'm walking on quicksand, and no relationship is possible."

Honor: one of the shining ideals — and there are many — that the white South teaches its children. And, like so many of the others, it lies shipwrecked on the realities of Southern society.

For here was James Rone — a human being like ourselves, a man we should have been able to call brother, a man with whom we should have been able to have a relationship. How wonderful it would be if we *could* be a brother to all men, at all times; and in our ideals we may be. But in the field of practical action, in the field of reality, we in the South have split our society in two. There were two groups of men, two opposing forces, in Louisville in 1954 — as there were all over the South. And Carl and I could not maintain a relationship simultaneously with them both. We might in our innermost feelings, but in the area of action we had to make a choice. Even if we took no action, we were by our very inaction making a choice.

Andrew Wade wanted a house. He had tried by every open and honest method to buy a house by dealing directly with the people who had built the houses he wanted to buy. There was only one way left for him to get a house, and that lay in deceiving some white owner as to its ultimate purchaser. To do that, he needed the cooperation of someone with white skin. He came to us, and we agreed to cooperate with him. If we had refused, we would have been cooperating with the white people who were refusing to sell to him. We would have maintained an honest and brotherly relationship with these people, but we would have been betraying a relationship of brotherhood with Andrew and the Negro people he represented. We could not have both relationships at the same time. We were faced with the choice: "Who is my neighbor?"

I tried to analyze it all later; I didn't then. Perhaps in every crucial decision we ever make, life has already determined the course we will take — long, long before the moment of choice arrives. In this complex in which we were caught, I was on the side of Andrew Wade and his people. It might have made me feel better later to think that I at least hesitated in that moment as Rone stood at the door of the South End Federal Savings & Loan Association offering his friendship as our new neighbor. But to be perfectly accurate, I don't think I did. We kept our silence. We thanked him for his courtesies; we shook hands with him as we left. And we drove directly from the bank to Rone Court where Andrew was waiting for us to bring him the key to the house.

Rone's wife was at the house when we arrived, scratching a "For Sale" sign from the window. She too offered neighborly solicitations and asked us to be sure to let her know if there was anything she could do to help us get settled. She did not question Andrew's presence there, and we did not explain it.

So hypnotized was I by the pleasantness of the Rones that, as we rode away, leaving Andrew in the house, I commented to Carl:

"Now suppose after all this that Rone tells us later he would have sold the house to the Wades himself, if they had just asked him."

Carl was more discerning than I.

"I doubt it," he said grimly.

I have often wondered, though, what our relationship with the Rones would have been if we had been moving into the house ourselves. Would we have found them congenial neighbors? Would we have become close friends? Would Mrs. Rone and I have sat and drunk coffee together in the mornings, as neighbors do, and discussed our children and our houses and our yards? Would we have borrowed sugar and flour from each other and baby-sat for each other and helped each other? Would we have ever known what savage emotions lie just under the surface in people who seem so kindly and civilized?

We never, of course, had a chance to find out. It was on Monday, May 10, 1954, that we completed the purchase of the house and turned the key over to Andrew. On Tuesday and Wednesday, he began moving a few things in, painting the walls, and waxing the floors. No one questioned him at first. Perhaps it was because Andrew is quite light-skinned and they did not know immediately that he was a Negro. Or perhaps they thought he was doing work on the house for us. By Thursday they knew.

That afternoon, Rone approached Andrew as he was working in the house.

"Say," asked Rone, "are the Bradens renting this house to you?"

Andrew took a deep breath and answered.

"No, they are deeding it to me."

Rone's blue eyes stared.

"Deeding it to you?" he said incredulously. "Who is?"

"Why, Carl and Anne Braden, of course," Andrew replied calmly. "They're the ones who own it, aren't they?" Then he changed the subject. "Now, I believe Carl said you were planning to repair that defective tile in the bathroom. Do you think you can get to it soon?"

"I haven't got time to think about that now!" Rone shouted. "I've got things to do." With that he dashed out of the house.

This was in the late afternoon. Andrew drove into town to get his wife, and they returned to the house immediately after supper to do some work together on the floors. By the time they returned, there were several strange cars in the Rones' yard. Within a few more minutes, other cars began to arrive until there were twenty or more parked near the Rone house. Men and women were milling in and out of the house. Andrew and Charlotte watched from their windows apprehensively. Andrew tried to reassure Charlotte.

"Don't worry. They're surprised," he told her, "but they'll be all right when they get used to the idea. I've known white people better than you have, Charlotte — they'll come around. Now we'll stay right here. We won't drive away. We won't let them think we're scared."

The evening wore on, but the crowd did not approach the Wades' house. Finally, they all came out of the Rone house, got in their cars and drove away. That night, just before midnight, Carl answered a knock at our door and looked out to see our front yard filled with milling, mumbling men and the street in front of our house blocked with cars. More people were sitting in the cars — some of them perhaps women, although Carl couldn't be sure in the darkness. Rone and Hudson were standing on the front porch.

"Mr. Braden," Hudson said, "is it true you've sold that house on Rone Court to colored?"

"I've sold it," Carl answered calmly. "Does it make any difference what color the people are?"

There was a growl from the crowd. Rone looked frantic and bewildered, anger mingling with his confusion.

"But there aren't any colored out there," he said lamely.

"What difference does that make?" Carl asked.

Another voice from the crowd broke in: "But I've saved up for years to buy the house I own out there."

"So has the man I sold that house to," Carl replied evenly.

The crowd was becoming angrier.

"You'd better get those niggers out of there!" someone shouted.

A big man with blond hair stepped up on the porch.

"Do you own this house here?" he asked.

"Yes."

"Do you have any children?"

"Yes."

"Well, you'd better watch out."

Carl stiffened then.

"Now get out of my yard and quit trampling on my grass," he said. "If you want to come back and discuss this thing calmly, I'll be glad to have you. But when you come back, act like gentlemen."

The crowd drifted away. I had been downtown that night to a concert which lasted late, and it was several minutes after the departure of the men when I arrived home. By that time Andrew and Charlotte were there to compare notes on what had happened. Listening to Carl's account of the event, I thought again of Rone and how he had smiled at Jimmy and wanted him to have a pony. What had happened to him in that moment when Andrew told him we were deeding the house to him?

It would be easy to say that Rone left the Wade house that afternoon to go out and organize a mob against us and the Wades. But I don't think that this was his conscious purpose. Obviously, he had called the people — or at least some of them — who were at his house that night: otherwise no one would have known that Wade was buying the property. But it seems unlikely that he altogether realized what he was doing or why. I think he was acting from panic more than anger.

When he approached Andrew late that afternoon, he was a safe man in a safe world, building his life in an ordered way behind the walls society had built around him, building his future secure with each stone that he laid in his little ranch-type houses on Rone Court. With Andrew's announcement of his plans to move into the house, a new and terrifying thing entered Rone's little world. A new and unknown thing impinged upon his life, frightening because it was the unknown and the unfamiliar more than because it was bad. It was as if a dike somewhere had broken and Rone was suddenly engulfed by the dark mysterious floods of a world that was too big, by problems beyond his ken. And as the dark floods swept over him, all of the old myths that were waiting in his unconscious — myths that he had learned sometime far in the past, myths that he had never examined and had never even had occasion to think about very much — loomed before him like giants in the darkness: Negroes are a lower breed of humanity; white people who amount to anything don't associate with colored; Negroes want to marry our white women; Negroes in a neighborhood lower property values — all of the old myths that were a part of his heritage in a Southern society. And his head reeled in the darkness. His dream of the future on Rone Court seemed wrecked; his security was shattered; he was panicked.

Doing as men often do when they are alone and panicked before forces too big for them, he had to flee to his kind. It was company he wanted, I think, when he called his friends that night to come to his house, not a mob, but company to surround him, to fill his world again with the known, the safe, and the sure, to make him feel secure again in a world he understood and with which he was familiar, which lay within the bounds of his old habits of thought. And it was company that those who answered his call to come to his house that night wanted too — company that Ben Hudson, the real estate man, wanted as he faced the specter of ostracism because he had violated the codes of the real estate business by letting a restricted block be broken, the threat of what he thought was ruin for his new and booming business; company that was wanted by the man who told Carl he had saved for years to buy his house near Rone Court; company that all of the others wanted as they saw their safe little world threatened by the new and the unknown. The crowd at Rone's house became almost transformed into a mob because these people did not know what else to do with their frustration, because acting as a unit and together gave them back some of the sense of security they had lost by the looming of a new factor in all of their lives.

There may have been another more conscious motive for Rone's calling the crowd together that night. I got a clue to it in a conversation I had with Rone the following Saturday afternoon.

On Friday morning it had become obvious that our trouble was just beginning. Our telephone began to ring constantly with anonymous threats and ultimatums to "get those niggers out of that house." Wade steadfastly continued moving his furniture in. I began making telephone calls myself, and on Saturday I decided to call Rone, to try to talk reasonably with him, to try to see him if possible.

I soon saw there was no use in trying to see him, but we talked for about fifteen minutes on the phone. And I remember the points I was trying to make clear. I told him I was sorry this thing had surprised him so, but that there was no other way Andrew Wade could have got a house. I told him I felt sure that if he gave himself a chance he would like the Wades as neighbors. I asked him to try to understand how the Wades felt, that they were just people like himself who wanted a nice house for their children, as he did for his children and grandchildren.

"But why did it have to be my house? Why did it have to be me?" Rone asked almost plaintively. "Everybody out here is blaming me for it."

Everybody out here is blaming me. . . . I saw now that Rone had had to oppose the Wades' occupancy of the house, he had had to organize the crowd to come to our house, in order to prove to his friends and neighbors that he was not a part of this terrifying thing that had impinged upon all their lives, not responsible for it. And each man who joined the motorcade to our house that night had undoubtedly had to come along in order to prove, each man to his neighbor, that he was opposed to this new thing, that he was a part of the old safe world and bore no responsibility for the new. How much so-called prejudice is maintained from generation to generation because every man must prove to his neighbor that he thinks as he thinks his neighbor thinks?

We had another instance of this vicious circle of social pressure in the actions of Rone's twenty-year-old son, Buster Rone. On Friday afternoon, the elder Rone approached Andrew again and asked him to sell the house back to him. With him was Buster. Andrew refused, politely but firmly. Then he tried to explain to the two Rones how he felt.

"I'm not trying to force myself and my family on you," he said. "You don't have to be my friend or ever come on my property if you don't want to. But how can you say I don't have a right to live in the same neighborhood with you? Try to put yourself in my place for a minute. I'm an American citizen. I fought for my country. I'm a person, like you. I want a decent house to live in. Will you say that in a democracy I can't have a decent house to live in, that I can't live where I want to, just because my skin is a different color from yours? We can all get along in the same world. That's what democracy means." He turned to Buster Rone.

"You're still young," he told him. "Perhaps you haven't yet been in the service. When you do go, you'll find that you will be living and working with people of all national groups and all colors. You may not be close friends with all of them, but you'll find yourself getting along with them. And you'll be happier, because you will find that you can make new friends among all people. You will grow too. We all have something to give each other."

The younger Rone nodded. As he and his father left, Buster and Andrew shook hands.

"I understand," Buster said.

And yet, the next night, Buster Rone with some of the other young men in the neighborhood went out and burned a cross in the vacant lot next door to the Wade house.

He admitted the burning of the cross to a grand jury investigating the case several months later and was asked why it had been done.

"It was just an idea brought up," he replied. ". . . I don't know . . . there is nobody thought they should move in the neighborhood."

6

Shots in the Night

The cross burning occurred late Saturday night, May 15. It was part of a night of terror at the Wade house that climaxed two days of threats from residents of the Rone Court area.

At dawn on Friday morning, May 14, the morning after the crowd visited our house, our telephone rang. I got out of bed to answer, and a woman's voice, unidentified, spoke:

"Get those niggers out of that house. We won't have them out here. You put them in there. You get them out. We'll give you forty-eight hours, or you take the consequences."

I started to argue with her, but she hung up. The ringing of the phone had awakened the children, and I went to get Anita out of her bed and change her diaper. I had just had time to remove one diaper pin when the phone rang again. This time it was a man's voice.

"We'll give you forty-eight hours. Get those niggers out of that house."

From then on, the phone rang constantly — sometimes the calls no more than four or five minutes apart. Sometimes there was a tirade from the other end. Sometimes only a brief statement: "You'd better watch out!" "Get the Wades off Rone Court!" I was afraid to just let the phone ring, or leave it off the hook, thinking the Wades or someone else with something important to say might call, so I kept on answering — getting the children's breakfast and settling Jimmy in his sandpile and Anita in her playpen outside in between the rings. When Carl got up — he always slept later than the rest of us because of his night-work hours — we took turn about on answering the calls. Sometimes the caller was a woman; sometimes it was a man. It seemed to me, however, that there were not many different voices. Probably no more than four or five people were doing all the telephoning. And whenever I could catch the phone between rings, I made calls of my own to people I thought might offer the Wades support.

Andrew had no phone at his Rone Court house at that time, but the same kind of calls came to him at his place of business. He remained calm. On Friday he had planned to move the rest of his furniture into the house, and he proceeded with his plans.

First, however, he called the county police, in whose jurisdiction the house lay, and told them of the threats. He talked to the captain of the police district; his father talked to the chief of county police, Colonel Walter Layman. Both Wades told these men that Andrew was moving into the house on that day, that there had been threats, and asked that police be on hand to nip any trouble in the bud. Both the captain and the police chief replied that they did not have sufficient men on the force to maintain a constant guard but they said they would patrol the area and be on watch.

If any police car did patrol the area of Rone Court that day, when Andrew was moving his furniture in, or the next afternoon and evening, after he returned to the house, Andrew did not see it.

By Friday night, the furniture was all in the house, but Andrew and his family did not stay there that night. The next morning, our phone again rang early. At 7 o'clock a voice said, "Braden, watch out. Something's going to happen at twelve o'clock." The calls continued at intervals all morning. Close to noon they became more frequent. "Braden, one hour." "Braden, fifty minutes."

About 11 o'clock Carl was eating his usual combination breakfast and lunch, and I sat down to drink a cup of coffee with him.

"I guess it's all a bluff, don't you suppose?" I asked.

Carl, as usual, was perfectly calm.

"Of course it is," he laughed. "You don't think if they were really going to do something they'd call us up and tell us in advance, do you?" He turned to talk to Jimmy, who was telling him in great detail about the house he had been building in his sandpile. It was only in recent months that Jimmy had learned to express his thoughts adequately in consecutive sentences, and he was thoroughly enjoying his newly acquired ability to communicate. His brows puckered slightly over his serious blue eyes as he talked. He always came in from playing in the yard when he heard Carl's voice in the kitchen and knew he was up and about. He was a complete Daddy's boy.

"Well, maybe we ought to call the police just in case . . ." I suggested tentatively at the first break in Jimmy's tumble of words.

"Might not be a bad idea," Carl said, paying more attention to the piece of toast and jam he was fixing for Jimmy than he was paying to me. "I'll call them in a little while if you want to."

He finished eating and took his time about washing his breakfast dishes. Finally, he went in the living room and called the city police — our house, unlike Andrew's, was within the city limits — and they said they would send a car to drive by our house around noon. Then Carl sat down in the big chair and relaxed to read the paper. By this time it was 11:45, and the telephone was ringing every few minutes: "Braden, watch out." "Braden, fifteen minutes." Finally I took the phone off the hook.

I looked at Carl, as he sat quietly reading the paper. My mind told me his unconcern was sensible and that the voices on the phone were only trying to scare us. But this business of facing physical threats was something new to me and I had not yet learned to shrug it off, as I finally did later. And besides, I was not sure — and am still not — just how much of Carl's nonchalance was a reflection of courage and how much of it was pure phlegmatism in the face of danger. His whole life experience had been different from mine. He had grown up in the jungle atmosphere of Louisville's Portland, where the gang of boys on his block was always in a state of running physical warfare with gangs from surrounding blocks. In my world, although I knew now that it was shot through with its own terrible kind of viciousness, it was a viciousness that was always smoothly covered with a façade of gentility and soft voices, where physical violence was something beneath discussion. The violence that permeated the South in those days was far removed from my insulated world — far away and under the cover of darkness, hardly a muted whisper of it reaching the rarefied atmosphere in which I lived. Now that it had burst into my own life, I was startled and dismayed.

The children had followed us into the living room, and I busied myself with them for a few minutes. Anita was sitting on the floor by the long bookcases that lined one wall of the room and glee-fully pulling out books — our most precious possession and the one thing in the house that was taboo for the children to touch. I rescued the books and diverted her attention to one of her own picture books. Then I sat down on the arm of Carl's chair.

"Look," I said, "I don't want to be a scary-cat, but don't you think we ought to go out in the yard or something about noon? Suppose they've set a time bomb under the house."

Carl laughed and pulled me down into his lap and kissed me.

"Anne," he said, "you're being silly."

I returned his kiss and got up.

"I know it's silly," I said. "But I don't see any use in being foolish either — not with the children anyway. I'm going to take them out in the yard."

I picked up Anita and suggested to Jimmy that he come out in the backyard and I would push him in his swing. He was delighted, and we left. Carl did not protest, but he shook his head and turned back to his newspaper.

Of course he was right. I saw the patrol car that the police had promised drive by several times as I pushed Jimmy in the swing. But noon passed, and nothing happened — not at our house.

Late that afternoon, Andrew and Charlotte went to Rone Court to spend their first night in the new house. Because of the threats, they decided to leave their two-year-old daughter, Rose-mary, with Andrew's parents for the night, but they took with them a young friend, Carlos Lynes. When they arrived, the front picture window had been broken out with a rock: they found the rock inside the living room. Around it was wrapped a piece of paper on which was written "NIGGER GET OUT." Andrew and Carlos Lynes checked around the house. There was no other damage, except that the grating of one of the small air vents under the house was broken out. It was the vent where dynamite was to be placed six weeks later.

The Wades and Lynes spent the evening arranging furniture in the house. About 10 o'clock they heard a noise outside. Andrew stepped onto a side porch and saw a cross burning in the field next door. Around the cross five figures were dancing. He could see that they were adults, and they looked like men, but he could not make out their faces. One of them shouted: "Get out while you still can!"

Andrew had a gun in his pocket. He pulled it out but then dropped it to his side.

"So — you are burning your own American flag!" he called back to the men. In a few moments they left.

There was no telephone in the house to call the police or friends. Andrew looked out: there was no police car in sight. Charlotte, who was seven months pregnant, was quite worried. But Andrew told her it would be foolish to leave the house then — in the darkness and alone. The Wades and Lynes settled down for the night, Andrew and Charlotte in the front bedroom and Lynes on a couch they had put temporarily in the kitchen.

About 2 A.M. they were awakened by the sound of rifle shots. About ten shots rang out. There was the noise of glass breaking. Lynes heard one bullet zing past his ear. He dropped to the floor and lay there, waiting, until the shooting stopped. Andrew and Charlotte jumped from their bed and ran into the hallway. Andrew pushed Charlotte to the floor and crawled into the kitchen. Looking out the window, he saw a car pulling off about 200 feet away on Crums Lane. The glass in the kitchen door was broken. Bullets were lodged in the woodwork of the pantry. Everything was quiet. There was only the roar of the car's motor as it sped away.

The Wades and Lynes sat up for the rest of the night, waiting until morning came and it was light enough to go to a telephone. But the rest of the night was peaceful.

It was just after dawn that Sunday morning that Carl and I were awakened by loud knocks on our front door. That night had been a hectic one at our house too. The telephone rang incessantly up until 2 or 3 o'clock in the morning; sometimes there were the threatening voices on the other end, sometimes only silence. Carl was at work that night, and after the children were in bed I brought my ironing board into the living room where I could reach the telephone easily as I ironed curtains. When Carl came in from work at the usual time — about 2 A.M. — I persuaded him that we should sit up a while in case anything was going to happen, as we were both sound sleepers. It was about 4 A.M. when we finally went to bed. It seemed we had been asleep only a few minutes when the knocks on the front door awakened us. I pulled aside the shade at our bedroom window, which is on the front of the house, and looked out.

"That's Andrew," I told Carl, recognizing the Wade car parked in front of our house.

Carl jumped up and put on his bathrobe to go to the door and I dressed quickly. When I entered the living room a few moments later, Andrew was already telephoning the police. He appeared remarkably calm. Charlotte's pretty dark eyes seemed much larger than usual as she sat on our living-room couch, her arms folded around each other as if she were cold — it was a warm spring morning — but she too seemed in perfect control of herself. Jimmy and Anita ran into the living room in their night clothes, and Charlotte leaned over to talk to them, amusing them with an ornament on the purse she was carrying. Andrew told us quickly what had happened and soon got up to leave.

"We'd better get back out there, Charlotte," he said. "The police will be coming."

He turned to us.

"Telephone anybody you can think of who might give us some support," he said.

I followed him and Charlotte to the door.

"What are you going to do?" I asked.

"What are we going to do about what?" Andrew asked.

"About the house. Are you going to stay?"

Andrew looked surprised that I would ask the question.

"Of course we'll stay," he said quietly. "This will die down. It was probably only a few people; others will support us. And besides a principle is at stake — you just don't run away from something like this."

Charlotte did not say anything, but she appeared to nod slightly as he spoke. I looked at Andrew. He was a tall, slim man with a habit of carrying his head high in a way that made some people describe him as "arrogant." As I looked at him that morning, I had the feeling I had never really noticed how tall he was. I suddenly felt a flash of shame at my own fear the day before in the face of the telephone threats.

An hour or so later, the Rone Court property was overrun with police, reporters, photographers, and curiosity-seekers. Soon a *Courier-Journal* reporter called us and asked for our side of the story. Had we intended to live in the house when we bought it, he asked. Carl, who had answered the phone, replied that we had not, that we had bought the house for only one purpose — to transfer it to the Wades, because they had been unable to buy the kind of house they wanted for themselves. The reporter then asked us to make a statement as to why we did this. Carl said we would prepare a statement and he would bring it to the newspaper office within a half-hour.

This, I think, was the first time we ever tried to put into words even in our own minds the "why" of our action. Our decision when Wade asked us had been so automatic, the whole undertaking had seemed so minor in our lives that we had given the thing little thought. Now we went upstairs into one of the new attic rooms we had made into an office, Carl sat down at the typewriter and I looked over his shoulder — as we often worked when we were writing something together — and in five minutes and in one paragraph we tried to put into words what we thought our reasons were. Since that time, we have been asked the question "Why" many times by many people; we have spoken and written many words trying to explain. But I have often thought that this first statement, made in the heat of events and under pressure of a deadline — although it wasn't as carefully thought out as some of the things we said later — was perhaps the most valid reflection of our unconscious thoughts on the matter. The statement, which the *Courier-Journal* printed the next morning, said:

"We feel that every man has a right to live where he wants to, regardless of the color of his skin. This is the test of democracy. Either you practice what you preach, or you shut up about believing in democracy."

The next day the story of what had happened at the Wades' house was front-page news in a town where race relations had been seemingly quiet for many years. Rone Court had become a public issue laid on the doorstep of a sleeping, complacent Louisville.

7

Panic in High Places

It never came out who was responsible for any of the events of that Saturday afternoon and night except for the cross burning. By Kentucky law this is an indictable offense when done for purposes of intimidation. Two men, in addition to Buster Rone, confessed later to the grand jury that they were among the men who burned the cross. The two were Buster's brother-in-law, Stanley Wilt, who lived in the new house near the end of Rone Court, and Lawrence Rinehart, another resident of the same general area and a former county policeman. Rinehart also told the grand jury that he was in the crowd which came to our house on the night of May 13. But no one admitted throwing the rock through the window, or breaking out the grating in the air vent or firing the rifle shots.

It seems safe to assume, however, that all of these acts were the work of a relatively small number of people. The majority of white people in the area had not yet taken sides on the issue of the Wades' occupancy of the house, although they all undoubtedly knew about it. Even a week later, the woman who lived in the new house directly across Rone Court from the Wades' house was wavering. Approached by some white friends of the Wades in an effort to find potentially friendly people in the neighborhood, she smiled hesitantly.

"I don't know what I can do right now," she said. "I'm sort of caught in the middle here." She did not want to discuss it further.

A woman whose house faced on a street parallel to Rone Court and whose property adjoined the Wades' at the back was more communicative when called on the telephone by friends of the Wades.

"I don't object to having them here," she said. "I have children, and I would be glad to have them play with the Wades' little girl. But I don't see how I can be friendly right now. If I go to call on the Wades, some of those people who are after them will turn on me. I'll have to wait until things quiet down a bit."

Certainly, if there was ever a time when all of the events that followed could have been prevented, it was in the period immediately after that Saturday, May 15. In other places, the explosive possibilities in such situations have been dissipated. In Louisville, a somewhat similar crisis had been resolved only six months earlier.

On that occasion, a Filipino woman, Mrs. Nina Hardman — the widow of an American soldier — moved into one of Louisville's all-white neighborhoods. There were immediate threats from some of the neighbors. A petition was circulated under the sponsorship of one of Louisville's city aldermen demanding that Mrs. Hardman move, and most of the neighbors signed it. Before any violence could erupt, however, numerous liberal forces in the city sprang to the Filipino woman's defense. The *Courier-Journal* ran a front-page story about what was happening and a strong editorial defending the basic American principle of equality, noting that "until now Louisville has been blessedly free of this sort of hostility among neighbors." Church leaders spoke out in shock at the reaction of the neighbors. Labor leaders protested, and some of them organized a picket line around the home of the alderman who had sponsored the petition. In a few days, most of the neighbors who had signed the petition came to Mrs. Hardman's home to apologize. They brought her food and flowers and welcomed her into their neighborhood.

That this pattern did not repeat itself in the case of the Wades is due to many factors, the most obvious of which is that this woman was a Filipino and the Wades are Negroes. Nina Hardman, incidentally, was no lighter than the almost-white Andrew Wade, but she did not have the stigma that the word "Negro" carries in the southeastern part of the United States of America. That this should make such a difference defies reason, of course, but people do not act reasonably when settled mores are challenged. They are much more likely to act from panic; and the events on Rone Court

panicked men and women who might have been expected to proceed reasonably.

On the day before the shooting at the Wade house, that Friday
when we first began to receive threats, I telephoned all of the
Christian ministers I could reach in the Shively area. Unlike many
people concerned with social problems, I had not written the white
church off. I knew many of its shortcomings; it often seemed to fail
at the point of social challenge, and there had been a time —
during my final college years — when with the impatience of youth
I had drifted away from it. But I had gone back — not only for
personal spiritual reasons but also because I felt, for all its failures,
that it still held the potential for helping to make a better world.
It was the source of many of my own ideals and of whatever
strength I might possess, and I knew it played the same role in the
lives of many people. In recent years I had come to know more
churchmen whose religious beliefs were translated into courageous
social action, and I had hopes that it could yet play a redemptive
role in the white South. At this point it seemed to me that the situation in Shively was more a job for the church than for the police.

I described to the ministers I called how the Wades, a Negro
family, were moving into a white neighborhood on the outskirts of
Shively and that there had been threats from a few people. I suggested that perhaps if the ministers would talk to some of the
members of their congregations in the area, a few of the residents
could be convinced to come forward in a friendly way to welcome
the Wades into the neighborhood, and this would offset the
atmosphere being created by those who were unfriendly. If this
were done, I said, many of the people who had no strong feelings
either way would probably follow the leadership of those who were
friendly, and the tension would be abated.

All of the ministers naturally wanted to know what my concern
in the situation was. I explained that my husband and I were white
and that we were the ones who had sold the house to the Wades,
that we had bought the house for the specific purpose of selling it
to the Wades because they were unable to buy for themselves the
kind of house they wanted anywhere in the Louisville area.

It is an interesting sidelight, in view of later criticism that we
received, that none of the ministers at that time expressed any shock

or disapproval at this method of procedure. All of them, however, were hesitant as to what they could do to help.

"It is a terrible thing," one of them said earnestly, "a terrible thing that people can act in such an un-Christian way. Of course every man has a right to live where he chooses. I don't know though. I'm not sure I have any members in that particular area. This is a hard question to handle with people — they have such set prejudices. I'll see. I'll do what I can."

I called the priest of the Catholic parish of St. Helen's which I presumed included the Rone Court area.

"Of course we believe in equal rights for all people," he said. "This is a dreadful thing. But I believe this is out of my parish. Rone Court must be in the next parish, adjoining ours — St. Denis."

I called the priest of St. Denis parish.

"These things are very hard," he said. "Of course they are wrong. But I believe Rone Court must be in St. Helen's parish. I'll see."

I called almost every minister in the vicinity — certainly all of those of the largest churches — Protestant and Catholic. It was a strange thing. I am confident that most of the residents of Rone Court and vicinity were churchgoing people. But in all of my calls I could not find one minister who thought he had any members in that neighborhood.

They were not deliberately lying. The mind plays strange tricks when faced with a challenge that seems too big. Rone Court did lie on a borderline between two Catholic parishes. Undoubtedly each priest at that point honestly thought—perhaps because it was best to think — that it lay in the other parish. Undoubtedly each Protestant minister could not at that moment remember any of his members who lived in that particular area. Some of them explained their hesitancy quite frankly.

"People have such strong opinions on this color question," one of them said. "I am opposed to segregation of course, because there is no other true Christian position; we are all children of God. But I haven't tried to discuss it very much with my congregation. I know how they feel. I would just be pushing my head against a stone wall. I'd destroy my ability to influence them on any other question."

"I'm from the North," said another, "and it's hard for a Northerner to speak to a Southerner on this sort of thing. They think we are outsiders. They're not likely to listen to me."

I know how they feel . . . They're not likely to listen to me . . . People have such strong opinions. On a different level, it was again like the men who joined together to come to our house on that Thursday night. The actions of each man were guided by what he thought his neighbor thought, by what he thought his neighbor expected of him, and not by what he himself thought.

Early Sunday morning, after Andrew had told us of the events of Saturday night, I called all of these same ministers again. I reminded them of what I had said to them on Friday. I told them what had happened on Saturday night. I argued that the whole situation might be changed if the ministers of Shively would rise in their pulpits on that Sunday morning to condemn the violence and ask for Christian tolerance and neighborliness. If any of them did so, we never heard of it.

Some of them did move in small ways. At least one of them, I know, visited at least one resident of the Rone Court area. One of the Catholic priests later wrote a letter to the Shively community newspaper in which, though he took no clear-cut position on whether the Wades had a right to move into the neighborhood, he denounced the violent methods that had been used to try to force them out. The wife of one of the Protestant ministers also wrote a letter to the paper — a very courageous letter in which she strongly condemned prejudice and violence. But measured by the dramatic leadership that was needed, all that came from the pulpits of Shively was an appalling silence.

I was deeply disappointed. I felt it most keenly, I think, one day a few weeks later when Charlotte Wade told me about one of the ministers in the area who had come to see her. It was on one of the many afternoons that June when I took the children and went to Rone Court to visit with Charlotte and Rosemary so they would not be alone in the house. Charlotte and I would sit on the long porch and talk while the children played — Jimmy and Rosemary, who were about the same size, racing about the yard and Anita tagging along behind, trying valiantly to keep up.

"You should have met this minister, Anne," Charlotte said. "I guess he thought he was being friendly. He said of course he personally thought we had a right to live here, but in the present situation he felt the only thing for us to do was move. Said we couldn't be happy here and the only way to preserve peace in the community and for ourselves was for us to leave."

Charlotte's brown eyes flashed as she told me about it.

"I didn't like him at all," she concluded simply.

As she spoke, I felt a sudden stab of shame — almost a physical thing. Shame for my religion, shame for my world. And, with it, a burst of irrational anger at this obviously well-meaning minister whom I had never even met. He had failed so miserably, and with him I had failed; we had all failed and all we believed in had failed. And the flashing eyes of a beautiful brown-skinned woman were our judgment and our retribution. Why, why, I thought to myself, could he not have done something, why could he not have said something that would make it possible for me to look at Charlotte Wade and not be ashamed of my white skin?

And yet, even in my burst of anger, some calmer voice within me told me that I should not sit in judgment. This minister was undoubtedly a good man. Given what looked like an impossible situation, he saw that something had to be changed; in his view, it could not be the whole community, so it must be the Wades and their driving desire for a decent place to live. His motives were good; he simply did not have an answer big enough for the problem he was trying to grapple with. He like all the other Shively ministers was the victim of a myth, the myth under which so much of the South lives — the myth that every other man considers segregation holy and that no one can oppose it and continue to live and work in this environment. He like all of them was caught in a trap, and at this point in time there was no way out.

It was the same with other decent people and groups in the community who might have been expected to act. All caught in a trap. A trap partly perhaps of their own making, and yet so collectively created and over such a long period of time that it is impossible to pinpoint its beginning or to place the blame. We talked with many of these people. We called every individual we could think of with a reputation for liberalism. In addition to the churches, on the very Sunday afternoon following the shooting we turned to another organized force in the community with the power to influence public opinion. Carl called a number of labor leaders whom he knew well, both in the AFL and the CIO. He told them the situation and asked that they take a position supporting Wade's right to live in his house, that they speak to their membership, that they perhaps take decisive action such as the picket line they had thrown up in the neighborhood of the embattled Filipino woman.

They too expressed shock at what had happened and horror that it could occur in as "forward-looking" a community as Louisville. They said that of course this was something the labor movement should give leadership on. They recalled that both the AFL and CIO officially opposed all segregation and discrimination, that they knew division of the races weakens the labor movement, that the labor movement was and should be the staunchest defender of democratic rights for all American citizens. They promised to take the matter up in their meetings scheduled for the following week and to make statements to the press. But they never did.

Something that one of them said to Carl that Sunday may be a clue to their inaction.

"Of course this is a hard issue to sell to our membership," he said. "We can talk about equality on the job and things like that. But in housing it's different. They've got pretty set ideas. This gets into social equality and they don't believe in that."

We knew from our own experience with the Harvester union that this was not necessarily true for all eternity. We had seen there that, as set as the white workers' views might appear to be, they were not unchangeable. But the leadership of Louisville labor was not willing to try such a seemingly risky experiment on the Rone Court issue. It would have been a big step forward, and the Louisville labor movement had not taken some of the intermediate steps.

And, also, by the time the various labor bodies held their meetings later that week, the Louisville *Courier-Journal* had already set the course of an equivocating approach for Louisville liberals to follow.

The *Courier-Journal,* as it later said frankly, found itself in a very difficult position in regard to the issue of the Wade house on Rone Court. As the leader of liberal opinion on the race question in Louisville, it had always worked against discrimination — against discrimination in any field, in the schools, in public places, on the job. And also in housing. In 1951, it had written angrily of the riots against a Negro veteran who moved into an all-white section in Cicero, Illinois, and deplored editorially the fact that "Cicero's churches and civic institutions made no move to protect his constitutional rights or to speak for an American's right to live where he chooses." It had of course come to the aid of Mrs. Nina Hardman and supported her right to the house of her choice.

For all these efforts, the *Courier-Journal* was hated by certain sections of the Louisville population — the people convinced that desegregation represented a vital threat to their interests and their way of life. And yet, despite this vocalized hate, there was between the liberal forces of the *Courier-Journal* and its opponents on this question a kind of armed truce — a certain unspoken agreement to disagree without too much decisive action on either side. Partly this rapport was a result of the fact that officials of the *Courier* moved in much the same social circles as their opponents among the segregationists, and it is hard to clash too fundamentally with the people you meet at the country club. To the greater credit of the *Courier-Journal,* the relaxed relationship also resulted from a certain sensitivity on the part of the officials of the newspaper to the feelings of those who opposed them. These officials realized that when they challenged segregation in Louisville they were challenging entrenched traditions and strong forces. They were convinced they could not move too fast or try to bring about changes too quickly without stiffening their opposition and perhaps in the long run defeating their own purpose. They believed that the best way was to proceed gradually, inch by inch, altering the segregated pattern of Louisville life so slowly and imperceptibly that the die-hard segregationist would hardly realize things were changing — boiling the frog without his realizing he was being boiled.

In contrast to this quiet and imperceptible approach to change, the sudden move of the Wades into a white suburb — when all Louisville suburbs had previously been behind the color bar — was a drastic action. It was a shocking thing to the people profoundly convinced that the races must be kept separate. Further than that, it stepped hard on the toes of some of the most powerful supporters of Jim Crow, the real estate interests. Within the framework of its philosophy, the *Courier-Journal* would have found the situation a hard one to handle in any event. The fact that Carl was an employee of the newspaper made it almost impossible.

Officials of the *Courier-Journal* knew that the supporters of segregation tended to blame the newspaper for every step toward integration taken in the community. This at all times made it hard enough to maintain a placid and peaceful relationship with their opposition. When it came out that an employee of theirs had deliberately bought a house in a white neighborhood for the purpose of transferring it to a Negro, they knew immediately that their opponents would say — as they did say and are still saying — that the whole thing was a scheme devised by the *Courier-Journal*. The charge was as untrue as it was unfair, but it was inevitable. It was a frightening thing because it upset the whole world the *Courier* had constructed for itself of adherence to principle while maintaining a way of living with its opposition. Consequently, the *Courier* officials reacted in panic.

There was another and perhaps more subtle reason for the panic. Believing that segregation was wrong, the officials of the *Courier* had built for themselves a world within the bounds of which they could oppose it. They acted on conscience generally, and they moved steadily, if slowly, in the direction they thought was right. But the situation was always firmly under their control. When they decided the community was ready for a step forward, they planned it carefully and the step was taken. When they decided the time was not ripe for change, the status — if they could arrange it — remained quo. But with the independent action of the Wades and us, new forces beyond their control were suddenly hurled into their ordered world. The determination of Wade to claim his rights when he wanted them and not when the *Courier-Journal* decided it was wise, and the determination of Carl and me to act when Wade asked it and not when the *Courier* approved it, brought them face to face with forces they did not understand and could not fit into their scheme of things. Their situation was like that of many white liberals all over the South today — honest men and women who for two or three decades have been opposing segregation and discrimination in a setting in which they were in the driver's seat and their foot was on the accelerator. Now many of these men and women, confronted with the startling factor of a united Negro people moving ahead on their own and setting their own timetable, are suddenly recoiling from the final steps toward the desegregation they have been advocating all of their lives. I do not think this reaction indicates that these people were not sincere in all the years they worked against segregation or that they do not still believe in the same principles today. But they are shocked by a new factor that is beyond their control — as the *Courier* was shocked — and afraid that progress which is going too fast for them to control will present problems and challenges too great for them. And the *Courier* officials — not unlike James Rone, although for different reasons and on a different level — reacted with the fright which seizes most men when confronted with something new and strange.

The first impulse that grew out of their panic was to dissociate themselves somehow from the whole Rone Court situation. This they did in the first story they ran on the incident, on Monday, May 17, on the front page. It started with this paragraph — or, in journalistic terms, this "lead":

"Efforts of a white couple to place a Negro family in a home they could not have bought themselves brought violence yesterday that barely missed killing or wounding several persons."

Every newspaper person knows that a news story should never express an opinion, but this lead — which was written in the *Courier-Journal* office after the reporter turned in his original story — clearly expressed one. It stated quite plainly that the *Courier-Journal* had an opinion as to the cause of some violence out on Rone Court, and that this cause was the action of Carl and Anne Braden in buying a house for a Negro family — this "brought" the violence. Ordinarily, the *Courier-Journal* maintains high professional standards of objectivity, but panic had taken over. The lead was its way of saying to the world that the newspaper thoroughly disapproved of the fact that Carl and I had sold a house to a Negro family and that the whole thing was no doing of the *Courier-Journal*.

On Tuesday, May 18, the *Courier-Journal* in the same mood of panic ran the following editorial:

The relations between white and Negroes in America is a long, tortured story. Its latest episode in Louisville is the case of the Negro couple who have moved into a white neighborhood on Rone Court, near Shively.

This episode reflects no credit on the judgment or the respect for law of certain white citizens involved. If the Negro couple also made an error of judgment, it can be more easily understood as an emotional protest against segregation.

The real fault of judgment, in our opinion, lies with Mr. and Mrs. Carl Braden. This white couple bought the Shively house in their own name, with no intention of living in it, but for the sole purpose of getting it into the hands of Negro owners who could not have bought it directly. Whatever may have been the motives of the Bradens, we believe they gave poor service to idealism in forcing an issue of race relations in this artificial and contrived way.

Some of the white citizens of the Shively neighborhood have convicted themselves of having no respect for the law.

They are entirely within their rights, we believe, in protesting the purchase of property in their subdivision by Negroes. Regardless of the moral issue, there is no use denying that the value of their property will decrease as a result of the sale.

The right of orderly protest, however, is not the right to throw rocks through windows or to fire bullets into rooms where human beings are sleeping. These are acts in the spirit of lynch law.

The police can do nothing less or more than guard the Negro family against such attacks. They can by proper vigilance shield them from physical injury. The forces of law cannot, however, compel a change in the mental patterns of a neighborhood, or save a Negro family from the unhappy ostracism that will be their fate there.

There is a conflict here of moral, legal, and emotional issues. Such confusion of motives seldom brings out the best in human behavior.

The most we can hope for now is that violence will cease, and that the neighboring white families will be content to rely on proper legal procedures instead of stooping to terrorism and intimidation.

Those who brought about this situation have hardly served the best interests of the particular Negro family or of Negro welfare in general. Louisville has been doing a significant job of improving the standards of Negro life and dismantling the barriers of discrimination. We have seen the admission of Negro undergraduates to the University of Louisville, the first such instance anywhere in the South; the approval of Negroes for membership in the local bar and medical associations; the admission of Negroes to the summer performances at Iroquois Amphitheatre.

These reforms came about through careful, steady community effort. They were possible only because both white and Negro groups approached them with admirable calmness. Any one of these changes might have been destroyed, or at least set back for a generation, by an "incident" designed to force the issue. Those who have an interest in real progress, rather than agitation in the name of progress, would do well to go along with the developing pattern that has produced such good results in Louisville.

Ironically, the *Courier's* news story and editorial never convinced any of the paper's bitter opponents that the sale of the house on Rone Court was not a plot of the *Courier-Journal*. But the editorial did do several other things. First, it gave the strength of the printed word of a newspaper to the idea that was already wreaking havoc in Shively, the myth that property values are bound to decline when Negroes move in, although there is considerable evidence that this is not necessarily the case. Second, the editorial gave the sanction of approval to the right of the white neighbors of the Wades to "protest" their residence on Rone Court; the advice to these neighbors to rely on "proper legal procedures" to get the Wades out of their house may have sounded good on paper, but of course there *was* no legal way to get them out; the *Courier* must have known this, and later events proved it true. But third, and most important, the editorial gave the liberal white people of Louisville an excuse for inaction.

All that the editorial said about Carl and me may have been justified. And if we acted unwisely, criticism of our action was certainly in order. But the net result of the position of the *Courier-Journal* as the leading spokesman of liberal thought in Louisville was that the emphasis was now on the "wrong," if that is what it was, of our action in buying and selling the house. The wrong of those who had hurled rocks and fired rifle shots, though it also got mention in the editorial, was now secondary.

The *Courier-Journal* undoubtedly felt it was speaking out against wrongs on both sides. But it had given Louisville's conscience, already startled by a challenge of tremendous proportions, the out it needed. The onus was now on us for having started the difficulty in the first place. People could now deplore the violence on Rone Court piously and safely and at the same time excuse themselves for inaction in the face of it since this was a situation that should not have arisen anyway except for the action of two foolish white people.

It is interesting that Wade was much less criticized by Louisville liberals than we were. The *Louisville Times,* whose editorial policies always coincide with those of the *Courier-Journal* (they are under the same ownership), spelled this out explicitly in a later editorial:

> The family of Andrew Wade IV made, we believe, an understandable error when it moved into a white neighborhood in Shively. . . . Mr. and Mrs. Carl Braden, in our opinion, made an inexcusable blunder when they made that mistake possible by buying the home and then transferring it to the Wades.

The distinction is not surprising. In any controversy, most of us reserve our greatest anger for the people we feel should be on our side. The segregationists furiously called us "traitors to our race" — because we were white and so, they felt, should have been like them. The gradualists furiously called us "blunderers" — because we were white and liberal and so, they felt, should have behaved "gradually" as they did. And inversely, of course, I was always much angrier with the liberals, whose support I felt the Wades and we should have had, than I was with the segregationists, whose support I never expected.

This approach, that Carl and I were the most to be condemned in the situation, was also taken by four religious leaders — Catholic, Jewish, and two Protestants — when they discussed the episode on a regular radio feature, "The Moral Side of the News." The men, all of them in principle opposed to segregation, spent twenty minutes of their half-hour program denouncing us for the sale of the house and ten minutes deploring the violence. The housing problem of Negroes in Louisville that gave rise to our action in the first place got lost in the shuffle; the violence against the Wades got submerged. This attitude found its resounding echoes in Louisville's startled white community, liberal as well as conservative, throughout the summer.

Some weeks later I had occasion to discuss the editorial position of the *Courier-Journal* with its publisher, Mark Ethridge. I argued that perhaps they had failed in a vital moment when leadership was needed and could not completely disclaim responsibility for the further violence that followed. He countered by saying that no matter what they had said editorially they could not have had much influence on the people in Shively who were determined to get the Wades out of the house. This is undoubtedly true. But they did have a great deal of influence with many liberal citizens in the community at large who had spoken out in the case of the Filipino woman and who were very likely inclined in their consciences to speak out now. These people could have influenced others and ultimately perhaps the influence would have reached deep into Shively. Instead the *Courier* provided such people with a reason for remaining silent.

It may be that the situation was impossible. It may be that our step presented a challenge so formidable that Louisville for many reasons did not have the ability to cope with it at that point. A case can be made out that because of this our action was profoundly wrong and destined to do more harm than good. But no matter where the greatest blame lies, the hard fact — the important fact — is that in the week that followed the shooting no clear voice pleaded the cause of tolerance in Louisville. No rallying point was created for the conscience of a community.

It can be argued too, and has been argued by some, that we also failed in the field of decisive action when such action was needed. On the Sunday morning following the shooting, we were urged by many people to take out warrants for the arrest of Rone and Hudson and others who had visited our house on the preceding Thursday night, on charges of banding together to intimidate us. We did not know for a fact who was responsible for any of the events of that Saturday night, so no warrants could be taken for these actions. But many people felt it was reasonable to assume that some of the same people who had threatened us were involved. They argued that if these people were arrested promptly it would act as a deterrent to further violence.

Carl and I, after consultation with Andrew, refused. We felt at this point that such action would only drive the incipient bitterness in the Shively community deeper. We felt that putting people in jail was no answer to race prejudice. When newspaper reporters on that Sunday asked us if we planned to take out warrants we replied in the negative and the next day's paper carried our explanation: "We believe the cause of justice and tolerance would be better served by causing as little friction as possible." We knew that Rone and the others were people Andrew and Charlotte were going to have to live with as neighbors. We had seen people whose prejudices appeared to go quite deep change very quickly. We believed that if we acted with forbearance at this moment some of these people who were then so violent in their opposition to the Wades would someday become their strongest supporters.

Later events proved how wrong we were. And yet I have never resolved in my own mind whether our decision on this question at that particular time and in that context was right or wrong. Perhaps by our hesitation at this point, we too were partly responsible for the additional violence that followed later. Perhaps the arrest of Rone would have made no difference. Again it is impossible to pinpoint the blame. The overriding fact is that at this time no decisive action came from those who believed the Wades had a right to live in the house — either from the liberal leaders of Louisville or from us. The people who opposed us were not so lacking in leadership.

8

The Suburban Press Sees Red

On the Monday following the Saturday cross burning and shooting at the Wade house, our telephone continued to ring constantly. The *Courier-Journal* that morning had carried its front-page story on the Wade purchase and the violence, and many people thus learned our name and address. The voices of the anonymous callers were more varied now and apparently scattered over the city of Louisville instead of being concentrated in the Rone Court area. None of the threatening callers identified themselves. We refused to talk to them when they would not give their names; but we kept answering the phone, as some of the calls were now coming from people who did identify themselves and who sympathized with our action. We knew that every such caller was a potential ally for the Wades, and we did not want to miss any of these calls.

Finally it was about noon, I had not made the beds and was just beginning to vacuum the living room rug. At that point, when the phone rang for about the fiftieth time, I threw up my hands. I went to the front door and called to Carl, who was outside cutting the grass — Jimmy running along beside him fancying he was helping push the mower and looking, despite the differences in their coloring, like a small edition of his father, stocky and square-built.

"Carl," I called. "You'll just have to come in and get this one. I can't answer that phone another time."

He laughed and left Jimmy pushing futilely at the lawn mower, as he came into the house and picked up the phone. I soon deduced from his side of the conversation that the person at the other end was someone he thought it worth the time to talk to. I turned off the vacuum cleaner and sat down to listen. Carl was explaining patiently the reason we had bought the house and our feelings about racial discrimination.

"No," he said at one point, "the Progressive Party had nothing to do with planning this; in fact, as far as I know, there has not been a Progressive Party in Louisville in several years. This thing was not the project of any organization; it was just that Mr. Wade wanted a house and asked us to help him get it. . . . Yes, Anne and I used to be members of the Progressive Party, and I think Mr. Wade was too. But we never knew him in that connection. As a matter of fact, I think he had become inactive before we joined the organization. . . . Yes, I think Negroes and white people can live together peacefully in the same neighborhood — in fact there are Negroes living in the next block from us. . . . I believe experience has proved that when people of different racial groups live close together and get to know each other, racial tensions are reduced. . . ."

I looked at Carl questioningly as he hung up the phone.

"It was John Hitt, editor of the Shively *Newsweek*," he said. "That's the weekly newspaper out there. He didn't sound unfriendly."

"What was all the business about the Progressive Party?" I asked.

"Oh, he had the idea this might have been planned by the Progressive Party as a sort of a test case on segregated housing," Carl explained. "I think he understands now though that this isn't a test case of any kind — that it's just a matter of a man wanting a house to live in. I got the idea from the general line of his questioning that he plans to report the thing in such a way as to try to quiet things down."

It is amazing, in retrospect, how often we misjudged our opposition.

John Y. Hitt, as we learned later, was a comparative newcomer to the newspaper business at the time of the Wade incident. He later testified before the grand jury that he had come originally from Washington, D. C., where he formerly worked for the government. His grandfather was from Kentucky and when he died Hitt's mother inherited Kentucky property. The family moved back to Kentucky in the early 1940s. Young Hitt worked in an aircraft factory during the war, then in dry-cleaning establishments, and later set up a dry-cleaning business of his own. In 1948, he went into real estate. He moved back to Washington for a short time in 1949 but soon came back to Louisville to return to the real estate business. He built and sold a number of houses in the Shively area, and a subdivision there is known as Hitt Acres.

Two years before the Wades bought their home, Hitt started the Shively *Newsweek*. The Wade house purchase thus touched him in two ways — as a man with his own interest in real estate and as an editor of a suburban newspaper. It is commonly acknowledged that a weekly newspaper in an area covered by large metropolitan daily newspapers must depend on community campaigns of one kind or another to help build its circulation. The Rone Court issue clearly offered the possibility for such a campaign — and Hitt seized it.

Also, between the time when Hitt talked with Carl on the telephone on Monday morning and the time when his weekly edition came out on the following Thursday, coincidence had injected another factor into the entire situation. For, that Monday, the radio announced the momentous news of the United States Supreme Court decision declaring segregated schools to be illegal. It was May 17, 1954.

When we first heard the news of the Supreme Court decision that day, we thought that it would have the effect of quieting things down on Rone Court. Now, we felt, people would see that integration was the law of the land, and they would be more willing to accept it in their own neighborhood and suburb. It is easy to see, looking back on it, that the effect was bound to be just the opposite.

The people in Shively who had considered segregation an unchangeable way of life had already suffered a shock; the added shock of the Supreme Court decision compounded their panic — as it compounded panic all over the South. Further than that, the Wades' move rendered the Supreme Court decision a personal threat to them; if there had been no Negroes living close by, there would have been little likelihood that the schools their own children attended would ever be racially mixed. The presence of the Wades on Rone Court — and with it the terrifying possibility that other Negroes would follow suit and also buy or build in Shively — gave the Supreme Court decision a sinister immediacy in their own lives.

It gave it a sinister immediacy to John Y. Hitt, who as editor of the community newspaper undoubtedly saw himself as the guardian of what he thought was the community's interest. It would probably never have occurred to Hitt, who had lived in Washington and worked for his government, to attack the Supreme Court. This was before Senator Eastland and other powerful men in the South had blazed the way by attacking that judicial body directly. The Supreme Court was far away and beyond Hitt's reach. Rone Court was close by, and the Wades and we were little people like himself. It had been a disturbing and startling week for John Hitt and many others; in his panic and his frustration, as a real estate man and a newspaper editor, he struck out at the little people close by who looked like easy and fair game.

On Thursday, three days after he talked to Carl, the weekly edition of the Shively *Newsweek* came out. It carried a picture of the Wade house and a fairly objective story of the purchase and the violence on the top of the front page. Across the bottom of the same page was an editorial under Hitt's by-line. It read in part:

HAS WADE'S SHIVELY 'DREAM HOME'
TURNED OUT TO BE A NIGHTMARE

For the past week the most talked about news in Shively and this area has been our new negro neighbors. And it should be a leading issue too. When the Wades moved into their "dream house" on Rone Court they did so in a furtive fashion, sneaking around, with the help of their white friends, the Carl Bradens, who thought so dearly of these negroes that he went to quite a bit of "finagling" to purchase this house, then immediately transferred the deed into Wade's name.

We wonder if this is truly a move of friendship or an organized attempt to place colored people in a neighborhood that has in the past been all-white, and to cause panic or possibly bloodshed between the whites that have lived in this fair community, and the incoming Negroes. We doubt that this is the only couple who will make this crusade. The record shows that when, a few years back, Negroes purchased a home on 28th Street in Louisville, the property dropped in value for the balance of the white people who lived in that block, now the entire block has been evacuated by the whites and the colored people have literally taken over. Is this going to happen in the Shively area? . . .

Mr. Braden has said that he arranged the deal solely because of his friendship for the colored race and that his Progressive Party relationship had nothing to do with it; Wade and Braden were members of the party . . .

Braden did this, knowing that the Wades had been refused other houses in this area and also in New Albany by builders who would not sell to a Negro . . . is their real desire to force the issue of non-segregation? . . . is Wade, with the help of Braden, really looking for happiness, or is he being a martyr for a cause? What cause? The cause of non-segregation, or is it the cause which made Stalin the lion of Russia, or could it be the cause of the Communists in this country to encourage panic, chaos, and riot to lower the morale of the American people?

Mr. Braden, when asked whether he knew at the time of the planned purchase that there were no Negroes in this area, said it made no difference to him. . . . He also stated that he is color-blind when it comes to races and they are just like white to him. Just a little thought, Mr. Braden: the Russians and the Communists in this country are white, too. Should we ignore that fact and help the Communist Party get control of this country? From what I have learned of the Progressive Party, there were a few Communist sympathizers in that organization. Braden stated in an article in the Louisville Courier-Journal Monday that acceptance of the Wades in the Shively area would prove the "test of democracy." Democracy is the will of the majority, where the supreme power rests with the people. We don't think the opinion of the majority of the people in this area is in agreement with this Negro family. . . . what of the white race? In the instances where we do not wish to mix, which is "our Democratic right," isn't it being taken away from us when we are forced to do so against our will? . . .

We are an easy-going race and it is so easy to read about

incidents similar to this happening other places and shrug it
off with the thought "that it couldn't happen here." It has
happened here! Either you take a firm stand now or take the
consequences along with your indifference.

Stalin and Russia had found their way into the picture presumably because both Wade and Carl and I had at one time been
members of the Progressive Party. Once the idea of Communist
connections and a possible Communist plot had been planted in
the minds of the opposition, it never did us much good to point out
that the Progressive Party had long since disintegrated in Louisville,
that Wade and we had not been members at the same time, and that
no one besides the three of us who had ever been members of this
party even knew about the Rone Court purchase before it happened — that, in fact, no one else knew about it except some
Negro professional men whom Wade had asked for advice. In
fairness to John Y. Hitt, it should be said that it was the *Courier-
Journal* that first called attention to our previous Progressive Party
connections — in its first story on the house situation. It was apparently from that story that Hitt got his information on this point.
But it was Hitt who grasped hold of the idea and erected a whole
framework around it.

The approach was a real find for the uneasy consciences of the
Shively residents who opposed the move of the Wades into their
community. It is becoming increasingly difficult for men and women
of good will to oppose in good conscience the efforts of the Negro
people to win full rights as first-class citizens. Everything in the
American tradition and the ethic of the nation's religion cries out
against discrimination, and most Americans honor these traditions
and believe themselves to be fair and democratic people. Years
ago white Southerners could often disregard — at least in their
conscious minds — the conflicts between their ideals and the practices of their lives; they could sweep it all under the rug; they could
look the other way. But now with the Negro people much more
vocal, with their demands on the front pages of the newspapers
almost every day, white people can't do this any more. The only
way they can avoid a heartrending showdown in their own souls
is to dress up their old ideas of white superiority with some new

theory — some theory that can fit into their lives without bursting the bounds of their own consciences and their own best instincts. That, I think, is why all over the South today we hear white suprema- cists making the charges that the NAACP is engaged in a plot to upset the sacred American way of life and that the United States Supreme Court itself has been subverted by communistic and foreign ideologies.

Thus, the good Christian citizens of Shively could not oppose the Wades just because they were Negroes. But if it was true that the Wades' move to Shively was Communist-inspired, there was good reason for opposition. Christian men and women can oppose and are expected to oppose the efforts of a foreign power to en- croach upon the American way of life. It was around this conscience- soothing theory that Hitt and the *Newsweek* began to crystallize public opinion in Shively against the residence of the Wades on Rone Court.

Hitt himself made his theory quite explicit several months later when he appeared before the grand jury. He volunteered his thoughts on the subject on the first day of his testimony:

> HITT: . . . I was encouraged by several people who work for me to write what I thought about it. I feel as though the entire move was a Communist move. I feel it is Commu- nist backed. I think that the purchase was a premeditated fraud to cause trouble out there, which it has, and I wrote about it.
>
> Q: A question there. Don't you think the same thing could have happened any place in the city? Why would you think that because it did happen in Rone Court in St. Helen's [old name for Shively] that it was Communist inspired.
>
> HITT: Of course, we don't have a paper anywhere else. That's what I am interested in is Shively.
>
> Q: I mean in Rone Court.
>
> HITT: Well, of course it is true that the way this has taken place, the way it's been played, I have read a copy of *The Red Front,* and the way it looked to me, it looked to me like a pattern. Also, the Howards up in Chicago,

> when they moved into Trumbull Park, it was a pattern
> that's followed to cause trouble. I believe the whole
> thing was set out there to start a race war . . .

And later he testified:

> . . . A lot of church people use the moral issue. I don't
> believe in persecuting any negro — I have nothing
> against them — I have one working for me today. I don't
> feel she is Communistic, but a negro who is being mixed
> up in an effort to overthrow our government is the reason
> I started writing this . . .

I think that from the beginning Hitt believed his theory himself
— just as I believe some of my friends in Alabama, who told me
over a year later that the Negroes in Montgomery were perfectly
happy and contented until "outside troublemakers stirred them
up" into boycotting the buses, believed their own theories. The
barriers between the races make fantastic blind spots. If Hitt was
trying to build circulation for his newspaper, he was not doing it
cynically or dishonestly; he thought he was campaigning for what
was best for his community. And his norm of a healthy white-
Negro relationship in that community — if it is fair to judge from
his own testimony before the grand jury — was his own master-
servant relationship with a Negro in his kitchen. He did not think
she was "Communistic." In his writings and in his testimony, Hitt
never displayed more than the sketchiest knowledge of what Communism actually is. Obviously, when he said a Negro who worked
for him was not Communistic, his real meaning was that she had
never showed any tendency that clashed with his idea of what a
Negro should be, that she knew "her place" in the world in which
he lived. When Andrew Wade moved into the lily-white neighborhood of Rone Court, Hitt like many others was suddenly confronted
with the new and startling fact of a Negro who did not fit into their
pattern of thought, a Negro like those who moved into Trumbull
Park in Chicago — as Hitt drew the parallel himself — a Negro
who demanded certain rights. This was a troublesome thing, injected into a community where life had been plodding along more
or less peacefully. The only explanation for it was that the Negro

thus demanding his rights and all white people connected with him were acting as they were for the sole purpose of stirring up trouble. This was not the way good American citizens act, so some foreign ideology must be involved. It was a simple explanation, and it disposed at one fell swoop of all the inexplicable forces so new and startling to Hitt's circumscribed world.

Almost immediately, Hitt had his theory bolstered by a man more experienced than he in explaining the inexplicable in terms of a foreign ideology and in supplying a noble and patriotic motive for fighting the strange and the new and the startling. This man was Millard Dee Grubbs.

Grubbs did not live in Shively but he was a resident of Louisville of many years' standing. He had long been a militant advocate of segregation. Carl and I had met him six years before when we were both working for the *Louisville Times* and had gone to interview him about his activities in spearheading the Dixiecrat party in Kentucky in the 1948 presidential campaign. This was not the first time he had assisted in organized efforts to "preserve the white race." In 1946, Grubbs had been identified as national director of the Continental League for Christian Freedom in a petition naming that organization filed in Superior Court at Atlanta by the assistant attorney general of Georgia. This petition, filed in the period of revulsion against racism that followed World War II, charged the Continental League with being a front for the Ku Klux Klan. It read in part:

> This organization is attempting primarily to recruit veterans along violently anti-Semitic, anti-Catholic, and anti-Negro lines.
>
> Grubbs also is an active organizer for the Klan in Kentucky. Grubbs has been associated in "soft peace" agitation with the well-known German agent, Ernest Elmhurst, who was until recently in prison in New York.

Grubbs denied Klan membership and said he was defending the Constitution. The day that Carl and I interviewed him in 1948, we found him in his two-story frame home on one of Louisville's older "boarding house" streets. He took us up a narrow dark stairway to an upstairs meeting hall where he and his followers gathered. The walls of the stairway were lined with flaming red crepe paper. Two American flags were crisscrossed at the top of the steps, and a sign at the head of the stairs welcomed us to "CONSTITUTION HALL." The meeting hall itself was dark and somehow eerie, but in the dingy light we could see other American flags in evidence and a large Bible on the rostrum.

Grubbs appeared to be about sixty. He warned us direly of all the corruption in high places in our society: it was impossible for the "little man" to get a break. He said he had studied law hoping to help promote justice but had found it impossible because of the depth of the corruption. A tangle in the legal profession had led to his disbarment. Finally he had come to the conclusion that the whole problem resulted from a plot of Jews and Negroes and Communists to take over the country. Obviously a rebel, starting perhaps with honest motives, he had resolved all conflicts by finding a "devil" on which to blame the world's wrong — and his life was now devoted to an attempt to exorcise it. He waved his arms and told us he wanted to protect the Constitution from such things as President Truman's civil rights program. My memory of him is of a man with a fanatical light in his eyes, apparently a dedicated man with a mission to save the world from evil and unknown forces.

When the Wade episode attracted attention on Rone Court, Grubbs wrote a two-thousand-word letter to the Shively *Newsweek*. In it, much as Hitt had already explained away Wade and the whole movement toward desegregation, Grubbs wrapped up everything new and startling that had happened in America in the last twenty years — Franklin D. Roosevelt, the CIO, and the gradually stronger stand of the U. S. Supreme Court against segregation — put it all in a package with Wade's move into Shively and placed a big label on it: "MADE IN RUSSIA." It was a tremendous feat. In one letter, it put the unruly world back into bounds that honest men could understand. And then, in a simple call to action, he gave them a means to preserve the bounds of this world. He called for the organization of the American White Brotherhood to preserve the time-honored values that all men know are valid. Hitt, like a man who had found a refuge in a storm, printed the letter in full on his editorial page under a prominent headline, "WADE PURCHASE A PREMEDITATED FRAUD." The letter said in part:

The brazen discrimination against the White people by subversive pressure groups and crooked and controlled politicians should be brought to an end. . . .

The premeditated and corrupt fraud by a copy-reader for the Louisville Courier-Journal, to obtain title to a piece of real estate in an exclusive White community for a negro family was pursuant to a Communist conspiracy that has for its objective the establishment of a black beach-head in every White subdivision. . . .

The long and unbroken control in Washington by a sinister group of which Franklin Delano Roosevelt, Harry Solomon Truman, and Dwight David Eisenhower have been the top-bracket front men, has enabled these arch conspirators . . . to let Communist spies swarm over the ramparts to take key positions in government, and to bring about the distressing situation which now confronts the Caucasian Race. . . .

. . . indifference by our citizens to the shameful high crimes and misdemeanors by their public officials is largely responsible for the plight in which we find ourselves. The malfeasance in public office which was out in the open and plain for everyone to see has almost made government itself disreputable, as is evidenced by the abortive attempt of Justice William O. Douglas, of the U. S. Supreme Court to override the action of the court and save the Rosenberg traitors from the electric chair; the high-handed misconduct of Franklin D. Roosevelt and his directive which locked up the evidence for several years which finally sent Alger Hiss to the penitentiary, and would have brought Hiss to trial for treason and the electric chair had Roosevelt not impounded it until limitation had run; the despotic act of Harry S. Truman in his order to seize the steel mills to make the owners surrender to Walter Reuther and his C.I.O. mob; . . . And lastly, the unbelieveable and assine [sic] decision by a stacked Supreme Court which would abolish States Rights, destroy the U. S. Constitution, strike down and destroy the White Race. These have been the fatal signs and portents of the rising red bureaucracy over a betrayed people and republic. . . .

Today, not only in America, but throughout the world

the White people are hemmed in and surrounded by colored people. We live literally in a sea of color. The only chance or hope for the survival of the White Race in a world's population which outnumber it ten to one is by adherence to a strict rule of segregation. . . .

It was our Creator that fashioned the White and the Black races, and commanded that they reproduce after their kind. . . . In all of God's creation, man is the only creature that disobey the divine law of segregation.

The Marxist world plotters well know that non-segregation leads to miscegenation and racial mixture . . .

The most urgent need of the White people at present is a militant organization to counteract the subversive pressure mobs and stop the intolerable discrimination against white people. To meet this imperative need, the writer, Rev. Oscar Gibson, and others had a meeting a few weeks ago and launched the movement under the tentative name of the "American White Brotherhood." . . . We need your help and believe that you need ours. . . .

If you are a member of the Caucasian race this matter involves all that you hold dear whether or not you now know it. . . .

This organization exclusively is for loyal white people and no others will be allowed membership. If you are interested and can qualify we will be happy to hear from you.

> Millard Dee Grubbs
> In care of
> Shively Newsweek

Grubbs' letter appeared in the Shively *Newsweek* two weeks after the initial story on the Rone Court situation. Thereafter, throughout the summer, week after week, story after story, editorial after editorial appeared — most of them, like Hitt's first editorial, deploring the fact that a plot was under way to "stir up trouble" in Shively. On June 17, Hitt came up editorially with the theory that perhaps the shots fired into the Wade home on the night of May 15 were "self-inflicted." He then went on to propose a program for the people of "our community who want to stay white and do not care to interlive or intermix." He proposed that residents of white sections set up private clubs, and stated:

> Since the Supreme Court decision on segregation (at the time of Wade's moving) much has been said pro and con about the problem of segregation and negroes moving into the Shively area. . . . It is a fact that a negro can buy where he wants to, it is a fact also that the whites cannot legally move him once he is a property owner on their block or in their neighborhood. But by forming private clubs . . . there could be a vote taken as to whether a newcomer is to be accepted or not. . . .

Hitt was here much more frank than was the liberal *Courier-Journal* in regard to the impossibility of dislodging the Wades from their home by any "legal" means.

As the weeks passed and the campaign of terror and abuse against the Wades became more and more vicious and hence more difficult for Hitt to defend, the *Newsweek* was forced by the logic of its original position more and more to place Wade in the role of an innocent victim of a plot by outside white agitators. Thus, Hitt wrote in July:

> A normal man would think first of his wife and child; he would retreat in the light of present developments and await a gradual adjustment which is sure to come eventually. If Wade were allowed to approach the problem sanely, he would realize the tension he has created (unless that was his primary purpose). . . . the clear-thinking people of this formerly quiet community deplore all the violence and unrest precipitated by Wade and his "defenders." They hope that, since Carl Braden and the other whites who are degrading the entire human race by entering into such a campaign of hate promotion have apparently achieved their purpose, they will be satisfied and allow the Wades to quietly move away.

Outside of Shively, the editorials in the *Newsweek* had little effect on the Louisville community. Few people beyond the confines of the suburb read the paper at all; the few who did — generally liberal-minded people who read it out of curiosity and because of their interest in the Wade situation — wrote the words of Hitt off as making no sense whatsoever. No one dreamed at that time that in the following autumn Hitt's theories would be adopted as official policy by law enforcement agencies in the county. But there can be no doubt that in Shively itself, the constant campaign of the *Newsweek* played a large part in molding public opinion — much of it public opinion that might gradually have been won for the support of the Wades if a different kind of leadership had been forthcoming. This fact was dramatized to me in a telephone conversation I had with a woman in Shively during the summer.

This was one morning when Andrew Wade stopped by to bring us the latest copy of the Shively paper, as he did every week. I was fixing Carl's breakfast, and Carl, who refused to let any crisis or turmoil keep him from reading a little every day, was sitting at the breakfast table with his head buried in some book on history he was reading, occasionally culling out what he called the "nuggets" to read aloud to me. Jimmy came running in to tell us Andrew was coming. He thought Andrew hung the moon and always heralded his arrival with the singsong announcement, "Comes Andr-e-e-w!"

Andrew came in with his usual exuberance. He was looking tired around the eyes these days and sometimes his face seemed drawn with fatigue, and yet through it all he never that whole summer completely lost a certain gaiety that was a part of him, and he always found something to laugh about.

"Well, the latest report from the Shively *Newsweek* is that the *Courier-Journal* has fired Carl for buying the house," he laughed as he threw the paper on our table.

"What next?" I commented. "Could you use some breakfast?"

"No thanks," Andrew said. "Just coffee. I ate a while ago."

"Is this wishful thinking on Hitt's part?" Carl asked.

"No, it's not Hitt this time," Andrew answered. "Some woman in Shively wrote a letter to the *Newsweek* saying that's what she heard. She's mighty happy about it if it's true. She wants Hitt to find out." He pointed to the letter in the paper.

I picked it up and read the letter.

"I think I'll call her up and set her straight," I said.

"Tell her the reports of my death are highly exaggerated," Carl suggested.

"I wonder why the paper *hasn't* fired you," Andrew said. "They certainly don't like my being on Rone Court."

"They take the position that what an employee does on his own time is his own business, no matter how much they may disapprove of what he does," Carl answered. "I guess there aren't many employers who would take that position in this day and time. You've got to give them credit for it."

I put Carl's eggs on the table, poured Andrew's coffee and left him telling Carl about his latest harassments on Rone Court, as I went into the living room to look up the telephone number of the woman who had written the letter to the *Newsweek*. This was several weeks after the first incidents on Rone Court, and we had been living under the constant tension of the continuing threats and abuse. I guess I was feeling the effects of night after night without much sleep, feeling too somewhat persecuted and looking for someone to take out my frustrations on. It was not much to my credit as a way of helping the general situation. But I called the woman to scoff and remained in the course of the conversation to give her reaction the thoughtful consideration it merited.

She turned out to be a very intelligent young woman, apparently sincerely interested in the social problems of segregation and desegregation.

After we had disposed of the question of the reports of Carl's being fired, she said:

"I don't know you, and I don't know why you sold that house to the Wades. Did you really want to stir up trouble?"

"No, we didn't want to stir up trouble," I replied. "We sold the house to the Wades because they badly needed a house and asked us to help them get one and because we believe every person has a right to a decent home where he wants to live, regardless of his color."

"So do I believe that," she said earnestly. "And I believe the people in Shively believe that."

"I'm sure a lot of them do. But some of the people in Shively have tried to drive the Wades out of the neighborhood. Why is that?" I asked.

"I don't think it's that anyone thinks the Wades don't have a *right* to live out here, Mrs. Braden," she replied. "I've talked to

many of the people around here. They believe that everybody has
rights. Oh yes, many of them are for segregation. I've talked to them
about the Supreme Court decision on the schools. Some of them
don't like it, but they are going along with it. They'll accept it.
They'll learn to live with it and finally to like it perhaps. But you
see, many people feel this thing of the Wades moving to Rone Court
was not just a matter of a man wanting a house to live in. I've been
reading the Shively *Newsweek,* and a lot of people feel it was something else. They feel he and you and your husband too just wanted
to stir up trouble out here. That's why they're opposed to it. If he
just wanted a house why couldn't he buy one somewhere else?"

"He tried to buy one somewhere else," I answered. "He looked
all over the Negro sections of Louisville and across the river in
Indiana too before he bought out there. He didn't have much
money; he wanted a little new house with a low down payment.
And there just aren't any houses like that in the Negro sections of
Louisville."

The voice on the other end of the wire was insistent.

"But surely he could have got some kind of a house somewhere," the woman said.

"I don't know whether he could have or not," I countered.
"Maybe he could have. Maybe he could have got some old dilapi-
dated house somewhere that was not what he wanted. But you or I
would not have had to settle for something like that if we had gone
house hunting; because of our white skin, we would have been
able to buy what we wanted and where we wanted to. The Wades
wanted that same freedom of choice you and I have. In that sense,
you may be right — that they wanted more than just a house. They
wanted freedom — the freedom of choice that white people in
similar circumstances have. That's what all Negro people want —
freedom and the feeling they are equal human beings. But why
should anyone conclude from that that they want to stir up trouble?
The Negro people have plenty of trouble. Why would they want
more? The trouble out there has endangered the Wades' *lives* —
and ours too because we are being constantly threatened. Why
would we want that?"

"But Wade knew there were nothing but white people living
out here, and you did too," she insisted. "You must have wanted to
make trouble."

How could I answer her? What could I say? The idea had been planted in her mind, and it had taken hold. Andrew Wade had bought a house in a white neighborhood; trouble had followed; therefore, his purpose in buying the house had been to start trouble. I felt that I was fighting shadows; I took another tack.

"But Andrew Wade didn't make the trouble out there," I told her. "There wouldn't have been any trouble if someone hadn't burned a cross — if someone hadn't thrown a rock through the Wades' window and fired rifle shots into their house."

The line of thinking she was already pursuing forced her logically now to go one step further.

"I can't understand it," she said. "Why, I know some of those people who live around Rone Court. They're good Christian people. They wouldn't do anything against a person because of his color. I just don't believe it. I don't know . . . the *Newsweek* seems to think it may be outside groups that did those things — or maybe even Wade himself or some of his friends. That's the only explanation I can see. I don't believe the people out here would do anything like that. They might not like the Wades being there, but they wouldn't use violence. They are Christian people."

I saw that it was useless to argue further. A good, honest person, she could not accept the fact of seeming evil in the people she knew. It had to be an outsider. The theory of the Shively *Newsweek* had found fertile ground in her mind because of the very fact that she was good and honest. I tried one more approach.

"Then if you believe the Wades have a right to live in their house, would you go to them and say so?" I suggested. "Would you offer them your support and your friendship, let them know you will be with them morally in their decision to stay in Shively?"

"No," she replied. "I can't now. I think it's too late. They and their friends have stirred up too much bitterness. It will never work now. It's better for them and for everyone if they move."

As I hung up the phone, I began turning over in my mind what she had said. The Wades and their friends had stirred up the bitterness . . . believing that was their motive, she could believe anything — and excuse herself from all obligation to help them. And how could Andrew Wade convince her — or anyone whose eyes were blinded by the same assumptions — that he was simply a man who wanted a house and the feeling of freedom that would come with living where he and his family chose? It is the problem that always faces the people who demand their rights. Two years later, how could Autherine Lucy convince people that it was an education she wanted and not trouble at the University of Alabama? How could the Negroes in Montgomery, Alabama, convince their opponents that it was not turmoil that they sought but courteous treatment on the buses? How can anyone prove to another what his motives are?

Too late, the Shively woman had said. In a way, she was right. It was too late. She was a person who might have been an ally for the Wades, for democracy in housing in Shively, for a new kind of brotherhood in suburban Louisville. How many more like her were there in Shively? But the lines had been drawn; public opinion had been solidified the other way. The issue had never been presented dramatically as a challenge to decent, democratic citizens to make democracy work on a new level. Instead the issue had become the defense of the status quo against the encroachment of something new. And by now the defense of this position had been embellished with all the trappings of the flag and the sacred institutions of home and family and country; it was making its appeal not to the baser emotions of prejudice but to the noble emotions of right and patriotism. Good people can often be rallied to either side of a controversy, depending on how each side is presented. Here God Himself had been placed on the side of the status quo. A vacuum had been left where a truly creative leadership in Louisville might have been on the battle lines in the fight for the minds of the people in the community. The Shively *Newsweek,* with its appeal to honor and things as they are and have always been — forever and ever — had stepped into the vacuum.

9

The Myth of Property Values

The Shively *Newsweek* was not the only focus for opposition to the Wades. Within a few days after the house transfer became publicly known, we began to hear rumors that the real estate and home financing interests in the community were deeply concerned about the situation. On the Friday after the Monday the first story appeared in the papers we received what looked like a direct repercussion of this concern.

On that morning Carl and I had decided we would try to get our minds off Rone Court for at least a few hours. We took the phone off the hook, and Carl went upstairs to work at the typewriter; in addition to his job at the newspaper he ran a small business called Editors, Incorporated, doing editorial work for various Louisville businesses, and he was behind on the jobs he had to get out. I sat down in the kitchen to talk to Sonia, Carl's daughter, who was at home that morning.

Sonia was generally sympathetic to Carl's and my views on segregation and therefore to our venture on Rone Court — insofar as she thought about these things at all. But actually the turmoil of the past week had impinged on her consciousness very little, for she was sixteen and almost completely absorbed in problems of her own life. I tried as we talked to get my mind off my own troubles by listening to hers — which were plentiful since she was at that moment involved in a young love affair that was not working out too well. As she talked, she held Anita on her lap combing her hair. It was only in the last month or so that Anita had had enough hair to comb at all; and Sonia, who had been a real big sister to our children from the day they were born, was carefully rolling the strands around her finger trying to encourage their natural tendency

to curl. With half of my mind, I was pondering what I could say
to Sonia to help her see that a broken heart at sixteen need not be
fatal; with the other half, I was indulging in speculations about
what Anita would look like when she grew up, wondering if her
hair would stay blonde or would turn dark like Carl's, whose
brown — almost black — eyes she had inherited. Between these
two thought processes, I had just about succeeded in blocking
Rone Court entirely out of my mind — when the doorbell rang.

"I'll get it," Sonia offered, setting Anita down out of her lap; she
evidently realized that I was weary of jumping up whenever a bell
rang. In a minute, she called to me from the living room:

"It's a registered letter, Anne. You'll have to come sign for it."

I went to the door and took the letter. I read the return address
on the upper left corner of the envelope: South End Federal Savings & Loan Association. This is trouble, I thought to myself. I
called Carl to come downstairs.

I was right. The letter was a copy of one the bank had sent
to Rone. In it, the bank stated that it had received notice that insurance on the Rone Court house had been canceled and that unless
new insurance was obtained within ten days the bank would be
forced to declare the mortgage due and payable. Although our
transfer of title to the house to the Wades had been blazoned on
the front pages of the *Courier-Journal* where it could be read by
every literate citizen of Louisville, the South End's letter made
no mention of this circumstance; and it gave no reason for the insurance company's cancellation of its policy.

We called Andrew to relay the news, and he immediately began
a desperate search for a new insurer for the property. He approached many Louisville insurance agents and companies, and
either he or some of his supporters made numerous contacts with
head offices of out-of-town companies. One after another turned
the property down, but finally coverage was obtained through the
efforts of Charles Steele, executive of the Louisville Urban League.
The Louisville Fire & Marine Company — because its head, Eric
Tachau, personally held liberal views on the race question — agreed
to insure the property on principle. We mailed the new policy to the
South End Federal Savings, with a letter telling them formally that
we had transferred the property to Andrew Wade and his wife and

asking them to please address all further communications concerning it to the Wades.

Within a few days, on May 28, we received a reply from the South End saying that they were demanding full payment of their $8,000 mortgage anyway. The letter said that since we had transferred the property without written consent of the Savings & Loan Association, we had violated the terms of our mortgage contract with them. A few weeks later they filed suit for foreclosure in Circuit Court against the Wades and us, on the same grounds as those outlined in their letter: violation of contract. The suit made no mention of the color of the Wades.

The mortgage at the South End had been made originally by Rone and transferred to us. On the day we closed the deal to buy the house, this mortgage was already on file in the courthouse, so we did not read it. After the South End's notice of foreclosure, we looked it up and found that it did contain a clause that forbade transfer of the property without the bank's written consent. We also found that a number of banks in Louisville have similar clauses in their form mortgage contracts, although this is not a usual contract provision in real estate practice throughout the United States. The usual provision is that, regardless of transfer of the property, the original maker of the mortgage and all subsequent assumers of the mortgage retain responsibility for payment.

Our decision to transfer the property to the Wades by the simple act of making a deed to them, without conference with the bank, had been made on advice given to Wade by the Negro real estate men with whom he had been conferring on the matter. When he asked them later why they had not foreseen difficulty on this point, since a number of banks in Louisville include such clauses in their contracts as a routine practice, they replied that such clauses are simply never used and for that reason they had never thought of them. Of course, so far as any of them knew, this was the first instance in which a Negro in Louisville had obtained title to a house in a new white subdivision and attempted to assume a mortgage at a white-owned bank.

The Wades and we later stated, in answering the suit in the courts, that the bank was attempting to use the courts to enforce a secret restrictive covenant. We charged that the bank had seized upon this technicality for the sole purpose of depriving the Wades of their equity in the property because they were Negroes. Officials of the bank did not publicly deny this charge. They simply ignored it. Their only answer was to repeat their assertion that we had violated the contract, and that was that. But I don't believe there was ever any doubt in the mind of anyone in Louisville, on one side of the controversy or the other, as to the real reason for the foreclosure.

When hearings on the suit were held in Circuit Court some months later, an official of the South End virtually admitted that race was the reason — albeit in a somewhat reluctant and backhanded manner.

C. Ewbank Tucker, an attorney for the Wades and us, cross-examined J. H. Gold, vice-president and general counsel of the South End Federal Savings & Loan Association. This exchange took place:

> Q: If in this instance, Mr. Wade with the proper financial credit references and the establishment of a good citizen-ship record had made application for a loan on that property situated in Rone Court, which is a white settlement, would you have approved that loan to him?
>
> GOLD: I don't think I would have.
>
> Q: And that would be based upon the fact that Mr. Wade is a colored man, all other things being equal?
>
> GOLD: No, sir, I don't think it would have.
>
> Q: Maybe you haven't gotten the import of my question. I am saying that if Mr. Wade with the proper credit references required by your organization, together with a good citizenship record, had made application for a loan would he be denied that loan, and, if so, for what reason?
>
> GOLD: Our fear of the safety of our security would be the reason.
>
> Q: What would that be based on?
>
> GOLD: That would be based upon the fact that we know in other instances —
>
> Q: No, I am talking about this incident —
>
> GOLD: We know from reports and newspapers, not only in

> Louisville and in other cities, that where colored people
> move into white neighborhoods that trouble arises and
> property is destroyed.
> Q: And the denial of that application would be based upon
> the fact that Mr. and Mrs. Wade were colored people — ?
> GOLD: No sir. It would not be based on that. It would be
> based on the fact that Mr. and Mrs. Wade had bought
> property and moved into a white neighborhood.

Whether officials of the South End conferred with other banking and real estate men in Louisville concerning the action they would take and the extent, if any, to which others were a part of the subsequent actions against the Wades and us can only be conjectured. One clue lies in the fact that months later — after Andrew had refused to buckle under to the South End's action and insisted on keeping the house and fighting the foreclosure suit — the Wade Electric Company ran into trouble with other Louisville banks. Andrew and his father found that when potential customers of their electric company went to these banks to seek loans for big electrical jobs that required bank financing the loans were refused when the bank learned that the Wade Electric Company would be doing the work. This cut them out of many of the big jobs on which their business depended.

We got another clue, also months later, when Carl was on trial in Circuit Court in Louisville on criminal charges. Meeting Carl late each afternoon as court recessed for supper, I repeatedly noticed four or five well-dressed men standing at the prosecution table in earnest conversation with the prosecuting attorneys. These strategy huddles — if that's what they were — aroused my curiosity, so I made it a point to find out about these men. They were, I was informed, attorneys for several of the big building and loan associations and real estate companies in Louisville.

We knew something, of course, of the part played by Ben Hudson, the real estate man who sold the property to us, since he was one of the spokesmen for the group which visited our house on the night of May 13. There is every reason to think that even then he was acting not so much from personal prejudice as from pressures inherent in his profession. It is common knowledge in Louisville that the city Real Estate Board will invoke fines or even expulsion against a white real estate man who sells property in a white neighborhood to a Negro without prior agreement that the block is to be "broken." Some indication of the pressures on a man like Hudson lies in the story Andrew Wade tells about statements made to him by another white real estate man in Louisville, A. H. Curella. Andrew had discussed his housing problem with Curella before he ever came to us; and, as he later told the grand jury, it was actually Curella who had first suggested to him that he get a white friend to buy a house for him. Curella denied this, but, according to Andrew's testimony, Curella at first considered handling the transaction for him himself, but then changed his mind and said:

"Just get any white friend because I am in the business."

South End officials of course contended, as noted in Gold's testimony, that their fear was for the "safety" of the property. This never made much sense that I could see: the property was fully insured at all times except for the brief interval between cancellation of the first policy and the obtaining of a new one; it was fully insured at the time the foreclosure suit was filed and at the times when any damage was done to the property. Actually, the thinking and actions of all these people — the South End, Hudson, and the others in their professions who supported them — revolved around a set of myths. And while as members of the real estate and home financing world they were in a way among the perpetuators of this mythology, they were in another sense also its victims. None of them in the whole course of this case ever talked about the mythology publicly or put it in their official pronouncements, but it was there in the background, dictating their actions.

Part of the myth was put into words on that day when we sat in Hudson's office on May 10 — before anyone knew we planned to transfer the property on Rone Court to a Negro. Carl was looking over the deed, and Hudson's assistant, Mrs. Thomas, engaged me in conversation. She wanted to know if we would be interested in listing our own house for sale. She had seen the house one day when she brought some papers on the Rone Court property there for us to sign. I told her no, I did not think we would want to sell. But, out of curiosity, I asked her how much she thought we could get for it if we were interested.

"Well, I'm not sure," Mrs. Thomas replied. "I'd have to look at it more carefully. It appeared to me it's in very good condition. But of course you know there are colored living in the next block, and there's some talk that they may move into your block before very long — and that decreases the value of your property."

"Well, I don't know about that," I answered somewhat tentatively. "Some people say that, but I'm not at all sure it's true." It was hardly the time or the place for a full-blown argument on the subject.

"Oh yes," she said confidently. "Of course, I don't have anything against colored people, but lots of people do, you know. And real estate values in a neighborhood always go down when colored move in."

She spoke matter-of-factly and almost as if she were reciting an axiom by rote. Apparently it was a statement she had made many times. It is a statement that is often made by the people who deal in real estate — not only in Louisville but all over America. Every white home-owner has heard it at some time and it hangs over his head as a continuing menace, ready to strike whenever the racial exclusiveness of his neighborhood is threatened. And it was undoubtedly what was in the mind of the Shively man who came to our home on May 13 with the crowd from the Rone Court area and said to Carl: "But I've saved up for years to buy the house I own out there."

Intertwined with this idea is another theory also widely accepted as gospel. This is the belief that a neighborhood is "better" in some overall sense if no members of minority groups live there. This concept undergirds the real estate trade in America, and it has embedded itself deep in the public consciousness — compounding and solidifying the ancient myths of white superiority that flowed out of a Southern slave society.[1] The exclusively white — and

[1] For a detailed study of the way in which the real estate business in America has encouraged the mythology that underlies racial exclusiveness in housing, see *Forbidden Neighbors,* by Charles Abrams (Harper, 1955). Abrams points out that such exclusiveness was not a characteristic of American towns in the early days but developed with the growth of cities. In the 1920s, he says, the National Association of Real Estate Boards helped launch a series of textbooks on real estate that became the bibles of the profession, and these books stated for a fact that "certain racial

Gentile and Nordic — suburb has become the new American dream for those who can aspire to it; to live there has become the mark of being "somebody." And many a white man who would privately have no objection to a Negro as a neighbor would be terrified if one really did move next door for fear that he would lose "respectability." It was this terror too that haunted the residents of Rone Court.

And along with this intangible aspect of the mythology — for the comfort of those who may have uneasy feelings that racial exclusiveness results in unfair treatment of minorities — there is a further fiction. This is the belief that people are just naturally supposed to live in a neighborhood where everyone is pretty much of the same race, religion and economic status — that people of all groups are happier, more stable and better citizens if they live that way and that mixed neighborhoods are a detriment to the community.

Certainly, as far as Louisville is concerned, the idea that dollar-and-cents values of property decline when Negroes move in has little or no basis in fact, and time soon showed how wrong Mrs. Thomas' prediction was as to the prospects for our property. For in less than three years some Negroes did move into our block and in other blocks close by. In 1952 we had bought our house for $7,800; in late 1955 houses just like it in the neighborhood were selling for $7,500; eighteen months later when Negroes bought some of these houses they sold for $8,500, $9,000, and even $9,500.

In general, though there may be some exceptions, the pattern has been the same in other parts of Louisville. When Negroes begin to buy in a neighborhood the prices jump, often as much as $1,000 or $1,500. The reason is not far to seek: the supply of houses

---

types . . . diminish the value of other property in the section." Real estate men, Abrams points out, began to sell the "exclusiveness" of a neighborhood as they sold the tiled bathrooms in the ,houses — except that, unlike the bathroom fixtures, the promise of racial exclusiveness cost the builder nothing.

It should be noted that there are some real estate men who are exceptions to this general pattern: men who have moved on their own to open up housing regardless of race, and often at considerable personal risk.

available to Negroes is so short in relation to the bulging demand that the prices are forced up.

As to whether this same pattern holds for other communities I have no firsthand knowledge. It may be that in some — or in many — it does not. But I do know that studies in recent years by experts in the housing field have at least cast serious doubt on the widely accepted axiom that dollar values must decline when minority groups move in. For example, a study of comparable all-white and mixed areas in San Francisco in 1950-1952 showed that prices were on the average the same or higher in the mixed areas; this was true whether the sales were to white or non-white. A Los Angeles appraiser made a similar study and found that property values usually increase under the pressure of Negro bidding; he cited properties that rose 8 percent in value when Negroes moved in, while the general price index for the whole metropolitan area went down 13 percent; the higher prices, he further noted, were not a temporary phenomenon but held up after the transition to a mixed neighborhood. Similar findings have been reported in studies in Chicago, Philadelphia, and Baltimore. The *U. S. News & World Report,* in its issue of October 23, 1953, reported that "Evidence recently come to light suggests nonsegregated residential areas often add to, rather than subtract from, market values."[1]

Of course it is true in Louisville as elsewhere that sometimes a group of white property owners — hearing a rumor that Negroes are moving in, or might move in — become panicked for fear their houses *will* decline in value and rush to sell them to the first person who makes an offer: and then values do decline temporarily. What

[1] The San Francisco study, by Luigi M. Laurenti, was published in *The Appraisal Journal,* July 1952. The Los Angeles study was by Belden Morgan, reported in *The Review of the Society of Residential Appraisers,* March 1952. *Social Forces,* March 1949, published the Baltimore study made by Clifton R. Jones. All of these are quoted by Abrams in *Forbidden Neighbors.* The Chicago study, made by E. F. Scheitinger, is quoted in a publication of the American Friends Service Committee, "They Say That You Say: The Challenge of Houses and Race" (November 1955). This publication also cites the Philadelphia report made by George E. Beehler, Jr., and originally published in *Realty Review,* October 1945. Abrams also quotes an article by Oscar I. Stern from the January 1946 issue of *The Review of the Society of Residential Appraisers* as saying: "It is a fact, the axiom that colored infiltration collapses the market is no longer true."

Mrs. Thomas doubtless meant when she told me that the value of
our house was decreased was that if I had tried to sell it at that
moment to white people I would have had to take a reduced price.
And that could very well have been true. In fact, if I had been
somebody else altogether, in Hudson's office for a different purpose, I might have hurried home to scare my neighbors with Mrs.
Thomas' words about Negroes moving into our block. And then if
a number of us had listed our houses for sale at the same time, we
might all have had to sell at a loss. For this is exactly what does
happen in a spurt of this kind of fright selling: the rumor that values
are falling creates the fact. And this is one thing that helps perpetuate the myth of declining values.

But for the homeowner who keeps his head and his property
this won't happen — certainly not in Louisville. It is regrettable,
from a human relations point of view, that some white people feel
they must move out when Negroes move into their neighborhood;
it would be better for democracy, better for everyone, if they would
stay and help the neighborhood become a truly integrated one —
as they do in some cases. But those who feel they must move have
every right to do so — as the frightened residents of the Rone
Court area had that right, a right which they rejected in favor of
efforts to force Andrew Wade to move. If they do choose the course
of moving — or move later for some unrelated reason — they
may be cheating themselves of an opportunity in creative living;
but they can do it without fear of losing on their financial invest-
ment — provided they sit out any initial panic and wait long enough
to sell. In fact, the man who told Carl "I've saved up for years . . ."
could probably, had he but realized it, have waited and sold his
house at a profit. Prejudice, unfortunately, sometimes "pays" in
material terms.

If it is not true then that Negro occupancy necessarily decreases
property values, why are many real estate and home financing
people so eager to maintain segregation? Why did they become
so aroused in Louisville when a single Negro family broke out of
the pattern and moved into an all-white suburb? A Negro business-
man explained one theory to me this way:

"It's a money-making proposition, pure and simple. They want
to keep the Negro housing market short. That way, when they do

decide to open up a neighborhood to Negroes, they know there'll be plenty of customers — and they can ask inflated prices. And when they do that they do everything they can to make it all-Negro. Because each time a white family moves they make money twice: they sell him a new house in the suburbs, and they sell his old house to a Negro."

It would appear on the surface that this might be the whole story. Money is made this way, there can be no doubt. And it is demonstrably true that real estate operators generally make every effort to get all of the white people out of a changing neighborhood. Many times white families who had originally intended to stay change their minds under this pressure. White people in my own neighborhood who decided not to move told me that for a period of months they had no peace — morning, noon, or night — because of real estate men coming by, calling them up, urging them to sell. They never bothered us, of course, because they knew it would be useless. (In fairness it should be said that Negro as well as white real estate men apply this kind of pressure, but usually the white companies manage to corner the lion's share of the business.)

And yet I think it is an oversimplification to say that the financial motive is the only one — that real estate men merely cynically "use" the property value myth to perpetuate segregation and make money out of it. For one thing, there would be money to be made too if the segregated pattern of housing was broken generally. The tremendous bottled-up Negro demand might force prices up in many areas and it would be a long time — at least in a place like Louisville — before the demand was so fully satisfied that this pressure would stop operating.

The complicating factor is that other aspect of the myth of property values — the intangible one, the one that says that people are happier and better off when they live among "their own kind." This aspect of the myth, I think, the real estate and home financing people involved in the Wade case honestly believed; and it was in this sense that they too were victims.

There are powerful arguments against this part of the myth too. It can be pointed out that living in a neighborhood where all of the people are pretty much alike can be a deadening thing — that a few families of different nationalities and races might broaden everyone's viewpoint and make life much more interesting, to say nothing of being more in line with the real American ideal of equality and democracy. It can be argued that people who live only among people exactly like themselves cannot be truly the best citizens, since an important part of good citizenship is the ability to understand and work with people of diverse groups. And there is the point that a neighborhood based on racial exclusiveness is not really a desirable place to rear children if it nourishes prejudice and snobbery rather than respect for one's fellow man.

But these are intangible arguments, as the myth itself is intangible. Their acceptance or rejection depends on the life experience of the one who hears. And if nothing in your experience had ever opened up these channels of thought, if you had heard always that people are happier and better off if they are divided, if you had learned this as one of the basic principles of your profession, you would be quite likely to abide by it and consider it a bulwark of a stable society. You could defend it without feeling at all that you were harming your fellow man. And being solidly convinced that your general approach was to the best interest of society and for the welfare of all, you could accept the money-making possibilities inherent in the situation as a natural piece of good fortune and without any conscience-pricking thought that you might be hurting others in your pursuit of profit. You could do this, that is, until it was called sharply to your attention or until you had to look at one of your victims at close range and see him as a human being.

The officials of the South End had to live with the Rone Court situation much longer than Ben Hudson or any of the others. They had to defend their actions in long-drawn-out court proceedings; they had to defend them in the public mind as the case became widely known over the nation and many people saw the South End as an ogre trying to drive a Negro from his home. I think it began to eat at their consciences.

This was indicated by a conversation Andrew Wade had with Frank Able, the secretary-treasurer of the bank, a few months after the suit was filed. Andrew had gone to the bank to see if some sort of satisfactory settlement could not be worked out. He told us later that Able went out of his way to be cordial and to prolong the conversation, assuring him anxiously that he had nothing against Negroes. Maybe, Able said, the South End could have worked out a loan for Andrew if it hadn't been that "this fellow Braden messed it up."

"But of course when I pressed him on that one and suggested that they just drop the suit and transfer the mortgage to my name," Andrew said, "he began to hedge."

One of our attorneys, Conrad J. Lynn of New York, who is a Negro, had a similar experience in the spring of 1956 when he went to the office of one of the attorneys for the South End, Lee Blackwell, to serve him with a copy of a brief in the case. Lynn told us Blackwell would not let him leave and almost begged him to sit down and talk a while. He told Lynn he was much concerned about the housing problem of Negroes in Louisville and was thinking of helping launch a new suburban low-cost housing development for Negroes; he wanted Lynn's opinion of the plan. Blackwell was almost wistful as he talked, Lynn said, apparently longing for some indication of approval — assurance from Lynn that even though he was attorney for the South End Federal Savings & Loan Association in the action against Andrew Wade he was not such a bad fellow after all. When Lynn simply threw cold water on his plan — telling him segregated developments were no answer to the housing problem of Negroes and that what was needed was an open market in all new developments — he appeared crushed.

These were not evil men; they, like the men who burned the cross at Andrew Wade's house and like some of the paralyzed liberals of Louisville, were trapped men. They were not the ones who had created the myth that a segregated housing pattern is the best for all concerned, but they had learned it as they learned their ABC's; they had absorbed it with the air they breathed. They had accepted it as one of the rock-bottom axioms of the professions which they had entered as their lifework. And when the time came to act on it, they acted — convinced, or nearly so, that the values they accepted were eternal ones.

10

Black Against White

The Wades were not without their supporters in their venture into Shively.

News of the house purchase spread rapidly even before the newspapers came out with their reports. Something like a thrill of accomplishment seemed to sweep through the Negro community. Louisville's Negro population, enclosed in its ghetto, seemed to sense that escape was possible. Here was a man who had broken through the wall. Here were white people who had helped him do it. It looked momentarily like the coming of a new day.

All that first Sunday, the Wade house was crowded with visitors. It was perhaps ominous for the future that most of them were Negro. Some of them were friends of the Wades; more were people they had never met. They came out to offer their encouragement, to say they were glad this family had been brave enough to do what it had done. The next day, the Negro Baptist ministers of the city sent a committee from their weekly meeting to call on the Wades and on us and to offer support. The local branch of the NAACP sent a letter to the newspaper backing the Wades and asking full police protection for the house. On Thursday, the weekly Louisville *Defender,* the Negro paper, ran a front-page editorial rejoicing in the move and saying, in part:

> By working together they [the Wades and the Bradens] pierced the vicious practice of not allowing a Negro freedom of pur-chase of the home of his choice. . . .The Wades in satisfying a personal desire to live where they choose are also fighting the housing battle of all of us. . . . Negroes must have access to acquire first class homes, and Kentucky may as well face it.

The big question in everyone's mind was whether the Wades planned to stay in the house. Andrew answered that question in an interview with the *Defender* that same week. He was quoted as saying:

> I will never sell, not even for $150,000. I feel that the principle of living where you are able to buy is too great to sell out. I would not be doing justice to my wife who loves the house or my children who are entitled to the best. . . . If our neighbors do not like our being here and feel they cannot live beside us or around us, then let them move. We are not moving. . . . We intend to live here or die here.

The spontaneous support among the Negro people quickly found an organizational form. On Friday night, less than a week after the first incidents at the house, a group of citizens, again mostly Negro, met at the YMCA to form a Wade Defense Committee. There were two immediate reasons for the formation of such a committee at this time. One was the cancellation of the insurance on the house. The committee set as one of its aims the finding of new insurance or if necessary the raising of cash to pay off the mortgage so that Andrew Wade could keep the house. The other immediate need was physical protection at the house. Angry groups of neighbors gathered in the vicinity all day the Sunday after the shooting. Cars of people shouting threats continued to ride by all week. It seemed obvious there might be more trouble. After the shooting, the county police did place an around-the-clock guard at the house. But Andrew, remembering that the police had known of the threats against him before that Saturday night and noticing the friendly relations between the police and the Rones and their friends, felt that this guard did not assure the safety of himself and his family. The people who formed the Wade Defense Committee proposed to meet this danger in two ways: (1) by attempting to find friendly white people in the neighborhood who could influence others, and (2) by sending volunteers to stay at the house at night to help Andrew watch all approaches to the house. The committee also hoped to enlist as much public opinion as possible in favor of the Wades. It planned approaches to community organizations among the white people and a series of radio programs. A Negro minister,

Dr. M. M. D. Perdue, was elected chairman of the committee. Prominent Negro attorneys, the publisher of the Louisville *Defender,* and other leading citizens in the Negro community were among its members. The committee started with a zeal. As one attorney said at the first meeting:

"We have got to keep Wade in that house. If we let the Ku Kluxers run him out, Negroes in Louisville will be set back ten years. We've got to keep him in that house."

The fatal weakness of the Wade Defense Committee from the beginning was the sparsity of its white support. The Negro members did not want it that way: they wanted white support and they sought it. They approached white ministers. They appealed to white trade union leaders. They approached numerous other white citizens who had reputations for disapproving of segregation. They sent letters to all of the white churches asking for support.

But the white response was always meager. There were exceptions, of course. The assistant pastor of the city's largest Unitarian Church attended several meetings. A white minister, pastor of one of the largest Presbyterian churches in Louisville, made a trip to Shively to express his sympathy and support, but he never came to any of the meetings of the Wade Defense Committee and never did anything else that was heard of. Probably he did not know what to do. A few white individuals sent money to the committee, along with explanations as to why they could not be active in its work but expressing interest.

But the prevailing answer to the appeals of the Wade Defense Committee among Louisville's white citizenry was silence. A few insulting and almost obscene letters came back to the committee in response to the mailing to the white churches, but these were the exception. For the most part, Louisville's white Christians and liberals simply looked the other way. The *Courier-Journal* had already indicated a line which the more cautious Louisville liberals could follow — that this was a situation in which it was not really necessary to take an interest, since it should not have happened in the first place.

Consequently, the few white people who did come actively to the support of the Wades were isolated from the beginning. There were a zealous few who did come, who devoted that summer of

1954 to the situation on Rone Court. They came with a certain sense of dedication — each one perhaps moved under some compulsive drive, not too different basically from the compulsion which had demanded of Carl and me that we buy the house in the first place, each one with an overpowering emotional demand within himself that he defy segregation. The situation on Rone Court had presented a challenge, a challenge that seemed to them a test as to whether they really believed what they said they believed; they like us could not refuse to act. But inevitably, perhaps, they were also already to some extent marked in the community as people who were "different" and sort of radical. For the most part they could act only as individuals and had little or no organizational backing from large and influential groups. Some of them had, as we did, past associations with organizations easily labeled as "left wing"; this gave the segregationists a powerful weapon to use against them in the attacks that came later.

One of them was Vernon Bown. He was a truck driver. Before settling in Louisville several years before, he had been a riverboat worker on the Ohio River. He had become convinced of the wrong of segregation in his activities in his union while working on the river. He had known us casually since he had lived in Louisville, although he had known nothing of our plan to buy the house on Rone Court; but when he read in the newspaper about the Wades' trouble, some impulse told him to go and visit them and offer his help. He later tried to explain his reasons to the grand jury:

> . . . over a period of time, I might have been away from home and working out on different jobs and so forth, I have gradually come to the conclusion that Negro people have been pretty badly treated in this country. They are persecuted in many areas, and even in Louisville where the people are much more enlightened than they are further south. Still there is a lot of prejudice and segregation, and I believe that colored people have the same rights and should have the same rights as anyone else, and that includes the right to move into a house wherever they wish, regardless of whether it is in colored neighborhoods or white neighborhoods. White people can move in any house where they wish, why should white

people try to tell colored people where they should live? I think it is a question of the Constitution. We are all supposed to be human beings. We are all guaranteed certain rights under that Constitution, so if Mr. Wade had moved out there and been no violence whatever, I probably would have paid no attention to it, but after the violence started, it seemed to me that Mr. Wade needed help. He wasn't going to be able to carry on this fight himself, and in view of my ideas on the question, I decided to go out and see what I could do to help, even if it wasn't more than moral support. I don't know what I could do, I just went out to see them. . . .

Bown's chance to help soon came. Andrew asked the Wade Defense Committee to find volunteers who would stay at Rone Court during the day while he was working so that his wife and child would not be there without a man on the premises. This was after the county police, despite protests from the committee, had decided to withdraw its daytime guard and leave only the night guard on duty. Bown and another man, a Negro, volunteered to stay days at the house — both of them worked at night and had their days free. Andrew picked Bown because he had no family and the other man did. So Bown gave up his room in town and moved to the Rone Court house and stayed in the extra bedroom. It was an act that the most hostile person could hardly deny required some physical courage, as those were tense days on Rone Court. But it was a white man moving into the home of a Negro couple, and this was an act that later proved incomprehensible to many people.

Another white person who came actively to the defense of the Wades was Lewis Lubka. He was a native New Yorker who had moved to Louisville and married a Louisville girl only two years before. He worked at the big new General Electric plant, where he had earned himself a reputation as a radical by being active in the organizing drive of the left-wing United Electrical Workers. This union lost the GE election to the CIO International Union of Electrical Workers, and Lubka became a shop steward in the latter union. In New York, Lubka had moved among people who actively opposed segregation. He was young and somewhat head-strong. It never occurred to him — as it does to so many trans-planted Northerners who become more "Southern" than Southerners, once they have crossed the Mason-Dixon Line — that he should act differently in Louisville from the way he acted at home. Long before the Wade incident, he had made many friends among the Negro people in the GE plant. He read of the Wade incident, and he also felt he had to do something to help. He went and volunteered his assistance. From then on, throughout the summer, he often spent two or three nights a week at the house. Often his wife, Thelma, went with him. She had been brought up in the Louisville pattern of segregation, but, like so many of us in the South, she had never really felt easy with it. And, like so many of us, she had begun to sense the wrong of segregation from what she learned in Sunday School. As she told me during that summer:

"We used to sing a hymn — did you ever hear it? — that went 'God loves all His little children, All the children of the world, Red, yellow, black or white, They are precious in His sight: God loves all the children of the world.' I have never forgotten that. It never seemed right to me that Negroes should not have the rights I had."

Like many white people in the South who sense the contradictions between what they are taught is right and what they see practiced around them, Thelma grew up keeping her opinions mostly to herself. She thought, as so many do, that perhaps she was the only one who felt that way. When she met and married Lubka, she had for the first time found someone with whom she could express her real feelings. She entertained his Negro friends in their home and enjoyed it. She went with him to the Wade house and came to like Charlotte very much.

Lubka told me later that he debated long with himself as to whether to tell his fellow workers at the GE plant that he was going to the Wades' house and supporting them. He knew many of them were violently anti-Negro.

"Finally I decided I had to tell them," he said. "That's part of fighting this thing in the South — not just doing it but letting people know you're doing it. You and your husband didn't keep your actions a secret. I couldn't either."

As is always the case in this sort of thing, he found a surprising number of his friends and acquaintances who agreed with him. But there were many others who were enraged. They had of course known that Lubka had Negro friends and was always talking his belief in racial equality. They had let that pass. After all, that was more or less his own business. But to go to the house of a Negro family that had committed the unforgivable sin of moving into a white neighborhood and support the family in this move! That was too much.

A group of workers in his department got up a petition to remove Lubka as shop steward. Some of them came to him on the side and told him there was only one way he could clear his name of this stigma — he must join with others in "really fixing" the Wades' house.

"I told them they could kill me but I would never do anything like that," Lubka said later.

He stood his ground. He argued the issues. He told them why he opposed segregation, why he thought America meant equality for everyone, why he felt that all people, white included, could live better if there was real equality. He also had his supporters. And others, while not agreeing, believed in his and every man's right to his own opinions. The attempt to remove him as steward was defeated, and as the summer wore on, Lubka continued to argue his viewpoint with his most determined opponents.

"I've won in a way," he told me in August. "At least some of those guys who couldn't talk about it in June without the veins popping out on their foreheads can sit down and discuss the thing calmly with me now. Some of them have changed their minds."

It was a case, as Andrew Jackson said, of one man with courage being a majority. It was also proof that it is *not* necessary for a Northerner who moves South to conform to what he thinks Southern mores are in order to live and get along with Southern white people. Some Northerners do fail when they don't conform, but usually this is not really because of their views on segregation; it is because they consider Southern white people stupid, and Southerners sense this and would resent anything they said. Lewis Lubka had none of this arrogance. He liked the men he worked with and he respected them as people; hence, it was possible for him to disagree with them on an issue without its affecting his good relationship with them.

Another of Wade's white supporters was LaRue Spiker. She too had a strong emotional drive against segregation. She was a student and had read deeply into the history of the abolitionist movement. At the time of the Wade incident, she was writing a book on Elijah Lovejoy, the Presbyterian minister-abolitionist who was killed by a mob. LaRue felt that the current situation in twentieth-century America required white people who were willing to take their stand as strongly as had the white abolitionists of the last century. She had formerly been a social worker in Indiana where her strong feelings about segregation and other things she considered social evils had led her to join several organizations that later ended up on the U.S. Attorney General's list of subversive organizations. Because of these associations, she had lost her job. Unable to get another job in Indiana or in social work, she had come to Louisville and had gone to work in a flour mill, where she became active in and finally president of her AFL union. There she tried to influence the white men and women she worked with to feel as she did about racial discrimination. Some of them responded. When Mrs. Nina Hardman was under attack six months before the Wades moved to Rone Court, LaRue was one of those who joined the picket line in her support. When the attack on the Wades came, she went to Rone Court to call, and persuaded some of her own white neighbors to go with her. She began to call on some of the neighbors of the Wades to try to influence them to be friendly. She visited people in other parts of Shively. A number of them responded favorably. One white couple she visited went to call on the Wades and offered to try to organize others to support them. This couple came back several times, but they later became discouraged when they talked to the minister of their church who advised that there was little that could be done because there was so much opposition.

LaRue shared an apartment with Louise Gilbert, one of the city's leading social workers and also chairman of the Louisville branch of the Women's International League for Peace and Freedom. Louise presented the Wade situation to this organization, composed mostly of other social workers, a few librarians, teachers, and persons in similar professions. The WIL decided it wanted to do something to help. It was already on record in the community as opposing segregation, having taken the lead in getting the Iroquois Amphitheater to admit Negroes to its summer operettas. The WIL decided to send a letter to hundreds of residents in the immediate vicinity of the Wade house asking for neighborliness and tolerance toward the Wades. The letter became a big issue in the case. When Carl was later tried on criminal charges, it was filed — although he had nothing to do with writing it or sending it — as Exhibit No. 1 against him. It read in part:

> We have no connection with the Wade family, but this letter is a plea for tolerance. Our organization has been working for 40 years to bring peace and freedom to all people through non-violent means. We do not know how you feel personally about this family moving to Shively, but we know that to many of you this was a new and shocking experience. We know, too, that many people have opposed the outbreak of violence and have seen with dismay this example of man's hatred to man.
>
> The Wades are, of course, just human beings among other human beings. The purchase of a home for the Wades by a white family was, due to a circumstance we have forced upon them, the only way they could acquire a home such as they wanted. . . .
>
> As members of an International organization, organized in the United States in 1915, by Jane Addams of Hull House, we have come to know people of all races and creeds. We find that color of skin makes no basic difference in people. Were you to become acquainted with the Wade family, you would find them having the same kind of home life, ambitions and ideals as yourselves. The very fact that they wanted to live in the kind of neighborhood you also chose to live in shows this had to be so.
>
> Some Shively residents have feared that the presence of a Negro family would decrease property values in the area. Negroes already reside in Crescent Hill, the Highlands and other sections of East Louisville, and have for a long time, yet property values have gone up rather than down in these areas.
>
> Many of you in Shively are of German or Irish extraction. Your grandfathers or great-grandfathers probably came to the United States to escape oppression, as did those of some of us members of the Women's International League. We be-

lieve that after you have thought this situation over you will want the Wades to have the same right to live decently that your forebears came here to attain.

This may be a new idea, but in the United States we have learned to accept new ideas . . .

How many of the recipients ever read the letter and how much it influenced them, if at all, never became known. But the letter caused a great deal of trouble later for its senders. The WIL also tried to get other Louisville organizations to support the Wades. But they were a small organization, composed of women whom many felt to be impractical idealists, and their influence was not great. Very little came of their efforts.

There were a few other white people who helped in various ways. For example, there was Alberta Ahearn, a young widow whom Carl and I had worked with in a number of interracial organizations, as well as peace organizations. We asked her to join the Wade Defense Committee, and she became quite active in it, serving as chairman of a committee which enlisted other women, white as well as Negro, to go to Rone Court and spend an afternoon or a day with Charlotte so that she would not be without company in a hostile neighborhood.

There was a white pressman at the *Courier-Journal,* Donald Renner, who in his spare time published a home-printed magazine; he tried to enlist support for the Wades through his magazine and went to the Wade house himself and spent several nights there. A leader of the CIO Textile Workers went to call with LaRue Spiker. A few of the white people Wade had formerly known in the Progressive Party made token gestures. But the white support was scanty. It came mostly from people who were not in a position to influence many others or to do anything very effective on a large scale. The people who might have had more influence never moved.

And gradually, in the face of this lack of effective white support, many of the Negroes who had originally supported the Wades in the first burst of enthusiasm also drifted away. In the beginning it had appeared to be a winning battle and a righteous one. A man had a right to live in the house of his choice — surely no one could deny that. Leading Negroes in Louisville felt that at least some of the city's white citizens would support this cause. In contrast

to the situation deeper south, Louisville Negroes were accustomed
to hearing pleasant words from at least some whites on the subject
of segregation. Perhaps they, like us, completely underestimated
the drastic implications the case involved — did not realize how
many white people who support desegregation in principle have a
tendency to shy away when an institution as sacred as the white
neighborhood is challenged. As it became obvious that the cause
was not really popular and that victory was not certain, when it
became obvious that the few whites who were supporting the
Wades were people without prestige or influence, then the personality conflicts which so often develop under the pressure of frustration began to strain the unity of the Wade Defense Committee. Its
Negro ranks also dwindled, especially among the men and women
who were considered by white Louisville to be leaders and spokesmen for the Negro community — not all of these leaders, for
some stayed, but some of them. Such personality conflicts were of
course only a surface manifestation of the underlying trouble; and
it would be too facile to say that this underlying trouble was an
unconscious fear. Many of those who left were people who had
proved themselves to be people of courage. It was probably more
a subconscious sense of futility. Not many people want to be
martyrs to what appears to be a losing cause.

Another factor was a rash of divisive rumors that so often seem
to crop up in the Negro community when some individual or group
takes a new and unexpected step toward equality. Wade, it was
said in some quarters, thought he was better than the rest of his
people and he had moved to Rone Court because he wanted to get
away from Negroes. Then again, when the Wade Defense Committee tried to raise money to pay off the mortgage, the story went
around that Andrew had started the whole thing just "to get the
public to buy him a house." Whether such rumors are planted by
the opposition or whether they arise spontaneously is hard to say,
but they do tend to appear in a situation of this kind. Mrs. Louise
Gordon, the Negro mother who gained nationwide attention two
years later when she tried to enroll her children in the all-white
school at Clay, Kentucky, told me that the part of the episode that
hurt her the worst was the way many of the Negro people turned
on her — saying she was trying to get her children away from
their own people. In places where mass movements have developed

against segregation, the Negro people have often been able to nip any such false rumors in the bud through tight organization within the community, frequent meetings, and constant communication between leaders of the movement and the people generally. But in Louisville, Wade's supporters had no such far-reaching and compact organization. People who knew Andrew and Charlotte personally knew that such rumors were false, but they continued to circulate and may have been a factor in reducing some of the Wades' Negro support.

Many Negroes, of course, stayed — as more and more Negroes all over the South today are pushing ahead on their own and alone, in the face of what must appear to them almost complete inaction among even the whites who claim to be their friends. Those who stayed were of course the more determined, the less easily discouraged — probably also those who had had fewer illusions about the liberal white citizens of Louisville to begin with, illusions that most Negroes deeper south have never had about the white world around them. Naturally from this it followed that those who stayed were also the ones who had little hope that their aspirations for equality would ever be achieved through the joint efforts of Negro and white working together. When a decent white person appeared they were glad to see him, but they considered him something of a freak — and from the white race in general they expected nothing. The white world was the enemy, and what rights they won they must get for themselves.

During that first week after the shooting, Wade said to several visitors in his house:

"People should not think of this as a fight of black against white. This is a fight of the broad-minded people against the narrow-minded people, regardless of color."

That was the way he saw it and wanted it. That was the way many of the Negroes who first flocked to the Wade Defense Committee wanted it. They did not want a fight of black against white. They wanted a struggle of what they considered to be the democratic-minded people against what they considered to be outmoded prejudice and undemocratic ways of life. But white Louisville defaulted, and the Wade case did become for the most part a case of "black against white."

11

The Bombing

As June, 1954, wore on, things seemed to quiet down on Rone Court. For six weeks after that Saturday night, May 15, when the shots were fired, there were no more acts of violence at the Wade home.

To be sure, the atmosphere remained tense. There were the continuing anonymous calls — at the Wade business office and, after a phone was installed, at the Rone Court house; there were the people driving by in cars shouting threats; there were the constant rumors: the Negro woman who told Wade she overheard a white man in a downtown store saying the house on Rone Court would be blown off the map; the man who told a friend of Wade's he had overheard two men in a bar talking about blowing up the house; the woman who called us up and related that she had heard some women in a Shively store talking about "when the police leave we'll drag them out of the house and kill them." There was the day when Andrew Wade's father and some other men were replacing the broken picture window at the house and a car of young men drove by, one of them shouting, "There's no use putting that window back in — we're going to break it out again tonight!" There was the worker in the GE plant who told Lewis Lubka, "I tell you, Lew, you'd better warn the Wades: they've already bought the dynamite."

The Wades learned to live with such rumors and gradually began to ignore them. Charlotte calmly went about fixing up her house and making drapes; Andrew cut the grass and weeds in the field behind the house and planted grass seed in the front yard. Around the middle of June, police told Andrew they thought the worst danger had passed and they would remove the daytime guard. The Wades and the Wade Defense Committee urged that the guard be continued, but it was ended anyway. The night police guard was still maintained. In addition, the volunteer guards, mostly Negroes but with a sprinkling of white people who had offered their services, also continued to stay in the house at night; but even this took on more and more the nature of a social gathering. The guards sat in the kitchen all night, talking and laughing and joking; sometimes they went to sleep. There was progressively less attention paid to keeping watch on all approaches to the house, as had been done in the beginning. Finally, toward the end of June, even the threatening rumors began to die away.

At our house, too, life became quieter. From the middle of May to the middle of June, it seemed that our telephone had rung constantly. The same voices — the same threats — steady — unending: "You'd better watch out!" "You're going to get it like the Wades did!" "Get those niggers out of that house!" On some nights strange cars drove back and forth in front of our house, circled the block and came back again — up until the wee small hours of the morning. One day a woman called to tell us she had heard some men in Shively saying they would come to our house some night and take us out and lynch us.

My mind told me these were idle and meaningless threats. Carl seemed able to ignore them, and I felt — as I had felt that Saturday I insisted on taking the children out in the yard when the callers threatened something would happen at noon — that I should ignore them too. In retrospect, measured against all that has happened since, they seem a little silly. But it was hard to ignore them then. It took time for me to learn to live with this new experience: the facing of possible physical danger. I found that it was quite different from the other thing I had long ago learned to live with and accept — the facing of verbal criticism and disapproval from some of my friends for the things I believed in. In the abstract, I had always rather assumed that if need be I would be willing to give my life for the things I thought were right. But I found now that there was a great deal of difference between vaguely assuming this in the abstract and facing the actual possibility in a concrete situation. I kept telling myself the people in Shively were just carrying on a war of nerves against us. But suppose some of them did actually kill us, I found myself thinking. What would happen to Jimmy and Anita? Suppose the children — I could not even finish the thought.

Finally and gradually, I was able to conquer my fear — or at least to live with it — and I don't think anyone, except probably Carl, even knew that I had it. No man or woman ever knows what fears he can conquer or live with until he faces the necessity. There were a number of resources I was able to draw on. And not the least of these was the example of Andrew and Charlotte Wade.

It started that first Thursday night, May 13, when the crowd came to our house and I came home soon after they left, to find Carl and Andrew and Charlotte discussing what had happened. Listening to Carl tell about it, I found myself shivering — shivering so violently that I was afraid they would all notice it as they looked at me. My mind said it was not afraid of the threats of a mob; I tried to laugh as Carl and Andrew were doing; but my body just ignored my mind and went right on shivering. I looked at Charlotte and Andrew. I knew they had sat three or four hours in their house that night, expecting a hostile mob any minute, and yet they seemed to be completely calm. I got up and went into the kitchen on some pretext so they would not notice my shivering.

As time went on and I watched the Wades making their house a home in the constant face of death, I discovered that I could learn to live with the threats too. I found out later, when I came to know Charlotte better, that she was not really as calm inside as she appeared on the surface — and I'm not sure that Andrew and Carl were either. But in a situation like this each man and woman, cloaking his own fears, perhaps imparts courage to his friends — each one in turn drawing some strength from the other, strength that not one of them standing alone might have had. I began to busy myself with the little things that one finds one must do at such a time. After the shots were fired into the Wades' house, I formed the habit of moving Jimmy's and Anita's beds into the downstairs hall each night. This was the spot where we thought they were least likely to be hit by bullets that might be fired through windows or doors. We moved Sonia into the new upstairs bedroom that we had just completed furnishing. Carl and I had originally planned to use this room ourselves and give Sonia the front bedroom downstairs, so that Carl would have a quieter place to sleep in the mornings. But with the threats and the tension, we thought it would be safer for Sonia not to be in the front bedroom on the ground floor and we also thought it would be better for us to be downstairs where we would be more likely to hear prowlers. Even at that, I was afraid to go to bed for fear I would sleep so soundly I might not hear a disturbance until it was too late. So I made it a practice, during this period, to sit up each night at least until Carl came home from work about 2 o'clock. These were warm summer nights, and I usually sat in our side yard where I could keep an eye on both the front and the back of the house. On many nights, Andrew would ask visitors leaving his house to pass our house on their way home to see if everything was all right. These practices became routine; I soon found that I was accepting them as routine, and thinking little of the danger any more; I had accepted it as a new way of life.

Often on these summer nights, some of our neighbors would come and sit in our yard and keep watch with me. Most of the white people in our neighborhood were, in varying degrees, sympathetic to Carl and me throughout this whole episode. Many of them did not completely agree with our views on segregation, but they were used to us. They had heard us express our views many times, and they had seen our Negro friends coming and going at our house from the time we moved in some two years before. So news of our part in the incident on Rone Court came as no great shock to them. Some of them, in the years that they had known us, had come around to deciding that we were probably right in opposing segregation — or perhaps, to put it more accurately, to deciding that their own belief in segregation was not as firm or as rockribbed as they had thought it was. But even among most of those who had not altered their own views, there was — after the Rone Court trouble started — a certain sympathy for us because we were their friends and we were under attack. The only exceptions were two women who lived up the street from us a little way. They quit speaking to us after news of Rone Court appeared in the press. But they were women who at one time or another had been mad at almost everybody in the neighborhood about something and had earned reputations as "cats." They never had much influence on others in the neighborhood who were inclined to be friendly to us. And some of the women in the neighborhood even came and asked me to take them out to see the Wades so they could express their friendship and offer moral support.

From the beginning of the difficulty, Andrew Wade and other of our friends urged me to keep a gun in the house. They thought this especially important because I was alone with the children at night while Carl was working.

I have a strange feeling about guns. I was horrified at the thought. I had never owned a gun, had never shot one. I felt that I would die if I had to fire a shot. I presumed that I could aim at a prowler's feet — but suppose that by some quirk I fired in such a way as to hit him where it would kill. I felt I could not live with myself for the rest of my life feeling that I had killed a person — no matter who it was, and even if he had intended to kill me. I found that one of those things I had always believed in the abstract I still believed in the concrete: that if someone planned to kill me I would rather be killed myself than be the one who killed. I knew of course that the Wades had guns in the house on Rone Court. I also knew that the Rones had guns in their house; on the Sunday after the cross burning I had been on Rone Court and had seen Mrs. Rone carry several shotguns from a pickup truck into her house. The Wades had to protect themselves. I knew they would not shoot unless they had to, and then not to kill if they could avoid it. I certainly did not criticize them or condemn them for it. I simply felt I could never be the one to fire a shot. And I refused to have a gun in our house.

I changed my mind one day early in June after Carl took Jimmy along on a ride to Rone Court to see the Wades on some piece of business. As he and Jimmy left the Wade house, a car with two young women in it followed them. Up the road a way, the other car pulled in front of Carl and forced him to stop. One of the women called out:

"You'd better be careful!"

"I can take care of myself," Carl replied.

"Then you'd better watch out for that child—something's going to happen to him!" shouted the woman. The car then sped away.

When Carl came home and told me of this incident, I made my decision. I suppose there is a point beyond which most people of pacifist inclination cannot go, although there are some who can take a complete pacifist position. I don't know how many mothers could hear their child threatened and not take defensive measures. I only know that I could not. That day I called Andrew and asked him to bring me the gun he had been offering to lend me.

Later our opposition tried to imply that we had furnished the guns the Wades took to Rone Court. The truth was of course just the opposite. Andrew brought me a small pistol, a .32-caliber I believe it was. All that summer I kept it on top of the bookcase near the front door each night or else beside my chair as I sat in the yard. I never had to use it, but it was there.

With all the turmoil that June, however, life went on somewhat in its normal way. There were the usual little crises, such as the day Jimmy fell off the new over-sized glide swing we had bought him — scaring his mother much worse than he hurt himself. There were the usual little thrills: Anita was at the age where we were waiting for her to begin to talk, and every once in a while there was a moment of excitement when she would speak — or I thought she did — a quite distinct and bona fide word. I was always busy: besides my duties with the children, I was helping to write radio scripts and news releases for the Wade Defense Committee — part of the job the group assigned to Carl and me as members of the publicity committee; as often as possible in the afternoons, the children and I rode out to Rone Court to be with Charlotte and Rosemary. On other days I took the children to visit Carl's mother, who was always eager to see her grandchildren and delighted in feeding them cookies and orange juice. It was restful for me too to sit in Mom's kitchen and talk with her: she never questioned anything Carl or I did or asked for any explanations as to why we had got ourselves so involved. She had a slight notion that our purchase of the house for the Wades had been a rather foolish thing to do. But she did not have the least doubt that the Wades had a right to live where they wanted to. She had always had a somewhat blind faith that anything her son did was basically right, and she treated me as if I were her own daughter; it was a good relaxing atmosphere.

Despite these interludes, however, I was physically exhausted by the end of June. On most nights Carl and I would sit up for a couple of hours even after he came home from work — until we were sure it was too late for anything to happen that night. Sometimes it was almost dawn when I finally went to sleep; Sonia always got up and prepared her own breakfast, but of course I had to get up when Jimmy and Anita awoke and I could never get them to sleep later than 8 o'clock in the morning. Ironically, on Saturday, June 26, I decided this was one time when I was going to get a good night's sleep. There had been no telephone threats for a week or more. Everything seemed quiet. It looked as though the whole nightmare might soon be over. The Wades had decided not to fight the foreclosure suit filed by the South End but to try instead to get new financing for the house. The deadline for us to file an answer to the suit was the first week in July, and our plan was to present the South End with its money in lieu of an answer. Wade and his friends and the Wade Defense Committee had been looking everywhere for the past weeks for a lender willing to take up the mortgage. Of course none of the white-owned banks in town would touch it, but just that week a Negro insurance company had given virtual assurance it would take up the bulk of the mortgage and had scheduled a board meeting for Monday, June 28, to give final approval. It looked as if the problem was solved, and this had been announced publicly at a meeting of the Wade Defense Committee that week. No one stopped to think that there might be danger in letting people in Shively know that the court efforts to get the Wades out of the house were about to fail. On that Saturday, Andrew had called to tell us he had secured promises of enough loans from individuals to make up the rest of the mortgage that the insurance company loan would not cover. For the first time in weeks, it seemed we could all relax. As Carl kissed me goodbye on his way to work that afternoon he rubbed his hands across my eyes.

"I don't like those deep circles under your eyes, Anne," he said. "You've got to get some sleep. Why don't you go to bed early tonight? Everything's over."

"I'd like to," I said. "Maybe I could get up in time to get to early church in the morning."

The quiet of the early morning Communion service had always meant something very special to me, but it was held at 7 A.M. during the summer months at our church, and that summer I had rarely awakened in time to make it. I had been settling for the late morning service, where it seemed to me that the hubbub destroyed some of the peace and calm that gave the services of organized religion their special appeal to me, and sometimes with all the confusion at home I did not even get to late services.

"And besides," I added, "I must be tired. I'm beginning to snap at the children. It's not right to take this thing out on them."

"Not only Jimmy and Anita but Mike," Carl said. "You've got to look out for him too."

Mike was our third child — or child-to-be — who was now apparently finally on the way. We had already named him, as we had named the other two before they were born, hoping we had guessed right on the sex as we had with Jimmy and Anita.

"Oh, don't worry about Mike," I said. "He's lucky — by the time he gets here this should all be ancient history."

"Yes, but we don't want to lose him before he's born," Carl insisted.

"I don't think there's much chance of that," I answered. "You know I never even threatened a miscarriage with the other two. I'm pretty strong that way."

"But you've never been under this kind of a strain before. I'm not worried about it, but I do want you to get some sleep," Carl said.

I told him I would. That night I went to bed at 10 o'clock and slept soundly.

I was awakened by the ringing of the telephone. I don't know how long it had been ringing when it finally roused me. I stumbled into the living room to answer.

"Anne . . ." I recognized Andrew's voice. In the instant that he hesitated before saying anything else, I wondered what time it was and why he was calling in the middle of the night.

"We're all all right —" he continued. It is strange how fast the mind can function at a time like this. He spoke steadily, but I recall that I had time to speculate that perhaps he was about to tell me that everything was all right on the loan from the insurance company. In my state of semi-sleep, it did not occur to me to wonder why he would have been calling so late about it or where he would have got such information on Saturday night since I had last talked with him. Then —

"— but they just blew the house up."

Suddenly I was wide-awake.

"When? What happened? Are you hurt?"

"Just about twenty minutes ago. Nobody's hurt. We're just a little shaken up." His voice was steady and controlled.

"But Rosemary . . ." I asked.

"Her bedroom's torn up, but she isn't here. We took her to

Mother's so she could go to Sunday School in the morning," he replied.

That's all I recall of the conversation except that he also told me the house was half-destroyed — all one side of it blown to bits. I told him Carl was still at work but that he would probably drive on out to Rone Court when he got home.

"No, I think he'd better stay there," Andrew answered. "They may try something at your house too tonight. You'd better look around."

I agreed and hung up. I went to look at the clock. It was not quite 1 o'clock. I checked the children's beds to make sure they were sleeping soundly. Then I took my little pistol from its place on the bookcase and a flashlight and went outside. The street light two doors from our house, which usually cast the light of day on our front lawn and which had been on when I went to bed, was broken out. I walked around the house with my flashlight and gun. Everything looked normal. I came back and sat on the front step with my gun until Carl came home and I could tell him what had happened. We sat up the rest of that night, but everything was quiet.

It was not until the next day that I heard the details of what had happened at Rone Court. I heard it from the Wades and from the others who were at the house. They had to recount the events many times subsequently — before the grand jury, in criminal and civil courts of law. The story never varied in the telling.

On Saturday morning, Charlotte and Rosemary had left the house about 8 o'clock to ride into town with Andrew as he went to work. The police day guard was of course no longer there. Vernon Bown had left the afternoon before to go to his night job and had told the Wades he would be leaving directly from work to drive to Wisconsin for a family reunion and be gone over the weekend. So on that Saturday morning, for the first time since the Wades moved in, the house was left unoccupied and unwatched. It was empty until about 1 P.M., when Charlotte and a friend and Rosemary and Andrew's father returned. Andrew's father stayed only briefly, and the two women and little girl were there alone during the afternoon. About 7 P.M., Andrew came out from work, bringing two Negro friends, Tellus Wicker and Melvin Edwards, who were to serve as guards for the night. Andrew, feeling perhaps the same relaxation of tension that Carl and I had felt that day and being relieved about the imminent solution of the mortgage problem, suggested that he and his wife and daughter and his wife's friend take a picnic over to the Indiana side of the Ohio River and spend the evening. It was to be the Wades' first night out for recreation since their move to Rone Court. Wicker and Edwards said they did not mind watching the house alone.

The Wades stayed in Indiana until late in the evening. Then they returned to Louisville, took Charlotte's friend home and dropped Rosemary off at the home of Andrew's parents, as they often did on Saturday night. They got back to Rone Court shortly after midnight. Andrew recalls that it struck him as a little strange to observe as they drove into the court that every house in the neighborhood was dark. This was not usual for midnight on a Saturday night. As they passed the Rones' house, he saw the policeman on duty sitting in a chair in the Rones' driveway — the spot where the police guards always stayed. He apparently had no police car with him, and so of course no radio set.

When the Wades drove into the driveway, Wicker was sitting on a small side porch that opens from the kitchen of the house. Edwards was asleep on the couch in the living room. Andrew went into the house to get some soft drinks from the refrigerator and went back outside to talk to Charlotte and Wicker. He asked Wicker if everything had been quiet. Wicker said it had been quiet, but that there had been an odd flashing of lights just a few minutes before. First, he said, a light had flashed from the Rone yard near where the policeman was sitting. It looked like someone flashing a flashlight, and he thought it appeared to be a woman holding it. And then a little later another light had flashed. This came from the barn behind the Wade house, directly across Rone Court from the spot where the first light flashed in the Rone yard. Then Wicker had seen a third light. This one was out in a field on the opposite side of the Wade house, the side opposite the one in view of the policeman's position in the chair. A person in the position where the third light flashed could not have seen the flashing of the first light, because the Wade house would have obstructed the view. He could, however, have seen the second light; and a person in the barn where the second light appeared could have seen the first light in the Rones' yard. The three together made a large triangular formation, which enclosed the Wade house.

Wade and Wicker talked a while and speculated upon what the flashing lights could mean. They had not had long to wonder when a deafening crash tore the air and almost shook them off their feet. When they pulled themselves together, they realized that the house had been blown up. Charlotte began shaking uncontrollably, and Andrew tried to calm her before doing anything else.

The worst of the explosion had been on the side of the house opposite where they were sitting. Apparently, dynamite had been placed in the air vent where the grating was broken out six weeks before when the window was smashed. This was the side where the two bedrooms and bathroom were. These rooms were virtually destroyed. Huge holes were blown in the floor and some of the flooring boards crashed through the ceiling. In the rest of the house, windows were broken and floors were buckled by the impact. Edwards, who had been still asleep on the couch, emerged from the house dazed and stunned — but unhurt.

The policeman ran in from across the street and started calling on the telephone, which for some reason was still in operation. Soon the premises were crowded with police. One of the most interesting aspects of that night came out in the testimony before the grand jury of the officer, William E. Blevins, who had been on duty in Rone's yard:

A JUROR: At the time of this explosion, did any of the white neighbors in the neighborhood come around to see what had happened to this house?

A: Not while I was there they did not.

A JUROR: Was the explosion very loud?

A: It was loud where I was at.

A JUROR: Is there white people living on either side of this house?

A: Yes.

A JUROR: And none of those people were disturbed at that time?

A: As far as I know they weren't.

Up until that night of June 26, Andrew and Charlotte Wade had been struggling valiantly to make their Rone Court house a home.

Despite the burning cross and the shots and the rock with its "Nigger Get Out," despite the streams of curiosity-seekers riding by each day, despite the fact that their house was a public issue and they seemed to be living in a goldfish bowl, despite the fact that the house was filled each night with the volunteer guards talking in the kitchen, exploring the refrigerator, watching television in the living room — guards they wanted and welcomed even though they did make life somewhat inconvenient — despite all these things, the Wades persistently tried to create some semblance of normal living. Charlotte hung the drapes for her living room windows; she shopped for rugs and debated with herself over what color slipcovers to buy for her living room. She had dreamed of a home of her own for many years. Like any woman, her greatest delight was in fixing it up the way she wanted it. She was expecting the new baby very soon and she wanted everything perfect by that time. She was not a person especially interested in causes. She had no desire to fight a crusade. She simply wanted a home and wanted to live in it in a normal way.

On June 27, all these dreams blew up with the house. Neither she nor Andrew ever felt the same about the house again. The possibility of a solution on the mortgage problem was blown to bits with the concrete and plaster of the house. The Negro insurance company's board met as scheduled that Monday but of course reported regretfully that it could not take up a mortgage on a house when it was in damaged condition. The Wades and Carl and I filed an answer to the suit of the South End Federal Savings & Loan Association and prepared to fight it through in the courts. The Louisville Fire & Marine Insurance Company announced that it was liable for the damage and would pay, but because of the pending litigation over the foreclosure they turned the money over to the courts, saying they did not know to whom the property legally belonged; and the house continued to lie in ruins. It appeared that final settlement of the whole tangle lay a long time in the future.

Andrew Wade told the newspapers the day after the explosion: "We'll still be here even if we have to pitch a tent." He did not intend to move. But the house had now become — completely and finally — a cause and a symbol. It had ceased to be a home.

12

The Failure of the Police

For the first week or two after the bombing of the Wade house, it appeared that the county police were making a serious investigation and were preparing to make an arrest.

Events moved rapidly in those two weeks. In view of later developments, they are important.

On Sunday morning, June 27, the *Courier-Journal* carried a front-page story on the bombing. In Monday's papers there were pictures and more stories. The *Courier* and *Times* both ran editorials; they again put their emphasis on the original "wrong" that had been done in our purchase of the house for the Wades but they also expressed horror at the bombing and urged that those responsible be brought to justice. Louisville's Negro community was electrified and angry, demanding action by the police; many white people too were momentarily shocked out of their lethargy.

On Monday night, June 28, the Wade Defense Committee held a large meeting where most of the leading Negro citizens of Louisville came — even those who had begun to drift away and who as time passed during the summer would drift away again — although still only a few whites. The committee called for a probe by the Federal Bureau of Investigation; the FBI did make some preliminary investigation, but the Justice Department in Washington later informed Wade by letter that they could not enter the case because no federal law had been violated. In the meantime, the Wade Defense Committee decided at that same meeting on June 28 to try also to get action on the local level. They voted to send a committee to the county courthouse on the following day to urge quick arrests.

This committee, made up of Negro ministers, lawyers, and members of the Wade family, duly visited the courthouse the next day, Tuesday, June 29. They buttonholed every available official of the county, and, because they could not finish their work in one day, they went back the following day, Wednesday. They visited the county judge, the police officials, the county attorney and the prosecuting attorney, known in Kentucky as the Commonwealth's Attorney, whose name was A. Scott Hamilton. Hamilton invited the committee to lay the matter before the county grand jury which was to be in session the next day. He told them to come back at 1:30 P.M. on Thursday, July 1. Since the calling of this grand jury investigation was later denied by officials, it is significant that an announcement of the fact that it had been scheduled appeared in the Louisville newspapers at that time.

There were at that time already some indications that the county police were investigating. On Thursday, July 1, a story in the *Courier-Journal* stated that "County detectives yesterday took statements from all residents of the Rone Court area." A *Courier-Journal* reporter, Phil Harsham, told members of the Wade Defense Committee that county police were also investigating a report concerning John Y. Hitt, editor of the Shively *Newsweek*. According to the information Harsham had received, the police guard on duty at the Wade house at the time of the explosion had said that Hitt had stopped to talk to him about midnight on Saturday night — about half an hour before the explosion went off. Harsham said Hitt had reportedly asked the patrolman if "anything has happened at the Wade house yet."

At 1:30 on Thursday, July 1, Andrew Wade, other members of the Wade family, and various members of the Wade Defense Committee reported on schedule at the courthouse for the grand jury probe. When they arrived, Commonwealth's Attorney Scott Hamilton approached C. Ewbank Tucker, attorney for the Wades and the Wade Defense Committee. Hamilton said:

"I think we should postpone this grand jury investigation today. The police tell me they have found out who blew up the house and there will soon be an arrest. If we have an investigation now, it may hamper instead of help their work."

Tucker agreed, reported this development to the others who had come for the investigation, and everyone went home.

Carl had been among those asked by the Wade Defense Committee to go to the courthouse for the grand jury investigation. I had stayed home to take care of the children. Shortly after 3 o'clock that afternoon, Carl and Andrew came back to our house, their arms full of bags of hamburgers and soft drinks they had bought on the way and their spirits high.

"They've got the man who blew up the house," Andrew announced, and they proceeded to tell me what had happened at the courthouse.

I was becoming more suspicious of our opposition.

"Sounds like a stall to me," I commented.

There were events which soon indicated I might be wrong. While Carl and Andrew and I were still eating the hamburgers, our doorbell rang. At the door was a member of the Louisville city police force. He stated that the chief of city police, Carl Heustis, wanted to see Carl in his office right away and had sent him down to provide transportation as a convenience. Thursday was Carl's day off from work, but he was planning to stay home with the children that afternoon while I went downtown on some errands. He asked the officer at the door to come in while he called Colonel Heustis to see if whatever he wanted could be postponed until the following day. Carl had known Heustis well since his police reporter days twenty years ago.

Heustis' voice on the other end of the telephone was insistent.

"Carl," he said, "you come on down here this afternoon. It may be the most important thing you ever did in your life."

Carl went. When he arrived at the police chief's office, he found that Heustis had all of his captains of detectives from various parts of the city on hand for a conference.

"We have received authoritative information," Heustis said to Carl, "that some of the people who blew up the Wade house are planning to blow up your house. Now I want to say right here and now that we are not going to have any bombings within the city limits of Louisville. I am going to put a twenty-four-hour watch of plainclothes men at your house until the danger passes. And I want you to take certain precautions."

"Where did you get your information?" Carl interrupted to ask. "I just heard the county police are on the trail of the people who blew up Wade's house."

"From the same place you got your information, I suppose," Heustis said, "and we think the situation is serious." Carl took this to mean that Heustis had received the information from the Commonwealth's Attorney. Later developments indicated it probably came from the county police.

Heustis then asked Carl to buy a floodlight and string it up in our back yard and to turn it on to signal for police if we heard any prowlers. He advised him to move our children out of the house at night.

"And watch your car — if you've left it parked any length of time in an isolated place," he added. "Even if it is locked, there are ways to open the hood and put explosives inside, under the hood. Lift up the hood and check it before you start the motor. And don't accept any package that might be brought to your house if it's someone you don't know."

We never doubted that Heustis was sincere in his efforts to prevent more violence. He undoubtedly disapproved personally of our part in the Wade house transaction. But Carl knew from his long acquaintance with him that he was an honest police official, dedicated to the job of maintaining a law-abiding city.

When Carl came home and told me of Heustis' warning, we set about taking the precautions he had urged as a routine matter. We had been living under tension so long that this new threat was no great shock. Threats were a part of our lives now; Heustis' report did not come as any startling revelation, since the anonymous telephone calls had started again on the day after the explosion. We put up the floodlight. We arranged for Jimmy to spend his nights at the home of a friend some distance away; we took Anita to sleep in the home of a neighbor. Before dark that night the detectives Heustis had promised were on duty — two of them in the State Fairgrounds that lay across the street from the front of our house, two of them in the alley behind our house. The fear that I had felt six weeks earlier was all gone now. I don't think I had had any sudden spurt of courage. It was just that I was tired; I no longer had the strength required for any emotion — fear or courage. I found that my reactions were reduced to cold calculations as to how we could best lessen the danger.

As we sat in our living room that night — Carl reading and I folding freshly washed clothes — I found my mind turning over various possibilities and figuring out ways to cope with them.

"Carl," I said, "you know Andrew has always thought those people out there around Rone Court might have tapped onto his phone to find out when he was going to be at home or away. Do you think they might have tapped our phone too?"

"They might have," Carl replied without looking up from his book.

"Well, I guess we ought to try to find out," I said. "If they have, we should probably be careful about what we say on the phone — not let them know when we plan to be away or at home. Did you ask Colonel Heustis if he thought they might have?"

"I never even thought of it," Carl replied, still reading.

"Well, I'll go down and talk to him about it tomorrow," I said. "And maybe I can find out when he thinks there'll be an arrest."

The next morning I went to Heustis' office. I told him my concern about a telephone tap.

"Oh you don't have to worry about that," he replied. "You'll see what I mean when you see who these people are. They're just a bunch of ignorant hoodlums. And they wouldn't be able to tap a telephone if you gave them the equipment and told them how to do it."

Then he volunteered:

"Besides, this is all going to be over in forty-eight hours — and I'll pull the guard off your house — because the people will be under arrest by then."

All through that July 4 holiday weekend we expected momentarily to hear that the arrests had been made. So sure were we for a few days that the police were ready to take action that Carl and Andrew and I had a long and serious discussion as to what course to pursue when arrests were made.

"You know," Andrew said, "I'm glad they're really going to arrest those people. And yet it's funny — I don't feel vindictive toward them, and I'm not really going to enjoy sending anybody to prison for a long term."

"I know how you feel," I said. "It's the same thing we felt six weeks ago when people were urging us to take out warrants against that crowd that came to our house."

"Maybe it wouldn't be the right thing to insist on sending them to prison," Carl commented. "Will it just drive the prejudice deeper? We know that putting people in jail isn't going to eliminate race prejudice."

Andrew looked thoughtful.

"And yet something has to be done to let people out there know they can't blow up a man's house and get away with it," he said.

"I know it," Carl agreed. "I wonder if there's some other way." He sat silent a moment. "They've got to be arrested, and they've got to be tried and convicted — there's no doubt about that. But what do you suppose would happen if, after that, you asked that they be placed under a bond — a peace bond — in other words, under obligation to keep the peace on Rone Court so that —"

"A peace bond?" I interrupted. "Now look, Carl — let's don't go off the deep end. This is a little different from the question we had on the warrants anyway — that was just threats. What are you going to do? I'd sure hate to think about those people walking around with more sticks of dynamite in their pockets."

"Well, just wait a minute and let me finish," Carl said. "Don't you see? That way, these people would be put in a position where it was their responsibility to see that there wasn't any further violence on Rone Court. Then, if there were any more threats or trouble, their bond would be revoked and they'd be sent to jail."

"Sure, Anne," Andrew said. "What Carl means is that this way the people who blew up the house would have an interest now in protecting it. Just think — I wouldn't have to fool with having guards any more. *These* guys would be my guards."

Jimmy had come running into the living room while we were talking, and I had leaned over to tie his shoelace. I looked up quickly at Andrew to make sure he was joking. He was laughing.

"No, all kidding aside," he said, turning serious, "I think it might be worth trying. At least it would let those people out there know I'm not trying to be their enemy or pick a fight — that I just want them to let me alone and I'll let them alone."

"I can see that," I agreed. "It might work. Even if it didn't win over the people who blew up the house it might have a good effect on some of the neighbors."

"Well, we don't have to decide right now," Andrew concluded. "Let's all sleep on it and see what we think when they're actually arrested."

It would have been a charitable course of action. It would

probably also have been in the eyes of many people a very foolish one. I wonder to this day if it might not have worked. But of course, as it happened, there was never an opportunity to find out.

The forty-eight hours that Heustis had mentioned passed with no arrests, and we began to wonder. On the following Wednesday morning, July 7, I got up early and prepared as usual to go and get the children from their respective sleeping places with our neighbors and friends. When I went out the front door, I noticed that the detectives, who had been on duty constantly since the day Heustis first talked to Carl, were gone from the Fairgrounds across the street. They were nowhere in sight. I called Carl to tell him, and later in the morning he went down to talk to Heustis again to find out what the situation was.

"I couldn't leave them there any longer," Heustis told him. "They were all getting chiggers over there in the Fairgrounds. I've got twenty detectives with a bad case of chiggers. And we've got to have some of those men for other duty. I feel sure we can watch your house adequately now by patrolling the area. If anyone is still planning to try anything, they'll think the guards are still there — but hidden. That will scare them off."

"But just what is the situation on the arrests?" Carl asked.

"The county police have a confession from the man who set the dynamite," Heustis replied. "This man told them there were several others involved and some of these people were planning to dynamite your house. He also told them the dynamite was obtained somewhere in southern Indiana, but he didn't know exactly where. But the trouble is the county police are afraid to proceed with arrests just on the basis of this confession. They've had too much experience — we all have — with going into court with just a confession. The man may repudiate it in open court and you're likely to lose your case. They feel they've got to have some more corroborating evidence. And they're trying to get it. They're checking all the quarries over in Indiana to see where the dynamite might have come from. They think they will have enough evidence to move soon."

Along about that same time, County Police Chief Walter Layman made a statement to attorney Ewbank Tucker and to a committee from the Wade Defense Committee which confirmed the things Heustis had said. Layman stated:

"We could put our hands right now on the man who did it. But we think we've got to get some more evidence before we can be sure of a conviction. We're making progress."

It is significant that the information about a confession to the county police was given not only to those of us who were involved in the case or on the Wade Defense Committee. The same day Heustis put the guard at our house, he called the executive editor of the *Courier-Journal* and *Times,* James Pope. He told Pope about the guard at our house and asked him not to mention it in the newspapers since publicity might aggravate the situation. In the course of the conversation, Pope later said, Heustis told him that county police had obtained a confession from one of the men involved in the bombing and that there would soon be arrests.

That was in early July. July wore into August, and August into September, and no arrests were made. A few months later Colonel Layman was denying that any confession had ever been obtained.

Strange as it may seem, in all of the court litigation that followed in the subsequent fall and winter, neither Colonel Heustis nor Colonel Layman was ever asked to testify about the statements they had made during this two-week period following the bombing. Finally, in February 1956 — a year and a half later — some additional light was cast on the situation when we called Colonel Heustis as a witness during the presentation of defense for us and the Wades in the foreclosure proceedings over the Wade property. One of our attorneys, Conrad J. Lynn, asked Heustis if he had placed a guard at our house during that first week of July 1954, and, if so, what prompted him to do it. This exchange took place:

HEUSTIS: The Chief of the Jefferson County Police Department, Colonel Walter Layman, had advised me of the dynamiting and that . . . he thought that it would be advisable that we place police officers, preferably detectives, in the vicinity of the Braden home . . .

Q: . . . in your conversation with Colonel Layman, did he tell you that he had an admission or a confession from anyone who admitted bombing this home of Wade's?

HEUSTIS: He told me at the time that he warned me of the condition, or the possibility of trouble occurring at the Braden home, that they had an excellent suspect whom

they believed they would make a case on; as I recall, he
mentioned the name of Rone. . . .

What happened during that period in late July or early August
of 1954 to halt the investigation? Why did the police, apparently
at one point on the brink of making an arrest, pull back? The complete answers to these questions may never be known. But there
are a few clues.

In the first place, many of the men on the county police force
lived in the Shively area. The people in the Rone Court section
who were hostile to the Wades were people some of them knew
personally, people they liked. For example, one of the men they
were apparently investigating was Lawrence Rinehart. He was a
friend of Buster Rone's and one of those who later confessed he
helped burn the cross in May. And he had once been a county
policeman. He had left the force several years before the Wade
incident and was now working in a government arsenal in southern
Indiana. Whether he was a man who was highly respected by
members of the police force I don't know. But certainly he was a
man they all knew; he was a person much like themselves.

The relaxed and easy relationship between the police on the
one hand and the people hostile to the Wades on the other was
apparent from the beginning. I saw an example that first Sunday
afternoon after the rifle shots. Rone Court was alive with people —
friends and well-wishers of the Wades on their property, hostile
crowds milling in and out of the Rones' yard and on the surrounding property, curiosity-seekers riding by in cars. Interspersed in the
crowd were members of the county police force. I was struck immediately by the difficulty in distinguishing the policemen from the
hostile crowds that centered around the Rone house. This was the
time I saw Mrs. Rone taking several large shotguns into her house,
and I went over to report this to one of the policemen. He was sitting
in a patrol car joking with five or six of the neighbors when I walked
up.

"Forget it, lady," he said nonchalantly, after I had presented
my complaint. "People got a right to have guns in their own house."

He turned back to the men and they all laughed together. I was
not sure whether their laughter was at some joke they had been
sharing when I walked up or whether they were laughing at me.

It did not matter much. The point was that these men were the policeman's friends, the people he knew well and identified himself with. I was not his friend — and neither were the Wades.

This same camaraderie between police doing guard duty and the Rone family and their friends continued throughout the following weeks. Usually the patrolman guarding the house sat in the Rones' yard. When people questioned this procedure, they said that this was the best vantage point from which to watch the house. It may have been. But it was also pleasant for them. The Rones served them coffee at intervals and passed the time of day with them in conversation.

This was in sharp contrast with the relationship between the police guards and the Wades. Generally both the Wades and the police tried to keep things civil and polite, but the real feelings on both sides came to the surface in the early morning of July 22, 1954. On that occasion, the police made their one and only arrest on Rone Court that summer: they arrested Andrew and a Negro friend, a man named Wallace Tircuit, on a charge of breach of the peace.

During this period, Andrew was spending each night in the damaged house, and usually there were friends and guards there with him. The arrests on July 22 grew out of an argument as to whether the police would allow Tircuit to go into the Wade premises. The police claimed his name was not on a list of approved visitors Andrew had given the police. Andrew claimed that since Tircuit was in his company this did not matter. Then, without provocation — according to Andrew — one of the officers said: "I'm going to settle this thing right now — I'm going to take you to jail." According to the police version of the episode, Andrew precipitated the arrests by becoming belligerent and accusing the officers of "not doing your job right," and Tircuit said, "To hell with the police!"

When the case came up in court, Tircuit was fined $20. He did not bother to appeal. Andrew, however, was given a fine of $100 and a 30-day jail sentence. This sentence was appealed and later set aside.

Regardless of whether one accepts as fact the police version of the events leading to the arrests or Andrew Wade's version, one thing is clear: there was mutual hostility between Wade and the police guarding the house. He did not have confidence in the police and never felt sure they were on his side. For their part, the police did not relish their job of guarding the house and did it only as an unpleasant duty.

This attitude was put into words in the testimony of the mayor of Shively before the grand jury that investigated the case. Rone Court lay just outside Shively's city boundaries, and the mayor was called to testify as to the attitudes of people in the community. He was asked if he felt that the Jefferson County police had done a good job in protecting the Wade family, and this colloquy followed:

> MAYOR: Every time I passed there, I always see a car there, and I have spoken to the Shively police and they have stated that they have been very effective and on the job all the time, although they didn't appreciate it very much, I understand, but they had to do their job. . . .
>
> Q: What do you mean, the Shively police didn't appreciate having the County police there?
>
> MAYOR: No, the County police didn't appreciate the job that they had. That's what I mean.

All of this adds up to the fact that when the Jefferson County police force was called upon to protect the property of Andrew Wade and bring to justice the people who destroyed it, they were being called upon to turn on people who were their neighbors and in some cases their friends, their own kind of people. They were asked to do this in the name of protecting a man whom they did not know, whose color most of them did not like, and with whom none of them really identified themselves. To meet this challenge would not be an easy task for a man of greatness, and it is not likely that any of the county police officers fell within the category of greatness. Under the circumstances, it was easy for them as the summer weeks passed to begin to feel that the bombing of the Wade home was not the terrible crime many had said it was in the beginning. After all, no one had been killed. It was an act that obviously, under the rallying power of the Shively *Newsweek,* had the approval of many people in the Shively community. The Wades had brought it on themselves by moving there in the first place.

The easy way was to ride with the tide, and that apparently is what the police did.

Considering all this, the really perplexing question would appear to be not why did the serious investigation stop — but why was it ever started in the first place? Why did the police proceed almost to the point of making an arrest in that first couple of weeks after the bombing? Certainly, in almost every case of the bombing of a Negro's home — not only in the South, but in cities all over America — the crime has gone unpunished. One does not know of course in just how many of these cases there was a spurt of investigatory activity by police immediately after the crime. I can only speak of what happened in Louisville, for this I know. And in Louisville it is a fact that for a time the police did plan to make an arrest.

I think what happened was that the initial shock of the crime tended temporarily to shake loose the traditional and long-standing relationship of the police and the anti-Negro people in Shively: the relationship that made for indifference to such crime. It did this because there was a spontaneous outburst of indignation and protest from decent opinion in Louisville, white as well as Negro. Louisville was shocked, momentarily, and the demand was heard everywhere — in the streets, in the bars, in the churches, wherever people met — that the bombers be caught.

The police responded to this voice of public opinion — not as a matter of being pressured, not as a result simply of the delegations the Wade Defense Committee sent to the courthouse, but by the very atmosphere in the community of Louisville at large, an atmosphere which for a moment said firmly: "This cannot happen in Louisville."

But as time went on, the protest died down — as protests so often do. The crime became less terrible as it faded into the past. People began to talk more again about how the whole affair should never have happened in the first place. Demands that the bombers be caught tapered off. And, with the relaxation of the atmosphere, the older and more firmly established relationships of the police to the people in Shively who condoned the crime reasserted themselves. The public opinion that had been encouraged in Shively by the suburban *Newsweek* spoke more strongly than did the voice of liberal opinion in a white Louisville that had lapsed again into silence and was beginning to look the other way.

When criminals go unapprehended, it is never just the police who are to blame. Generally speaking, the laws which are enforced are the laws the public wants enforced. There are many, many laws on the books, but the ones which live are those which have force in the public consciousness. Murder, rape, robbery: these are crimes which galvanize a police force almost anywhere into action, and few police officers will be swayed from arresting the culprit in such cases even if he is someone they know and like. But this is because the public almost everywhere considers these to be heinous crimes and expects the laws regarding them to be enforced. But we know, for instance, that anti-gambling laws are enforced in some communities and ignored in others; it depends not on what is in the statutes but on whether public opinion in the respective communities considers gambling to be a crime. And, even in the case of murder, as I learned so well at the Birmingham courthouse, the crime may be treated quite differently depending on the color of the persons involved; the lawbooks don't say that color should make a difference in regard to murder, but public opinion often does.

It was not that many people in Louisville did not consider the bombing of the Wade house a crime. They did. But generally, after the first shock died away, most of them — if they were white — wanted to forget. Rone Court was an unpleasant name, an unpleasant incident, for many reasons, and white Louisville did not want to think of it any more.

Only Andrew Wade, and those who were his staunchest supporters, could not forget. Neither could many other Negroes longing for decent housing — and a chance for a better life.

13

The Making of a Crusader

At the time of the Rone Court incident, the Negro families that had moved into the previously all-white Trumbull Park housing project in Chicago had been living for almost a year in a virtual state of physical siege — under constant attacks and threats similar to those that plagued the Wades in Louisville. During that summer of 1954, one of these Trumbull Park residents, interviewed by a magazine writer, made this statement:

"I didn't come in as a crusader. I came to get a place to live. I'm a man of principle, but no man wants to die for it if he can live. But I'm going to stay. I had to become a crusader after all."

That quotation struck me when I read it because it seemed to describe so exactly the situation of Andrew Wade. When he went house-hunting in the spring of 1954, he was not in any way a crusader; he was simply a man who wanted a house to live in and, along with it, a little breath of freedom for his family. He was ready, if necessary, to put up with some difficulties to get what he wanted; but it was the needs of himself and his family that were uppermost in his mind and in that sense he was certainly not a man with a cause. In the months that followed, however, he did begin, under the pressure of events, to develop into a crusader. It was a development that he did not always relish, and it was not without its painful aspects. But perhaps that is the way all crusaders are made.

The first step in this evolution came immediately after the burning of the cross and the firing of the rifle shots — when he told the reporter for the Louisville *Defender,* "We intend to live here or die here." But the evolution was not complete. The statement to the *Defender* was partly rhetoric, and, as we shall see, Andrew later forgot he had made it. He was determined to stay in the house, and

153

he was willing to risk danger to do so. But his primary hope still was to make the house a home. Throughout that latter half of May and these first weeks of June, he lived constantly in the shadow of death but dreamed always of the peaceful day he felt sure would come, the day when it would be all over, when he and his wife and child could settle down to living a normal life in their little ranch-type house, the guards and curiosity-seekers gone — an average suburban family in an average suburban home.

With the bombing, it became suddenly apparent that this day was not soon to be and perhaps never to be. It became apparent that there were strong doubts, which any realistic person including Andrew had to admit, as to whether the Wade family could ever live a completely normal life there. With the spotlight of publicity so dramatically centered on the house, could it ever — even in the distant future after it was rebuilt — cease to be a landmark? With the bitterness in the neighborhood so deeply rooted and punctuated so sharply by the repercussions of the dynamite blast, could the Wades ever again entertain the hope of eventually being quietly accepted into the neighborhood?

In the face of a situation like this, there were only two courses for a man to take. Either he could decide that the house could probably never become the quiet home he had started out to seek for himself and his family, and he could therefore give it up and move back to the ghetto; or he could decide that the house had now become a symbol, the embodiment of a principle, and that for him to retreat now would make it more difficult and perhaps impossible for other Louisville Negroes to break out of their walled-in world. Andrew's decision was automatic and immediate; I do not think it was until much later that he analyzed his reasons. The smoke was still smoldering from the explosion when he made his reply to the reporters: "We'll still be here even if we have to pitch a tent."

Living in the shell of a house was impossible. Charlotte and Rosemary moved into town to live with Andrew's parents. But Andrew was determined that the people in Shively should know and that his supporters in all of Louisville's Negro community should be assured that he was not giving up the house. He was determined that lights should burn in that house each night. And each night he returned to the house, and he stayed there until dawn. It was not an easy thing to do. The dynamiting had again set in motion far-flung forces of hate; the anonymous telephone calls had started again at his house and his place of business as well as at our house. This time some of the callers were more direct in their threats: if Andrew continued to come to the house, he would be killed. If he didn't give up, his little daughter might be kidnapped. Andrew took precautions to protect his daughter. He asked the city police, in whose jurisdiction his parents' house lay and in whom he had always had more faith than he had in the county police, to watch his parents' house where Rosemary was. But for himself, he defied the threats and drove each night at dusk over the lonely country roads that led to Rone Court. Most of the time the friends and guards continued to come to the house to spend the nights with him, but sometimes he stayed alone — if no guards were available. One night, his father and Charlotte, becoming worried because he failed to answer the telephone when they called, drove to Rone Court and found him alone and asleep in his car in the driveway — physically exhausted but still at his house.

During this period, there were some liberal white citizens of Louisville who made an effort to settle the whole unpleasant affair by persuading Andrew to give up the house on what seemed to them fair terms. They told Andrew they would try to help him work out a settlement of the foreclosure suit pending against him in such a way as to prevent his losing any money, on the condition that he would give up the house. And they would try to help him get located elsewhere. But by that time Andrew felt that his objective was more than a house for himself; fate and circumstances had placed him somewhat in the role of a representative of all his people who needed housing and freedom. He approached this proposition to help him much as a union negotiator might approach the bargaining table. After he had thought it over for a few days he came and told us about it.

"I think I might give up the house," he said, "if they could assure me that some efforts would be made to provide new housing for Negroes — all Negroes, not just for me. And it would have to be on a non-segregated basis. Segregated housing is no answer; there can never be enough of it. You see, there has to be something like this as an alternative if I am to give up the house. If I leave that house now, I am saying to the Ku Kluxers, 'You've won; you blew up my house and I left; the way to get a Negro out of anywhere you don't want him is to use violence.' If I say that, I'm just fixing it so that no other Negro can move into a white neighborhood and live peacefully. I can't do that unless when I do move I can help provide some other answer to the housing problem."

When he proposed this idea to those who were offering to help him — that efforts be started toward new integrated housing in Louisville — no one saw how it could be done. The deal fell through.

"I have no choice but to keep the Rone Court house," Andrew told us later.

He was finding no pleasure in his role as a martyr — although some of his opponents said he was and maybe they really thought it. I don't think many of the people who are forced into such a role do find pleasure in it. Opponents of the martyr often say he enjoys his role; to say this and to think it helps to ease the consciences of those who slightly suspect they may have helped push him into the role in the first place. But what they forget is that every martyr is human. As a human being, he has the same desires for a pleasant and peaceful life for himself that every man has; he has the pulls from people he loves who may not understand the thing he is doing, from people who see his course only as "foolish"; sometimes he begins to wonder himself if he is foolish. Andrew was very human, and he had many pulls on him.

First, there was Charlotte, whom he loved deeply. There was not the least trace of the crusader in Charlotte. After the house was blown up, she sometimes did not altogether understand why Andrew had to keep on fighting in the way he did.

I began to know Charlotte fairly well during those summer months. It was something of a new experience for both of us. From her point of view, I was the first white person she had ever known intimately as a friend. But from my point of view too, it was something new. For Charlotte was the type of person few white people ever have an opportunity to know well — one of those Negroes who never come around interracial gatherings, who studiously avoid places where white and Negro people might mingle, who stay as far away from the white world as it is possible to stay.

Building a friendship was not an easy task for either of us. For Charlotte it meant overcoming the habits of a lifetime in which every white person was an object of dislike and distrust. For me, it meant trying to understand a viewpoint with which I had had no previous direct experience, which did not manifest itself in other Negroes I had known well — Negroes who were willing and eager to strike down racial bars. But we made some progress. Charlotte began to let down some of her defenses with me because Carl's and my action in buying the house for her and Andrew — an action that had amazed her — inspired in her a tentative trust of us; and I very much wanted to be her friend. There were the beginnings of a friendship there — a friendship that might have grown had it not been for the storms that broke around all of our lives the following September before it had a chance to develop fully.

I found out that Charlotte was one of that large group of Negroes who, confronted in childhood with the bleak walls that hem in their world, decide the wall is not worth fighting. She was one of those who decided early that the best course lay in building for yourself the best life possible behind the wall, in acting as if it and what lay on the other side did not exist. That never quite worked, of course; you could never completely forget the wall, for it rose up to strike you in the face at every turn; and each time it did you grew more bitter toward the people on the other side. But you never tried to challenge it because that would be futile and silly.

Charlotte's family had treated the wall that way, and Charlotte learned the lesson early. She learned that white people were something to be avoided insofar as possible because they were the source of trouble. Forget them; ignore them, go about your business — that way there was some chance for happiness.

Charlotte was a beautiful girl, and she found as she was growing up many of the normal bits of happiness any pretty young girl finds in any world. She had many friends, and she was loved by all who knew her — she had a sweet and warm personality when she let down her reserve, with the people in her own world. When she married Andrew, she set out to raise a family in the same pattern in which she had grown up — behind the wall.

It was when she and Andrew set out to try to get a house in

which to rear that family that she finally found that the wall made life unbearable. Moving into a white neighborhood would have been the last thing in the world she would have ever imagined herself doing. But she wanted a house; and she had her heart set on a ranch-type house. First, she hoped she and Andrew could build, and Andrew spent many evenings drawing up plans for the kind of house they wanted. But when he investigated the price of lots and costs of building he soon found this was beyond their reach. It was then they started looking for a house to buy — in the Negro sections of town. When they were unable to find it, the determination to get the kind of house she wanted became the overpowering emotion in Charlotte's life — stronger now than her lifelong aversion to white skin. She was elated — and incredulous — when Andrew told her he had found a white couple willing to buy a house for them. She was delighted when it was purchased. On the morning after we bought the house and turned the keys over to Andrew, she woke up (Andrew told us at the time) with stars in her eyes; and the first words she said were: "We own the house!"

Even the burning cross and the shots did not shake her much. This was probably, as I realized later, because she in contrast to Carl and me and even Andrew had expected some trouble. Very likely, this was because she had fewer illusions about interracial harmony than any of the three of us, all of our eyes somewhat blinded as they were by our own dreams.

"I knew there would at least be a cross burned," Charlotte told me later. "I don't see why you didn't think so, Anne."

She took it in her stride, and it did not change her attitude toward her new house. As far as Charlotte was concerned her interest in Rone Court and Shively stopped at her property line. She had no interest in the neighbors and never expected them to be her friends; she expected their hostility and planned to handle it as she had always handled white people — by shutting them out of her mind and world. She planned to do on Rone Court what she had done all her life: build her world behind a wall and rear her children in it, have her own circle of friends she had always had and let the rest of the world go by. None of the Rones or other hostile Shively neighbors who probably feared the Wades were going to try to force themselves into familiarity with them need have had any worries about Charlotte. I am sure that had their residence there been peaceful and lasting Charlotte would have never moved an inch to initiate a friendship with anyone in the neighborhood, and anyone who wanted to make friends with her would have had to go 99 percent of the way.

But when the house was blown up, Charlotte's whole feeling about it changed. The house was in ruins, and there was no possibility of living in it. A house was to live in — so why continue going back to this one? She became frantic with worry about Andrew's safety as he drove back to the house each night. Her unborn child was due almost any time, and she worried about that — worried that she might lose it or that it might be born abnormal because of all the strain.

During the latter part of that summer she talked with me often about her worries because she felt that, as a woman, I would understand.

I think I did understand. For in those weeks following the bombing I had lost Mike after all. It was in that period after the police guard left our house and the threats persisted and I had resumed my nightly vigils of watching our house — the sleepless nights and the tense days. I had been so healthy all of my life, I had been so sure that a miscarriage could not happen to me, that I ignored the warnings of Carl and my friends. And then, all of a sudden before I realized what was happening, in one bewildering night of pain Mike was gone. I still had a good supply of physical stamina, I suppose, and I recovered quickly — in body, but it took longer for the spiritual wound to begin to heal. I was only two months pregnant, and a two-months baby does not yet have the identity in the mind of its mother that an eight-months baby like Charlotte's does. And yet my babies always had something of a personality in my mind from the moment I suspected I was pregnant. Later Carl and I often said that little unborn Mike was the only physical casualty of the war on Rone Court. We were thankful from the beginning that the casualty was not greater, that it had not included some child already born. We were acutely aware that things might have been much worse. But we wanted Mike too. It helped me to understand Charlotte's feelings. But I thought I at least partially understood Andrew's too.

"Why is Bubba doing it, Anne?" Charlotte asked me one

night as I sat talking with her on her mother-in-law's front porch — they always called Andrew "Bubba." Her baby had come by then. It was a beautiful — and perfectly normal — little girl, and everyone breathed a sigh of relief at that. But her arrival had made Charlotte even more anxious for Andrew's safety. "Why does he keep going out there every night? What is he trying to prove? What good does it do?"

"I'm not sure, Charlotte," I said. "I don't know that as a white person I could ever completely understand. But I think perhaps he feels that if he gave up under this kind of fire he would be letting down his people."

"But what of his wife and children?" Charlotte asked. "What's going to become of us if he gets killed? Doesn't he care about that?"

"Yes, I'm sure he does," I said. "But maybe he is thinking about making the world better for them when they grow up."

"Better? How?" Charlotte's voice was cynical.

"A world where they won't have all these walls to fight. A world where every person can be free."

"Oh, Anne!" Charlotte looked at me as if to ask how I could be so naive. "It's not ever going to be that way, and you know it. Things aren't going to change, and it's silly to try. All you do is ruin your own life. That's what Bubba's doing, and maybe you and Carl are too. And what good does it do?"

I listened and wanted to answer. I wanted to say that I was sure it did do some good, that I was sure someday things would be different. But life had proved so conclusively and so recently for Charlotte that I was wrong. I felt that any words I spoke would be mockery. When I remained silent, Charlotte went on, her eyes afire.

"Look, it's not easy the things you have to go through when you're colored. Sometimes it makes me so mad that I can hardly stand it. It makes me mad now just thinking about it. Why *can't* we have a house? Why *can't* we live on Rone Court? Why *can't* I go anywhere I want to? Of course, I don't like it. But I've learned to put up with it. I've learned because I have to. And I think it sometimes only makes matters worse to fight against this thing."

There was nothing I could say. But as I listened to Charlotte and watched her, I thought of all the segregationists who — ob-

serving her on the surface — would have said she was truly satisfied with things as they were. I thought of all the other Negroes like
her who had retired behind the wall and whom the segregationists
call "content." And yet, never had I seen in the eyes of Andrew, the
fighter and the militant, the bitterness that burned in hers as she
spoke of the discrimination she hated but had accepted because
there was no way out. The very fact that Andrew had hope and saw
somewhere in the distance a way out — the fact that he was consciously moving toward that door of escape — had somehow
swept away any bitterness he might once have known. It occurred
to me that perhaps Charlotte Wade and people like her — the
silent ones who appear to have accepted the inevitable, the people
who have no apparent desire to oppose the status quo — are the
greatest challenge of all to the conscience of the white world that
built the wall around them and stripped them of all hope that it
could be torn down.

But I did not say these things, because it was the white people,
not Charlotte, who needed to hear. And she did not want to hear
anything. She only wanted her husband to quit risking his life, to
come home to her and try to live a normal life. She told him this
all during the summer of 1954, and it was not easy for him to go
against her wishes. But something pulled him on, and he did. In
the end, because she loved him, she agreed that he must do the thing
he felt was right. But she never completely understood, and she
never approved.

Andrew's mother too was among the forces pulling him back.
Unlike Charlotte, she was not gripped by a sense of complete
futility, and living with a man who insisted on fighting for his
rights was not a new experience for her. Andrew's father is like
that, and he never wavered in his support of the course Andrew had
chosen. But when the house was bombed and Andrew's life was
threatened, Mrs. Wade was seized by a mother's natural fears.
Many of the anonymous phone calls threatening him with death
came to her house, and it was more than she could bear. She urged
him to give up the house completely, and she urged everyone who
knew him to do the same. It was under pressure from her that I
finally did the thing I had vowed I would never do: I asked Andrew
to move out of the house.

From the beginning of the difficulty, Carl and I had taken the position that it was not our place to advise Andrew one way or the other as to whether he should stay in the house. And we had scrupulously avoided doing so. But in that week following the bombing, Mrs. Wade called me on the telephone. She told me all of her fears for his life.

"Anne," she said, "you all have got to tell him to get out of that house."

I thought I knew how Mrs. Wade felt. I remembered how I had reacted when Jimmy's life was threatened, how it had caused me to go against the beliefs of a lifetime and get a gun in the house. I knew in my heart that one's feeling for one's son does not change when he grows to be a man. But what right did I have, I thought, to try to tell Andrew what to do? At first I tried to dodge the issue.

"I don't think Andrew would pay any attention to what we might say about it, Mrs. Wade," I told her. "He's made up his mind he's going to stay. Why should he listen to us?"

"Oh, I know he's bull-headed," she replied. "He always has been. But I think if there is anyone who can persuade him, you can. After all, you all bought the house for him. He would consider your wishes."

"That's just it," I said. "Can't you see? — We don't feel that we have any hold over Andrew just because we bought and sold that house. That's all in the past now. It's his house. The future is his to decide. We're certainly not telling him to stay, but I don't see how we can tell him to leave. Don't you see what you are asking us to do? You are asking us, white people, to 'tell' a Negro what to do. That's the kind of thing I've been opposing all of my adult life. And you have opposed it too, Mrs. Wade. You know you have."

She had. I had known Mrs. Wade for years, longer than I had known Andrew. But she was in no mood now to consider abstract principles. She was a mother, her son was in danger, and she was grasping at straws.

"But if he stays he may be killed," she said. "I believe you could get him to move. If anything happens to him, I want you to know I will feel that you are to blame — because you could have made him move."

As I hung up the phone I felt that I was in a daze. I guess I was tired from the weeks of strain, and I was probably not completely rational; but I felt that it would be more than I could stand to have the responsibility for a murder placed on my shoulders too. About that time Carl came in, bringing the children from his mother's where they had spent the morning, and I told him what Mrs. Wade had said.

"The next time I see Andrew I'm going to try to persuade him to move," I told him.

"I don't think you have any right to do that, Anne," Carl said, laying Anita down on the couch and preparing to change her diaper. "I know how Mrs. Wade feels; of course she's worried. Mom's worried about us too; she was talking about it today. You'll be that way about these children all of their lives too; I guess any mother is. But every generation has to live its own life, and make its own decisions."

"Your mother's different," I said irrationally. "She's gotten used to you taking risks and endangering yourself — ever since you were a little boy getting into fights in Portland."

"No she's not," Carl replied. "She's not any different. But that's not the point anyway. It's not a matter of whether Mrs. Wade is right or wrong. She may be right. But the point as far as we are concerned is that we don't have any right to try to tell Andrew what he should do. He was asking me the other day what I thought he ought to do, and I told him just what I always have: that I don't think it's up to me to try to influence him to stay or to leave but that whatever decision he makes I'll support him in it. That's the position I've taken, and I'm going to stand on it."

"But she said she'd blame us if he got killed," I persisted. "Suppose something does happen. I can't live with that the rest of my life."

Carl finished pinning Anita's diaper and came over to my chair and put his arms around me.

"Look," he said, "you're worn out. You aren't thinking straight. Why don't you get some rest and think this thing over a few days? It may look different."

I didn't answer, and I suppose Carl saw he had not changed my mind.

"All right," he said, returning to the couch to straighten the baby's diaper. "But whatever you tell Andrew, make sure you're just speaking for yourself. And anyway, I can tell you right now he's not going to listen to you. He told me yesterday he had decided definitely to stay, and I got the impression nothing's going to change him."

If a few days had lapsed before I next saw Andrew, I might have decided to take Carl's advice. But, as it happened, he stopped by our house that very afternoon while I was still in an upset state of mind, and I did as Mrs. Wade had asked.

"Look, Andrew," I said hesitantly, "wouldn't it maybe be better to give up this whole business? Your mother's worried about you; your wife's worried about you; you may be killed. I understand why you feel you can't give up the house; I know you feel you are fighting for a principle. But maybe you've done your share. Maybe it's somebody else's turn to fight. I think you should give up the house." I was ashamed of myself as I spoke, and I am ashamed now.

Andrew gave me an *"Et tu, Brute"* look and shook his head.

"Can't do it, Anne," he said. "You know I can't."

I had embarked on a path of shame, and I drove it to its logical conclusion.

"Do it for me, Andrew," I said. "Do it as a favor to me. Four months ago you came to us and asked us to do you a favor, to buy the house. We did it. Now I'm asking you to do me a favor. Move out of the house."

"That was different, Anne," he replied. "I asked you to do me a favor for my benefit — to make my life better. If you ask me to do something for you, I'll do it. But you are asking me this favor for my own welfare. I think I have to decide what is best for my own welfare."

I knew so well, even then, that he was right. I did not urge him further.

Others did, though. Even among the Negro people, there were many who disapproved of Andrew's determination to stay in the house. It was just foolish, they said. What good could come of it? A man ought to think of his wife and children. Those are not easy criticisms for any man to hear. They were not easy for Andrew, and we knew he was going through many inner tortures of soul. But there were the other Negro people, those who wanted him to stay, those who felt something vital would be lost if he gave up now —

not always people who were willing to do very much to help him themselves but who were depending on Andrew. He felt a sense of obligation to them and to his own principles and a sense of obligation in a larger sense to his own children; and probably for this reason he was able to turn a deaf ear to the people he loved who were urging him to give up. He had decided to follow the course of a fight for principle: he had become a crusader.

Probably no man who does this ever quite understands what makes him do it. And, for this reason perhaps, there was to come a time when Andrew — under tremendous pressure — would have momentary doubts that he had ever really been a crusader at all, would wonder if the idea to crusade had been his own or someone else's.

But I could not foresee this in that summer of 1954. For then it appeared to me that Andrew had answered his critics conclusively one day as he sat in our living room. We had been sitting there talking about the case, and Andrew started trying to sum up what it meant to him.

"A man owes his children many things," he said. "I owe mine a freer world. I know that often I feel a flash of resentment against my own parents and their parents and their parents' parents. If these people had done more for freedom, I wouldn't have to be fighting this way today for a house to live in. This battle wouldn't have fallen to my generation. I remember my father telling me later how ashamed he was when he had to tell me when I was a boy that he couldn't take me to Fontaine Ferry Park . . ."

Andrew sat quiet a moment, as if remembering. Then he went on.

"I don't want to have to look at my daughters as they grow up and feel ashamed because I have to tell them they are second-class citizens," he said. "And I don't want them to grow up and have to do the work I should have done. I want it to be done in my generation so that they can enjoy some of the fruits of it. That's the greatest gift I can give them. And — and, if I have to die in the effort, they will still be better off than if I passed the whole burden on to them."

Having made up his mind to keep the house, Andrew had no choice but to continue his efforts to get the police to arrest the people who had bombed it. Toward the end of August, he moved his furniture out thinking it was going to be possible to begin work on rebuilding in the immediate future, and he and Charlotte were able to rent a small cottage near his parents' home from people who were going to be away for the winter. As it turned out, the hope of immediate rebuilding fell through, as the court refused to release the insurance money — even direct to a contractor. But Andrew was as determined as ever that as soon as possible he would rebuild the ruins and move back to Rone Court. And he knew that he would never be able to persuade Charlotte that she could be safe there as long as the people who had once bombed the house were untouched by the law.

The Wade Defense Committee agreed with him, and they would not let the matter die. They kept sending delegations to the courthouse to see what was being done, when arrests could be expected. They kept the matter before the public — a public that wanted terribly to forget.

It must be remembered that in all likelihood a small group of persons — perhaps four or five or six — actually planned and carried out the bombing of the Wade house. A dozen or so more perhaps knew of the plan and how it was carried out. Of the rest of Louisville's white population many paid little attention to the affair at all. The great majority of those who did might roughly be divided into two categories: (1) Those who unconsciously approved of the bombing but could not admit this fact to themselves and for this reason had very uneasy consciences about the whole business, and (2) those who definitely disapproved of the bombing but for one reason or another failed to say so or to do anything about it or at best tried to forget the matter after the first shock reaction died away — and who for that reason also had quite uneasy consciences.

All in all, white Louisville's conscience was in a very bad way. If Andrew had been a less determined young man, if after the bombing he had been willing to quietly give up the house and move away, Louisville's conscience might have forgotten the matter and rested easy. It is always so simple to say that peace can be maintained if only the people challenging the status quo will keep quiet. But if Andrew had been less determined, the case would probably never have started in the first place, as he would have been content to live forever in the cramped quarters of Louisville's Negro ghetto.

The fact that there are Andrew Wades in the world is one of the main factors that effect social change. They are appearing all over the South today, and throughout history their like has always arisen. And yet their appearance is always new. It is always startling to the defenders of things as they are. It is always a trial even to those who know the Andrew Wades are right but who long for the easy and the safe and the quiet, for those who are not quite ready, despite their abstract ideals, to rise to the challenge an Andrew Wade presents. White Louisville hoped in its inner heart that Andrew Wade would just go away — remove himself from their sight. But that could not be. It is the nature of Andrew Wades that they do not go quietly away. Louisville had to find some other balm for its conscience.

14

"There But For the Grace of God..."

It was the local prosecutor, A. Scott Hamilton, who provided the balm for Louisville's conscience.

In late August 1954, Hamilton announced that he would ask the September grand jury to investigate the bombing of the Wade home. He made the announcement after constant prodding by the Wades and us and the Wade Defense Committee. Later we realized that he made it partly in exasperation — tired of being bothered each week by a delegation from the Wade Defense Committee urging him to do something about the bombing.

On the opening day of the grand jury investigation, he announced his theory of the bombing which was quoted in the press.

There were two theories about the bombing, he said. One was that neighbors of the Wades had done it to drive the Wades out of the neighborhood. The other was that it was perhaps an inside job, carried out by friends of the Wades — maybe even a Communist plot designed to create an incident and stir up race trouble in Louisville.

As time went on, so far as Scott Hamilton was concerned, this second theory became the only theory. It soon became apparent that, according to this theory, the plot had been a *white* plot — a plan carried out by us and other white people who posed as friends of the Wades but who were actually agitators who wanted to stir up trouble between the races. In fact, Hamilton said, this whole idea of the Wades moving to Rone Court had been dreamed up by the white Bradens who wanted to make trouble; we had planned it and told Wade what to do and used him as a tool. Finally, perhaps without Wade's knowledge, we had plotted the dynamiting of the house.

Our first reaction to this theory was one of shock. We could not believe that anyone would seriously entertain such an idea. It was over a year — a year of watching Hamilton in action, a year

168

of watching and studying reactions in Louisville — before I finally came to the conclusion that Hamilton very likely believed his own story.

A number of circumstances would indicate that Hamilton, before he ever started his grand jury investigation, was in possession of information as to the identity of the bombers (or bomber). For one thing, there were Hamilton's own statements and those of the county police in early July that the police knew who the culprits were. There was also the statement by City Police Chief Heustis (in that same July period) that this knowledge was based on the fact that one of the bombers had confessed. There is another piece of evidence, later in date than these statements, which would indicate that even later in the summer neither the police nor the prosecutor had changed their minds as to the identity of the bombers. Sometime in late July or early August, Heustis was discussing the case casually over coffee in a restaurant near the courthouse with Robert W. Zollinger, an attorney who at that time had no interest in the case but who later became a prominent figure in it. On that occasion, Heustis made the statement: "We know who blew it up, but we can't get a conviction." Present during this conversation was one of Hamilton's assistants who later helped prosecute charges against Carl. The assistant did not take part in the conversation at that point, but he expressed no surprise at the statement by Heustis and he did not question or contradict it. It would be fairly safe to assume that what an assistant prosecutor knew in a matter of this kind Hamilton also knew.

An additional, albeit negative, piece of evidence that the bombers were known lies in the conduct of the September grand jury investigation itself. During two and a half weeks — in seven days of testimony covering eight thick volumes — neither County Police Chief Layman nor any other member of the county police force was questioned regarding the early reports of a confession by one of the dynamiters or about the statements they had made as to the identity of the criminals being known. City Chief Heustis was not even called as a witness before the grand jury — although his statements in July were brought to the attention of the jury and the prosecutor during the testimony. If the belief and the statements of the police in early July had been merely a false lead which was later discredited, as some have speculated, it would certainly seem that all of the information surrounding this early investigation would have been brought out before the grand jury which had asked the Police Department to lay before it all possible information and clues.

But despite all the external evidence indicating that Hamilton knew who blew up the house, there are certain internal factors in his personality and his background supporting the view that, by the time he became embroiled in the September investigation, he had forgotten the real meaning of what he had known in July. This may sound fantastic, but I don't think it is. The human mind works in strange ways. Simple and objective facts often play a smaller part in a man's thinking than the emotional pattern of a lifetime. All too often a man's philosophy of life, evolved through the years, dictates his conception of truth in any given situation. If the facts of that situation do not conform to his preconceived ideas, he is more likely to arrange the facts to conform to his ideas than to try to change the lifelong pattern of his thinking to conform to the facts. He can do this quite sincerely and honestly, convinced that he is thinking and speaking the truth. After all, judging by Chief Heustis' statement in the latter part of the summer that "we can't get a conviction," the police had never been able — either because of indifference or obstacles that were too great — to gather adequate evidence for a conviction against the people they were originally convinced bombed the house. For one in Hamilton's position, it might have been natural to assume that since such adequate evidence was not forthcoming the entire suspicion had been erroneous in the first place; and even the reported confession he might have written off as the words of a crackpot — although some gnawing inner doubt probably made him hesitate to take the risk of laying the earlier investigation openly before the grand jury. It might have been quite possible for him to discount in September what he had known for a fact in July. This would be a very natural pattern of thought if you needed desperately, because of all your life experience, to believe some other theory — and I have an idea that Hamilton did need desperately to do so.

I do not know Scott Hamilton. His life touched mine and threatened to wreck it; and I suspect that my life and those of other people on my side in this case affected his life too, because he lived and breathed the case for three years. But we could not know each other; we met as opponents. I saw him as the man who put me in jail, who sent my husband to prison, who broke up my home, who stood in the courtroom and before the bar of public opinion and denounced me and my husband as menaces to the community and to civilization itself. He undoubtedly saw me as a person who had caused him no end of trouble, and as a threat to all he considered right in the world. Life works in such a way that it builds another one of those walls between us and the people who come on to our horizon as our adversaries. We cannot know them; we cannot meet as human beings.

And yet, as the case progressed, I gradually came to the conclusion that I must understand the people who opposed us. This came to seem more important to me, in this complex of racial tension in which we were involved, than the justification of my own position. I wanted to know Scott Hamilton; I wanted to know what made him do the things he did. On some days I would sit in the courtroom and watch him as he paced before the judge's bench — big like a lion but flabby of muscle — as he paced and argued to the judge what dangerous characters Carl and I were, how great a crime we had committed, how Carl's bond should not be reduced so he could be released from prison; I would watch him and I would find myself wondering about him, wanting to get beneath this bombast and find out what was underneath, to find the human being under this surface. I found myself gripped by an almost overpowering impulse to get up out of my chair and go over to him and say: "Look, be quiet a minute. Sit down a minute. I want to talk to you. I want to know you. I want to know what you think. I want to know what your life has been. Sit down a minute and tell me about yourself."

But I was a defendant in a criminal action; he was a prosecutor. A defendant in a criminal action does not say something like that to a prosecutor. I suppose, if I had, the judge would have remanded my case on the grounds that I was insane — or at least in need of mental treatment.

Once, while the case was at its height, I had just momentarily a snatch of a real conversation with Hamilton. That was on an occasion when I went to him while Carl was in prison under $40,000 bond and asked him to agree to a bond reduction. He refused, but as we sat in the judge's office and talked, I suddenly felt a little sorry for him. He seemed to be ill at ease; he avoided looking at me as he talked. And I remembered having heard that since his attack on us and other white friends of the Wades he had been carrying a gun everywhere he went, because he was afraid of reprisals from some of the people he had attacked. I had heard that he had floodlights burning each night in his back yard and had some of his detectives there to guard the premises. I knew how it was to live with floodlights in your back yard and to keep a gun close at hand.

"Look," I said to Hamilton after we were through discussing the bond situation, "I hear you've got your yard all lit up with floodlights at night, because you think somebody connected with this case might try to do something to you. I know how it is to live with that kind of fear. I spent months last summer never knowing when somebody might blow our house up. I'd like to tell you that you can take the lights down and ease your fears. We're not going to try to do anything to you."

His face flushed and he looked embarrassed.

"I haven't got them up any more," he said.

"Do you really think we are the kind of people who would try to blow up your house or harm you in any way?" I asked him, really curious.

His face flushed again and his eyes avoided mine as he answered.

"Oh, I don't think you would, but somebody might," he said.

Somebody might. Who? But I was the person he had said was one of the most dangerous people in Louisville — even more dangerous than Carl, it was said by some. I wouldn't try to hurt him — but who then? Some dark and nebulous force that he could not explain, some enemy lurking in the shadows? Some evil that he had conjured up out of his own fears when he, like Rone, was suddenly confronted with a new factor in his life that he could not explain? Except that he, in contrast to Rone, was a prosecutor; and as a prosecutor he was in the habit of explaining evil in the world by the fact that there were some criminals somewhere causing it. And so, as a prosecutor, he was able to localize this sudden new and evil thing that had arisen in his world, to give it a "local habitation and a name," to center it on two people named Braden and convince himself that here, in these two people, was the source of all the trouble. Once he had them safely pigeonholed as criminals, the world seemed back in its old bounds.

Now because of the turn of the conversation, I had jumped out of my pigeonhole and become for an instant at least partially a human being. I think that is why he did not want to look at me. He didn't want the neat arrangement he had made of his world upset again. The moment passed quickly. He rushed to regain control of the situation and turned the conversation to a subject where I was back in my pigeonhole and he was on familiar ground. He began to try to go into various aspects of the charges against us. I had no desire to discuss these things with him without a lawyer present, because I knew I could not be sure that something I said would not be misused later, so I told him I thought there was nothing more for us to talk about and that I would leave.

As I opened the door of the judge's office, I turned to look at him again. He was standing by the judge's desk, one hand nervously fingering a paper there, his face still flushed, his eyes staring in the direction of the judge's tall shelves of books but obviously seeing nothing. Circumstances had dictated that this man and I meet as enemies. But far beneath the surface — in the regions of our souls where we could never meet — were we so different after all? Was the enemy he thought he saw in me really perhaps only a guilt that grew out of his own being and which he had transferred to me? And, by the same token, was the enemy I thought I saw in him only a buried aspect of my own life? If circumstances somewhere in the past of both our lives had been different, would I perhaps have been on his side in this battle or he on mine?

From then on, when we met, it was usually in the courtroom, where there was no opportunity — even for a fleeting moment — to talk with him as human being to human being. In my efforts to understand him, I had to fall back on my own resources — on the few facts I knew about his life and on a few buried strands that I could unravel from almost forgotten memories of my own past.

The facts I knew were meager. He had grown up in Louisville, the son of a rather well-to-do family that lived in one of the "better" sections of town. People familiar with the complex stratifications of society told me his family — having come from humble beginnings in a rural part of the Bluegrass area — was not exactly a part of what considered itself the Kentucky "aristocracy." But Hamilton's father was a lawyer and apparently a brilliant one. As a young man he became a member of the state General Assembly and when Scott was a small boy moved to Louisville to become Collector of Internal Revenue. He later practiced law in distinguished law firms in the city and finally became a federal judge, earning high respect on the bench. The family was politically influential and apparently attained as much social prestige as it is possible for political power to convey.

I once talked to a man who had been in the younger Hamilton's class at elementary school. The school was one that drew from a socially wide range of families. It served a section of Crescent Hill, a part of Louisville populated at that time by fairly wealthy people, but it also served a section on the fringes of Crescent Hill where poorer families lived. The man I talked with came from one of the poorer homes; his recollection of Hamilton was that he was "always off in a corner somewhere with the rich boys."

"They never associated with us," the man said, "and we never liked them too much; we thought they were snooty and sort of spoiled by their families."

As to Hamilton's current circumstances, he lived in one of the more exclusive suburbs of Louisville. So far as I knew, he was in no sense in the economic class with the really wealthy people of the city, but I had been told by people who knew him that his social contacts were almost entirely among people who considered themselves somewhat of the elite. To be sure, he had political contacts — contacts in his business and professional life — with people from various walks of life. Any politician has to — votes come from all sections of the population. But when he went to dinner parties, when he went to other social gatherings, it was reasonable to assume that the people he met were of the upper crust socially.

I knew too that Hamilton often said he had lost money when he gave up his private law practice to become Commonwealth's Attorney but that he had been willing to do it because he felt it was a service he owed his community.

Lawyers who dealt with Hamilton often told me he was essentially kindhearted.

"He really doesn't want to hurt anybody," one of them said. "It's just that he doesn't think you and Carl are people."

I found out further in the course of this case that Hamilton did not consider himself anti-Negro — in fact, that he had what seemed to be a compulsion to assure people he was not. For example, during the questioning of one witness before the grand jury, he made this statement: "Now I think that all of us . . . are equally interested in the welfare of mankind, so to speak, and I have just as much feeling, I believe, for an unfortunate colored family as you do have."

As the case progressed, Andrew Wade and his father had occasion to talk with Hamilton often. They rarely had a conversation with him, they said, that he did not assure them he had nothing against "colored people," that he had "known colored people all his life and liked them." Sometimes Hamilton used the term "Nigra" instead of "colored people." Andrew during his troubles became a little cynical about the people who opposed him but who had "known and liked colored people all their lives."

"Every one of them says that," he commented to us one day. "Usually they had a colored mammy when they were children too. I never knew there were so many colored mammies in the world."

And most of the Negro people in Louisville who had any dealings with Hamilton, I found out, did not agree with his own view that he was not anti-Negro. As one of them said to me:

"Sure, he likes us all right if we stay in our place."

Negroes in Louisville tell with a kind of wry amusement about the time Hamilton agreed, in line with the policy of the Democratic organization, to appoint a Negro attorney as one of the assistant prosecutors in his office. That arrangement lasted a very short time when the Negro attorney turned out to be one of those who would not "stay in his place." A case arose involving what the Negro attorney thought was a violation of a man's constitutional rights because of the color of his skin. He insisted on taking the side of this man in police court, maintaining that the chief duty of a prosecutor was not to get convictions but to see that justice was done in the public courts — and Hamilton protested. The upshot of it was that the Negro attorney announced in the police court that he would resign from the staff of the prosecutor's office, and Hamilton immediately told the newspapers he was accepting the resignation — before the attorney even had time to turn it in. After that, Hamilton was apparently reluctant to take any more such chances; and, as a matter of fact, it was not until long after Hamilton's actions in the Wade case had aroused the ire of Negro voters that the Democratic organization persuaded him to appoint another Negro assistant in an effort to smooth the troubled waters.

And as I thought of these things, my mind went back to all the other people I had heard talk about how much they "liked colored people" and how they felt for "an unfortunate colored family." I thought of the warmth in my mother's voice as she spoke of the Negro woman who worked for her for many years: "You know there's nobody in the world, Anne Gambrell, that I love more than I do Mary." I thought of my father paying the hospital bills for Willie, his yard man. I thought of a friend in Alabama saying: "You know they have a real wisdom — I guess in a way I learned more from my nurse than I ever learned in school." All these gentle people — whose bodies stiffened, whose faces hardened, whose eyes became suddenly cold when they picked up the newspapers and read where Negroes were demanding to go to "white" schools.

And as I thought of these things and pondered Hamilton's actions in our case, my mind went back again to my own childhood. Was it perhaps a little like his? There were remote points of contact in our respective backgrounds: in his early days in Louisville, his father had been in the law firm of a former governor of Kentucky under whom my own great-grandfather had served as lieutenant-governor in the early twentieth century. How many people, those from the poorer families, in the school that I attended perhaps saw me as a girl who "was always off in the corner with the rich children — sort of snooty and spoiled by their families"? And as my mind went back to the past, a memory began to stir. Buried for years in the forgotten recesses of my mind, it gradually worked itself to the surface. And finally I remembered — the first time in my life that I had heard of Negroes organizing to demand their rights.

I must have been in my early teens. Now in my memory I could hear the adult voices, soft and guarded, in a discussion that was not for the ears of the young:

"Have you heard what's happening? All the nigger cooks are getting organized into clubs."

"Clubs? What are they doing?"

"They're forming Eleanor Clubs. The story is that they're going to ask for higher pay and start disappointing their employers by not showing up for work unless their pay is raised."

"No!"

"Yes, that's what I heard. Of course it's not the niggers' idea. I know my cook would never do anything like that and I don't think any of the others would either. But Eleanor Roosevelt is getting them stirred up and organizing these clubs. That's why they're called Eleanor Clubs. The story is that she may be a Communist or at least she's under the influence of Communists."

Rumors of Eleanor Clubs were widespread in the South in the late 1930s and early 1940s; they cropped up periodically as long as the Roosevelts occupied the White House. Anniston was no exception. It was a period of upsurge of organization among all workers, white and black, farm and industrial; and it is possible that in some parts of the South domestic workers too were attempting to organize themselves — obviously without the direction of Mrs. Roosevelt; but if such an organization movement did exist in the Deep South, it was unfortunately short-lived, and I'm afraid it never had much strength in Anniston. Yet the very rumor was enough to scare wealthy white women. These women considered themselves kind to their servants and some would even give them a pay increase if they asked for it in a "respectful manner"; but when they looked at the cook in their kitchen and fancied that she might be taking matters into her own hands — planning her own future and joining with others like herself to bring it about — these white women were thrown into turmoil. Such a development upset their whole world, their whole concept of a society in which control rested in the hands of a benevolent elite. Obviously, "good niggers" didn't act that way and "we white people in the South know our niggers." Obviously, it must be somebody from the outside "stirring the niggers up" — some white person undoubtedly, because everyone knows that a nigger only does what some white person tells him to do. And who could it be? Why, Eleanor Roosevelt, of course. Good normal white Americans wouldn't want to do an evil thing like stirring up the niggers, but of course the rumor is that Eleanor Roosevelt has Communist tendencies, and lots of Communist friends, so that could explain it. As everybody knows, these people who go around talking the way Eleanor Roosevelt does about rights for niggers have more than likely been influenced by

Communists. Communism is one of those foreign doctrines and the North and East are overrun with it. It's getting to the point where the South is the only place left where you can find real good loyal, white Americans. And now they are coming down here and trying to stir up our good niggers; you know that's bound to be it, because our niggers wouldn't think of turning against us on their own.

Again, all of these things were not put into words. But they were implied. And some of it was explicit. It was the first time, I believe, that I ever felt the impact of the word "Communist." An evil word, a dark word, but a word that somehow explained the startling fact that "our niggers" would do something like organizing clubs to improve their conditions — something they could not possibly do on their own because they were so "contented."

And as this episode now worked its way to the levels of conscious thought, I tried to remember what my reaction to these stories had been at the time. I tried to peel away all the layers of thought that had come since, all the things I had learned since I began to glimpse a world without walls; I tried to think again as I had thought as a young girl and to remember whether I had believed this simple explanation of the unrest that was even then seething beneath the surface in the South.

I think I probably did. I think I did because I needed to — needed to even as the adults from whose shocked lips I heard it needed to. I, like so many other white young people in that world, already had unconscious worries about the South — worries that were eating away beneath the surface of my mind. . . . *And still I was a part of the white world too.* I loved my family and I loved my friends, and all of these people believed — or said they believed and thought they believed — that a Negro's proper role was to be subservient to the white man. And yet, if the Negro people were really discontented in this role and were organizing to improve things for themselves, then it must be that the white people in my world were somehow mistreating them. But the white people in my world did not mistreat people! They were good people; they were kind people; they believed in treating their fellow man right. I believed that. I had to believe it. If it weren't true, my whole universe was upset. So it must be a fact that it was just a matter of some outsider stirring up the "niggers," making them do things they didn't want to do. After all, maybe it was just my imagination that our washwoman's little daughter looked uncomfortable in my castoff clothes; maybe she was really quite happy. She had never said she was not. No Negro I had ever had any dealing with had ever done or said anything that would indicate he or she was not content with things as they were. They deferred to me as they deferred to all white people in that day and in that setting in the South. And I fought off the truth; I fought it even to the point, I think, of accepting a fantastic story like that which told me that anything that was wrong was all the doing of Eleanor Roosevelt.

Before many years had passed, the truth did catch up with me. But suppose my life had taken a different turn. Suppose I had never met the young actress in New York; suppose I had never had an opportunity to step out of the walled-in world of my childhood and come to know people who were not of my own environment, where the people had been so sure that the welfare of humanity rested safely in their benevolent hands and that no one outside their circle should have a thought of his own; suppose I had never met, as I did in Louisville, Negroes who treated me as an equal, who did not call me "Ma'am." And suppose under these circumstances I had come to live in Louisville. I might have come here anyway; it was the city where my family had come from and where I was born; my family had many old friends and relatives in Kentucky. Suppose I had come to Kentucky and married some son of one of their friends and had settled in one of the elite suburbs of Louisville — a segregated suburb, far from any contact with Negroes except the servants or perhaps on some charity drive. My path might well have crossed Scott Hamilton's — we would have met perhaps at the country club or at the home of some mutual friend. And I would have undoubtedly seen him as a successful lawyer and a fine citizen and a pleasant man. And if I heard him say he had "suffered financially by giving up private law practice to become Commonwealth's Attorney" but that he "owed it to the community," I would have been quite impressed. I would have thought what a fine thing it was for this man to make this sacrifice for the community, and I would never have realized what a limited concept of "community" we both had. I would not have realized how our concept left out so much of humanity — all of the people not in our economic bracket and certainly all members of minority racial groups. I would have thought, as he thought, that I was concerned for the "welfare of mankind, so to speak." But I would have been confident, as he was confident, that it was the people in my narrow little world who knew best what was right for the "welfare of mankind"; and I would have been startled and shocked when I saw some other group in mankind moving in its own way to shape its own destiny.

Then one bright morning, while the Negro maid was clearing off the breakfast things, I might have read in the paper that some colored man, some Wade, had bought a house in a nice white neighborhood — that a white couple had bought and sold him the house. Suppose thereafter there had been violence and the house had been bombed. What a troublesome thing in a community where I had always thought that race relations were so peaceful! And then suppose I had chanced to sit by Scott Hamilton at a dinner party and he had told me what was really going on — how a committee from this thing called the Wade Defense Committee, colored ministers and lawyers and such, kept coming to his office every week, not asking but *demanding* that he do something about this bombing, keeping the thing alive when everybody with any sense just wanted to forget about it. But Nigras do not act this way; we have always got along fine with our Nigras in Louisville. What about this Andrew Wade? Why would he want to move into a neighborhood where he must know he was not wanted? Nigras don't think of doing things like that on their own. Somebody must be working behind the scenes on this thing, telling the Nigras what to do, trying to stir up trouble. Who is this white couple that bought him the house? Could they be stirring up the whole thing? Maybe they are Communists. Usually where you have this kind of agitation among the Nigras, there are some white Communists around stirring it up.

These are some of the things, I think, that would have gone through my mind. For if my life had taken this course, the memories of my early questionings would have been pushed far down into my unconscious mind. I would have long since blotted out of my memory the little girl who looked uncomfortable in my dresses; I would have long since rejected the stirrings I felt in a larger self as I sensed the existence of a God that was big enough to encompass the brotherhood of all mankind. And because I had rejected these things and blotted them out, all that would have been left of them would have been a sense of guilt eating away in the dark recesses of my soul. And because of that guilt I would have had an even greater need than I had when I was growing up to believe that all was well with this white world I lived in, to believe that if there were any storm signals on the horizon it was because some agitator — probably an outsider, maybe some foreigner — was stirring up trouble.

And then, if I had picked up the newspaper one morning and read that Scott Hamilton had advanced a theory that solved the Wade bombing — that it had all been a plot by a bunch of white Communists to stir up race trouble in the community — I would have breathed a sigh of relief and I would have believed it. I would have believed it as I think Scott Hamilton believed it and as did many others in his world.

For we must remember that Hamilton's theory about the bombing was already implicit in the unconscious of many people in Louisville. In a sense, Hamilton only gave voice to something that already existed in their minds — waiting there like an undeveloped film.

We knew in the days immediately after the bombing that a story sprang up, apparently quite spontaneously, that the Wades had bombed the house themselves. LaRue Spiker heard it in the flour mill where she worked.

"Some of the women I work with are saying they think the Wades blew up the house themselves," she told us at the time. "I can't understand it. They don't know anything about the case except what they have read in the papers. They can't give any reason as to why the Wades would have wanted to do that. But that's what they're saying."

The same idea was expressed by others — some as far removed from the situation as the women in the flour mill, and including many residents of Shively. It was implied — although not to the point of libel — in the first article John Hitt wrote in the Shively *Newsweek* after the bombing. Several weeks before, Hitt had already presented his theory that maybe the shots fired into the Wade house on the morning of May 16 had been "self-inflicted."

We marveled in those weeks immediately after the dynamiting as to how any reasonable person could believe the Wades might have destroyed their own house. There was absolutely no evidence to support such a theory. It was expressed by widely separated people far from the bombing and in possession of no facts that could have substantiated it. Gradually we realized that it sprang not from any facts but from their own psychic needs. Most of the people who expressed these opinions were people who were violently opposed to the Wades or any Negro family moving into a neighborhood they considered all-white. In their own unconscious, they had already committed a crime of violence against the Wades themselves; they in their hearts had blown up the house. But on the surface they were good and peaceful and law-abiding citizens. They could not admit either to themselves or to their neighbors — but mostly to themselves — the violence of their own natures when confronted with the problems of desegregation. They had to find an out for their own consciences. And when they could convince themselves that it was not people like themselves but the Wades who had blown up the house, they had found that out; they had lifted the burden of the crime from their own shoulders.

Scott Hamilton, when he announced his theory, simply carried this kind of thought process a step further. It was a little hard to justify the charge that a man would destroy his own house. Further, if one accepted this, one had to cope with the idea of a Negro who did not fit into the picture of the docile Negro on which much of white Louisville based its concept of race relations — who did not fit into the pattern of thinking of people like the person I might have been if my life had taken that different course. Andrew Wade and all he represented had to be explained away too. By placing the blame for the bombing on the white people who had apparently supported the Wades, Hamilton took care of several problems with one stroke. He removed the onus of the bombing from the anti-Negro segment of Louisville's population. And by decreeing that Wade's move into a white neighborhood had all been a plot by Communistic whites, he removed the troublesome thought of the Negro people demanding equal rights as citizens. By the same stroke, he handed Louisville liberals a final excuse for their in-action in the face of the terror on Rone Court throughout those summer months — handed it to them to use if they could believe the unbelievable — and some of them did for a while because they also desperately needed to do so.

On the surface the theory seemed to settle all problems.

The Braden trial. Judge L. R. Curtis is on the bench. The Bradens' "subversive" books are stacked on the center table. Robert Steinau C-J & LT, December 3, 1954. Louisville *Courier-Journal.*

At the defense table. *Left to right*, Attorney Bob Zollinger, Carl Braden, Anne Braden, Attorney Louis Lusky. John Cunningham C-J & LT, December 11, 1954. Louisville *Courier-Journal*.

Carl Braden.
Gene Baron C-J & LT,
December 9, 1954.
Louisville
Courier-Journal.

The Wade house, after bombing. From "Louisville Travesty," pamphlet published by the Emergency Civil Liberties Committee, New York, 1955.

Andrew Wade IV, Charlotte Wade, and their children. From "Louisville Travesty," pamphlet published by the Emergency Civil Liberties Committee, New York, 1955.

15

The Crime: Bombing or Beliefs?

Carl and I were among the witnesses called to testify before the grand jury on the opening day of its investigation, September 15, 1954. It was Jimmy's third birthday.

We were glad the case was finally being investigated and approached the affair with what seems in retrospect an amazing lack of foresight as to the turn it would take. Looking back on it later, we could see that there were at least two indications which should have warned us that the investigation was going to develop into an attack on us.

For one thing, during the month of August, Carl had been indicted by a previous grand jury on a charge of voting twice in the primary election that summer. The double voting was one of those foolish things that should never have happened. Our polling place had been moved that year, and on election day Carl went to the wrong precinct and voted. Poll officials discovered his mistake as he emerged from the voting booth and told him he should go on over to his correct precinct and vote again; they said they would deduct his vote from the total in their precinct. Carl realized later that he should not have taken this advice, since it would have been impossible for the election officials to deduct his first vote from the total, as they would not have known for whom he voted unless he told them. But at the time, the matter seemed of little importance. There was no real contest in the primary that year, the outcome being a foregone conclusion. Carl's interest in voting was mainly a matter of having his vote recorded, for he prided himself on a nineteen-year perfect voting record. He went to his correct precinct and voted again. And he thought no more about it until a week or so later we heard that Scott Hamilton was investigating the incident. When the indictment was returned by the August grand jury, on a charge carrying a possible six-month jail sentence, people in Louisville generally concluded the action was a reprisal against Carl for his part in the Wade house situation — especially since there had been a 75-vote discrepancy in another precinct for which no one was ever prosecuted. The double-voting charge was later settled quietly when the judge hearing the case stated from the bench that he thought Carl had made an honest mistake and that it was the election officials who were at fault. But by that time, the subsequent actions of the September grand jury had made clear to everyone the motivation behind the original indictment.

The second incident that should have warned us as to Scott Hamilton's intentions with the bombing investigation was his refusal a week before the September grand jury hearings to excuse me from testifying. Carl and I had both received subpoenas. It always presented problems for us to be away from home at the same time because of the children, and I went to see Hamilton to ask if I might be excused. I explained to him that we wanted to help in every possible way but that my testimony in regard to the house would actually duplicate Carl's. He insisted that I appear, saying he wanted the jury to hear all possible viewpoints, but he did so politely and was solicitous in arranging for me to come in the morning and Carl in the afternoon so there would not be a problem about the children. I agreed and went away, still not suspecting what was up. On the day of the investigation, I left home in the morning calculating that I would be home in time to make Jimmy's birthday cake before he got up from his nap; I had invited the children next door and Rosemary Wade to come in late that afternoon to eat cake and ice cream with him.

It was actually not until I was in the grand jury room, called as the second witness of the day — the first had been the policeman on duty the night the house was bombed — that I became suspicious. As soon as the routine questions about my name, address, age were out of the way, Hamilton said: "Now, Mrs. Braden, you understand that under the Constitution of the United States, that a person is not compelled to answer any questions that they believe might tend to incriminate them. . . ."

I looked at him in amazement. I was aware of the constitutional protection against self-incrimination, of course, but I had not considered that I was coming before this grand jury as a possible

defendant or as a subject for investigation myself. It seemed odd
that Hamilton should be advising me of my privilege not to incriminate myself. I replied:

". . . I am perfectly willing to tell them everything that I know
that would shed any light on the bombing of Andrew Wade's home.
I believe that is what is being investigated. Is that right?"

The foreman of the grand jury replied "That's right," but
Hamilton went on:

> Now, Mrs. Braden . . . there are two ideas about this
> explosion. Some people think the white neighbors or the
> residents out there in particular may have set this explosion,
> in order to scare the Wades out of the neighborhood. On the
> other hand, others seem to think that the Wades did it them-
> selves, or their friends did it, to more or less focus attention
> on the affair and to start up trouble and that sort of thing.
> And actually, I might go this far and say that there are rumors
> that it was Communistic-inspired . . . that is the reason I felt
> that I should explain to you about the rights not to incriminate
> yourself.

In a flash I saw what was happening. I looked at Hamilton.
He was a big man with a slightly pudgy face; it was flushed now as if
he were holding down some hidden anger. He was seated on one
side of me and his young assistant, Lawrence Higgins, was on my
other side, leaning forward eagerly in his chair. The grand jurors
were on either side of the long table in front of me; they looked
like normal everyday people. But suddenly I had that surrounded
and suffocated sensation I had felt once on Rone Court when I had
pulled into a driveway to turn my car around and found my exit
momentarily blocked by two carloads of men and women, staring
at me with fury and hatred in their eyes. I had entered the grand
jury room a few minutes earlier thinking I was among friendly
citizens who were going to help us find out who blew up the
Wades' house; now all at once I felt that I was in a room full of
enemies.

I was therefore not surprised when, some minutes later, Higgins
interrupted me as I was telling of events at the Wade house and
began asking me questions about the Wade Defense Committee.
Who formed it? Why was it formed? Who attended meetings?

Then, questions about my own interest in "racial matters." Why was I interested? What other things had I done in the past on this question? And then:

"Mrs. Braden, do you belong to any organization here in Louisville whether — where the colored and white meet?"

And a moment later by Hamilton:

"Now, Mrs. Braden, have you ever been a member of the Progressive Party?"

The questions followed in rapid-fire succession then: Had I ever been a member of the Civil Rights Congress? Had I ever been a member of the Labor Council for Negro Rights? Had I ever belonged to the League of American Writers? Had I ever belonged to the National Negro Labor Congress? Had I ever belonged to the Communist Party? Did I read the Communist paper, the *Daily Worker?* Did I subscribe to it?

I had heard and read a great deal about investigations of the kind the grand jury seemed to be embarking on. I knew that in recent years there had been Congressional committees whose main function seemed to be to go about the country asking people the kind of questions the prosecutor was now asking me. I thoroughly disapproved of such investigations — I felt they violated basic principles of American freedom and that what a person believed and the organizations he joined were a matter only between himself, his own conscience, and his God. But I had never seriously expected that I myself might some day be facing this kind of inquisition. Carl's and my activities that might have seemed "subversive" in some people's books had seemed to us too insignificant and unimportant to matter to anyone or to attract any attention — as indeed they were until we sold the house to the Wades. But now when it happened, my reaction was immediate and spontaneous: these people had no right to ask these questions; it was none of their business; I would not, I told myself, tell them a thing. I would not answer anything.

Some of the organizations Hamilton mentioned I had never heard of; others I had heard of but never joined; others I had belonged to or given money to. But, whether I knew of them or not, I refused to answer all the questions. I told the jury I thought the questions were completely irrelevant to the bombing of Andrew Wade's house.

I tried to make my reasons explicit when Hamilton took me before the circuit judge, Leroy Curtis, asking him to hold that I was in contempt of court if I refused to answer the questions. Judge Curtis ruled that I should answer some of them but did not have to answer others. This exchange took place:

MRS. BRADEN: Well, I would like to state to the judge right now that I do not intend to answer these questions and it is up to him what he wants to do about it, but I feel I should have an opportunity to state my reasons. I feel that this Grand Jury is acting beyond the bounds of its rights and powers and duties to investigate any affiliations I might have in any organizations, or any reading habits I might have, or for anything except the bombing of the Wade house. I think we have enough McCarthys in this country without the Grand Jury turning into one. I think it is not the business of the Grand Jury what organizations I belong to or what I read. . . .

JUDGE: Well, Mrs. Braden, the decisions I have made, some of which say you should answer certain questions. I made other decisions that you don't have to answer certain questions. And most of the questions to me seem to be very remote, yet in view of the wide scope of this investigation dealing with various issues and questions, I have ruled that you must answer certain questions, as indicated, and if you refuse to answer those questions you will be in contempt of court and the court will have nothing else to do except to send you to jail for contempt and keep you there until you purge yourself of the contempt.

MRS. BRADEN: I will not answer. . . .

For some reason, they did not put me in jail for contempt. Instead Hamilton told me to go on home so Carl could come down and testify. By that time, it was too late to make Jimmy's birthday cake in time for that afternoon, so I postponed the little party I had planned — telling Jimmy we would have it another day. Carl went on to the courthouse, and when he entered the grand jury room the same process repeated itself. Hamilton asked the same questions, and Carl refused to answer — on the grounds that the questions had nothing to do with the bombing of the Wade home.

We immediately called the newspapers to tell them what had taken place in the grand jury room. We felt that the best antidote for what was going on was the strong glaring light of publicity. In the next morning's *Courier-Journal,* the story was front-page news, and on the following day the paper ran this editorial headlined "The Crime Was Bombing, Not Beliefs":

> This newspaper finds itself in a difficult position with respect to Mr. and Mrs. Carl Braden. Mr. Braden is an employee of The Courier-Journal. In common with all employees, he is entitled to his own political convictions and social associations. These are no business of ours so long as Mr. Braden does his work and pursues his other interests in his own time.
>
> He does both of these things. But his personal activities frequently make news and provoke controversy. They become matters to be reported upon and to occasion editorial comment. Although this comment is seldom flattering to the Bradens, many people have chosen to regard them as agents of The Courier-Journal. They base this odd conclusion on the reasoning that, if they aren't working deviously in behalf of the newspaper, Mr. Braden would be fired for the unorthodoxy of his political views.
>
> We cannot recall that any employee of these newspapers was ever discharged because he disagreed with us politically or even because, on his own time, he made himself a political nuisance. We do not think the day will ever come when a man will be fired by us because we dislike his beliefs or his friends. Let us make it quite clear that we think both Mr. and Mrs. Braden are politically misguided; that they stir up difficult and potentially dangerous community situations in pursuit of their beliefs, and that they derive a certain satisfaction from the public criticism which attends their actions.
>
> But they have a right to be misguided and professional martyrs on their own time if they so desire and we have the right to criticize their activities as severely as we see fit. We felt strongly, and said clearly, that the Bradens' action in buying by subterfuge in a white community a house which they then turned over to a Negro friend, was deplorable.

Instead of advancing the cause of better race relations, a cause which had progressed here without benefit of the Bradens' shock treatment, they have harmed its advancement perhaps irreparably. They have embittered and endangered their friends the Wades and have set in motion forces of ugliness and bigotry that will not soon be stilled.

But having made this clear, we must manifest the deepest disapproval of the line of questioning followed by the Commonwealth's Attorney A. Scott Hamilton, during a grand jury investigation of the recent explosion at the Wade house.

On the pretext that both the house purchase and the bombing may be part of a Communist plot, Mr. Hamilton asked Mr. and Mrs. Braden a series of questions on their political beliefs, their associates, their reading habits and their membership in a number of organizations.

In our opinion, the refusal of Mr. and Mrs. Braden to answer these questions is quite correct. Mr. Hamilton has produced not the slightest evidence to uphold his theory of a Communist plot. He has paid very little attention to the alternative and much more likely theory that the bombing was the work of hoodlums who resented a Negro's purchase of a house in a white area. If he has any facts or indications to back up the Communist plot idea, it is his duty to lay these before the Grand Jury. The questions he has asked the Bradens seem designed to force them either to call themselves Communists or, by refusing to answer, to give him the right to call them so.

But even if both the Bradens had said yes to all of Mr. Hamilton's leading questions, this is still a far cry from proving the existence of a plot or their connection with such a plot. We regret deeply that Judge Curtis lent himself to this display of local McCarthyism and we hope that before the witch hunt proceeds any further, the Judge will recall to his associate the real objectives of the inquiry. The matter under investigation is not what the Bradens believe or read. It is the wanton destruction of a man's house in the middle of the night by persons who only accidentally avoided the further crime of murder. Questions which throw light on this affair are urgently needed. But questions which merely establish the self-evident fact that the Bradens hold unpopular views are in the highest degree irrelevant. They are, moreover, symptoms of the prevalent hysteria which this community has previously escaped and into which it should not be dragged now by a prosecutor who does not seem very clear either as to his duties or the rights of witnesses in a democratic society.

It was a courageous editorial. In view of the strong disapproval the *Courier-Journal* editorial board felt toward Carl and me, it also reflected a high degree of devotion to principle. But it was also too late; the two months during which the *Courier-Journal* had sat silent in the face of official failure to catch the bombers of the Wade home had taken their toll; and paradoxically, the editorial probably sealed our fate with Scott Hamilton.

It is my opinion that when Hamilton launched the investigation he did not have any intention of indicting anyone. It is much more likely that he intended the "investigation" to be a hit-and-run attack on Wade and his supporters. I think he intended to say to the public that many of Wade's supporters were possibly Communists. He was then going to conclude that this, ipso facto, proved that the whole affair on Rone Court was very likely some sort of an effort to stir up trouble. And then, in his calculation, the grand jury could issue a report saying the situation was so completely confused that it could not be determined at this time who bombed the house. That, he probably felt, would have ended the whole troublesome affair for once and for all.

But with the publication of the *Courier-Journal* editorial, the lines of battle were drawn. The *Courier-Journal*, in the minds of Hamilton and other Louisville citizens who believed in segregation, represented the voice of liberalism. Despite the fact that these two groups usually managed to live together in cordiality, the segregationists disliked the newspaper and what it stood for; they disliked it much more than they disliked Carl and me; we were only two small individuals who constituted no real threat to their way of life; the *Courier-Journal* constituted a major threat. The way in which the Wade case had developed had suddenly created a break — a temporary one, as it turned out — in the usual truce between liberals and segregationists in Louisville. The *Courier-Journal* had spoken; the object now was to "get" the *Courier-Journal*.

No politician, if he is in his right mind, attacks a powerful monopoly newspaper directly. But if Hamilton could make his attack on Carl stick, he would have convicted the *Courier-Journal* in the public mind, because Carl was an employee of the newspaper. All of the *Courier's* protestations that Carl and I were not their agents had not convinced the paper's enemies. Hamilton was now forced into a position where he had to "put up or shut up." He had to prove that the bombing had in fact been a plot that revolved around us.

But Carl was at work the night the house was blown up, and I suppose that Hamilton and the grand jurors, even in the high state of fancy that gripped them, found it a bit unbelievable that I, a woman, would sneak out in the dead of night and place dynamite under a house. It quickly became evident that it would not be we who would be accused of actually placing the dynamite but another white supporter of Wade, Vernon Bown.

We got the first inkling of this on the first day of the investigation when Andrew was called to testify. Andrew told us after he left the jury room that day that the prosecutor and the jurors — they were all white, mostly men — had seemed amazed that Bown, a white man, had moved into his house and lived there for several weeks. They spent a great deal of time, he said, asking him who Bown was, where he came from, why he moved into the house, what he brought with him. They asked him what made him trust Bown to stay in his house. Andrew said he told them he had no reason in the world to suspect Bown.

Bown himself was called before the jury on the second day of the investigation. The prosecutor's and jury's questions to him brilliantly illuminate the reasons for their suspicions. After Bown had explained to the jury how he felt an inner duty to offer his help to the Wades when he read in the newspaper of their trouble, this exchange took place:

Q: You just read the newspaper and went out there?
A: Yes.
Q: And nobody asked you to go?
A: That's right. I assumed the Wades were in need of help so I went there and offered my assistance.

Q: Would you do the same thing for a white family?

A: Yes.

And on a subsequent day, when Bown was recalled before the jury, this was the testimony:

Q (BY A JUROR): You mean you just picked up the paper and you saw an account in the paper about this, and you decided to go out and you didn't move in at that time, did you?

A: Oh, no, no.

Q: You moved in later?

A: That is right.

Q: And you had no conversation with anybody regarding your going out there, any mutual friend or anybody?

A: No.

Q: Mr. Wade had no idea who you were?

A: No, he didn't.

Q: He didn't know that you had mutual friends?

A: I told him after I went out there that I knew Mr. Carl Braden. I had read in the paper that Carl Braden had bought this house for him.

Q: And you didn't speak to Mr. Braden about it before you went?

A: No, I didn't.

Q: Just moved out there and that was it?

A: I didn't just move out. I just drove out there that evening.

Q: And then you told us you gave up your room and took all your effects out there?

A: You see, the way it happened, I went out to see Mr. Wade sometime — I hadn't been out there for a week or so, I don't remember the exact time.

Q: You mean after your first visit?

A: Yes.

Q: You didn't move in right away?

A: Oh, no. I believe it must have been a week or two afterwards, and Mr. Wade, we were discussing the question of people staying out there to kind of keep watch on the place, so nobody could slip up on them and do them any harm, and he said he had enough people, friends of his, who could stay there at nights, but didn't have anybody to stay there in the daytime with his wife while he was working, and I volunteered, if he didn't mind, I'd stay out there with her. He said he had an extra bedroom so that's the way that came about.

Q: Of course, you have always felt, as you just said, I believe, the Negroes as well as any minority group has the right to live any place he wants to?

A: That's right.

Q: And there are a number of people I think you will agree who feel the same way you do in principle?

A: I believe there are.

Q: However, their way of doing it is different from yours. They feel that those things are best effected over a long period of time. You evidently are of the school of thought where you don't think so?

A: I think you are assuming —

Q: I am not assuming. I am asking you the question if that is what you think.

A: You see, this wasn't my idea for Mr. Wade to move out there, and once he had moved out there I felt he had the right to stay, and if I could help him to stay there, I thought it was my duty. . . .

The questioning of Charlotte Wade throws further light on the incredulous attitude the prosecution and jury felt toward Bown's residence in the Wade house. The assistant prosecutor, Higgins, asked Charlotte how it came about that Bown moved into the house. Charlotte explained that it was arranged by her husband and Bown. This exchange followed:

Q: Are you telling this jury that he talked to your husband about it and your husband didn't talk to you about it?

A: Yes, he did.

Q: What did your husband tell you about it?

A: He told me there was a man who, Mr. Vernon Bown, Mr. Bown was coming there, that he thought it would be a good idea to have some man around the house and that this man had volunteered to be there with me until he came home.

Q: You knew it was a white man?

A: Yes.

Q: Now, he stayed in the back bedroom?

A: Yes.

Q: Well now, what did you originally have that room set up for?

A: I really didn't have it set up for anything. It was just no more than a bedroom.

Q: You mean this white man just moved into your house there and took over one of your two bedrooms and you didn't even discuss it with him at all?

A: The man came as a friend, and we needed friends.

And later:

Q: You only had two bedrooms in the house?

A: That's right.

Q: That is a comparatively small house, isn't it?

A: Yes.

Q: For a total stranger to move in, that's an unusual situation, isn't it?

A: Well, under the circumstances —

Q: Isn't it an unusual situation for someone you don't know to move into one of your two bedrooms?

A: Under the circumstances, I don't think so.

And questioning of Charlotte by one of the jurors:

Q: Did you have a lot of people coming to the house at that time?

A: We had quite a few people coming there. I guess some of them from curiosity.

Q: Did they come into the house? Did they come up to the door, ring your doorbell and come in?

A: Some of them did. Some of them just passed up and down in front.

Q: How many came into your house and told you their names and identified themselves? How many white people, I am talking about.

A: I wouldn't be able to say.

Q: How many approximately?

A: I wouldn't be able to say approximately.

Q: A hundred?

A: I don't think it was that many.

Q: Can you give us the name of anybody besides Bown, the man who moved in?

MR. HIGGINS: If there were so many that came up there, you'd remember one of them.

A: I just can't remember now. I mean, this all happened, and I was quite confused then, and it's kind of hard for me to remember back.

Of course, as we have seen, there were a number of white people other than Bown who did go to the house. Not as many as there should have been — but some. But none of the others had moved into the house and taken up residence there. That was the thing that was completely incomprehensible to the prosecution and jury. Why would a white man have done it? He must have had an ulterior motive.

A radio provided the missing link. Pieces of a portable battery-type radio were found scattered in the debris under the wrecked side of the house. It seems obvious that the pieces must have fallen through the holes torn in the floor at the time of the explosion, as numerous other articles from the house did. But when the prosecutor discovered that this radio had been the property of Vernon Bown, that he had brought it along with his other belongings when he moved into the house, the crime seemed solved. By the third day of the investigation, rumors were rampant over the courthouse that Bown would be accused of setting off the dynamite with his radio.

The most important key to the grand jury's activity lies in a study of what it did *not* do. In the first place, it made no effort whatsoever to delve into the early reports that the dynamiter had confessed. The July statements of City Police Chief Heustis and County Police Chief Layman were called to the jurors' attention by a number of witnesses, and on the day after the investigation opened Heustis, reminded of the matter by reporters, made the following statement in the press:

It was my impression that a semi-confession had been made and that County police were in a position to make an arrest. I don't recall that I used the word "confession."

Despite this, Colonel Heustis was never called before the grand jury. Chief Layman was called but was asked no questions about the report of a confession and, in fact, very little about what his department's early investigation had netted. There were persistent references throughout the testimony to "statements" the police had taken from neighbors of the Wades immediately after the bombing, but no police officer was ever asked what these statements contained.

Furthermore, the grand jury apparently made no effort to probe into the unusual circumstance that all of the houses in the Rone Court area were dark on the night of the bombing, nor the strange flashing of three lights shortly before the bombing — although they were told about these things. John Y. Hitt, editor of the Shively *Newsweek,* had been on Rone Court that night — he volunteered this information almost as soon as he got in the grand jury room, explaining that he often stopped there in search of news — but the policeman on duty was not questioned at all about this or about the report that Hitt had asked "if anything has happened at the Wade house yet." Nor was any attempt made to inquire further into this same policeman's statement that the deafening noise of the explosion apparently aroused none of the neighbors.

Wade had given Hamilton a list of people he had reason to be suspicious of — people in the neighborhood who were hostile, people who had driven by his house often shouting threats or looking at him and his family in a threatening way and whose names he had obtained by checking license numbers. A few of these people were called before the jury; many were not. No neighbors who had not been on his list were called at all. All of those whose cars had reportedly been in the neighborhood denied they had ever been there and were promptly excused; some claimed the only way they could explain the fact that their cars had been seen in the vicinity was that their grown sons often drove their cars. None of these sons were ever called before the jury.

One intriguing bit of testimony came out in the questioning of Ralph Diemer, operator of a hardware store in Shively:

Q: Mr. Diemer, did you ever hear a conversation by anyone in your store or elsewhere, relating to the fact that there was going to be, or might be, an explosion at the Wade home?

A: I don't recall.

Q: Well, now let me ask you if you ever made this statement to anyone, or a statement containing the substance of this — I am going to read this statement to you: "About June 1, 1954, I had occasion to be in Diemer's store and there were several men — about five — talking about negroes in Rone Court — and the place should be blown off the map. Mr. Diemer, owner of the store, said the dynamite already had been bought in the County and was stored in Rone Court." Now did you make that statement?

A: No sir.

Q: Now, did you ever hear anyone make a statement that the Wade home in Rone Court should be blown off the map?

A: I may have.

Q: Are you positive you never made the statement that the dynamite had been bought somewhere in the County and was stored in a basement in Rone Court?

A: I did not.

Q: Are you positive?

A: I am positive.

Q: Are there any other Diemers interested in the hardware store?

A: Only my wife.

Q: Do you know a man named William O'Keefe?

A: I met him, I guess, three or four weeks after the explosion when he accused me of making the statement.

Q: And what did you tell him?

A: That he was a liar.

BY THE FOREMAN: What kind of fellow is O'Keefe?

A: A police officer, I believe.

MR. HAMILTON: He is a member of the Jefferson County Police Force.

After a few more questions, Diemer was excused. He was not asked to explain further his statement that he "may" have heard someone make the statement that the Wade home should be blown off the map. And William O'Keefe was never called before the grand jury.

The most significant thing about what the grand jury did *not* do was its failure to indict the three men who confessed before it that they had been among those who burned the cross on the first night the Wades moved in — Buster Rone, Lawrence Rinehart, and Stanley Wilt. All three said they burned it to let the Wades know they were not wanted in the neighborhood. In Kentucky, burning a cross for the purpose of intimidating someone is a crime; but none of these men was indicted.

The questioning of Buster Rone and Rinehart and Wilt and all the other neighbors whose names Andrew gave to Hamilton was quite brief. They were simply asked if they had any knowledge of the bombing, if they had ever bought or detonated dynamite — questions of this kind — and when they replied in the negative, they were excused and that was that. The main bulk of the eight volumes that finally made up the grand jury transcript is devoted to lengthy hours of questioning of Wade and his friends. In the early days of the investigation, the attack centered almost equally on Wade and his Negro friends on the one hand and on his white supporters on the other. As the investigation progressed, the concentration was more and more on the white people.

It is noteworthy that the grand jury transcript contains not the least scrap of evidence that any of the persons under investigation were in fact Communists, as Hamilton had suggested. It contains not the least scrap of evidence that any of these people actually had anything to do with the bombing. I therefore think that the actions of the grand jurors, as well as those of the prosecutors, can be explained only in terms of the preconditioned pattern of their thinking. They had certain blind spots; there were certain things they could not understand; and because there were things they couldn't understand, they were able to believe the unbelievable. The transcript itself pinpoints these blind spots.

First, they were completely unable to understand Andrew Wade and his determination to live in his house. Constantly, throughout the investigation, they were probing, probing — trying to establish that this house purchase was not Wade's idea but that it came from someone else, that it came perhaps from the white Bradens or that it came from some organization that wanted to start a general movement of Negroes into white areas. Thus, after Andrew had told of his first visit to us:

Q: Had you discussed the purchase of a house, not this particular house, but the purchase of a house with the Bradens before that house?

A: No.

Q: You hadn't talked buying a house with them at all?

A: They didn't even know I was going to buy a house.

And later:

Q: But this idea of moving out there, I mean you had reason to believe because of the refusal on the part of other agents to sell you properties that you desired, this idea, was there any idea at all of the sort of crusading that you would start a movement, I mean we were out there the other day, there's all that vacant ground around that house, you know.

A: That's right.

Q: And of course, I imagine Mr. Rone always intended there should be other houses built, but if there was any idea on the part of you or your friends that perhaps, well, if I move out there, then others will follow, or there will be an opportunity for others to follow?

A: . . . I had no idea of crusading, no, because I wanted a little family of my own and a little home of my own . . . I want to enjoy life while I'm young . . . I conscientiously was working toward the point of a little home and quietness. And there was definitely no one concerned in our plan, no one at all. . . .

. . . .

Q: And nobody but your wife and yourself encouraged you as far as moving out there was concerned?

A: That's right.

And in the questioning of Andrew's father:

Q: Did the Bradens encourage you and your son in this?

A: No sir, it was our own idea.

Second, the prosecutor and grand jury were utterly unable to comprehend the loneliness a Negro family feels when it is under attack and surrounded by a hostile white world. This loneliness is a difficult thing for any white person to understand — the hemmed-in feeling, the trapped feeling, the feeling that one must depend on one's own resources for there are no friends on the other side of the wall. Thus, the grand jury could not understand the fact that the Wades felt it necessary to keep guns in the Rone Court house, the fact that they were never sure they could trust the police. The jury apparently was not interested in the fact that none of these guns was ever fired — except once, and then a single shot into the air on a night when a friend of the Wades saw a man crawling toward the house on his stomach. The very fact that the guns were there meant to the jury and the prosecutor that the Wades were hoping for a race riot. This concern over firearms cannot be attributed to pacifist inclinations among the jurors and prosecutor. If this had been the case, they would have been concerned also about the fact that the Rones had guns in their house and that John Y. Hitt testified himself that he had a gun in his house at the time that he was writing his editorials about Rone Court — and that somebody had fired rifle shots into a human dwelling place the first night Andrew and Charlotte stayed there. But these facts never aroused the interest of the jury. Only in the Wade house were guns a provocation to trouble. Many pages of the grand jury testimony are taken up with efforts to determine just how many guns were in the house, who provided them and why they were there. For example, during the questioning of Andrew's father:

Q: What was the reason for having weapons in your son's house?

A: Because we had been threatened over the telephone.

Q: Well, you had the police out there.

A: When you live with a thing like this, there is a certain amount you must do for yourself. . . . Now I know how hard it is to get evidence on policemen and they live in the vicinity and we got to know the ones and had seen them in the office, and knowing they were in sympathy with the neighbors, we did not know what might happen . . .

Third, the grand jurors were unable to comprehend the feeling of solidarity that arises among the Negro people when one of their number is under attack as Andrew Wade was. They could not understand the numbers of Negroes who risked their lives to spend time at the house as guards and companions. In their questioning, they probed for some sinister clue to it all — for some indication that someone had organized the support for the Wades in an effort to stir up more trouble. For example, they questioned Tellus Wicker, one of the Negroes who was at the house the night it was bombed, as to his reasons for being there that night and on preceding nights:

Q: You went out to keep him company, is that right?
A: That's right.
Q: Keep who company?
A: Keep the Wades company, and I told Wades — they was having trouble out there, and I told them, I said . . . "Well, if the people overpower the police, I will be out to help in any way I can."
Q: Did you actually feel that the few people, the families that lived out there, were going to overpower the police, as you said?
A: I didn't know how. They form a crew. I don't know.
Q: Where did you get the idea?
A: Simply from the fact I thought what had happened would happen again.

• • • • • •

Q: Isn't this a little far-fetched from the kind of life you generally lead, and we generally lead; we live in a cosmopolitan city, we have watched the city grow up, we have watched the Police Department give the kind of protection to citizens year in year out. I am trying to find out if you were incited into this thing through someone talking about it, and where did you get your original information from? I mean how did this idea create in your mind?

A: This idea was created in my mind because I thought if the police was overpowered and those weapons was out there, I could be of some assistance. That was my idea to go out there, was to assist them if things went beyond their control.

Q: If there were some Indians and cowboys that wanted to shoot, that you'd be subjected to shots and might get killed? Did you think about that?

A: I did.

Q: Is that good?

A: That might not have been a good idea, but it was my idea of it.

And in the questioning of Anna Harris, a young Negro woman who was Charlotte's friend and who often stayed at the house with Charlotte during the trouble:

Q: What about yourself? Were you afraid to go in a house where you knew people were going to shoot into it?

A: Was I afraid to go?

Q: Yes.

A: No, they are my friends.

. . . . . .

Q: There was no idea of danger to yourself?

A: No, I don't think so.

Q: Where a situation like that was present, didn't it occur to you from a standpoint of friendship that probably, at that particular time, after there was a disturbance, that women should not be there? Did it occur to you to try to urge your friend to leave there, her or the little girl?

A: Well, I did not urge her to leave. I will just put it like that, because it was not my business.

Q: No, but you did probably discuss that with her, so you realized the danger there to yourself and to her by being there?

A: Sometimes you don't imagine the danger. You just go on and do what you think is right in your heart to do.

Fourth, and perhaps of the greatest importance, the most incomprehensible thing of all to the prosecutor and the grand jurors was the attitude of white people who associate with Negroes. The major theme that runs through the entire transcript of proceedings is expressed in the question that was asked over and over, of both white and Negro witnesses: "Have you ever attended any meetings here in Louisville where white and colored meet together?" After Bown became a center of attack, the jury subpoenaed his foreman at his place of employment and many of his co-workers. They asked them all about his association with Negro workers. They asked his foreman:

> . . . I wonder if you could tell us whether in your observation of his movement and activities, does he seem to seek the company of Negro workers? I mean, does he seem to sort of congregate with them, if he sits down and eats his lunch does he sit with them or does he —

The foreman interrupted to say no, that Bown ate his lunches in the white restaurant where all the white workers did. But the prosecutor pursued the subject with Bown's other co-workers. For example, he questioned a Negro fellow worker of Bown's as follows:

Q: Has he [Bown] ever visited in your home?
A: That's right.
Q: He has?
A: Yes.
Q: On many or few occasions?
A: Very few occasions.
Q: How many times within the past 12 months, would you say?
A: I should say about twice.
Q: About two times in the last year, is that right?
A: That's right.
Q: Who came with him if anybody on those occasions?
A: Nobody else, only himself.
Q: Do you have lunch with Bown very regularly or not?
A: Have lunch with him?
Q: Yes.
A: I haven't had lunch with him.
Q: Have you ever gone out and eaten with him?

A: No.

Q: Dinner, supper, or breakfast?

A: No.

· · · · · ·

Q: How did he come to visit in your home?

A: He was a stranger in town. I work with him. He seems like a nice fellow.

The prosecutor and jury, for reasons that are hard to understand, appeared to be infuriated by the letter sent to Shively residents by the Women's International League for Peace and Freedom. They called before them Louise Gilbert, the social worker who was chairman of the Louisville chapter of the League, and her roommate, LaRue Spiker, who had also tried to organize white support for the Wades. The questioning of Miss Gilbert is illuminating:

Q: Do you know Andrew Wade IV?

A: Not well.

· · · · · ·

Q: How long ago did you first become acquainted with him?

A: Oh, probably — I don't know exactly but it was since the original incident.

· · · · · ·

Q: How did you happen to meet him? How did you happen to make his acquaintance?

A: A friend of mine, my roommate and I, went out to their house to call on them. That's the first I met them.

Q: You went out to Wade's home to call upon him, you say?

A: Yes.

Q: How did you happen to go out there and call upon him? Did someone ask you to go?

A: No.

Q: Well, if you don't mind, just tell the jury how you happened to go out there?

A: I was concerned about the situation and thought that an expression of interest from other people would have some value.

Q: I don't want to appear facetious, and I hope you will take

this in a way — but for the record, in other words, this
record may at some date wind up in the Court of Appeals
or somewhere like that, but you are a white person and
the Wades are colored?

A: Yes.

The blind spots that obscured the vision of Hamilton and his
assistant, Higgins, and the jurors come out clearest perhaps in the
questioning of Donald Renner, the white printing pressman at the
Courier-Journal who in his spare time published the little home-
made literary magazine called *Louisville Writers and Poets*. We
did not know him before the Wade incident, but after Rone Court
became community news, he asked Carl to write a story about the
situation for his magazine which he had just recently started. Carl
did, and Renner published it in his July 1954 issue, along with
an article he had written himself on "The Causes and Cures of Race
Prejudice." He was already a member, although not a very active
one, of the NAACP, and he became very much interested in the
Wade situation. He volunteered to do guard duty at the Wade house
and stayed there several nights during the summer. As he told the
grand jury:

> I felt if I believed in doing something, along with the way I
> talk, the way I believe, I should do something occasionally
> . . . I thought I ought to go and make a gesture of doing,
> as well as going around and saying, telling people that I
> believe in this, or I believe in that.

Later the Women's International League secured his services to
duplicate their letter to Shively residents on his multigraph machine.
All of these circumstances got him called before the September
grand jury. Pages of the transcript are filled with the prosecution's
efforts to determine his motives. Questioning by Hamilton:

> Q: Let me ask you this question. Don't answer it if you
> don't want to. But I notice in your publication here just a
> couple of titles, and also your interest in the Wade sit-
> uation. Now, I think that all of us in this Grand Jury
> room are equally interested in the welfare of mankind,
> so to speak, and I have just as much feeling, I believe,
> for an unfortunate colored family as you do have, but

> why is it that people will bend themselves over in a
> situation of this kind, that is, some people, to protect a
> colored man's family and yet not do the same thing for a
> white family . . . In other words, would you go to this
> much trouble to help a white man whose house had
> burned down, or whose house had blown up as you
> would to help Wade?
>
> A: Well, that's a hard question to answer. I never thought
> that I would do more for a colored man than I would for
> a white man.
>
> Q: Have you ever gone out to protect a white man's house
> where his home may have been entered by burglars, or
> where he was mistreated or thought that he was mis-
> treated?
>
> A: No. But as far as I can remember, I have never known a
> white man that wanted anybody to guard his house.

The questioners were interested in finding out Renner's reasons
for starting the publication of his little literary magazine. Was it,
they asked, to give expression to some particular point of view,
to spread his ideas? Renner explained patiently that his primary
purpose had been to build up a little independent business of his
own, to make eventually a little extra money; he said the magazine's
main function was to entertain. But the search for motive persisted.
Higgins questioned him:

> Q: Mr. Renner, you stated that you became a member of the
> National Association for the Advancement of Colored
> People one night as a lark out here with your minister
> and Sunday School teacher.
>
> A: I didn't mean to call it a lark. We did join.
>
> Q: As a matter of fact, you have been interested in this ques-
> tion of the black and white races for some time, haven't
> you?
>
> A: Yes.
>
> Q: Over a period of years?
>
> A: I would say so, yes.
>
> Q: Isn't it true . . . that the primary purpose of disseminating
> this literature here [the magazine] is to disseminate your

views as to the discrimination, or whatever you want to call it, between the white and black people?

A: No sir, it is not true.

Q: Isn't it strange that in your early articles — in your early publications, those articles appear, one by Braden and one by you? . . . At least if that wasn't your preliminary issue, you took an early opportunity to present your views, didn't you?

A: That article I probably would have written maybe a couple of years from now. I wrote it now because I wanted to put it with the Braden article.

Q: You did have it in the back of your mind, then, to use the medium for your views of colored people?

A: At some time or other, I intended to write an article on it, yes.

Confronted with so many elements they could not understand or even imagine, Hamilton and Higgins and the jurors often found themselves in a state of angry frustration. The transcript is punctuated with irrational outbursts. In them, with the frustration is mingled the compulsive need of Hamilton and the people he represented to remove the onus of the bombing of Wade's home from the anti-Negro segment of Louisville's white population. Thus, when Hamilton took Bown before the judge to determine whether he would be required to answer certain questions, this exchange took place:

JUDGE: Unless you have some substantive evidence that it was an inside job, and it was done by the Communists —

HAMILTON: Judge, if I can butt in, that's what the Grand Jury is trying to find out, who did it, and that's what the Grand Jury is investigating, and that's what they are trying to find out. I think it is unfair on the part of anybody to assume that the white people out there did it any more than to assume that somebody else did it, and that's what the Grand Jury is trying to find out and trying to determine.

JUDGE: . . . I don't know what evidence you have to connect Communists with this bombing.

BOWN: Mr. Hamilton, suppose you did establish somebody's political affiliations, that wouldn't establish who did the bombing.

HAMILTON: It might.

JUDGE: There ought to be some link.

HAMILTON: You have got just as much link in this —

JUDGE: No, that's my ruling. It is too speculative. It is guesswork.

HAMILTON: Judge, it is no more guesswork to believe that these people were mixed up in it than it is to speculate that the white people in Shively were so low down that they would try to chase these colored people out by blowing the house up . . .

Hamilton's state of mind at that point is further indicated by the exchange that occurred between him and Bown when they returned to the jury room:

HAMILTON: Well, Mr. Bown, in view of the court's ruling that you don't have to answer that question or any of those questions . . . there is nothing more I can do. I have no more questions to ask you.

BOWN: Mr. Hamilton, if you have any concrete evidence —

HAMILTON: Just don't say anything to me. I am asking the questions. You can answer them or not. I don't want any speeches.

That happened on September 24. It was the day of Bown's second appearance before the grand jury. It was also the day that I had finally decided — after a hectic nine days in which there had been no time even to think — that I had put Jimmy off long enough about his birthday party. On that morning I had dropped everything else and made his cake. It was Carl's day off from work and late in the afternoon he had bought the ice cream; the children next door had come over and Sonia had come in from another home in the neighborhood where she was baby-sitting at the time; I had gone to pick up Charlotte and Rosemary and Carl's mother in the car, and we all relaxed watching the children enjoy themselves for an hour or so. It was well past suppertime when the party was over. When Carl and the children and I returned to our house from taking his mother and Rosemary and her mother home, our phone was ringing. Carl answered. It was a deputy from the county jail calling to say that Bown had asked that we be notified that he was in jail on a charge of contempt of court.

We later learned that early in his testimony that day Bown took the position that he had been placed in the role of a defendant and would answer no more questions on any subject, on the grounds of possible self-incrimination. The judge, as noted above, upheld him in this position, and he was excused from the jury room. After he left, however, the prosecution found that early in the proceedings he had declined to answer one question merely on the grounds that it was irrelevant, rather than claiming the privilege against self-incrimination. It was a minor question — how many times had he seen us in the preceding two weeks? — and actually careful study of the transcript later showed that he had answered the question at one point, saying he had seen us twice, before he refused to answer when the question was asked a second time. But his failure to answer once was all the pretext the grand jury needed. They indicted him, and he was arrested that night at his place of employment.

On the same night, police and representatives of the Commonwealth's Attorney's office went to Bown's apartment and raided it; they had no search warrant. After the bombing at Rone Court, Bown had moved back into town and had taken an apartment with a retired riverboat captain named I. O. Ford. Bown and Ford had known each other for several years, but Ford had played no part in the Wade case. He was seventy-nine, too old to get out of his apartment much and spent most of his time reading. But, as he soon thereafter told newspaper reporters, he had once been a Communist. In fact, he had run for mayor of Cleveland on the Communist Party ticket years before, he said. He told reporters he was no longer a member of the Communist Party. But the raid on the apartment occupied by Bown and Ford netted boxloads of Communist literature — works of Marx, pamphlets by Lenin and Stalin and by American Communists, copies of the *Daily Worker*. The next morning's *Courier-Journal* carried a front-page story on the raid with a picture of some of the literature — books bearing Stalin's picture prominently displayed. Hamilton announced to the press that he had now "hit the jackpot" in the investigation of the

bombing and that the finding of this literature "more or less con-
vinces me that this thing was Communist inspired."

That was the turning point of the grand jury investigation. After
that, there was not the least chance — if there ever had been any —
that the probe could become a cool appraisal of the facts surrounding the bombing. The community was electrified; hysteria began to
mount. Few people stopped to consider the non sequitur in Hamilton's statement — to wonder how the finding of any kind of literature proved anything at all about the bombing of Wade's house.
The thing that was uppermost in everyone's mind was that here
in Louisville had been uncovered evidence — or supposed evidence — of people who might be Communists. Not in Moscow or in
New York or in other faraway places where Communists were
supposed to be, but right here at home on Louisville's doorstep.
And the people who seemed to be Communists were the very
people who were opposing segregation, who were connected with
the movement of a Negro into a white neighborhood. The result
was an explosive merger of anti-Negro and anti-Communist hysteria that was to become the hallmark of the Louisville case and
which has since become a distinguishing feature of much of the
opposition to racial integration throughout the South. It was an
atmosphere in which it was almost impossible for a voice of reason
to be heard. One Louisville radio commentator who dared to label
the whole investigation a "witch hunt" was summoned before the
grand jury the minute he left the air and practically accused of
obstructing justice. Others who were inclined to think reasonably
remained silent. Bown stayed in jail because no one in Louisville —
who had the money or property for it — dared to post his $3,000
bond.

One night early the following week Carl came home from work
and sat down in the living room to eat a dish of ice cream, as he
often did before going to bed.

"Well," he said calmly, "I ran into a friend of mine who works
at the courthouse today. The latest rumor is that Hamilton has
unearthed an old state sedition law and is going to indict us all
under that."

"Sedition law?" I asked incredulously. "I didn't even know
Kentucky had one."

"Neither did most other people. It was passed back in the

early 1920s during the Palmer Raid days — as a matter of fact, as a weapon against the Socialist Party at the time my dad was active in it," Carl said wryly. "It was never used though."

"Sedition — but why would he accuse us of sedition?"

Carl went on steadily eating his ice cream.

"Very simple," he said. "He says the purchase of this house and the bombing were all a Communist plot to stir up trouble between the races and by that method to create riot, insurrection, and bring about the overthrow of the government."

Surely, I thought, I will wake up in a minute and find that I have been dreaming.

"What's the penalty?" I asked.

"Twenty-one years in prison and a $10,000 fine," Carl said quietly.

I seemed to feel an icy hand clutch at the pit of my stomach. It *must* be a dream, I thought. I suppose I looked a little startled, because Carl put down his dish of ice cream and came over and kissed me. For a moment he sat silent on the arm of my chair. On the surface, he was calm and unperturbed, as he always was. But we had grown very close in our years together, and often each of us knew what the other was thinking without any exchange of words. That sixth sense told me now that Carl too was somewhat shaken beneath the calm. This knowledge, for some paradoxical reason, made me feel a little better. Finally he spoke quietly:

"If I have to be indicted for sedition," he said, "I'm glad it's with you."

I presume there are more romantic compliments that a husband has paid to a wife after six years of married life. But at that point I could imagine none that would have meant so much to me. The icy hand relaxed its hold around my stomach.

Fortunately, perhaps, there was little time that week to think or to brood; events moved too rapidly. Our telephone rang constantly. Reporters called; friends called; enemies called. Conferences with lawyers. Frantic efforts to raise Bown's bond. The continually changing rumors coming out of the courthouse.

On October 1, the last day of the investigation, Carl and I were summoned to appear again before the grand jury. When we got to the courthouse that morning, we found it filled with people. The investigation had become the biggest news in the community, and curiosity-seekers swarmed to the scene. Most of them stood around in little groups talking quietly, occasionally throwing hostile glances in our direction. The immediately preceding days of the investigation had been devoted almost entirely to a fishing expedition in search of Communists; the bombing seemed to have been lost in the shuffle. I saw Andrew's father that morning sitting in the witness room, a piece of paper in his hand.

"This is a list of questions I want to give them," he explained to me, "questions they haven't looked into — about the Ku Klux Klan elements that caused the trouble out there. I've been sitting here two full days now waiting for them to give me a chance to talk."

He never got his chance; he was still sitting in the same chair late that afternoon when I left the courthouse to go home and check on our children who had been left in the care of Andrew's mother. I had time only to stop at our house briefly, make sure the children were well and happy, and drive to the Wades' house nearby to compare notes with Charlotte and Andrew — when Carl called me there to tell me we had been indicted for sedition and that the judge was setting bond at $10,000 for each of us. He told me to take a cab to the police station and meet our lawyer there. I hesitated momentarily wondering if I should go back by our house and try to explain to the children. But I had just told them when I left a few moments before that I would be gone awhile, and they were all right there with Mrs. Wade. I might make matters worse, I thought, by going back — for there is really nothing one can say to children three years and one-and-a-half years of age to explain this sort of thing or make it easier. I called a cab to come for me at the Wades.

Four people besides Carl and me were indicted for sedition: Vernon Bown, I. O. Ford, LaRue Spiker, and Louise Gilbert. Bown was also charged with actually setting the explosion. The sedition indictment charged us with no specific act; it simply quoted the words of the statute, in effect saying we had "advocated sedition" — or, as one writer commenting on the case later noted, accused us of sedition in that we were seditious. But there was little doubt in the minds of the Louisville public as to what seditious thing it was we were supposed to have done. And another grand jury a month later made it more specific when it returned a second indictment against us, charging us with conspiring to dynamite Wade's house for seditious purposes. LaRue and Louise were not included in this second indictment; the charge was against Bown and Ford and Carl and me and one additional person, Lewis Lubka, who had also been among the white guards at the house. And the report submitted by the grand jury at the time of the first indictments made quite explicit the meat of the charge against us. The report stated:

> It is very significant to this Grand Jury that this case seems to follow the pattern used by the Communist Party in this country to create trouble between the respective races in this country, and that one of the specific methods of doing this is by the purchase of property for negroes in areas which normally are occupied by white persons, and then causing incidents such as this.

There are two features of the grand jury indictments that are especially noteworthy. One is that not every white person who supported the Wades was indicted. Most of the very active ones were, but a few, like Donald Renner, who were also quite active, were not included. The dividing line seemed to be whether the person had refused to answer questions before the grand jury. Those who did not feel the same kind of repulsion we felt about official inquiry into our personal affairs and who therefore answered all questions were not indicted. All of those who refused on one ground or another to answer some of the questions were indicted. The refusal to answer was treated as if it were an admission of guilt. Those who refused were apparently indicted on the theory that it would be easiest to prove that they were Communists and to bolster the contention that white people who oppose segregation are bound to be Communists.

The second noteworthy thing is that no Negroes at all were indicted — not Andrew nor any of the leaders of the Wade Defense Committee nor any of the Negro guards who practically spent the summer on Rone Court. This of course was in line with the theory that Negroes on their own do not oppose segregation, that it is always the white radicals who pull the strings, and that if the white people so inclined could be silenced the whole disturbing problem would be eliminated. For the Negroes connected with the Wade case and for Louisville's Negro population generally, the grand jury had some fatherly advice. In its report, it stated:

> One of the appalling facts determined by this investigation is that the ultimate purchasers of this house apparently surrounded themselves with persons reported to be Communists or Communist sympathizers. We desire to emphasize at this point that all people, white and negro, have fared better in this country under the democratic form of government, than any country in the world, and we are certain that the colored people will only harm themselves by relying upon persons having Communist tendencies.

It was somewhat bleak advice for the Negroes of Louisville. As everyone knew, the only white people on whom the Wades could have "relied" were those who were later to be accused of having "Communist tendencies," for no other white people in the city, as we have seen, offered any active help. But the grand jury report — whether this was the conscious intent of the prosecutor and the jurors or not — was worded in such a way as to strike fear into the hearts of Louisville, Negro and white — and for a time it did.

16

Back to the Crossroads

As I rode toward the police station in a cab on the night that we were indicted, I could hear police sirens shrieking a few blocks away. Like most people, I rarely noticed the cry of police sirens in the night — unless they happened to sound at a time when someone I loved was away in an automobile and the possibility of a traffic accident occurred to me. Now, suddenly, they took on new meaning. I remembered with a start that Carl had told me the judge was issuing bench warrants for our arrest. The police were probably on their way to our house, not knowing that I was coming to headquarters voluntarily. The sirens were looking for *me,* crying out in the night, looking for me to put me in jail. They seemed to be screaming my name.

In that moment, I came to the final realization — a realization that had started painfully as I sat in the grand jury room sixteen days before — that not only the frustrated private citizens of Shively but all of the forces of law and order were arrayed against us.

How strong is the umbilical cord that ties us to our background and early environment. I thought I had long since cut the cord; I thought I had examined the values of the world in which I grew up, had found many of them wanting and had established new values. And in a sense I had. But now at a time when this world reciprocated and turned on me in a furious effort to tear me to shreds, I found that in many ways I was still a privileged-class woman of the white South. My mind knew better, but my nerves and my reflexes still expected the protections and immunities that went with the place in society to which I had been born.

All of my life, the forces of law and order had been on my

215

side. Before I ever started to school, I had learned that policemen were my friends — kind men who helped children across the street safely and protected our house from men, presumably black men, who might want to burglarize it. Later they were on occasion men who might try to give one a traffic ticket but could usually be talked out of that if one smiled at them in a nice way. Prosecuting attorneys, as I grew up, were the fathers of the boys and girls I met at school dances and country club parties. Later they were the pleasant men in whose offices I often sat as a newspaper reporter, discussing the news, passing the time of day. Grand juries were legal bodies which returned indictments against criminals but never the people I knew. Almost before I could talk — at the same time I was absorbing the myth that white people were superior to Negroes — I learned that I was free. By the time I was old enough to express an idea, I knew that I lived among people who could go anywhere they wanted to and say anything they wanted to — within the bounds, of course, of good manners and good taste — and that when I had outgrown parental restrictions I too would have these freedoms. When I learned in school about the Bill of Rights, it had real meaning for me, and I was quite emotional about it. It meant just what I had always known — that I lived in the most wonderful country in the world, and the reason it was wonderful was that in it people were free — free as I was to think what I wanted to think, read what I wanted to read, and say what I wanted to say. And when I was in the ninth grade, I won an oratorical contest sponsored by a civic club in Anniston on the subject of the Bill of Rights. That was in 1937, and in my address I drew a sharp contrast between freedom as I knew it in America and the situation in Germany and Russia where people were not free.

It was not many years after that, of course, that I began to realize consciously what I had known even earlier unconsciously: that not everyone in America was as free as I was, that the color of a man's skin or his economic status often made a great difference. I realized that the police were often the enemy of the Negro and that the prosecuting attorneys I knew as my own friends did not always dispense "equal and exact justice to all men of whatever state or persuasion." At that point, I started to develop a social conscience and came to feel that my own freedom was an empty and degrading attribute as long as it was denied to others of my fellow men. Finally, I began to do what I could, according to my lights, to correct this situation. In the course of these efforts, I unlearned much that I had learned as a child; especially I learned that the whiteness of a man's skin and his family tree and his economic position did not make him superior to his fellow human beings and were, in fact, much more likely to make him inferior if he valued these things too highly. And I came to know situations too — especially in working with trade unions and with Negroes striving for equal rights — where it was sometimes my own friends who were arrested by police. I even had a brief run-in with police once myself — in Mississippi while attempting to see the governor on behalf of a Negro I believed unfairly sentenced to death; but this episode passed quickly. And through it all, the one lesson of my childhood that I never unlearned, one that I clung to without analysis, was the conviction that for me personally the law and its enforcement agencies were on my side.

I think this undoubtedly is one of the reasons I joined or contributed to organizations on the Attorney General's "subversive" list without ever batting an eyelash; it never occurred to me that I did not have the right to join any organization that appealed to me. I know many people who in joining such organizations have acted on the basis of a hard-won conviction of the individual's right to his own personal beliefs. Even people who do not agree with them should, if they are honest, admire their courage. With me, the motivation was nothing especially admirable and it was not courageous. It simply grew out of my childhood assumption of personal privilege.

Just how firmly the concept of immunity to the ire of the law was implanted in my mind, as late as August 1954, is illustrated by my reaction when we first learned that authorities were investigating the fact that Carl had voted twice in the primary election. Scott Hamilton had questioned one of our neighbors, who was a poll official, about it, and she reported the questioning to us.

"Why that's ridiculous," I told Carl. "Why don't you just write a letter to Hamilton and explain to him how it happened?"

It seemed to me that would settle the matter. Despite everything in my adult experience that told me different, I could not —

when confronted with a brush with the law in my own life — escape from the pattern of my childhood thinking that told me no prosecutor would consider indicting me or my husband. If there had been a misunderstanding, all one needed to do was write a letter and explain the matter and clear things up.

Carl took my advice and wrote the letter. But I don't think he ever thought, as I did, that it would do much good. He had had no clashes with the law in recent years, but his childhood experiences were quite different from mine. In his earliest memories, the agencies of law enforcement were not his friends. His first recollections of police, in contrast to mine, were when they chased him and his friends out of the streets which were the play space in Louisville's crowded Portland district. Later, to Carl, the police and their counterparts in the National Guard were the people who broke his father's strike at the Louisville & Nashville shops. He was not surprised when, despite his letter, the grand jury returned the indictment anyway charging him with voting twice; but I was amazed.

It was on that first day when I appeared before the grand jury that this remaining strand of the umbilical cord to my past began to tear apart. Here was a prosecutor who was suddenly my enemy — mine, not the enemy of someone I did not know or even of someone else I considered a friend, but of me. Here was a grand jury that was investigating me. Since that day many people who believe in civil liberties have praised me for the "courage" I displayed in resisting the grand jury's efforts to pry into my personal beliefs. This has always amused me slightly, because of course it was not courage at all. It was nothing but indignation that any arm of the government should presume to interrogate me about matters which I had always been so sure were my private business, to challenge the freedoms I had always been so sure were mine.

Now as I sat in the cab on my way to the police station and heard the sirens screaming my name the strand finally snapped. Today, long afterward, I never hear police sirens in the night that I do not feel they are looking for me. At that moment, however, by the time I reached the police headquarters, I felt only numb. As I went through the process of being booked, fingerprinted, and photographed, my only emotion was one of great weariness. For two and a half weeks, I had been fighting back with defiant statements, refusing to believe that this could happen to me. Now it had happened, and it was as if my nerves finally relaxed and all of a sudden I knew how tired I was. I realized that I had been under a strain for five months. I felt at that moment as if I had not had a good night's sleep since May 13, the night the mob had come to our house and all the trouble started. Tonight, I thought, in the quiet of a jail cell, at least I can sleep.

When I reached the jail, it was evidently past bedtime, for everything was quiet and dark. The matron led me back through a long hall to a small cell furnished only with a commode and a narrow cot. To me, at that point, the cot looked as welcome as the most luxurious bed I had ever seen. I stretched out on it, and no innerspring mattress ever felt any softer. The matron was a pleasant young woman, and she stood talking a few moments after she closed the heavy door of iron bars. She knew that my arrest had something to do with the grand jury investigation that had been going on at the courthouse.

"I guess you didn't answer the questions to suit them," she commented matter-of-factly. She had had LaRue Spiker and Louise Gilbert in the jail in the last few days when they were held in contempt for refusal to answer the jury's questions.

"I guess not," I replied. "I didn't answer them at all. Anyway, they indicted me."

"What are you charged with?" she asked.

"Sedition."

"Sedition?" she said. "What's that?"

"I'm not sure," I answered. I was too tired to try to explain. "It has something to do with overthrowing the government."

The matron looked at me doubtfully. I had to smile. I probably did not look much like a person who was about to lead a revolution.

"What did you do?" she persisted.

"I'm not sure about that either," I said. "I sold a house. No, that couldn't be it. I'm not sure."

"Well, you go on to sleep," the matron suggested solicitously. "Things will look better in the morning."

After she left, I turned her question over in my mind. What had I done? Sold a house? How much can they do to you for

selling a house? Threaten your life for five months, kill your unborn child, and then put you in jail for twenty-one years? All for
one little house?

As I drifted off to sleep, words out of the past mingled with
the words in the grand jury room and together they raced back and
forth in my mind: Don't call niggers Mister . . . Did you ever
belong to an organization where the white and colored meet? . . .
Colored sit in the back of the bus; you sit in the front . . . Did you tell
Mr. Rone you were going to sell to colored? . . . We eat in the
dining room; niggers eat in the kitchen . . . Do you have colored
in your home? . . . You use that door; niggers go in there . . . Do
you eat with colored? . . . Never call a colored woman lady . . .
Why did you sell it? . . . Niggers sit in the balcony . . . Did you tell
Mr. Rone? . . . Watch out, be careful . . . Did you ever belong . . .
Do you read. . . .

And in the distance, police sirens still shrieking, coming for
me, putting me in jail. . . .

When I awoke I knew it must be morning; somewhere I could
hear people talking. Soon, I thought, someone will come and
bring me breakfast. But the minutes passed into what seemed like
an eternity, and no one came. There was nothing to do but sit
there and come to grips with my own thoughts.

Now, with a night's sleep behind me, everything began to come
into focus. Suddenly I was ashamed of my feelings of self-pity the
night before. Now the answer to the matron's question seemed perfectly clear. Of course I was not here just because I had sold a
house. I had challenged a whole settled world, a way of life, and
this world had struck back. What had I expected? Had I really
thought, I asked myself, that this argument over segregation was
some sort of a pink tea where people of opposing viewpoints would
state their respective positions and then sit down and drink a
friendly cup of punch together? The people defending segregation
were desperate; they were convinced that they were right and that
the defense of their position was the defense of civilization itself.
If I believed in my position enough to challenge them, I must expect
to pay a price.

Almost every person with a social conscience reaches a point
in his life when he must decide whether he is willing to make a

sacrifice for the things he believes in. When he makes that decision, he casts the die as to whether he will be a dilettante, a parlor reformer — or a person of action. I have been thankful since that it never fell to my lot to face such a decision. Events made the decision for me. Sitting there in the jail that morning, I suddenly felt that now that what seemed like the worst had happened, it was too late to be afraid. When the cord that still tied me to security had snapped the night before, I had been set adrift. But now I felt that some way — somehow — I would land on my feet.

My next thought was that I must let Carl know I was all right. Finally, a matron came to bring me a dish of peaches floating in thin syrup and coffee in a tin cup for breakfast. I asked her if she could send a letter for me to the other side of the jail where I knew Carl was. She said she thought she could, and in a little while she brought me some paper and pencil. I wrote to Carl:

> The matron brought me this paper and a pencil and says she thinks she can get this note delivered to you without its having to go through the mail. I hope it reaches you today.
>
> The main thing is I want you to know I am all right. I am worried for fear you are worried about me. I guess everyone finds in a crisis that there are deep wellsprings of strength within him that he didn't know he had. I suppose I will need a lot of strength — but I am confident I will find it.
>
> I am reminded of that last letter I had from Harriet. I don't believe I ever took time to read it to you in the rush of the past two weeks. She was talking about a character in a play who was always saying he "had to go back to the crossroads." Her observation was that in a very serious fashion there come times in everyone's life when he must go "back to the crossroads" — to determine who he is, from whence he came, what he believes in, and from this knowledge to draw the inner strength that he needs to meet the challenges of life. . . . I think perhaps this is a traumatic experience that has jolted me back to the crossroads, so to speak. I think I am in the process of finding some of the things I need. I will write you more about it as it all comes clear to me. But for now, just be assured that this has not knocked me off my teeter-totter.

I know you are all right. There has never been any doubt in my mind about your strength.

That's all for now. Except to tell you I have never loved you as much as I do right now.

Back to the crossroads; back through the years. I was not sure just where the crossroads were; I did not know at exactly what point I had taken the path that led to a jail cell. But I could see now that it had long been inevitable. Since the day I met Carl and found that I was not alone, that there were people in the world doing something about the wrongs that plagued my soul? Since the day I had seen death on the table in the Birmingham courthouse and had felt its chill closing in on my own heart? Since the day I had glimpsed a world without walls with my young actress friend in New York? Or perhaps was it still further back than that? The day perhaps that I had learned in the fashionable little Episcopal church in Anniston that all men are brothers in God and I was my brother's keeper. Or perhaps it was the day I was born with the makings of a conscience into a segregated society. Back to the crossroads — so long ago.

I went back literally, a week later, when I was released from jail on bond and went to Anniston to see our children, who had been taken there by my parents after we were jailed.

I had not expected to be released from jail this soon. The bond of $10,000 seemed to me utterly out of reach. Most of our friends owned no property, and those who did had it mortgaged. I could see no alternative to remaining in jail until we came to trial. Having accepted this as inevitable, I began to adjust to jail life. Jail has its own routine, and once I relaxed from the pace of the outside world, I began to fit into the routine. The second day I was there I was moved from my cell to a dormitory with several other women. There was plentiful conversation to pass the time, and I ordered books from the jail library. For the first couple of days, I worried almost constantly about the children. Carl and I had arranged for friends to take Jimmy and Anita to their home if we were indicted, and Sonia was living with one of our neighbors where she was baby-sitting full time. I knew Sonia would be all right, because she was old enough to take care of herself and she had always con-

sidered Carl's mother's house a second home and could go there
if she felt the need of family. But with my own children it was of
course different. I kept thinking of the way Jimmy had looked one
morning a few days before we were indicted: he was on the couch
in our living room and I — stupidly forgetting for an instant that
he was there — said something on the telephone about the possibility of our being put in jail; I realized what I had done when I
looked up and saw him sitting there forlornly, sucking his thumb.

A fall cold snap had set in after our arrest, and I worried
foolishly for fear our friends would not find the children's warm
clothes where I had packed them away for the summer. But there
was nothing I could do. For the first time in my active life, I was
helpless to deal with practical problems; it was a strange new experience, but I adjusted to it. I wrote a friend: "I remember once
when I was playing in the ocean when I was a little girl; a big wave
knocked me down. There was no use fighting against it; the only
thing to do was to relax and let it roll over me, to ride with it until
it had spent itself. I feel that way now."

I knew from the beginning that my mother and father would
probably be in a position to make my bond, but I did not want
to ask them to do it. We disagreed completely on the subject of
segregation, I knew that they thoroughly disapproved of all my
activities in this field, and I felt that I had no right, now that I was
in trouble, to call on them for help. During the summer months, I
had told them nothing of the Wade incident. Although the affair
was big news in the Louisville papers, it was evidently not widely
reported elsewhere in the South, and some way they never heard
of it. I saw no reason to worry them or upset them by telling them
about it. But when it became apparent in September that we would
be indicted, I realized that this would be in the papers everywhere
and that they would have to know. On the Sunday before the
indictments were returned, I sat down and wrote them a letter.
At that time, we had not heard the rumors about the sedition law,
but we thought we might be indicted for contempt. I held the letter
for four days after I wrote it — until I knew there was no longer any
doubt that some sort of indictments would come — and then I
mailed it. The letter said in part:

. . . I think I should tell you about some trouble we have been having. You are not going to understand it all, and I am sorry. But you should know. It has been going on for some time, but I have thought it would soon blow over, and I would not have to bother you with it.

Some time ago, some Negro friends of ours asked us to buy a house and sell it to them in a previously all-white neighborhood, and we did so. Now, you will never understand, I am sure, why we agreed to do such a thing. But your standards and mine have been very different for a long time . . .

. . . Now, I suggest that you stay out of this thing entirely . . . No matter what happens, I will see that the children are well taken care of . . . Don't come up here. Don't call. Write me if you want to. If you don't, I'll understand . . .

But of course they did come. They came for our children, to whom they were devoted. At that point they could not post my bond, since the judge was refusing to accept anything but Kentucky property. But seven days later, when the court finally agreed to accept cash, our lawyer came to the jail to tell me that my father had called to say he wanted to make my bond.

"Call him back," I said, "and tell him not to feel he has to do this. He may anyway. I know Daddy. I'm his daughter, and he would do anything in the world for me. But, if he decides to go on and do it, he must realize that I cannot be under any obligation to change my position on segregation."

I presume our lawyer relayed the message to my parents. And they made the bond anyway. I can pay them no higher tribute than to say they did it with no strings attached.

Of all the people whose lives were touched with tragedy by the Louisville case, I think I feel the greatest pity for my mother and father. I was one of two children, an only daughter. Mother and Daddy were people whose adult lives had been centered around providing opportunity for their children. Daddy worked long and hard — rarely taking any time off for recreation unless it was to do something with or for his children — in order to give my brother and me an education and all the other things we might want. Although Mother was a woman who always participated to some extent in community affairs, her children came first in her time and attention. In my childhood, Mother and Daddy showered me with material things — and with affection. They were proud of my achievements, my outstanding record in school, my ability to make friends. They did all the things they thought were right in rearing me, and by all odds they should have been able to look forward in their advanced years to watching me live a successful life in the terms of their world. Instead, suddenly, in my thirty-first year, I was in jail — indicted for sedition and because of actions that in their circles were probably a worse disgrace than an indictment for murder.

It might have been different if we had not been a close family, if I had always had a tendency to rebel against them just for the sake of rebelling. But that was not the case. Despite the abundance of their affection, theirs was not a possessive love. They encouraged me to think for myself, to make my own decisions, the possibility I suppose never occurring to them — enveloped as they were in the security many Southern segregationists felt fifteen and twenty years ago as to the invulnerability of their racial views — that any of my decisions might overstep the bounds of the accepted mores of Southern society. Until I was seventeen or eighteen years old, we had a relaxed and easy parent-child relationship. I felt completely free to discuss all my early love affairs with Mother, to share with her and Daddy my joys and my problems, to go to them for advice — knowing always that the final choices would be mine to make. If I can have as good a relationship with my son and daughter when they reach adolescence as my parents had with me in that period, I will feel it has been an achievement.

Then, when I was in my late teens and early twenties, I made up my mind on segregation — and after that, my parents and I could not communicate any more. This question has divided many Southern families, past and present, and it divided ours. At first we tried to discuss it, to argue our opposing views, but this always resulted in a violent family argument. So we agreed to quit talking about it. When I went home for visits, we talked about other things. But when we agreed on this pact of silence, we closed the vital channels of communication between us. For it was segregation that was uppermost in all our minds. They knew it, and I knew it. The South was in turmoil. They moved in their direction to defend the status quo; and I moved in my direction to oppose it. But with each other, we kept our silence. And as we did, the relationship between us became more and more sterile. The range of subjects we could discuss became more and more narrow — the one thing that was so vital to us all, also so vital to practically every other subject in the world, pushed back into the shadows while we play-acted with ourselves and pretended it was not there.

And now this thing had burst from the shadows and erupted in all of our lives. It had erupted in my life in a form that I could handle. The terrible thing that had happened to me had happened because of the things I believed in. It had happened too because of the things Mother and Daddy believed in. And that was the most tragic part of all. For, I think it could not have completely escaped them that they were a part of this world that had turned savagely on the daughter they loved and sought to destroy her and that it was a part of them — and that if they had not reared me so narrowly within the bounds of this world, I might never have felt the need to oppose it so fiercely.

I still don't know just how much of this they faced consciously in their own minds. Segregation eats ugly sores into the soul of every white person in the South — although he may never analyze it or admit it to himself. Often the sores fester in darkness beneath the surface for a lifetime without the person ever realizing what is wrong. Some of us are fortunate enough to have been able gradually to cut the sores away, painfully, one by one. Few people, I think, are ever hurled into a situation, as Mother and Daddy were, where the protective covering is suddenly pulled from the sores through no doing of their own — leaving them exposed to the raw and biting wind. I got some vision of what this means, I think, in a conversation I had with Daddy during that visit home in October 1954.

At that point, I was trying to look ahead and plan in my own mind for whatever the future might hold. In the event that both Carl and I had to go to prison for a long period of years, what about the children? I was quite satisfied to have them with Mother and Daddy that winter as a temporary expedient. But what if it ran into years and years? I knew that Mother and Daddy adored them and would give them loving care, but I strongly doubted that I wanted them to grow up there. If they did, I felt, they would almost certainly have to develop in one of two directions: either they would become little Ku Kluxers in their outlook, or they would reach the point as I had where they would have an almost neurotic compulsion to devote their lives to fighting segregation. I had hoped they could grow up accepting the equality of all peoples as a natural thing, where it would be a part of their lives, a normal thing, a relaxed thing. I had not discussed my feelings on the subject with Mother and Daddy, because I did not want to hurt them any more than necessary. But they had sensed at least a part of it. And Daddy had discussed it with William Stoney, the minister of their church, with whom they were very close. One day as Daddy and I sat talking in the living room while the children were outdoors playing, he broached the subject.

"Anne Gambrell," he said hesitantly, "I hope just one thing. No matter what happens — if you can't raise these children yourself — I hope you will let us have them."

I did not answer. I did not know what to say. Daddy went on.

"I know you don't want us to have them," he said. "I talked to Bill about it the other day. You can ask him. I told him, 'Anne Gambrell doesn't want us to have her children because she is afraid I will give them my prejudices.' And I told him — and I had tears in my eyes when I said it — 'I will promise her this: I will never, never give her children my prejudices!' "

There were tears in my father's eyes now as he spoke. And, as I listened, I felt the hot tears rush to my own eyes. What he must be suffering, I thought. Never before had I heard Daddy admit he *had* any prejudices; always he had been one of those Southern white men who consider themselves the "colored man's best friend." How far he had come. Because I loved him, I wished there were some way I could put balm on those sores, to shield them from the raw wind. I wished I could say, "That's all right. It doesn't matter." But it did matter; I could not lie about it. But I realized too, as we sat there, that I could not pour salt in the sores either. I could not speak the truth I knew: that no matter how much he meant what he said, no matter how hard he tried, a child living with him would soak up his prejudices, absorb them by osmosis as I had done. So I remained silent. I passed it off by saying it was a bridge we didn't have to cross yet and perhaps we never would.

I think the soul-searching was temporary. I don't think Mother

and Daddy ever had to examine the sores very closely or make any
effort to cut them away. Anniston itself — conservative Anniston,
their own circle of friends — provided the balm I could not provide
as it rallied around them.

White upper-class Anniston was of course a-buzz with talk of
my indictment. This was something that just did not happen to
people in Anniston or to people who came from there. People there
sometimes went crazy; they sometimes ran off with each other's
wives; sometimes they killed themselves. But no one from a "good"
Anniston family ever went and got himself indicted for sedition and
put in jail. The attitude of my parents' friends toward me was one
of deep distress. In no sense did they turn on me in hatred. After
all, the Wade house incident had not happened in Anniston, and
Louisville was pretty far away. This was more than a year before
the Montgomery bus protest, and white segregationists in Alabama,
generally, felt fairly secure in their conviction that, despite the
United States Supreme Court, the social order would remain stable
in Alabama for all time to come. As for me, it was wholly regrettable that such a "nice girl" as I had been — such a "smart and
attractive" one — had got herself into such a mess. Obviously, I
had just got mixed up with the "wrong people."

To Mother and Daddy, these people's hearts went out. After all,
being a parent is a risky business; rear your child the best you can,
and you just never know how he is going to turn out. Much in the
way they would have rallied around parents whose daughter had
had a baby out of wedlock or whose son had gone haywire and
embezzled funds from the bank, they closed ranks around Mother
and Daddy in their tragedy. It was one of the most conservative
men in Anniston who came to Daddy when he heard I was in jail
and handed him a check for $10,000 to post my bond.

Anyone who has lived in a small town knows how, when there
is a death in the family, all the neighbors and friends bring gifts of
food — delicious casseroles, cakes, pies — to the bereaved family.
The custom is partly based on the assumption that the family will
be too grief-stricken and too busy to have the time or the spirit to
cook; and it is also a concrete expression of heartfelt sympathy. By
the time I got to Anniston on October 9, this was happening at our
house. Friends of Mother and Daddy were arriving in a steady

stream carrying tasty dishes of food; some of them also brought flowers.

I do not mean to poke fun at these people. Their actions were an expression of a deep-seated kindness that is a part of their natures. And kindness is one of the greatest attributes of the people in this stratum of society. If its expression is sometimes limited by the social blinders that are a part of their way of life, this does not alter the fact that the source of the kindness is good and that it is a virtue not to be sneered at. I have often thought that perhaps the exaggerated generosity these people heap on their friends and relatives is a release for the native goodness that the rigid bounds of their social views have bottled up inside of them.

But after I watched for a few days as the visitors came with their gifts of food and flowers, it occurred to me that the only thing wrong with this picture was that the corpse was here too, alive and healthy. I decided that the best thing for me to do was to go on back to Louisville as soon as possible, and I did.

Before leaving, however, I went back to the little Episcopal church I had loved so as a child. I felt that I wanted to take the Communion service there, and I asked Bill Stoney, who was my old friend, to give me a private service early one morning.

My religious ideas had changed drastically since I attended services in this church as I was growing up. While I was in college and in the years immediately after, I had gone through the period of doubt and agnosticism that most young people possessed of an intellectual bent experience. When it was over, I had discarded my childhood concept of a private God Who dispensed favors or withheld them depending on whether one was good or not. In its place, I had substituted another concept — of a God Who was a spiritual force, the central wellspring of good and love in the universe — a force which served the double function of uniting all mankind in a common bond of brotherhood and of providing a perpetual source of creative energy that flowed through the life of every individual, flowed to a greater or lesser degree depending on how completely a person was able to open up the channels of his life to it. I have never found out whether my reconstructed concept of God is compatible with Episcopal theology, and I have not especially wanted to explore the matter, for I have been afraid it may not be. I am one of the many people who need symbols for their religious beliefs, and, for me, because they were the first I knew, the symbols are those of the Episcopal Church. I had come to the conclusion in recent years that the teachings of Christ and the symbols of the Christian church were only one of a number of possible levers by which a man, whether he realized what he was doing or not, could open the channels of his life to the creative power which is God. But in my own life, this was the lever by which the channels had first been opened, and I cherished it. I had found that the symbolism of the Communion service with its dominant theme of the unity of man with the Divine — "that He may dwell in us and we in Him" — fitted my adult concept of God as well as it had fitted my childhood ideas.

Sitting there in the Anniston church on that autumn morning in 1954, I thought I understood why the symbols had been so lasting, why they had survived so well my changing life and thought. The windows of the church were open, and outside I could hear in the distance the busy morning sounds as Anniston went about its daily work — the blowing horns, the voices calling. Outside was Anniston as it had always been — the cramped world and with a strait jacket around its soul. But here inside the church I felt again the joy I had felt there as a child as I sensed vaguely the larger horizons of a world that included all mankind. It was here in this church that I had first learned that all men are One. The people who taught me these lessons had not mentioned what this concept did to their society's fetish of the color line; perhaps they never analyzed it, and at first neither did I. But I am sure that the seed that was planted in my mind and heart here was the thing that made me able to seek a larger world later — that, in fact, made it imperative that I do so. This staid little church — so fashionable and often so worldly on a Sunday morning! And yet it was the most far-reachingly decent influence in my walled-in childhood — and probably the most radical in my life. No wonder its symbols had so well withstood the test of time in my life. No wonder I turned to them now in an hour of crisis. I left Anniston to return to Louisville, feeling that perhaps this little Southern town that had given me so many weaknesses had also given me the reserve of strength I needed to meet what lay ahead.

17

Terror in the Community

It was thus two whole weeks after our arrest before I felt at
first hand the full impact of our indictment on the atmosphere in
Louisville.

I had known that hysteria was rising in the community during
the grand jury investigation. I had felt it sharply that last day of
the investigation among the hostile crowds in the courthouse —
smoldering fury directed at all those under attack but centering on
Carl and me. I had realized too that the hysteria probably reached
a new height while we were in jail and the prosecution raided our
house, as they had raided Bown's and Ford's apartment.

We had felt, of course, that such a raid was probably inevitable
from the night of the Bown-Ford raid. In fact, one of our friends
with sources of information at the courthouse had called us one day
that last week of the investigation to urge us, if we had any books in
our house that might be considered Communistic, to get rid of them.

"Absolutely no," I replied. I was in one of my defiant moods.
"I'm not going to let anyone make me start burning books."

When I told Carl about the telephone call, his response was
just as emphatic.

"I won't move a single book out of this house," he said. "I'm
going to fight this thing out if it takes all winter."

As things developed, of course, it was to take much longer than
that, and there was to come a time when we would wonder if it
might take twenty-one winters.

The first raid at our house came on the fourth day we were in
jail. Two days later, there was a second raid. Our library contained
hundreds of books — the lifetime collections of both Carl and me,
books representing almost every conceivable viewpoint, political,
economic, philosophical and literary. There were, of course, many
books by Marx and Lenin and Stalin and other Communist writers,

231

as well as many books on socialism by non-Communists. The raiders selected all these books and left most of the others, and again there were the pictures and headlines in the newspapers letting the world know that there were supposed Communists in Louisville.

And yet, although I knew that this must have further charged the atmosphere, I was still not prepared for the situation I found when I returned to Louisville two weeks after our arrest. By that time, most of the city's business luncheon clubs were passing resolutions praising Scott Hamilton for his conduct of the grand jury investigation and his diligence in rooting out dangerous elements. The executive committee of the Louisville Bar Association gave its approval; American Legion posts were joining the chorus. These things of course were to be expected. But the appalling thing was that practically no one in Louisville — white or Negro — seemed willing to speak out in our defense.

There were exceptions, to be sure. Several Negro ministers, including the Rev. M. M. D. Perdue, chairman of the Wade Defense Committee, and a few other leaders in the Negro community were consistently outspoken in our support. A few white people were too. But the number of those who were willing to speak was small; it was not an indication of any general trend. This is not to say that everyone in Louisville approved of what the prosecution was doing; in many circles the disapproval was strong. But, for one reason or another, most of those who disapproved were silent. The minister of our own church, the Rev. J. Irwin McKinney, remained loyal to us throughout, and several other white ministers in town expressed sympathy privately; but when one of them got up in the Louisville Ministerial Association while we were still in jail and made the mild proposal that the Association ask for prayers that those indicted "see the error of their ways if they are wrong and be vindicated if they are right," he met only a stony silence from the organization. The *Courier-Journal,* which had itself come under a blistering attack in a special report by the grand jury which indicted us, refused to fire Carl but, even when he was later released from jail on bond, refused to let him come back to active work; and its editorial columns lapsed into silence on the case. The trade unions and most of the organizations of the Negro people were mute.

Some of the silence was due to fear. This was especially true among many people who had been our friends and acquaintances and who now feared that they themselves might be convicted of guilt by association.

I felt this fear reaction at close range when I called an old friend, a white man, soon after my return to Louisville and told him I'd like to stop by and visit him and his wife some evening. They had always been firm opponents of segregation, and this among other things had been a bond that created a common meeting ground between them and Carl and me. I wanted to see them because I thought they might have some suggestions as to where I could turn for help on raising Carl's bond.

"Suppose I meet you downtown for lunch tomorrow," the man suggested when I called. I agreed, and when we met the next day, I asked him where his wife was.

"This thing's got her pretty upset, Anne," he said, his face flushing. "I didn't ask her to come along." I tried to hide my shock; she was a woman I had thought would never be afraid of anything.

I felt it again when another friend stopped by to see me one evening after dark. She had not wanted to telephone, she said, because she was afraid my phone might be tapped. But she wanted me to know she was thinking of me. There was nothing she could do to help, she said, but she wanted me to know she was with us — in spirit.

These instances multiplied as the days passed. As time went on, I came to realize that the fear was quite understandable. Hamilton was calling many of our friends to his office — questioning them, asking them what we talked about, asking them insistently if it weren't true that we appeared to be Communists. More people were called before the grand jury. One woman wrote a letter to the newspaper supporting us, and on the day it appeared she received a subpoena to go before the grand jury. Even Sonia had been questioned.

I found out about that one day soon after my return to Louisville when I was having lunch at Carl's mother's house. Mom was her same old self — visibly upset because Carl was in jail, but possessed of her unchanging confidence that her son, although somewhat foolish, was probably right about most things. Sonia was there, and we were all talking about the raid at our house. Hamilton had said in obtaining the warrant to search our house that he had got information from someone who knew us well which led him to believe we had "seditious material" in our house, and we were all speculating among ourselves as to where he could have got such a report.

Suddenly Sonia's face paled. "You don't suppose he could be talking about that statement I signed, do you?" she said.

"What statement?" I asked.

"That statement I signed the day I was down there — that time he questioned me three hours," she said. "I told your lawyer about it right after it happened."

"Well, I haven't had a chance to talk to him much since I got back," I replied, "and I guess he didn't want to bother me as I was leaving for Alabama — I was in such a hurry to get down there and see the children. What did the statement say?"

"She doesn't know," Mom interposed. "She didn't read it."

"You see," Sonia explained, "he just asked me a lot of questions and some woman took it down in writing — what he said and what I said, I guess — and he told me to wait and sign it. I guess I shouldn't have. I probably shouldn't have gone down there, but you see they sent two policewomen out there where I was baby-sitting, and they said I had to come, and I didn't know what to do." Sonia had quit eating her lunch now and was sitting with her head in her hands, deep in worry. I felt very sorry for her.

"That's all right, honey," I said. "You didn't really have to go, but it's not your fault. You didn't know that. He shouldn't have sent for you that way. What sort of questions did he ask you?"

"Oh, it was the same questions over and over," she said. "He wanted to know who all came to our house to see you and Daddy and what you all talked about at home and things like that. I told him I never paid much attention because I was away so much — either at school or baby-sitting. And then he asked me if you all had had those two colored boys staying there at the house one weekend last year — when I came over here so the boys could have my room. I told him yes on that. I don't know where he found out about it, but he thought it was awful. You remember — it was when that NAACP youth convention was in town."

I nodded.

"You didn't mind, did you?" I asked. I recalled that at the time Sonia had been delighted, as she always was, to have an excuse to spend the weekend with Carl's mother, whom she loved. Sonia had never showed any inclination to bother about the color of our visitors, one way or the other.

"No, of course not," she said, "but I guess Hamilton thought

I did. And then he asked me — this is what worries me — if you all had a lot of books in the house and what kind of books they were. I told him I didn't know much about what kind they were because I never paid much attention to them but — this is what I'm afraid he used for the warrant — I did say you had an awful lot of books, all over the house."

I had to smile. There was not much of a specific nature that Sonia could have said about our books. Our efforts to make an intellectual out of her had been a dismal failure; she was much too interested in boys and movies and having a good time. If she had ever opened one of our books to read it, I had not seen her.

"I hope I didn't do anything wrong," she went on. "I wouldn't do anything to hurt you and Daddy for anything in the world."

I went over and put my arms around her.

"Don't worry about it," I said. "If Hamilton wanted to get into our house, he'd have found some way to do it anyway."

Many people in Louisville did worry about it though. Before long, Hamilton announced publicly that it had indeed been a statement by Sonia Braden from which he had got the information to request a search warrant to go into our house. When people learned that a sixteen-year-old girl had been questioned about her parents and their home and their books, the panic in some sections of the population was compounded. More than one Negro domestic servant whom we knew told us of occasions in some of the city's wealthier homes where they worked when their employers had carefully gone through their libraries, picking out books that might be questionable, and had wrapped them up in old sheets, weighted them down with rocks, and thrown them in the Ohio River.

I began to sense the reaction of Louisville's Negro community to our indictment one night in mid-October when Andrew spent the evening — one of many he so spent — at the telephone calling people he knew to ask them to put up property or money toward Carl's bond. Andrew, I knew, was somewhat shaken himself by our indictment, but he was apparently determined to stick by his friends, and he insisted on helping me in my efforts to raise bond.

"He said his property is mortgaged," he commented wryly, as he hung up the phone after about the twelfth futile conversation of the evening. "I know that's not so, and he knows I know it. He's afraid, because you've been called a Communist."

"Maybe not exactly afraid," I answered. "Maybe it's just that he and others too don't feel they can take on a fight over sedition and Communism with all the other troubles they've got." It had not yet become as apparent as it was a year later that every move toward desegregation in the South was going to be labeled as "Communistic" by some of its opponents.

The impact of events on Negro-white relations in Louisville was dramatically illustrated when the local branch of the NAACP held its annual meeting in December. Always at these meetings in recent years there had been a fair-sized representation of white people present. Always this predominantly Negro organization had named at least a few white people to its executive board; I had been one of three white members at the time of my indictment. When the annual meeting was held this year, no white people at all turned out for it. When the nominations for the 1955 board were presented, no white people were included, and none were added from the floor. Obviously, in view of events, the white liberals of Louisville thought it safest to stay away. Obviously too, the Negro leaders thought it safest to get along without white support — apparently reckoning with the possibility that any white people they did nominate to the board might be labeled "Communists" before the year was out. Whether or not the opponents of desegregation had consciously planned our indictment as a tactic of divide-and-conquer, it certainly looked that way — and that was how it worked, temporarily.

The majority of Louisville's Negro people, I ultimately discovered, strongly disapproved of the prosecution's action. Most of them saw the whole affair as an attempt to cover up official failure to arrest those really responsible for the bombing of the Wade house. There were exceptions to this too, of course. There were some Negroes who believed what the prosecution said, who believed that the bombing had been a plot by white people who posed as Wade's friends. These were generally those Negroes whose deep distrust of all white people made them doubtful from the outset of any white person who appeared to be a friend of Negroes. But their number was relatively small. As one Negro leader put it to me, "The Negro people know who blows up their houses." Actually, in the aftermath of the prosecution, we found that many Negroes trusted us more than they ever had before. The abuse to which we had been subjected seemed to place us closer to their world. Their feeling was perhaps articulated by a Negro minister almost a year after the indictments when Carl started to leave a gathering of Negro ministers saying he thought maybe they wanted to discuss some things in private. "Oh, sit down and stay," the minister said, smiling, "you're practically colored anyway."

But despite their disapproval, most Louisville Negroes were silent in that period immediately following our indictment. This was of course partly because hysteria in the community had reached such a pitch that anyone who came publicly to our defense ran the risk of instantly being called a Communist himself. And among the Negro people the fear of this kind of attack was not always — perhaps not predominantly — a personal thing: it was also a fear for their cause. Knowing the tremendous odds they already faced in their efforts for equality, many of them felt that to invite the additional burden of this kind of smear meant needlessly jeopardizing their struggle. The small minority who did speak up in our support took a quite different position. They argued that it was dangerous to be silent just because white people who opposed segregation were labeled Red; they said this simply further encouraged the use of this tactic and imperiled the chances of joint Negro-white efforts toward integration. But the view of this minority did not gain widespread acceptance.

There were also other more complex factors involved in the silence of the Negro people. For one thing, our imprisonment did not loom nearly so large in the eyes of the Negro people as it did in our own eyes or in the eyes of some other white people. For the Negro people generally, frame-up is no novelty. Negroes have been unjustly imprisoned in the South for generations. Jails are an old story to them and sometimes to be expected.

For another thing, their silence reflected a certain stoic patience. As one Negro minister told me a year later:

"Of course we know this has all been a way of getting around arresting the people who blew up the house. We want those people arrested, because no one can really be safe in Louisville until they are. But don't worry. The truth of this thing will come out eventually. It will all come out; justice will win in the end. We can wait."

The Negro people in America had been waiting for justice for three hundred years; they could wait a little longer.

Among the white people too who disapproved of the prosecution's action, fear of the Red label was one of the predominant reasons for silence. But here also there were additional, more complex factors — different from those that operated among the Negro people. Generally intellectuals who considered themselves liberals, these white people were profoundly shocked by the grand jury investigation, the indictments, the raids on private houses. To them, the whole sequence of events seemed a grave injustice. Of course, as every lawyer and newspaper reporter knows, rank injustices occur every day in most courts. But in this case the victims were people who could not be conveniently classified as criminals and forgotten. Furthermore, the victims were people who were vigorously protesting what had happened to them. The case itself was community news — and later would become national and international news. All of these factors called the affair sharply to the attention of liberal citizens on whose lives neither the justice nor the injustice of the courts ordinarily impinged. They were astounded and concerned and they felt they should do something.

Some of them did do something. Some of them raised the money for the defense to buy the expensive transcript of the grand jury proceedings. Several months later, some of them organized a chapter of the American Civil Liberties Union in Louisville, stating that the experiences the community had been through had convinced them of the need for such an organization.

But most of these people were not willing to extend their protest about the case to a personal defense of the defendants. They were concerned — and many of them said so frankly — about the violations of civil liberties that they saw, but they strongly disapproved of the defendants themselves. Basically, no matter what reason they gave, this cleavage turned on the segregation issue. At best, they thought our action in buying the house for the Wades was extremely ill-advised. At worst, they thought that in a way we had actually asked for the trouble that befell us and deserved little help. In fact, some of them felt a deep resentment against us because they thought that in a way we were to blame, by our radical actions on the segregation issue, for the prosecutor's subsequent attack on civil liberties — an attack which potentially threatened them all and had disturbed the peaceful live-and-let-live atmosphere that had prevailed in Louisville. The touchstone of their attitude is that

practically none of these same people had been concerned enough
about the events on Rone Court during the summer to come to
Andrew Wade's support in any way. They were aroused by the
later attacks on civil liberties, but they had not been aroused by
the attacks on a Negro's right to live in the home of his choice —
at least not to the point of taking any action.

The most notable exception to the pattern of silence throughout
the city was among the Louisville lawyers who were willing to come
to our defense. We never had any shortage of lawyers. The Negro
attorney of the Wade Defense Committee, C. Ewbank Tucker,
remained firm through the whole storm. Later another Negro
attorney, Harry S. McAlpin, entered the case as one of my lawyers
and to defend Vernon Bown on the bombing charge, and he
worked long and hard on our behalf. Other Negro lawyers offered
their services in various ways.

But among the city's white lawyers too there were those — for
different reasons perhaps — who were willing to act. The first
white lawyer to enter the case was Grover G. Sales, for years past
the Kentucky attorney for the national office of the American Civil
Liberties Union. Years before he had risked his life to go into
eastern Kentucky to defend the besieged Harlan miners during their
early efforts to organize a union. Through the years he had come to
the defense of unpopular people whose legal rights he thought were
being violated. The logic of his life and his beliefs led him into the
courtroom at the moment when the hysteria surrounding the grand
jury investigation was at its height. He came as an observer for the
ACLU and later became defense counsel for Louise Gilbert.

Because Sales' health prevented his continuing to take an active
part in the case, he later arranged for another Louisville lawyer,
Louis Lusky, to carry on the work of the ACLU in the case. Lusky
came of a very conservative Louisville family, and for the most part
he was quite conservative in his own views. But he had a deep
belief in civil liberties; his philosophy of society and government
held that the public good is best served if people of all points of
view have the right to express their opinions freely, this being the
only way to assure that social changes are effected peaceably. He
possessed outstanding legal talent, and for years he had been a
student of constitutional law as it relates to civil liberties; he had
written articles on this subject for law reviews. This case presented

an opportunity to carry his scholarly interest in the subject into the arena of action. It presented the opportunity under somewhat trying circumstances, since his family was in the real estate business, and it was the real estate interests in Louisville who were among our strongest opponents. But when the challenge came, he never flinched. Once he had entered the case, he never faltered. In the early months, he served only as an observer for the ACLU and argued a motion for dismissal as *amicus curiae*; later, however, after Carl's trial he was appointed by the ACLU to serve as Carl's co-counsel on appeal, and no man was ever more faithful in the lawyer-client relationship. And he risked his career to do it.

In addition, two other white lawyers, Robert W. Zollinger and George Ambro, entered the case. Both were criminal lawyers with practically no previous experience in civil liberties cases. And both went through considerable soul-searching before they decided to take part in the defense.

Zollinger was one of those criminal lawyers who appear in almost every community, whose legal careers are as much a crusade for justice as a profession. For years, he had been struggling, sometimes almost singlehandedly, against what he felt were abuses of justice in Jefferson County courts, fighting each client's case with devotion and refusal to compromise. He had a deep belief in the United States Constitution and the principles of Anglo-Saxon law as the best system ever devised by man to protect the rights of the individual. But he felt that always there were people who sought to substitute the rule of men for the rule of law and that a constant battle must be made to re-establish the rule of law. Usually, when he fought that battle he was fighting in the context of cases in which few people besides himself and his client were interested. He had little help. He was attracted to our case because here he saw a case where the violations of individual rights could not occur under cover of darkness and community indifference. As he later wrote himself, "The wonderful thing about the Braden case is that the abuse of civil liberties occurred to people . . . vocal enough to fight back." But it was also a case full of danger and the certainty of disapproval from many in the community. It was not an easy case — and he didn't have an easy time making up his mind.

Carl and I had known Zollinger casually for a number of years, so it was natural that when trouble loomed during the grand jury investigation it was to him we turned. For two weeks, he hesitated. One day he would be available when we called. Then three days would go by and he would not return our calls. Finally, he would call again, often late at night, and after we had talked together awhile he would sound more confident. On the last day of the grand jury investigation, when we were subpoenaed to appear again, we did not know whether he would be on hand or not.

When we got to the courtroom, he was there. As we stood talking, I commented on the charged atmosphere in the court and said to him:

"I guess you are getting a lot of criticism around here for representing us."

"Oh yes," he replied. "But suddenly I don't care any more."

I saw that something had happened to him since the last time we had talked with him.

"You know," I told him, "there's a hymn we sing in the Episcopal Church; it starts off with the lines, 'Once to every man and nation, comes the moment to decide; In the strife of Truth with Falsehood, for the good or evil side.' "

Zollinger's eyes lit up.

"That's my favorite poem," he said. "I was reading it last night."

And then he quoted back to me a stanza of that poem which our church has made into a hymn, written appropriately enough by James Russell Lowell in regard to the abolitionist movement of a century ago: "Then to side with Truth is noble when we share her wretched crust, Ere her cause bring fame and profit, and 'tis prosperous to be just; Then it is the brave man chooses, while the coward stands aside . . ."

I knew that he had made up his mind.

Somewhat the same conflicts raged in the mind of George Ambro, who eventually represented LaRue Spiker. A Catholic and a strong humanitarian, Ambro led an exhausting life as a lawyer because he identified himself emotionally with all of his clients and lived through their ordeals. He had a strong urge to help the underdog. He was not especially concerned with all the issues in our case; but we were under attack and we were the underdogs. He was afraid and said so frankly, but he felt he had to help. And in the end, he too made up his mind.

Perhaps for us the most appalling thing of all, in that October

1954, was the realization that for much of white Louisville, among the people who did not know us personally, we had become the personification of all Evil. The week after our indictment, the Shively *Newsweek* ran a question-and-answer interview with Scott Hamilton. And this was the first question and answer:

> Q: If the Bradens are convicted, what is the maximum penalty they can receive?
>
> A: They can serve up to twenty-one years in prison, receive a $10,000 fine, or both.

The luncheon clubs continued to pass their resolutions. People wrote letters to the newspapers congratulating the prosecutor. The street talk and the gossip were more expressive than the formal resolutions and the written word. One woman employee in the courthouse stated openly that a trial was too good for us, and that we ought to be tortured and killed. A white minister who was a friend of ours told me in a shocked voice of hearing people at his country club — people he had thought to be "civilized men and women" — saying that they really thought "in a case like this lynching might be a good thing." I recalled with a start the remark about lynching from my gentle friend so long ago in Alabama — one of the episodes that had made me know that I must oppose segregation; it seemed that my life had come full circle.

Appalling too was the realization that to others who did not know us we had become the personification of Good. Often as I walked along the streets in the Negro sections of town some man or woman I had never seen before, recognizing me from newspaper pictures, would stop me and say softly words to this effect: "I want you to know I am praying for you. I can't do anything, but I'm praying. Thank God people like you and your husband are alive."

It was a situation that was to spread as the case progressed and became more widely known. To some people we were the Spirit of Evil; to others, we were the Spirit of Good. It was appalling because we knew so well that we were neither one. We were simply two people who believed, rightly or wrongly, in certain things and had to act on our beliefs. But our actions had hurled us into a situation where the social problems that beset the South and the nation were dramatized. And we became symbols — symbols that had not too much relation to reality.

Finally, on October 22, we made Carl's bond. His mother's house covered part of it. A Negro couple, long friends of ours whom we had helped in a previous difficulty of their own, braved public criticism to post their house, and we were able to borrow $2,000 cash to make up the difference.

Louise Gilbert and LaRue Spiker had been released from jail before me, their bonds posted by a friend of Louise's and by LaRue's family. Lewis Lubka's family was able to make his bond quickly after his indictment. By early November, all of the defendants were out of jail except for Bown and Ford, who were to remain many months longer. Talking into the wind of the hysteria around us, we all kept saying that the only real issue was the question of who blew up the Wade house. Bown, charged with actually setting the explosion, firmly maintained he had been in Milwaukee on the night of the bombing and demanded immediate trial on the bombing charge. Later he was to file in the court sworn statements of three persons who testified he had been with them in Milwaukee that night at the exact moment when the explosion occurred. But in the hysterical atmosphere of that fall of 1954 he and we were like voices crying in the wilderness. "Sedition" had become the issue of the day. The prosecution announced it would try Carl Braden first on the charge of sedition.

We felt we were living in a fantasy. We knew the whole theory of the prosecution was ridiculous — but how much of white Louisville knew it, Louisville that had needed a scapegoat so badly? Even some people who were generally friendly to us adopted a wait-and-see attitude. We were caught up in an hysteria we could not dissipate. It was like fighting shadows, and sometimes the shadows seemed to engulf us. At that time few people away from Louisville had had time to hear about the case, and we had as yet little assistance from outside Kentucky. We did have lawyers. We had the Constitution of the United States on our side. And we had the facts on our side. But these seemed scant protection when we knew that so much furious public opinion was massed against us, and most of that which was not against us was silent. We proceeded to prepare for trial — to fight in the courtroom a battle that we inwardly knew would never be decided finally in the courts but only in the hearts and minds of men.

18

The Great Exorcism

Carl's trial opened on November 29, 1954, and lasted thirteen days. It is not my purpose here to argue the legal points or to express an opinion as to whether the evidence against Carl or the law supported his conviction. These points have been adequately argued — for him and against him — in the courts. I am more interested in the atmosphere that surrounded the trial and what the trial meant to Louisville. For by this time, Carl and I — our guilt or innocence — did not matter very much in the larger scheme of things. We had become symbols.

On the opening day of the trial, the courtroom was filled. I sat on a bench at the rear of the big room during the jury selection and watched the people leaning forward avidly to hear the proceedings. I soon realized that these people had not come as our friends and most had not come out of simple curiosity. They had come because they had some inner need to see a witch burned. And they waited breathlessly as they watched. I heard a feminine voice near to me say:

"Why do they bother to try the nigger-lover? He's nothing but a Communist — he should be lynched."

I turned to look in the direction from which the voice came. I was startled when I saw the woman who was speaking. She was an elderly woman, and the lines of her face were gentle. But there was a light in her eyes that was out of keeping with everything else in her face.

The jury selection was finally completed; it was an all-white jury of course, for the prosecution had used its challenges to eliminate the few Negroes on the panel. The actual trial started

with Scott Hamilton's opening statement to the jury. He stated that
the prosecution would prove Carl was a Communist, and then he
moved on to the crux of the case:

> Now another argument or policy or theory of communism is
> . . . the communists want to create class conflicts throughout
> the world. In other words, they want to see trouble between
> the colored and the white races in this country. . . . Now, in
> view of that, the evidence will show that last March Andrew
> Wade IV and his wife entered into an agreement with Carl
> Braden and his wife whereby the Bradens would buy a house
> here in what you might refer to as a white residential section
> out here near Shively. . . .

He then went on to outline in minute detail the purchase and resale
of the house on Rone Court. The tone of the prosecution was set.

It soon became apparent that the prosecution had two major
objectives in the trial. The first was to prove that Carl was a Communist. The second was to prove that racial incidents are deliberately planned by Communists to arouse class conflicts. As the
assistant prosecutor, Higgins, put it later — quoting Benjamin
Gitlow — in his closing argument to the jury:

"He told you the Negro problem was founded in Moscow itself."

This sweeping statement that blotted out three hundred years
of American history was a simple explanation, and Louisville needed
a simple explanation.

The technique adopted by the prosecution to attain its first
objective — proving Carl to be a Communist — was threefold:
First, they introduced books taken in the raid at our house, works
of Marx and Lenin and Stalin and other Communists, as well as
other books by non-Communist socialists. Then, second, they
introduced personal papers such as letters taken from our house
to show our connection with what they described as Communist-
front organizations — the Progressive Party, the American Peace
Crusade, the Negro Labor Council, and others. Then they tied all
this together by putting on the stand nine paid professional ex-
Communist witnesses all of whom testified that the books and papers
that had been introduced would only be found in the home of a
Communist. These witnesses came from all parts of the country;

none of them claimed to have any personal knowledge of Kentucky, and none of them claimed to know Carl.[1]

The technique by which the prosecution sought to attain its second objective — showing that Communists deliberately stir up racial conflict and that therefore as a Communist Carl had plotted the incidents on Rone Court to cause trouble — was also threefold. First, they set the stage with their first witness. This was Mrs. Martha Edmiston, an ex-Communist from Ohio. She testified, among other things, that she had been taught in the Communist Party to provoke racial incidents and racial strife wherever possible. Immediately after her testimony, and as the second link in the chain, the prosecution put Andrew Wade on the stand to tell about the purchase of the house on Rone Court. The story itself was simple and factual, but the tone which had already been set by the prosecution now gave it sinister overtones. And then, as the third step, the series of ex-Communist witnesses followed the testimony of Andrew Wade to corroborate what Mrs. Edmiston had said — that a primary purpose of the Communist Party is to create racial conflict.

The high point of the trial tension came on the fifth and sixth days of the testimony when Manning Johnson and Leonard Patterson testified for the prosecution. Johnson and Patterson both identified themselves as ex-Communists, and they were both Negroes. The following is an excerpt from Johnson's testimony:

Q: Mr. Johnson, what was the program of the Communist Party on the Negro question in the United States?

A: The program of the Communist Party on the Negro question in the United States is that of bringing about in the South of a Negro state or government, Negro republic. As the program states, that the party must organize the Negroes in the Black Belt of the South, involve them in struggles for the purpose of cutting out of the South a state. This state would begin on the eastern shore of Maryland, running a zig-zag course across the former Confederate states, driving a wedge into Texas. This whole area in the South is to be united into a Negro

[1] The nine witnesses were Mrs. Martha Edmiston, John Edmiston, Arthur Paul Strunk, Benjamin Gitlow, Maurice Malkin, Manning Johnson, Leonard Patterson, James Glatis, and Matt Cvetic.

republic where the Negroes will establish their own army, their own police force, the executive, judicial and legislative instruments of government; to take the land from the white landowners, give it to the Negroes, confiscate the factories, the mills, and the mines, and make them the property of this Negro state. . . .

Q: What is to happen to the properties that belong here in Kentucky, for instance, to the white people?

. . . .

A: The program calls for taking away the land from the white owners in the South and distributing it among the Negroes.

. . . .

The program calls for the arrest of all the State and local officials of government, their imprisonment, and their liquidation.

. . . .

Q: Now can you give us some of the methods and techniques which were taught and used by the Communist Party from your personal knowledge, to bring about this racial rebellion?

A: Yes, we had a number of discussions in the school at the time on the tactics, techniques, and methods of bringing about a general rebellion of Negroes in the South. We were told that we were to utilize any grievance that the Negro has in the South, to stir up situations that would provoke acts of violence, that could be utilized by the Party to incite the whole populace against the constituted authorities in that particular area.

And in Patterson's testimony:

Q: Just briefly what was the purpose of the Communist Party in inducing Negroes to join from your own knowledge?

A: . . . I was told by the Communist Party of the United States and also by the Communist International that it was my duty as a trained Negro leader in the Communist Party to take the lead in mobilizing a broad Negro liberation movement in the United States, and in particular in the southern states to organize this movement and bring it under the influence and leadership of the Communist Party, and this movement being used to set up a separate Negro state in the southern states, a separate Negro government, with the right of such government to break away from the federated United States . . . and I was instructed in order to build up this movement that I must educate other Communist Party members to go and work together with this movement and raise the slogan in the southern states of confiscation of the land from the white landowners and give it to the landless Negroes. In other words, go into Kentucky, go into Alabama, and which I did go and attempt to put this into practice and get the Negroes together, and then in order to get them together we'll throw out the slogan, "We'll take this land from this white landowner over there and we'll give it to Negroes."

I was not in the courtroom on these days, as the defense attorneys were keeping me away from the trial thinking they might want me to testify later. But I felt some of the impact of the atmosphere that was building up when I met a friend of ours, a Negro minister, as he was leaving the courthouse. Most Louisville Negroes were following the trial very closely through the newspapers, TV, and radio, but very few came to the courtroom; he was one of the exceptions.

"I had to leave for a while, Anne," he said. "You just get to feeling uncomfortable — feel like you need some air. It's getting pretty bad — I think if somebody lit a match in there the whole place would explode."

It was hard to comprehend.

"What's doing it?" I asked.

"Johnson's testimony, mostly," he said, "and now Patterson — theirs has been the most damaging. I don't like the way those jurors are looking at Carl now. All that about taking the land away from the white people and giving it to the Negroes — that's what's getting them. They figure that's the thing you all did on Rone Court."

"But we didn't *take* land from anybody," I said. "We bought a house."

"Doesn't matter," he replied. "That's what they're thinking. It fits the pattern."

By the time the prosecution closed its testimony-in-chief, it was obvious to the defense that what was needed for its case was not only facts but a quieting influence in the courtroom. For four and a half days, it tried to bring that influence to bear. Carl took the stand to testify in his own defense; between direct and cross examination, he testified two days. He stated as simply as he could his reasons for buying the house for the Wades, his feelings about the injustice of racial segregation. He stated that he had never been a member of the Communist Party and gave his understanding of the purposes of the organizations to which he did belong. He took the books introduced by the prosecution one by one, explained what was in them, why he had them, what he thought of each one — whether it was objective or biased. After his testimony, a number of people who had known Carl and worked with him over a period of years took the stand to testify that they had never known him to advocate violence in any form, had never known him to be a "trouble maker." One of them, the founder and chairman of the Louisville Labor-Management Committee, a mediation body, testified that Carl had in fact helped in the organization of this committee and had rendered invaluable assistance in the prevention of several major strikes in the city. Gradually, the atmosphere became calmer. The crowd in the courtroom began to thin; the show was not going the way the audience wanted it to go.

When the defense rested at noon on the twelfth day of the trial, the prosecution announced that it would call one witness in rebuttal after the lunch recess. When we returned from lunch, the courtroom was crowded again. The word had evidently gone out that the show was going to be resumed. Alberta Ahearn, one of the white people who had been active in the Wade Defense Committee, took the stand. The prosecutor stated that the questioning would be brief, and that she was being called for restricted rebuttal purposes

— to contradict Carl's testimony that he was not a Communist. Mrs. Ahearn testified that she was an undercover agent for the Federal Bureau of Investigation, that Carl and I had recruited her into the Communist Party and that she had attended Communist meetings in our home. She testified specifically about six Communist Party meetings she said she had attended with Carl, all in the year 1954. She said she and Carl and one of our co-defendants, I. O. Ford, were members of a Communist cell. She made the general statement that at the meetings of this cell Communism, Marxist books, and related subjects were discussed; she did not specify exactly what was said on these subjects. In addition, she said discussions at the meetings centered around the American Peace Crusade, and she summarized the discussion by saying:

> . . . and briefly, we talked about peace, peace on Russian terms. That means abolition of the hydrogen bomb. In other words, to promote peace in the United States and things of that sort.

Nothing in her testimony bore on the situation surrounding the Wade house incident.

As she spoke, it was as if some magic rite were being performed in the courtroom. There was absolute silence among the spectators as they watched her, spellbound. The entire staff of the prosecutor's office was on hand for the occasion. As one of the assistant prosecutors questioned the witness, Hamilton and his other assistant stood near the judge's bench, excited and smiling in triumph.

Carl took the stand again to deny her testimony. He said that he did know Mrs. Ahearn and had long considered her a friend, that she had indeed visited in our home on numerous occasions, sometimes in the company of I. O. Ford. He said also that the Peace Crusade and some of the other subjects she had mentioned had been discussed when they were there together. But, he testified, the occasions were social gatherings or meetings of various committees and organizations, none of which included the Communist Party. This testimony made little impression in opposition to hers. It was his word against hers, and there was no doubt as to whom the jury wanted to believe.

By the time the prosecution began its final arguments to the jury, I had the feeling that the scene had ceased to be a courtroom; it had become instead some sort of mystic gathering, an ancient pagan sacrificial rite. The people who had gathered came filled with their guilts, their frustrations, their prejudices that they could not admit to themselves. All of the testimony had been a preparation service, and now in the closing moments of the ceremony the prosecutors summoned forth the evil spirits that plagued those who heard, spun them into a web and entwined them around Carl. The scene in the courtroom was staid and dignified; the judge sat on his bench in his formal black robes; the attorneys on either side spoke with courtesy and decorum. But as I sat there at the defense table and watched, I could almost see shadowy figures dancing around our feet and bowing before some sacrificial fire. And the high priests were intoning the words of a ritual.

Hamilton and Higgins divided the prosecution's closing argument between them. Hamilton took the first half, starting off quietly, listing the points he felt should be called to the jury's attention. He read from a book by Stalin saying that, for communism to conquer, all of "the class forces hostile to us" must become "sufficiently entangled" and "sufficiently at loggerheads with each other." Then he commented:

> Be sure and get that, and remember that when you go back to the jury room — "when all the class forces hostile to us" — certainly all good Americans regardless of their color are hostile to communism, and when and if we become at loggerheads with the colored people, the Jews, Catholics against the Protestants and that sort of thing, then we are at loggerheads. . . .

Next he referred to a letter the prosecution had introduced as having been found in our house. In it the writer had enclosed a newspaper clipping about a Negro's store being bombed in the small town of Manchester, Kentucky, and had asked that protests be made about the incident. Hamilton commented:

> I assure you that if a white man were accused of dynamiting that colored man's store, wouldn't that help to put us at loggerheads with each other?

It was Higgins who gave the final exhortation:

I say to you, gentlemen, as sincerely, as honestly as I can, that we should let this be a milestone in the historic fight of America today to stop this evil of pitting race against race, white against black, Catholic against the Protestants, Jew against the Gentile, rich against the poor. That's what they are trying to do. Let's stop it . . . It is a fact that, gentlemen, while we are playing, while we are sleeping, these people are digging, digging . . . for one purpose and one purpose alone, and that is to turn you against me, me against you, group against group, so that in our bitter struggles within ourselves we will become totally exhausted and when we lay prone, fatigued from our own inner struggle, they can descend upon us and conquer us. And ladies and gentlemen, I say to you when that happens, when that happens the darkness will descend upon this world that will make the blackness of the Dark Ages seem aglow. The entire world will become enslaved with despotic rulers and masters that will make the greatest tyrants of bygone history seem like benevolent schoolboys. Are we going to allow it to happen? I say that we will not . . . We must ruthlessly cut out this cancer of communism, and here is one place to start. And we will start it. We will start it, and we will do it, and you will do it gentlemen, just as sure as there is a living God to give you strength to do it . . . You will do it, gentlemen, when you retire to your jury room. No one is to enter that room with you, gentlemen, but the law in all its glory cannot prohibit Almighty God from sitting there with you . . . Ask His guidance when you go in there as to what to do. See what He tells you is necessary to prevent the destruction of His own houses of worship. And if you will follow through, if you, gentlemen, will perform your duty as jurors, this awful responsibility which your neighbors have put upon you here, you will find that man guilty as charged in the indictment and you will fix an appropriate punishment.

The jury's responsibility was clear. Carl had become the personification of Evil, the source of the troublesome race problem, the destroyer of sacred home and country. If he was destroyed, everything evil in the world would be destroyed. No one would have to worry any more about why Negroes' homes were bombed, why Negroes could not have decent housing in Louisville, why decent human beings could not live at peace with their fellow men. No one's conscience need trouble him longer as to why he could look at evil in the world and do nothing about it, why he could see a Negro's home bombed and keep his silence. Here he could strike a single blow and be rid of it all.

There was never any doubt in my mind, as I sat at the defense table waiting for the jury to return, as to what the verdict would be. The jury was out three hours, and I sat there alone most of the time; for Carl, according to court procedures, had been put in a cell when the case went to the jury, and even the few spectators who had been somewhat friendly to us were now apparently afraid to be seen talking to me. One person in the courtroom did bring me a grapevine report (for the deliberations in a jury room do reach the grapevine) that the debate holding the jury out was whether to give Carl the maximum sentence allowed by the law — twenty-one years in prison — or whether to give him only fifteen years.

Finally, the jury returned and announced its verdict: guilty, and a sentence of fifteen years in prison and a $5,000 fine.

The crowd in the courtroom had thinned again now. Many people had left, as it was suppertime, and had gone home to await the news of the verdict, which was a foregone conclusion, on their radio and television sets.

Before the verdict was announced, the judge told the remaining spectators there must be no demonstrations in the courtroom. For the most part they obeyed his orders. Only a kind of sigh and mumble of relief swept over the sparse crowd as the sentence was announced. Only one man shouted "Lynch him!" and ran from the building. Carl went away with the deputy sheriffs to the county jail. I sat at the defense table until most of the crowd had gone before I left with our lawyer. And white Louisville went home to its beds that night to sleep quietly — its duty done, its heart cleansed, and its evil exorcised.

19

The Shadow of the Wall

At the time of Carl's trial, many people were under the impression that Andrew Wade turned against Carl and testified to things that were damaging to him. That was not the case. Andrew's testimony was simple and straightforward. He told the story of his search for a house, his inability to find one, his seeking out of Carl and me to buy him a house as a favor. He said nothing at the trial that could have been construed as damaging to us in any way — except insofar as our willingness to buy the house for him could be made to appear sinister.

The impression that he testified against Carl arose because the prosecution read into the trial record a portion of a statement Andrew had made in Hamilton's office on November 8, 1954 — three weeks before the trial opened. This was quoted in the newspapers, and many people thought Andrew had made the statement during the trial. And, on November 8, he did express distrust of us.

From the moment we were indicted, the prosecution pursued one major strategy. That was to get Andrew Wade to turn against us, to get him to testify that it was we who had conceived the idea of purchasing the house on Rone Court, that we had put him up to it, that we had engineered the entire project from beginning to end — that he in short had been used by us. Hamilton and his assistants of course believed this to be the case. Otherwise, none of their theories would fit. But if this were true, everything fitted. To their minds it could not be otherwise, because a Negro who thought for himself and asserted his own rights was unthinkable. The only possible explanation for such a Negro was that some white man was telling him what to do. Their main object was to get Andrew to confirm their theories.

We knew from the beginning that this was their strategy. It never worried us. The thought that Andrew might ever turn on us was beyond the remotest possibility in our minds. Some of our friends and lawyers worried about it, but we told them to quiet their fears. There were two reasons for our confidence. One was that we knew so well ourselves that none of Hamilton's theories fitted Andrew — he had never in his adult life let any white person tell him what to do and would not have allowed us to do so even if we had wanted to. We could not therefore conceive of his saying anything that would support Hamilton's theories in this direction. The other was that we remembered so well the long summer just past, when the Wades and we had gone through such hell together, when we had faced the same hostile white world. Sometimes we felt we were no longer a part of the white world; we lived in Andrew's and Charlotte's world — a world of color and abuse. Living in the same world as we seemed to, we thought, there was no possibility that there could ever be mistrust between us.

We knew that Andrew was being called to the prosecutor's office often for questioning, and that he went when he was called. We felt that his appearances were unnecessary, since they were not in response to subpoena. But Andrew, we knew, thought it was better to go, and we did not seek to influence him. We felt that he knew what he was doing and could handle his own problems. He usually let us know after he had been to Hamilton's office and related something of the questioning. It seemed to be the same questions over and over — the details of events that had led to the purchase of the house, the details of events that had preceded the bombing. We even knew that he had been to the office on November 8. He told us immediately afterward that there had been two strange men there helping Hamilton question him. We learned later that they were representatives of the House Committee on Un-American Activities in Washington. They had helped Hamilton to prepare for Carl's trial, and indeed we learned later that it was through them that he secured the services of the professional ex-Communist witnesses who testified for the prosecution.

But we did not know of the transcript taken of the questioning of Andrew that day, or what it said, until Hamilton produced it on the third day of Carl's trial.

On that day, Andrew was testifying. He had stated, among other things, that he had never had any reason to suspect the honest motives of Carl Braden. He had said that he and Carl had worked toward the common goal of bringing "peace to Rone Court." Then Hamilton read from the transcript of November 8. He read as follows:

Q: Why did you leave the Progressive Party, Mr. Wade?

A: Well, it had started getting a smear, turning pinkish. . . .

Q: That was during the presidential campaign . . . When Henry Wallace was running as candidate?

A: That's right.

Q: And how did you go about leaving the Party, did you resign?

A: . . . I caught the attention of the bunch and made a speech and told them I was quitting. . . .

Q: And you said you were leaving because of the Red tinge?

A: That's right. . . .

Q: You say you left the Progressive Party because of the tinge that was connected to the party, and that would indicate to me you have some feeling about left-wing organizations operating in this country. In view of your background . . . how do you feel about some of this material in which you have become involved or some of these incidents, especially in the light of the stories which have been written by Carl Braden? Do you personally feel that you have been used by this group?

A: I feel I have been used by both groups.

Q: What other group . . .?

A: The people that originally started the trouble out there, made an open door to these people that came in. I believe if we American people wouldn't create friction among ourselves, we wouldn't welcome them so easily.

Q: You mean the people in the community in which you moved into?

A: I wouldn't generalize it that far. I don't think too many of the people were hostile, but it was instigated by Mr. Rone and any of the people he collected together. I think their attitude in the beginning made it an open way for the Communists to move in, if that is true, and the fact of all this literature confiscated I will say that I think it's a very bad situation, that it may be somewhat their right to have literature, but it looks mighty bad.

Hamilton then asked Wade if he had in fact made these statements on November 8. Wade replied that he had. He could not say anything else. Obviously, he had made them.

Hamilton was required to show the defense a copy of the transcript from which he had been questioning Wade. That afternoon after court recessed, we took it home and read it all. That night was the turning point of the trial for me.

I will never understand why Hamilton did not quote more of it into the record of the trial. There were parts of it much more damaging than the parts he read.

At one point, the questioners read from the article Carl had written the previous June for Donald Renner's little magazine. (This article was apparently what the House Committee representatives referred to when they asked Andrew about the "stories" Carl had written.) In the article, Carl had quoted several of the statements attributed to Andrew by the Louisville *Defender* in that newspaper's first interview with him after the cross-burning. The *Defender* had headlined its story in big black type with one of the quotes, "WE INTEND TO LIVE HERE OR DIE HERE." Neither Carl nor I was present when the *Defender* reporter interviewed Andrew, but it never occurred to us to doubt that the statements were authentic, since Andrew was pleased with the story when it was printed in the *Defender*. Later when Carl requoted the statements in the story he wrote, he seemed pleased again. Further than that, we had heard Andrew make similar statements in conversation throughout the period. The November 8 transcript in regard to these quotes follows:

Q: I have a manuscript here entitled, "Andrew Wade's House" [Carl's article in Renner's magazine], and you are quoted in this. For that reason, I want to make you familiar with the quotation. It says, "I will never sell, not even for $150,000," Wade declared. "I feel that the principle of living where you want to is too great to sell out. I would not be doing justice to my wife who loves the house and my children who are entitled to the best." Do you recall making that statement I just read?

A: I don't remember that exact amount of $150,000, but that was the idea.

Q: You don't remember ever giving any certain amount in a statement?

A: I might have, but I don't remember.

Q: Here is another question: "If our neighbors do not like our being here and feel they cannot live beside us or around us, let them move out. We are not moving." Did you make that statement?

A: I don't remember the statement, but I felt that way.

Q: All right, here is another statement. "We intend to live here or die here." Did you make that statement?

A: No.

Q: Now on the basis of these statements that I have just given to you and thinking about them, would you feel that anyone in writing such manuscript has tried to put words into your mouth or use you?

A: Yes.

Q: You have nodded your head in the affirmative, is that true?

A: That's right.

Q: Do you feel, Andrew, that Mr. Braden, when he wrote this, was trying to play this thing up bigger than it actually is?

A: Well —

Q: Trying to solicit sympathy or create agitation among races and people? Don't you think that, just from what he's read here, he's misquoted you several things through here, and I don't know if you've read it or not, that certainly indicate that. How do you feel about it?

A: I would say that what you think is true. There is no doubt that he was trying to, but I just don't want to, you know, before any trial, just condemn the man.

During that summer of 1954, Andrew had the habit of dropping by our house several times a week, sometimes every day. Sometimes he came on a specific piece of business, sometimes just to talk and discuss recent developments. Sometimes Charlotte was with him, and sometimes he came alone. After Carl and I were released from jail on bond, following the grand jury investigation and our indictment, we were rarely at home except to sleep. Jimmy and Anita were away in Alabama; Sonia had gone to stay with relatives in New York; we had constant business away from home, and our home life was practically nil. For this reason, we formed the habit of dropping by the Wades' fairly often to discuss developments with them as they arose. Andrew had suggested to us after our release from jail that we stop by there to eat if we were ever in need of a meal and didn't have time to cook. It never occurred to us that Andrew's feeling toward us might have changed, that he might not be as glad to see us as always. We of course did not know then all that had been going on during his questioning in Hamilton's office day after day; he certainly never gave us any indication that he did not consider the charge that we conspired to blow up his house as preposterous as we considered it. One day we heard a rumor that Andrew himself might also be indicted. We of course went to him immediately to tell him and to discuss with him the possibilities of raising bond quickly if he should be arrested. All these things came up in the November 8 questioning:

Q: Mr. Wade, in this statement, strictly from a point of fact, this sentence, "We have had dinner with them and they have visited in our home," is that a statement of fact that they have had dinner in your home?

A: Yes. We never invited them to dinner as a family, but on two occasions Carl — one, Carl called me and said, "How about us coming over to dinner?" I told him — after the indictments — I said, "At any time that you" — while Anne was out of town — "At any time that you are scuffling for a meal, you can drop by and eat with us."

Q: Just before that you said he called you and said, "How about we coming over for dinner?" Are we to understand that he invited himself to your house?

A: That's right.

Q: And that was after the indictments were returned?

A: That's right, and I graciously accepted, and my wife had to hustle up some food.

And later in the transcript:

Q: Have you seen Braden much since he was released from jail?

A: Yes, I used to go over to his house quite often in the day, but after this mess came up, I stopped going except on rare occasions, and lately he has been coming by my house, and my wife throws up both hands when he comes up.

Q: What does he say to you?

A: More so trying to find out how I feel, if I suspect them or not.

Q: What does he say to indicate that, to make you think he's feeling you out?

A: Well, "Isn't this preposterous? Look what they are doing to us."

Q: Does he ask you what goes on down here every time you come down?

A: Oh yes. He has some means of finding out, every time I walk out of here.

Q: He questions you pretty close every time you walk out of here?

A: Yes. Sometimes even tells me what happened in here.

Q. Tells you what happened in here?

A: Yes. He told me what was discussed in here. I remember one time, Mr. Hamilton said that they might bring down indictments against four or maybe five, and when I got home he contacted me and said "They are going to bring down indictments, I understand from the grapevine."

Q: Did he say who the indictments would be returned against?

A: No, he didn't call any names, but now Saturday night he said to me, he said, "Wade," he said, "you had better get somebody — get in touch with some people and see if you can get somebody to commit themselves on going your bond."

Q: Where did that take place, that conversation?

A: In my house in the living room, Saturday night.

Q: Who all was present?

A: My wife was in the kitchen. Only Carl and myself. They dropped by to give me those papers there.

Q: How long did they stay?

A: They invited themselves to eat again. They ate chili. He said, "I never have refused chili," and walked on in and they took over.

And still later in the transcript:

Q: Have you gotten the impression that he is trying to show you that he is your friend by bringing a great deal of attention to this, by his writing the articles, the press releases, the radio programs?

A: Yes. I am forced to agree with Mr. Hamilton there, and I have to do all my thinking in that line because that is the most dangerous angle. And naturally, while thinking in that line, I feel the way you just expressed. I am just reluctant about condemning them any further than I know. Everything I know, I try to tell it to you.

One of the things that the interviewers sought to establish was that Carl and I had actually written the statements that Andrew gave to the press from time to time. The only element of truth in this is that Andrew on occasion brought us some statement he planned to make and asked us, on the basis of our professional experience, to condense it and put it into a form the newspapers would be most likely to use. I don't remember that we ever suggested to him that he issue a statement to the press except once. This was on the occasion of our second indictment when we were charged with conspiring to bomb his house. On the day this indictment was returned, Hamilton had summoned Andrew before the grand jury and had told the newspapers that Andrew had been the only witness. The obvious result of this action was to give the public the impression that Andrew had given testimony that indicated our guilt of the charge. Andrew told us the next day that the questioning of him before the jury simply covered the same old ground he had been over scores of times. On this one occasion we did strongly urge him to make a statement to the newspapers, to make clear that he had not told the grand jury anything that would by any stretch of the imagination justify the indictment, and he did make such a statement. Our request for this statement came up during the questioning on November 8, and Andrew said at one point:

> A: . . . and Dad jumped on him [Carl] and told him, "I don't know whether you guys are guilty or not." He said, "Whether we are guilty or not?" He said, "Yes, I don't know you are not guilty. I don't know about my own grandfather, and until I find out and until the Court decides, that's the best way to do, just take it easy. . . ."

I am fairly certain no such conversation ever took place between Carl and Andrew's father, or between Carl and Andrew, or between me and either one of them. I was present when Carl talked with both Wades on the day in question, and I would have certainly remembered such a remark, because it expressed the exact opposite of what I thought they were thinking. But as I read Andrew's words in the transcript on that night during Carl's trial I realized that he had undoubtedly thought his father had made this statement because it was evidently what both of them were thinking and wanting to say at that point.

There was no statement of fact in the entire transcript that could have hurt us, for actually there was no harmful fact that Andrew could have stated. And I am sure he never lied about anything. But the tone of the interview was devastating. It was the statement of a man talking about a man and woman he did not trust.

When I had finished reading it that night, I felt that all of the fight had been drained out of me. I could not analyze my feelings at the time; I knew even as they overwhelmed me that they were subjective and that I should not give in to them. But I could not help it. I felt that the things we had been working for — a world without segregation, a world of understanding and brotherhood— had turned to dust in my hand. The more rational part of my mind chided my emotional self as it reacted. "What's the matter with you?" the rational self asked. "Is it that you wanted Andrew to 'appreciate' what you did for him? Haven't you got past that stage yet? I thought you'd always said you opposed segregation because

of what it did to you as much as for what it did to the Negro people.
I thought you always said you bought the house for Andrew and
Charlotte because you believed in a world without segregation,
because you wanted to live in that kind of world and wanted your
children to live in that kind of world. Did you really do it just for
Andrew, and was appreciation from him the price you charged?"
But my emotional self stood firm and unshaken and answered: "No,
it wasn't that I wanted him to appreciate us. Of course we bought
the house because it represented the kind of world we wanted as
much as he wanted it. But that's just it — he had to want that kind
of world too. I thought we did it because of an ideal we shared with
him. I didn't ask appreciation as a price, but I asked — I assumed
— that he trust us, that he feel as we did that we were all working toward a common goal. Now the dream I thought we had
shared is gone. If it was not his dream too, if he did not from his
point of view see us as the sharers of a dream, the dream did not
exist. We have been chasing shadows." I felt tired and defeated.

Carl was much saner in his reaction.

"Don't worry about it now, Anne," he said. "Remember that
we're all under tension. Wait until you can look at things more
calmly. And don't say anything to Andrew about it — not now
anyway. He has been under terrific pressure, don't forget. You
don't know what you would have done if you had been in his place."

I did not know, and I didn't care.

But I took Carl's advice. I did not mention the transcript to
Andrew during the trial. Some way I pulled myself together and
got through the trial. Outwardly I was not changed. I continued
to run errands for the defense lawyers and do what I could to help.
Inside I felt futile and empty.

Later, when the smoke from Carl's trial had cleared away, I
came to look at the incident more rationally. I began to see that it
did not represent the end of the world. I began to sense the terrible
pressure Andrew had been under on that November 8 when he was
questioned. I was seeing the Wades with a good bit of regularity
after Carl's trial, and nothing seemed changed. Carl of course was
in prison and I was at home alone, and Andrew called often to see
how I was getting along, to ask me to stop by and see him and
Charlotte.

Finally, several months after Carl's trial ended and while he was still in prison, I had occasion to be in the Wades' store late one afternoon when no one except Andrew was there. I felt that my emotions over the transcript were sufficiently under control for me to discuss it calmly, and I felt it should be discussed. So I brought it up.

"Andrew," I said, "there is one thing I need to know. Is there the least shadow of suspicion in your mind that we might have had anything to do with blowing up your house — or that we have used you in some way?"

"No." Andrew's answer was firm and sure and quiet.

"But at one time you did have that suspicion?" I asked.

Andrew hesitated.

"You don't need to tell me," I said. "I know. You had doubts on that day when the people from the Un-American Committee questioned you in Hamilton's office, didn't you?"

"I was afraid you'd misunderstand that," he answered. "That part about your using me. You see they kept harping on that, and I wanted to bring out the other side — Rone's side. That's why I said I had been used by both sides — " Andrew began speaking in a tumble of words trying to explain.

"No, there's no need to apologize or to make excuses," I interrupted him. "We aren't mad about it. I was hurt at first — but I had no right to be. It wasn't your fault. But I'm not just talking about that one statement — we read the whole transcript, Andrew. Where you said we invited ourselves to dinner at your house, and you were tired of having us come around and Charlotte threw up her hands when she saw us coming. And how we had put words in your mouth. And how we seemed to be trying to get you on our side — I had always assumed we *were* on the same side — but — "

Now he interrupted me.

"You read it all very carefully, didn't you?" he asked. He was clearly embarrassed by it.

"Yes I did. It shook me to the roots of my being, Andrew. At that point, I didn't even care how the trial came out — I had lost all interest in everything. But I had no right to feel that way. I see that now, and I don't feel that way any more. But I felt I had to talk to you about it. It won't stop me from fighting now — because

I have to fight. But I have to know where you stand. I have to
know whether you trust us now or not."

Then, as if a floodwall had broken, Andrew spoke and told me
all that had been on his mind in the previous months.

"No, I don't have any doubts about you and Carl — or about
Bown or any of the others that got indicted, Anne," he said. "I
never did really. But there was a time last fall when I was confused. I was tired. I was worn out. I didn't know what to think about
anything. It's hard for me to explain what it was like after you all
were indicted. Hamilton had me in his office every other day —
sometimes for hours at a time. I told him from the beginning that
I knew you all couldn't have had anything to do with blowing up
the house. He just pooh-poohed that. He said, 'Oh, that theory's out
— we've got the evidence on them.' He kept telling me you were
just using me. Over and over — like a broken record. 'These people
are using you — they're using you.' I didn't believe it, but I didn't
know what to think. And then he began telling me that if I didn't
see that you were using me maybe I was in on the plot too — that
I wasn't out of this thing yet. That went on day after day — until
I didn't know what I was thinking or saying."

"Andrew, I understand," I said. "You don't have to — "

"No — " he broke in — "let me finish — I want to tell you
the truth about how it happened. I did begin to wonder. Just for
a little while. I didn't believe you all could have wanted to do me
any harm — but maybe somehow you thought some good might be
accomplished by the house blowing up. Or somebody else might
have persuaded you it would do some kind of good. Suppose you
were Communists — then maybe someone higher up had told
you to do it. It seems crazy now — but that's the kind of thing
that went through my mind. And then that day I made that statement in Hamilton's office — when the men from the Committee
were there — it all seemed so official, they'd come in from Washington and all that. And they all said — Hamilton said it too — that
there wasn't any doubt that you all were Communists, and they
said that the only purpose you had in buying the house was to cause
trouble and work for the overthrow of the government. And they
wanted to know where I stood — was that my purpose too? That's
what they were asking me. Well, I knew it wasn't my purpose, and

I didn't want to believe it was your purpose, but I — somehow I just didn't know what to think. And if that *was* your purpose, then maybe you had blown up the house. That day, that's when I was at my lowest ebb."

He paused — as if exhausted, remembering. Then he went on quietly:

"After that — when Carl's trial came and I saw Hamilton didn't really have any evidence against you all — I saw how wrong I had been. I'd been fooled — and I don't think I ever will be again . . ."

I listened to his words, and gradually I began to comprehend. Not about the pressure he had been under, because I already knew that. Just as I knew that everyone has his moments when he can no longer withstand pressure and from sheer fatigue must temporarily ride with the tide. But the significant thing was something else. Some people had said that Andrew had actually turned against us at that point because, under pressure, he was afraid — afraid of what might happen to him. But I had always known that this was not the basic thing. He may have been afraid; anyone who would not have been, at least a little bit, under those circumstances, would be superhuman. But I had known that fear alone would not make Andrew weaken. I had seen him risking death each night 'to travel the dark roads of Shively to go back to his house and what it symbolized; I knew that he had the strength to conquer simple fear. No, the basic truth was that when the pressure mounted and Andrew was battered with fatigue, he distrusted us. It may be that the distrust did come to the surface under the impact of pressure and exhaustion, but it could not have arisen out of a vacuum. It had to come from somewhere. And now I knew for sure where it came from.

"I hope you and Carl understand," Andrew said. I realized that I had been sitting silent for a long time and that he might misinterpret my silence for anger.

"Of course, I understand. Carl has always understood," I said, "and I should never have reacted in the way I did. I certainly don't blame you — I know what you must have gone through. I was only thinking of what a hard job it is we face, those of us — you and Carl and me and all the others, Negro and white — who dream of a world without color bars. I wonder if we will ever achieve it, Andrew, ever in our generation. We think we're tearing down the

wall, but then in a moment of crisis the shadow of the wall rises up
to separate us. I've often wondered how I would feel if I were a
Negro — I've wondered if I could ever trust *anyone* with white
skin. It would seem that if there could be any trust across the color
line anywhere it would be between you and Charlotte and Carl
and me. We went through so much together — it would seem there
couldn't be any wall left between us. And yet in *your* moment of
crisis, the wall was there."

I hesitated briefly, trying to think it all through — turning over
in my mind the doubts Andrew had described. Maybe somebody
told us to do it, he had said; somebody else might have persuaded
us; maybe there was something else we were influenced by. We
had seemed to know each other as well as any human beings
could — and yet he couldn't be sure Carl and I didn't have some
purpose he didn't have.

"Andrew," I said, "you felt you couldn't wholly trust us. Not
that you trusted Scott Hamilton either — not really — and not that
you would consciously have joined his side — although the effect of
that statement of yours was that you temporarily did join his side.
But the truth was you were caught between two white worlds, and
you couldn't be sure that either of them was your friend. And the
real reason you distrusted us, Andrew, was not because people were
saying we were red — *it's because we were white.*"

His protest was immediate.

"No, I don't think that was it. If you'd been colored — and all
the circumstances and charges and pressures the same — I think it
would have been the same."

"I don't believe it," I replied. "Oh, I don't mean that you would
trust every colored person or that you do. But knowing us as you
did, if we had been colored, you could never have had even one
moment of distrust. I believe that. No matter how tired you were —
no matter what anybody said about us — they could have said we
were Communists — they could have said we were the devil
himself — but none of it would have convinced you that we might
think it would be a good thing to blow up your house. You would
have been sure — you would have *known* — that we saw things
as you did. But we were white, and you couldn't be sure."

He did not answer this time, and I could not help but feel that
his silence meant that I was right.

"It's not your fault — or ours either," I went on. "It's the fault of this — this disease of segregation — we all grew up with it and it has conditioned us for life. We fight it — we'll continue to fight it, but we can never completely erase its mark from our lives. In the lives of our children maybe it will be different. Maybe our two children and your two children can know each other as human beings — can judge each other by what each does and not by the color of his skin. If this can be, our efforts won't have been in vain."

He nodded.

"I don't think they are in vain," he said. "I think our children will live in a different world."

And we turned to talking of other things.

It was to be many months before I had a chance to have a similar conversation with Charlotte. Unlike Andrew, who with Carl and me had held illusions that the wall's terrible shadow could be dissipated and color forgotten in our time, Charlotte showed no reluctance to admit to herself and to me that she had found it hard to trust us because of our color.

I had long known this. It was one afternoon back in June 1954 — one of those afternoons when the children and I had visited her on Rone Court — that she told me of her feelings as we sat drinking coffee together.

"I like to talk to you, Anne," she said. "I feel I can trust you. I never felt that way with a white person before. In fact, I never really knew a white person before. White people have always been my enemy. You and Carl are the first white people I've ever really known. When Bubba came home and told me you all had said you'd buy the house for us, I didn't believe it. I couldn't believe any white person would do something like that."

We were feeling our way in those days. The walls were high, but we were beginning to break through them. She was glad she had found a white person she could trust; I liked her very much. We had a great deal in common. We had children the same age. We had some of the same problems — problems that are common to all mothers and wives regardless of color. We were groping our way to a friendship that could forget the existence of color. If it had had more time, the embryo might have grown.

But it did not have time. Our indictment and the state's charges against us intervened. Having always been amazed and incredulous that a white couple would be willing to help her get a house, Charlotte did not find it too difficult to accept — at least partially — the charges against us, to believe that we had had an ulterior motive from the beginning.

I don't think she thinks so any more. Charlotte and I can talk again now. Sometimes I feel that we are beginning to get close to each other again, beginning to pull at the wall. But it is very high. I think often of the friends we might have been; there is much to draw us together; but the shadow of the centuries stands between us; I am not sure that the embryo that once started will ever grow.

I thought of all these things during that winter of 1954-1955, after my conversation with Andrew, when I finally decided to tell Jimmy the truth about why he was at his grandmother's and why his daddy never came to see him any more. The children stayed in Alabama all that winter and spring because, through those months, we were expecting my trial to come up momentarily. As often as I could, I went down to see them for a day or two. They were both at an age where they were developing rapidly, and it always gave me a start to see each time I visited them how much they had changed — things you don't notice so much when you live with your children every day and watch them develop gradually. Anita learned to talk in sentences down there that winter, and I remember how it surprised me: one time when I arrived she ran to greet me at the car, and I asked her what she had in her hand — as one often asks a baby a rhetorical question expecting no answer. I was startled when she looked up at me and replied quite distinctly, "I have a chocolate cookie." She was adapting easily to her new home, for she was young enough to take the change in her stride. But Jimmy who was three and had been his father's constant companion since he was a tiny baby was having a hard time. He was also developing faster than I at first realized, and finally I saw that he was beginning to figure things out in his own mind. He was becoming very suspicious of the excuses I had been giving him about his daddy being very busy and away working — suspicious and a little hurt that his daddy would be too busy under any circumstances to come to see him. So I decided I should tell him the true facts.

I told him the story in simple terms I thought he could understand. I built it around the Wades' little girl, Rosemary, because he had often played with her. I explained to him that Mother and Daddy had bought a house for Rosemary because her parents could not get her one, and I told him that some people had got very mad at Mother and Daddy because of this and had put Daddy in prison; I explained that prison was a place where Daddy was warm and comfortable and had plenty to eat but that the men who were mad at him just would not let him out to come to see Jimmy.

Jimmy was fascinated by the story. Somewhat surprisingly he appeared to be more interested in the part about Rosemary and her house than he was in this new place called prison; perhaps it was because the picture of prison did not really register with him until later. And his questions went to the heart of the matter.

"Why couldn't Rosemary's mother and daddy get her a house?" he asked. "What's wrong with them?"

"Because some of the people who lived near the house didn't want Rosemary and her mother and daddy to live there," I tried to explain.

"Why?" he persisted.

"Because they wanted someone else to live there."

"Who? Why didn't they want Rosemary?"

"They just didn't. They had funny ideas," I answered and changed the subject.

What answer was there? No one had ever told Jimmy that some people don't like other people because of their color, and he had never had any reason to arrive at such a concept, because he had seen people of all colors in our house as our friends from the time his eyes opened on the world.

But I knew that he would have to know the answer soon enough. Society could not change that quickly. He would know and he too would inherit the bitter fruits. Maybe after all it would not be Jimmy and Rosemary and their little sisters who would know a different world. Their children, perhaps? Or their children's children. But some day it would come, and it was worth working for. I never doubted that it was worth working for, but there was a time when I wondered if the dream could ever be realized — wondered if the struggle was not utterly futile.

20

The Spasm Passes

The weeks immediately following Carl's trial are for the most part blacked out in my memory. It is the only period in my life in recent years when I cannot remember just where I went, just whom I talked with, just what was said.

I do recall that when I went home from the trial that night of December 13, 1954, after the conviction, the woman who lived next door was waiting up to talk to me. She had been kind and sympathetic from the very beginning of our trouble, from the night the crowd of people first came to our home a lifetime ago the preceding May. She wanted to put her arms around me and comfort me, and I remember asking her to please go away, saying I just wanted to be alone and would talk to her the next day. I went to bed that night and cried — something I would never have expected to do in these circumstances. I recall thinking how ungallant I really was — crying because my husband was in jail, put there for doing the things he thought were right, the things we both believed in.

That was on a Monday night. I know that on the next morning the *Courier-Journal* carried a brief boxed notice in its story of the conviction saying that, since Carl had been tried and found guilty by a "jury of his peers," his employment by the newspaper was therewith "at a permanent end." I know that this notice appeared on that date because I have the clipping in my files, but later I had no recollection of the moment when I first read it or of what my emotions at that time were. I know that on the following Friday I went to New York. I can establish that date because on that Saturday night I attended a party arranged by some people in New York to raise funds for our defense. But between that Monday night of the conviction and that Friday I can remember nothing.

Nor can I remember anything of that next week when I returned to Louisville until I left for Alabama to spend Christmas with our children. I recall very little of the few days I was in Alabama and nothing of the next week when I came back to Louisville again. Nor of the next week, nor the next.

I must have been going places during those weeks, must have been seeing people, talking with them. I could not see Carl because there was a rule at the jail that persons who had been inmates there could not come back to visit anyone else for three months, and it had been less than three months since my own release from jail. I doubt that I was seeing many of my old friends because the terror in the community had mounted all during Carl's trial and even months later I was making it a point not to try to reach any of these people unless they got in touch with me first, and most of them never did. But I must have been seeing my co-defendants, Carl's family, our lawyers, a few other people. And I must have been acting in an outwardly normal way, because if I had done anything irrational some of these people would have told me about it since.

But memory, in its kind way, seems to have blocked out that brief period of my life, as it often tends to block out the things we do not care to remember. And that was a period which I obviously do not want to remember and of which I am not very proud. Any person would like to feel that he can be heroic when the times and circumstances demand it of him; the times and circumstances demanded it of me then, and I was not very heroic. I felt that the things I had believed in and worked for — the world without walls — were will-o'-the-wisps, and it seemed that my life had been wasted.

Basically, I think, the fury that had culminated in Carl's trial had overwhelmed me. I kept thinking of the man with the skull in the Birmingham courthouse, and it seemed that he had won. And I think I understood now for the first time, really, how those Negroes feel who decide the wall is not worth fighting, who decide to ignore it and try to build some little personal lives for themselves on their own side of the wall.

I decided during this period that it was really not worth the time and trouble and effort to appeal Carl's conviction to the higher courts. I had begun to feel this way before the trial ended, and Carl and I had talked about it. After he was in jail, he wrote me that he wanted to do whatever would make me feel the best and that I should decide whether we would abandon an appeal.

And then there came a turning point. There may have been many factors, but the one I remember — my first vivid recollection after Carl's trial — is the evening I went to the home of one of our lawyers, Robert Zollinger, to tell him I had decided we would not appeal the case. He was shocked.

"Anne, you can't mean that," he said.

"Yes, I do," I replied. "We can't win — you know we can't. And it's just going to make things rougher if we try. Carl will be eligible for parole in five years. I'm bound to be convicted too, but I probably won't get any longer a sentence than his. If we don't appeal and are just quiet, maybe we'll both get paroles as soon as we're eligible for them. Otherwise, we probably won't."

"And of course there's always the possibility you might appeal and win," Zollinger remarked.

"So we appeal and win," I answered. "Then they're that much madder at us, and they try something else to get us. I just can't fight this any longer, Bob, and it seems to me this is the simplest way out."

He was looking at me intently, and I could see he had not quite made up his mind whether I was serious or not.

"You see," I went on, "five years isn't forever. In five years, Jimmy will only be eight and Anita will be just six. We'd still have time to live and raise our children."

I thought of the places we could go — away from the South, away from the ugly things that were too big to fight. There were interracial communities in America, and I knew where some of them were. Carl's sister lived in one; I remembered visiting her there and seeing the white and Negro children playing together on her block — and she had said, "You'd never have to worry about your children and segregation if you lived here, Anne." And there were others — that new interracial housing development some Quakers were starting near Philadelphia, maybe many more. I thought how it would be to raise our children, even if somewhat belatedly, in one of these places — raise them where they would never know the forces that had destroyed us, raise them in a healthy, insulated world.

Zollinger's voice brought me back to reality.

"But, Anne," he said slowly, "think of what may happen to all the other Jimmys and Anitas if this conviction stands."

"What do you mean?" I asked. I knew what he meant; I didn't want to think about it.

"Just what I said," he answered. Then he paused, sitting for a moment with his head in his hands, thinking. "Look," he went on, "I don't know whether we can win this case or not. I think we've got a good chance. I know that by everything in the law we should be able to, and I don't believe the higher courts are going to put up with what's been going on here. But nobody can be sure on something like this. And as for what else they might do to try to get at you — I wouldn't even try to guess. I haven't had any experience in practicing law in a police state, and that's what we've been getting close to in Louisville in the last few months. But . . ."

He got up and walked the length of the room and back. Then he sat down again.

"The thing is," he continued quietly, "you just don't give up without a fight. This isn't going to be a very good place for anybody to live, Anne, unless we can get this case reversed. I was talking to a man the other day — you'd know him if I told you who he was — he's one of the leading lawyers in this town. He said if this conviction is upheld, he's going to take his family and move to Canada — because nobody will be safe. There's a lot more involved in this thing than you and Carl and the children."

As he spoke, the telephone rang, and he went into the dining room to answer. I was left alone in the living room — alone with the words he had spoken. Words I didn't want to hear. Thoughts I didn't want to think. And more even than Zollinger knew. This case had always been chiefly a civil liberties matter to him; the segregation part of it had never particularly interested him, one way or the other. But now that he had driven the wedge, I had to think of this too. What of all the other Jimmys and Anitas? What of all the other children like Rosemary Wade who still needed houses? What of all the other white children in the South who would grow up with segregation blighting their souls if everybody gave up so easily? What of all the Negro children on the country roads and the city streets who were entitled to freedom and dignity and a place in the sun? I tried to tell myself it couldn't possibly matter what course we chose — it was just conceited to think we were all that important — there were plenty of other people who would carry on. But it didn't work. I knew it did matter. Not so much for what we could do if we chose to fight but for what we would be doing if we surrendered. Two people take a stand and then accept defeat, and people know and they are set back: and the next time it's harder.

I was not enthusiastic. I was in no mood to take on the problems of the world. But something arose from the reflex centers of my mind to tell me I could not think only of myself and my own children — at any time. Words came out of the past — words, I knew now, that had shaped my life.

I heard again the voice of the minister at Anniston reading from the New Testament: "Whoever shall seek to gain his life shall lose it, but whoever shall lose his life shall preserve it."

I heard again the words of my mother when I was still in elementary school: "You can never live a worthwhile life, Anne Gambrell, if you think only of yourself. It's the things you do for other people that make life worthwhile."

I heard again the words of the dean of my Virginia college: "What matters is not what you get out of life, but what you give."

White Southern society had injected much that was poison into my lifeblood; it had taught me much that was shoddy and much that was wrong; it had bequeathed me the sense of guilt that no honest white Southerner can wholly escape. But it had also had its ideals, and I had inherited those too. One of these was the principle that no man can live for himself alone, that each man has a responsibility to his fellow man. True, this principle was honored more in the breach than in the observance and at best it was covered with the veneer of *noblesse oblige*. But, underneath, the ideal was there for those who could see and hear — and I knew that I must follow that ideal now or succumb to schizophrenia, as so many did. I could not run away — not even for my children. And anyway, I thought, what would it really mean to my own children, even if I could arrange for them to grow up in a healthy insulated community? How would they develop any standards worth living by if they knew — as they soon would have to know — that their parents had run away from the responsibilities that were theirs?

I did not know what I could do at the moment that would be very constructive. I only knew I could not give in.

Zollinger had already come back into the living room, bringing us coffee and setting my cup on the arm of my chair. He was sitting quietly, drinking his own coffee — apparently realizing he had said all he could say and that this was something I had to work out alone.

"I'm wrong," I said finally. "Forget what I said. Of course we'll appeal. And we'll fight the case as hard as it's possible to fight it."

"I thought that's what you'd decide," he smiled.

And suddenly I had to laugh a little to myself. How the tables had turned. A few months before, when we were about to be indicted, it had been Carl and I who were bolstering Zollinger's courage. Now he was having to bolster mine. Zollinger, who had little concern for vast social problems and was somewhat amused at what he considered our crusades to save the world. But he had an honest lawyer's simple belief in the rights of every individual, and he had a passionate belief in the Constitution of the United States and in the system of rule by law instead of rule by men as the best way of protecting individual rights. And this simple belief was like a rudder that kept him charted on a straight and principled course when people more concerned with complex social problems might waver with the winds of time and circumstance.

Each of us must find a rudder somewhere. It was someway significant to me later — when my dejection of those early days of 1955 became more and more unbelievable to me as it faded into the past — that when the necessity arose I had found mine where I might have least expected it. Many people have tried to explain me by saying I learned the things I believe in from the radical movements of our day. But the basic things I know and believe in I learned, paradoxically enough, from the institutions of the white South. In recent years I have also learned much from radical movements, and I have learned to have a high regard for many of the people in them. But it was not the words of any of these people that came back to me in that moment when I seemed to sit among the ruins of my life and my husband's and had to decide where and how to begin to rebuild. Instead it was the words of the white South — the unpracticed words, the beautiful words. It is in our childhood and our youth that our reflex centers are shaped, and it is the reflex centers that decide our course of action in moments of crisis. Regardless of its decay and distortion, I find that I cannot completely write off the undeveloped potential of a society that still at least teaches its children a sense of obligation to all other children of the world.

As I look back, it is sometime soon after that conversation with Zollinger — along in mid-January — that my memory begins to function again. I began to fight back. Because of the very press of events, it of necessity became a fight for survival. I did not have the time nor the perspective to think in very broad terms; I could not look very far ahead. We had to take it a minute, a day at a time and do the things that had to be done at the moment.

We had no money, and the transcript of Carl's trial, which we needed for the appeal, was going to cost an estimated $4,000. We had to fight to get the court to grant him the right to appeal as a pauper. The lower court turned us down, but the State Court of Appeals upheld Carl's pauper status. That meant we could get the transcript without advance payment, although of course it did not help on the matter of attorneys' fees and the cost of printing briefs.

The next task was to get Carl out of prison. His appeal bond had been set at $40,000 — the highest bond ever set in Kentucky, so far as we could find out. We fought for a bond reduction through the Court of Appeals, but we lost that one. There was nothing to do then but to try to raise the bond, and that effort started.

Meantime, other things were happening. Andrew, recapturing his old indomitable spirit, renewed his determination to fight for his right to live in his house. Charlotte had declared that she would never live in it again, and Andrew knew that she would never change her mind unless the people who had driven them out before were brought to justice. He decided he must take steps on his own, since the prosecution would not. He himself swore out warrants for the arrest of Buster Rone, Lawrence Rinehart, and Stanley Wilt on charges of banding together to burn the cross the preceding May to intimidate him. But the court threw out the charges on the grounds that a previous grand jury had heard the evidence and failed to indict. That only increased Andrew's determination.

Meantime, too, the hysteria began to wear off a little in the community. A few people, first among the Negro people but to some extent among the white people too, began to speak out against what had happend. The American Civil Liberties Union, which at the time of Carl's trial had been in the case only as observers, now employed Louis Lusky to serve as Carl's co-counsel on appeal. He began to prepare Carl's appeal brief.

I lived in a constant state of tension during those winter months — continually pressed by the details of problems close at hand. We were expecting my own trial to come at any time. Vernon Bown was still demanding to be tried on the bombing charge, but Hamilton said he would try me next on February 28 on the charge of sedition. The trial was postponed until March 14 and then until April 18. Then, just before the trial date of April 18, the prosecution, for reasons that may never be entirely clear, announced that it would agree to the postponement of my trial and those of all the other defendants until Carl's appeal was decided in the higher courts.

That gave us time — time for many things and for the immediate job of raising the bond to release Carl from prison. Bown had finally been released in February; a Louisville Negro had posted his house as bond. In April, I. O. Ford's bond was reduced because of his age and poor health; the Emergency Civil Liberties Committee, which was already helping raise funds for the defense and providing all the defendants with the advisory services of its general counsel, Leonard Boudin, raised this bond and Ford was released. So now only Carl, of all the defendants, remained imprisoned. By this time, people all over the country had heard about the case and were willing to lend money toward the bond. Again with the help of the Emergency Civil Liberties Committee, it was finally raised. On July 12, 1955 — almost seven months to the day from the time of his conviction — Carl was released from prison.

We brought the children back to Louisville and tried to re-establish a somewhat normal home for them. But for us, the fight was just beginning. Major legal battles — in both the criminal and civil courts — lay ahead. We had to raise money for them — to pay legal expenses that beset all the defendants, to print Carl's brief, to fight the foreclosure suit on the Wade property. We had to let people wherever we could reach them know the facts of what had

occurred, in the hope that we could stir the forces of public conscience. And gradually through the months that followed Carl's
trial, people and organizations in all parts of the country — North
and South — offered us support. We no longer felt alone.[1]

The South End Federal Savings & Loan Association, as soon
as we were indicted, had proposed that all hearings on the foreclosure suit against the Wade property be held in abeyance. They

[1] Along with the actions of the American Civil Liberties Union and the
Emergency Civil Liberties Committee, the first real break in the silence on
the case came when the Rev. William Howard Melish preached a sermon
on it at the Episcopal Church of the Holy Trinity in Brooklyn. The Episcopal League for Social Action printed this sermon and distributed it by the
thousands all over the country. Later numerous church groups came to our
support — the American Friends Service Committee, church federation
leaders in various places, alliances of Negro Baptist and African Methodist
Episcopal and A. M. E. Zion ministers in numerous cities, the Methodist
Federation for Social Action, and groups of individual ministers of almost
every denomination. The Religious Freedom Committee filed an *amicus
curiae* brief.

Labor organizations also voiced protest and gave us help: most notably,
the United Packinghouse Workers and the United Automobile Workers,
and also the International Longshoremen & Warehousemen's Union, the
United Electrical Workers, and locals of the American Communications
Association, the United Shoe Workers, United Service Employees, Amal-
gamated Clothing Workers, the Mechanics' Educational Society of America,
the International Jewelry Workers Union, the New York Teachers Union,
the International Union of Mine, Mill & Smelter Workers; and a number
of CIO state and city councils, and also the Trades and Labour Council of
Belfast, Northern Ireland.

Other groups giving support included Southern liberal organizations,
especially the Southern Conference Educational Fund, as well as individual
labor leaders, ministers and educators all over the South; civil liberties
organizations such as the Bill of Rights Fund, the West Coast Committee
to Preserve American Freedoms, the Liberal Citizens of Massachusetts, the
Southerners for Civil Rights, and the National Lawyers Guild, which
filed an *amicus curiae* brief; the Women's International League for Peace
and Freedom, units of the NAACP and student organizations on various
campuses; virtually every left wing political organization in the United
States, including the Socialist Party. Several publications carried on active
campaigns in our behalf; these included the *American Socialist,* the *National Guardian,* the *Monthly Review, I. F. Stone's Weekly,* the *Southern
Patriot,* the *Militant,* the *Daily Worker,* and the *Witness,* an Episcopal
publication.

may have expected that because of developments Wade would voluntarily give up the property. But of course this did not happen. Immediately after Carl's release from prison, they asked the court to begin hearings again. These hearings continued off and on for more than a year. Meantime, Carl's brief was completed and filed in the Court of Appeals of Kentucky.

All of this had to be done — as a matter of survival. But gradually I came to feel, long before that year that followed Carl's trial was over, that none of the things we were doing — all these things we had to do — was really going to decide the basic issues involved in this case. I now knew again what I had known when we went into Carl's trial: that issues which must find their solution, for good or bad, in the hearts of men are never decided finally in the courts of law.

History had not been standing still while we were embroiled in our own troubles. Things were happening all over the South. The Supreme Court decision outlawing segregation in the schools, which had come down the same week the Wades moved into the house on Rone Court, had served to speed up the movement of events. In communities in every part of the South, Negro citizens were petitioning school boards for immediate desegregation of the schools. The White Citizens Councils were set up in Mississippi to oppose integration and were spreading all over the South, organizing at every crossroads. Negroes who spoke out for integration were being threatened with slow starvation by economic boycotts.

Emmett Till, at the age of fourteen, was murdered in Mississippi. And, in words reminiscent of our own case, the local sheriff advanced the theory — which later helped to acquit the men charged with his murder — that the whole incident had been a plot by the NAACP to stir up "race trouble" in the state. Negroes in Montgomery, Alabama, in a massive demonstration of unity, quit riding the city buses as a protest against abuses under the segregated seating system, and later turned their protest into an attack on segregation itself; homes of the leaders of the boycott were dynamited; and, again in a way reminiscent of the Louisville case, a grand jury indicted the people who were leading the boycott — not on charges of doing the dynamiting but for the act of organizing the boycott itself. Autherine Lucy became the first Negro to enter the University of Alabama, by court order, and a rioting crowd threatened to kill her; in the now familiar pattern, Governor James Folsom — probably one of the most liberal among the Southern governors — although deploring the mob violence, opined that it was the NAACP that was responsible for all the trouble in Alabama. And the Louisville *Times,* in words almost identical to those the *Courier-Journal* had used in condemning our sale of the house on Rone Court to the Wades, declared that the Lucy case had "worsened race relations in Tuscaloosa . . . where considerable progress had been made toward racial harmony." White ministers all over the South — some of them — were quoting the Bible to support segregation. Southern legislatures were searching for ways to circumvent — and, if necessary, to defy — the United States Supreme Court; the Virginia voters, by a two-thirds majority, were voting to allow their communities to abolish the public school systems if necessary to prevent desegregation. The White Citizens Councils were combining into a South-wide organization, and the Federation for Constitutional Government was established at a meeting in Memphis to bring together all groups wanting to "preserve our Constitution." Senator Eastland was going about the South declaring that the Supreme Court had been subverted by Communist influences and calling on all good white men and women to rally now to defend their way of life.

Some things were happening on the other side too, indicating that the white South was not as solid as some outside the region have always thought. In the spring of 1955, hundreds of Southern educators and community leaders, many of them white, were meeting in Houston to express support for desegregation of the South's schools. One third of the people in Virginia, again many of them white, were voting *against* abolition of their public schools. The white students of Georgia Tech were burning Governor Marvin Griffin in effigy because he had decreed that the school's football team could not play in the Sugar Bowl against a team with a Negro player. Two hundred leading citizens of New Orleans, some three-fourths of them white, were petitioning the school board of their city for desegregation of its schools. Many white students and faculty members at the University of Alabama were petitioning for the readmission of Autherine Lucy to classes. Many individual white ministers in large cities and in country roadside churches were calling for an end to segregation. The Southern Conference Educational Fund was presenting to Congress a petition signed by 2,500 Southerners, great numbers of them white, asking for a Congressional investigation of the violations of rights of Negroes in Mississippi. The Southern Regional Council was organizing Councils on Human Relations in each Southern state, attempting to bring together white and Negro people in support of the Supreme Court decision. Sugar workers in Louisiana were uniting, Negro and white, on the picket line in a strike that attracted nationwide attention.

But as the tension spread, there came from the majority of white Southern liberals — men and women who ten years before were actively talking and writing in favor of Negro rights — only a tremendous silence. Or if they did speak it was to the Negroes and not the white people, and to urge not compliance with the Supreme Court decision but "moderation" on the part of the Negroes. William Faulkner, in *Life* magazine, issued from Mississippi a frantic plea to the NAACP to "Go slow now," "Stop now for a time, a moment," lest by their haste they force all the Southern moderates, including him, into the camp of the segregationists. The Negro people went right on pressing their demands for first-class citizenship, and the voices asking for moderation were like a paper dam trying to stop the rush of history as it swirled around them; but among the white people these calls found their recurring echoes, and they had their effect. The white voices calling for desegregation seemed to become weaker; the few who refused to compromise, as in Louisville during the Wade case, were the more isolated, and their words were drowned out. Many white ministers who had spoken out for sanity lost their pulpits; many decent people lapsed into silence; others, growing discouraged and weary of it all, turned their eyes to what seemed to be a land of forgetfulness in the North, and left the South. Soon almost the only voice one seemed to hear in the South was that of the White Citizens Councils — its membership snowballing as the uncommitted thousands, in the absence of any strong clear-cut leadership on the other side, flocked into its ranks. And friends of mine in various parts of the South told me in 1956 that whereas it would have been relatively easy to desegregate the schools in their communities in 1954 — when the opposition was small and most of the people uncommitted — it would now be much harder. The Negro people continued to act with a courage and dignity that inspired the nation — but the South, like Louisville in 1954, was becoming more and more rigidly divided into "black against white."

And as the emotions in the Louisville case quieted with time and I was able again to turn my eyes to what was happening in the world around us, it became increasingly clear to me that the importance of the events in Louisville was that they encompassed in microcosm all of the conflicting forces that were raging on a gigantic scale in the struggle that enveloped the South. In Louisville there was Andrew Wade, and the Negroes who supported him. So there was in every part of the South a "new" Negro — unwilling any longer to plead or to beg from the white man's table, unwilling to compromise or to settle for second-best. In Louisville there had been the handful of people who burned a cross, fired rifle shots, and blew up a man's house. In the same way all over the South there were those — at first relatively few — whose shock at the appearance of this new Negro gave added power to the old Southern myths that made for a violent reaction. There had been the white neighbor of the Wades who said she would have been "glad" for her children to play with the Wades' little girl, the Shively woman who told me on the telephone that most people in that community did not oppose a Negro's right to a home and dignity, and all the other originally uncommitted people. In the same way all over the South there were the thousands upon thousands who could have been won to either side. But as in Louisville the liberal forces that might have provided a rallying point for support of the Wades had talked instead of how Wade had moved too fast and had "hurt race relations" — so the leading liberal forces in the South were asking the Negroes to be more "moderate" lest the South be thrown into turmoil. And as in Louisville there had been John Y. Hitt and Scott Hamilton, so throughout the South there were those who were providing people with an apparently patriotic and noble reason for their prejudices and capturing their imaginations for a crusade against desegregation. In Louisville the net result had finally been a community hysteria that ultimately appalled those who had silently let it happen and could expiate itself only in a sort of symbolic witch burning. Now the entire region seemed moving toward a pathological hysteria of which no man could predict the outcome.

The Louisville case, I came to see — like every incident in the South in recent times — needed more than court decisions. It needed to be understood. And just as the real problem could not be solved by shouts of "Communism" from our opposition, neither could it be solved by self-righteous shouts from us condemning the people who opposed us. Nothing could be accomplished by condemnation and denunciation; we need not — we could not — approve, but we had to try to understand.

When Carl was released from prison I found that he had been thinking, in his own way and under the pressure of different circumstances, along the same lines. We had not tried to discuss very many basic problems during those months when he was in prison and I was on the outside, visiting only briefly once a week — first through a window and then through a wire screen. It is not easy to discuss things under those circumstances; life is easier if you don't try.

But Carl had been thinking of many things. I did not know it until it was all over, but he had spent forty-two days in solitary confinement when he was first transferred from the county jail in Louisville to the state prison — leaving his cell only for the brief periods when I came to visit. He had not told me about it at the time because he thought I had enough to worry about without adding that.

"Being in solitary forces a man to come to terms with himself," he explained to me later. "You have to conquer yourself, your weaknesses and desires and eventually your own ego. Once you do that, you begin to see how unimportant you really are. You can think more clearly of the bigger problems outside yourself. And for the first time in your life, you can think of them without injecting your own subjective feelings into them."

It was natural that when Carl's mind turned to the world outside himself it should concentrate on the problems that had precipitated this case. And he concluded, as I had, that nothing was to be accomplished by condemnation from either side and that what was needed was deeper understanding all along the way. He expressed something of this when he said in a statement to the press on his release from prison on bond:

"I have no ill will toward anyone as a result of the opposition to my action in helping Wade. I realize that social change often startles those who have a vested interest in things as they are."

And then, finally, as if a spasm that had gripped the community had passed, the Louisville case came to an end.

The criminal charges against us were dropped after the United States Supreme Court, acting in the Pennsylvania Nelson case in April 1956, ruled out state sedition laws. In June the Kentucky Court of Appeals, apparently relieved that it would not have to pass on the other points raised in Carl's appeal, used this ruling in the Nelson case to reverse his conviction. The charges against the rest of us fell with this decision — including the charge that we conspired to bomb Wade's house for seditious purposes, since this had also been brought under the state sedition law. Only the case charging Bown with actually bombing the house remained as a valid indictment; faced finally after two years with the necessity of bringing this charge to trial, Scott Hamilton moved for its dismissal also.

Actually the charges against us had been dead in the public consciousness long before they were killed in the courts. Time someway had provided its healing balm; the hysteria had quieted, and people no longer talked in the streets and in the country clubs about how we ought to be lynched. It was as if the spasm, by its very fury and intensity, had burned itself out — as it will someday burn itself out all over the South. There were some aftereffects, of course, that could not be erased: all of the defendants had lost their jobs and none was ever reinstated; there were scars on individual lives that might never completely heal. But in the community at large, when the judge finally dismissed our indictments in November 1956, no one really cared any more except the prosecutor and the defendants. And we started the slow process of putting our lives back together again.

As for Andrew Wade's house, it continued to lie in ruins as the litigation over the foreclosure suit dragged on into 1957. Finally, as we had long felt was inevitable, the court ruled that the bank was entitled to foreclosure. It was ironic that it was the attacks of Scott Hamilton on us that finally enabled Andrew, despite the foreclosure, to gain clear title to the house. For the attacks had made the case known all over the country. And when the court ruled that the mortgage must be paid or the house sold at public auction, two people none of us had ever heard of before — Mr. and Mrs. David Simonson of Chicago, who had listened to Andrew and Carl on a radio interview sponsored by the United Automobile Workers — offered to lend Wade the money to pay off the mortgage. In the summer of 1957, Andrew started work on repairing the house.

But although we won, we lost. When the repair work was complete, Charlotte still insisted that she would never move back into that house with her children. Andrew had known for three years, of course, that she felt this way. The fact that the bombers had never been brought to justice and that now after so much lapse of time and all the furor over our case there was scant chance they ever would be — these things had not helped. His constant hope had been that as Louisville recovered from its shock, some of the liberal-minded people who had been silent in 1954 would feel pangs of conscience and give Charlotte some feeling of support. After the dismissal of the charges against us, he visited some of these people again; they were sympathetic; they deeply regretted all that had happened; but they were apparently afraid of renewing old bitterness and when he asked them for public expressions of support, they changed the subject. Once more after the house was rebuilt he tried again, and got the same answer. Andrew himself felt that if they moved back to Rone Court the situation would be quite different from that of 1954, but he could not convince Charlotte. She said she would never be able to sleep there peacefully for a night — not knowing what minute a bomb might explode again. As throughout the case it had been Charlotte Wade who had seemed to me the greatest judgment on the morality of Louisville, so it was in the end. And the failure of a community was recorded on a day in August 1957, when Andrew finally put a "For Sale" sign in the yard of his house at Rone Court.

And yet in the paradoxical way life works, it was also true that although we lost, we won. For Louisville, despite its failure on Rone Court, was not quite the same place in 1957 that it had been in 1954. Changes had come. Faster than many thought possible. In the summer of 1956 the parks were desegregated. And then the following fall, Louisville won national acclaim as it began desegregating its schools. School officials had said from the beginning that they would comply with the Supreme Court decision; the city's Negro leadership opposed a gradual approach and demanded that desegregation start simultaneously in all twelve grades; officials agreed. During the year preceding the start of the program, they encouraged discussion of the issue among students, teachers, and parents; they — as well as a number of other individuals and groups in the community — urged people to accept the "law of the land." When the change came in 1956, the smoothness with which it started was one of the most hopeful things that had occurred in the South since the Supreme Court decision.

It is significant that Millard Grubbs and the others who had opposed the Wades on Rone Court also tried to stop desegregation of the schools. They organized a White Citizens Council in that summer of 1956 and threatened opposition when the schools opened. But many of the white liberals were now speaking out. They let the police know in no uncertain terms that they wanted trouble nipped in the bud. It was almost as if they were determined that their city not be disgraced again. And on the day school opened, the police were on the job. The transition was peaceful.

Actually the Citizens Council movement never caught on in Louisville around the school issue. Much of the original fury that had followed immediately after the Supreme Court decision had spent itself, and if the Wades and we did nothing else by our venture on Rone Court we served as lightning rods for some of it. When 1956 and the beginning of school integration came, Louisville had in a sense been through it all before; I doubt that the spasm ever grips the same community more than once.

Much, it was true, remained to be done. The school desegregation was not as complete as it has sometimes been painted, and the state president of the NAACP publicly called it "token integration." To the deep resentment of the Negro people, there was no desegregation of teachers; and a flexible transfer system, which was sharply attacked by the Negro press in Louisville, cut down considerably the amount of actual integration among the pupils — as we found out when we began to look for a really integrated school for our children in our racially mixed section. But a start had been made.

In many other areas, too, the job was far from done, for in a number of important aspects Louisville was still segregated. Especially in new housing, the segregation was just as complete as it had been when Andrew first went house-hunting. True, a kind of limited progress had been made, for in the aftermath of the publicity that the Wade case brought to the housing shortage, construction started on several new subdivisions for Negroes. But it was segregated housing and — as will always be the case as long as segregation restricts the supply and forces up the prices of homes available to Negroes — it was too expensive for a family of average income. It was perhaps one of those ironic and inevitable injustices that Andrew was unable even now to buy one of the new houses that had undoubtedly resulted from his own ordeal. After he sold the house on Rone Court and paid the Simonsons the money they had loaned him, they gave him $1,500 to replace the down payment he had lost, to enable him to buy another house. But payments in the new Negro subdivisions were beyond his reach — the more so since boycotts were still taking a toll of his business. And he and his family began to look for an old house in one of Louisville's older sections, which white people were abandoning.

Yet I don't think Andrew Wade was ever bitter. I think he knew that in the final analysis and in the deepest sense he won. As the *Courier-Journal* later wrote, in regard to the racial situation in Clinton, Tennessee:

> The man who braves the mob is inevitably the winner. . . .
> It may be that in every community where the problem of constitutional and moral principle in this matter is to be solved, at least one such must arise and offer himself as the agent of testing. And if this happens, the fight will be won in the end, the resisters will be overcome not by force or writs but by compunction and shame.

21

Toward a New Race Relations

As we attempt to understand the kind of episode that happened in Louisville, we need to shift our mental gears to the pace at which history is moving in the South. There was perhaps a time when there was some comfort in the knowledge that the final solution to these problems would come only in the hearts and minds of men. Men's hearts and minds, it was usually assumed, change slowly; therefore we could sit back, relax somewhat, and wait for a change to come about — perhaps giving it an occasional helpful nudge. But today we don't have that kind of time. The places where the basic change must occur are the same, but more than a nudge is needed. And, as a matter of fact, it is only under the impact of action that human hearts and minds are ever altered anyway — only when some practical situation presents the necessity to think and feel in new ways, or at least to reexamine old beliefs.

First, I think we need to recognize that such conflicts as that which occurred in Louisville — and other incidents, different in form but similar in content, in other parts of the South — are probably inevitable. They are inevitable because of the existence of certain inevitable factors.

One of these factors is Andrew Wade and the people like him. The vision of freedom and dignity has today captured the imaginations of large numbers of Southern Negroes, and no force on earth — no words of caution or pleas for moderation — is going to stop them or swerve them in their determination to reach their goal. You would have to change the history of three hundred years of oppression to change this factor now, and wishful thinking as to how much better things would be if the Negro people would just "take it easy" is completely futile. In Louisville, it might not have had to be

Andrew Wade and his search for a house, but if it had not been this it would have been something else.

Another inevitable factor is the existence of James I. Rone, Scott Hamilton, and people like them. Race prejudice too has roots far back in the centuries, and I think we cannot afford to underestimate its force. It grew out of a slave society in which a white people who claimed to believe in freedom and God and the brotherhood of man took other human beings as slaves and then had to justify their actions by convincing themselves that the Negroes were an inferior breed of humanity. It was nourished by the strivings for economic gain, complicated and fired with emotion by the sex relationships that defied the man-made barriers, exploited by politicians who found it easier to talk about saving white supremacy than conquering hunger in the South. And it was passed along from one generation to another, to the child in his cradle. A number of able sociologists and historians have analyzed the complex strands of the web, and again we would have to change three hundred years of history to erase all of the effects now.[1]

But even as we recognize the inevitability of these conflicts, I think we must also recognize the fact that they need not result in disaster. For there is another constant factor too in this situation, and that is the potential for change in the white men and women of the South.

Actually, the white South has never been solid. There were whites who opposed slavery in the days before the Civil War; there were whites who worked with the Negroes in the Reconstruction governments of the Southern states after the Civil War. Today in this second half of the twentieth century, although the myth of white supremacy still hangs like a shadow over the region, much of its original force is gone. The slave society which produced it is far in the past; with many white Southerners, although the outward forms and expressions remain, the deep emotional need for them has eroded away with the passing generations. Often the persistence of the forms is more a matter of habit than of inner need and con-

---

[1] For an excellent study of the psychological roots of race prejudice, see Lillian Smith's *Killers of the Dream* (W. W. Norton, 1949); for a study of the political and economic factors, see W. J. Cash's *The Mind of the South* (Alfred A. Knopf, 1941).

viction; it may be the product of a lifetime in which no occasion ever arose to compel an examination of one's way of thinking; again, it may be the fear of social pressure and what others will say. And because the hold of the myth is tenuous, even at the moment when it appears very strong, we have the recurring phenomenon of people changing very quickly. There are countless white men and women in the South today who have completely reversed their positions on this question — sometimes with apparent suddenness. I speak with authority on this point, for I have seen it happen. I have not only seen it; I have lived it. I grew up with all the same conditioning that motivated Rone; if the circumstances of my life had been different, I might have been among those who set dynamite under Andrew Wade's house — or in the howling mob threatening death to Autherine Lucy; but new factors entered my life, and I changed. And I have seen others change — many of them.

Today the possibilities for change are greater than they have ever been before. This is true because the very actions of the Negro people in demanding a new kind of freedom are forcing this question to the conscious level of the minds of white people everywhere; no white person can any longer drift with the tide and act purely on habit; he must take a look at himself and decide where he stands. Many of course no matter what happens will in the process only become more enslaved to the myth of white supremacy, for there are those who cannot change. But many others can. How many do change — and how quickly they do it — will determine whether the incidents we are now witnessing are to produce disaster or will merely serve as growing pains.

And finally I think we must recognize the fact that these necessary changes will not come about unless the people who would like to see them happen, the people who believe in brotherhood — and the South has many of them — are willing to speak out and help them happen. This is the real key to the difference in the way Louisville reacted to desegregation in housing in 1954 and to desegregation in the schools in 1956. In 1954, the liberal white people sat silent, and those supporting segregation took the offensive away from them; by 1956, these liberal people had pulled themselves together, tapped new resources within themselves, and taken the offensive away from the segregationists; the result was that in 1956 and 1957 the imagination of the community was captured for a pride in successful desegregation instead of a defense of the status quo. If liberals all over the South sit silent as they did in Louisville in 1954 — appalled at the fury of what is happening, afraid of its challenges, wishing it would go away — they leave a vacuum. Human society, like nature, abhors a vacuum, and today the forces preaching white supremacy in the South are presenting their campaign as a great crusade, breathing a new life into the old myth, giving it a new and immediate fire it has not had for generations. People are always attracted to a mass crusade — a great movement working toward some big purpose that gives their lives new significance; Southerners especially have always had a weakness for them. The movement for equality, for a world where all people can live together in harmony, could be presented in that way too. But today in the South it is only among the Negro people that this is happening; among the white people the only real crusade in sight is that of the white supremacists.

In the face of this challenge, why are so many liberals silent in the South today? Why were they silent in Louisville in 1954? The reason they gave — and I think it was an honest one — was that the Wades' and our action, because it was too precipitate, would do more harm than good. We had "hurt race relations" in Louisville.

This, of all the charges that were made against us, was the one that concerned me most of all. We had been accused of everything. Some of the first threatening callers who telephoned us, after it became known we had sold the house, implied that we had made a financial killing in the deal.

"I guess you decided to make a little money by ruining our neighborhood out here," said one anonymous voice on the telephone.

"I know why you bought that house for those niggers," another woman caller said when Carl answered the phone. "That's your baby!" She was referring to Charlotte Wade's unborn child.

And then John Y. Hitt, together with Millard Dee Grubbs, and finally official spokesmen for the state of Kentucky had come along and said it was all a Communist plot.

Carl and I were able to laugh at all these accusations.

"Sex, money, or a Communist plot," Carl commented. "Everything has got to be one of these. It seems that some people can't conceive of anyone doing anything as a matter of principle."

But I could not laugh at the charge from some of our liberal friends — that our action had hurt race relations. This was the last thing in the world we wanted to do. The whole passion of our lives was for better relations among people. If our beliefs had led us into actions that worked against such better relations, something was basically wrong. I had to examine this charge.

To determine whether Andrew Wade's move to Rone Court could have hurt race relations in Louisville, we have to determine what good race relations are, and try to decide how the situation in Louisville, before the Rone Court incident, measured by this standard. The same test might be applied to Montgomery, Tuscaloosa, and other places where the charge has been made that some action "hurt race relations."

Obviously, different people will have many different ideas about what constitutes "good race relations." To the segregationists, good race relations mean an unchanging and unquestioned racially segregated society — the peace of the caste system. In their opinion, both races are happier and better off if they maintain separate institutions of society. That, to them, is a "good" arrangement.

The silent liberals of the Wade case and those who have argued in a similar fashion elsewhere would not agree, of course, with this position of the segregationists. Liberal is a broad term: it covers people who oppose all forms of segregation, and it also includes those who oppose it only in certain specific instances. But all liberals advocate some change in the segregated pattern. When they talk about "good race relations," I think they mean a situation in which an amicable atmosphere exists between the two racial groups — thus, they believe, creating a framework out of which change can grow. Many liberals develop a gradualist approach because they think that when a step is taken too fast it inflames the passions of those who oppose integration, breaks the supposedly amicable relationship, stiffens resistance, and thereby sets back the day of ultimate progress. And that is what many felt that we and the Wades did by our action.

It is certainly true that the events of 1954 in Louisville — like other incidents elsewhere in recent years — proved conclusively that this job of complete desegregation is not going to be an easy one. It is going to require resources of the heart and mind and spirit that none of us has ever had to tap before. This is a startling fact, and all of us — hoping ever for the easy solution to our problems — may be forgiven if we are temporarily frightened by such a challenge. But I question whether this startling fact is ever created by such a thing as Andrew Wade's move to Rone Court. I think it is much more likely that it is merely a fact that is inherent in our Southern society and which such incidents as the Wade case simply bring to the surface.

In Louisville, for example, it was true that some bits of progress toward desegregation had been made. A few bars had fallen, and Louisvillians of all colors had been meeting for years at interracial dinners and brotherhood affairs to talk of improved relations in their city. But how deep did the progress go? A man's life centers in his home, and a community's life centers in its neighborhoods. Even today, continued segregation in housing undermines school desegregation at its roots. For all of its apparent progress, in 1954 the great majority of the white people in Louisville lived in such a pattern that they never in all their lives had an opportunity to know a Negro as an equal. And — the other side of the coin — the great majority of the Negro people in Louisville lived all of their lives in such a pattern that they never had an opportunity to know a white man or woman as an equal.

I know of no gradual method to change the pattern. It is not that gradualism in its best sense and as an ideal is necessarily bad. The concept of gradualism has fallen into deep disfavor among the Negro people and among many of the whites who oppose segregation too because its phrases are mouthed by many of the same people who are actively seeking to perpetuate segregation forever. For example, John Y. Hitt on June 17, 1954, proposed editorially in his Shively *Newsweek* a plan for white citizens to form private "clubs" in their neighborhoods to keep Negroes from moving in; exactly three weeks later in another editorial he was advising Andrew Wade to retreat from Rone Court "in the light of present developments and await a gradual adjustment which is sure to come eventually." But gradualism is often sincere — not merely a semantic cover designed to thwart any progress at all. Many honest gradualists hold firmly to their ideal of steady, if slow, progress into the future, and this may be all right as a theory on paper. But how in the world could Andrew Wade have gradually moved on to Rone Court? And how could Autherine Lucy have gradually entered the University of Alabama — although, when one stops to think of it, what actually could be more gradual than one Negro student entering a university? But the entrance itelf could not be slow and gradual — no more than any Negro anywhere could gradually move into a previously all-white neighborhood. If he is going to move, he just has to move. Whenever he does it, it is something new. And something new will always seem startling, and it will never seem gradual, and it will always stir opposition. I can't see that the opposition would have been any less if the first Negro moved to break segregation in Louisville's white suburbs in 1960 instead of 1954 — if his move were the first, as Andrew's was. Whenever it happened, it was going to create a stir, because the seeds were there.

For the truth of the matter was, the bits of progress and the brotherhood luncheons to the contrary notwithstanding, *Louisville did not have "good race relations" in 1954.*

Different people may have different ideas on what good race relations are. The essence of a relation or a relationship, in my opinion, is that two factors are involved — otherwise it would not be a relationship. Therefore, when we are trying to determine what makes any relationship good, we cannot calculate with the opinions of only one of the factors. White men and colored men are involved in race relations, so race relations have to be a two-way street.

Obviously, as far as Andrew Wade was concerned when he went house-hunting, race relations in Louisville were not good — and they were not amicable. From his point of view, good race relations would have been a situation where he could have approached any white house-owner in the city as an equal, laid his down-payment on the table and received a deed to a house. That situation did not exist.

There is always a temptation to think that race relations are good when they are quiet, and that the terms are in fact synonymous. But the slaveowners of pre-Civil War America thought race relations in their time were good too. Two groups of people were living side by side; the relations weren't always as quiet as they have been generally considered to be because there were many slave revolts that get scant mention in the history books; yet no doubt many plantation owners enjoyed thinking all was quiet — and in many years and in many places, it was. But no one today, except perhaps a few really unbalanced people, would say that slave society constituted good race relations. The opinions of one factor in the relationship — the Negro slaves — had been omitted from the calculations.

At the time I grew up in Anniston, Alabama, race relations were quiet. I do not recall any race riots. I do not recall any serious race incidents. But I was in my late teens before I ever had the opportunity — and then far from Anniston — to meet a Negro as an equal. I do not think that was good race relations.

I think of a Negro minister in Louisville who about a year after Wade's move to Rone Court was looking for a house to buy. He was an elderly man and was soon to retire from active service at his church. He would then have to vacate the church parsonage, and he wanted to find a pleasant home in a pleasant neighborhood where he could retire. He had been a civic leader in his community. He had not only been a leading spokesman for his own people; I am sure he had been a part of every important interracial effort in Louisville in the past fifty years. He had attended many of the goodwill gatherings in this city where white and colored men met to tell each other how much they believed in brotherhood. And yet, wherever that man went to try to buy a house he was turned away. I can see his face now as he told me about it. The dignity of a lifetime spent in ministering nobly to the needs of others was being stripped from him. As each door was slammed in front of him, he became anew an outsider beating on a solid wall. I do not think from the viewpoint of that Negro minister that race relations were good in Louisville.

One argument of those who say that race relations are damaged when opponents of segregation push "too fast" is that such pushing may result in violence. They point out that Autherine Lucy might well have been killed by the mob in Tuscaloosa, Alabama; that members of the Wade family might have been killed in the explosion on Rone Court; and that murders of Negroes appear to have increased in Mississippi since the Supreme Court decision against segregation in the schools. This is an effective argument, because most of us who believe fervently in brotherhood among peoples, by the very nature of our beliefs, abhor violence.

What we may tend to forget, however, is that violence against the Negro people in the South is nothing new. In the past, it went on hidden in the darkness of night on lonely country roads and in the back alleys of Southern towns — and hidden too by the indifference and in some cases the ignorance of the world around. But the violence was no less terrible and no less fatal to its victims.

The man whose skull I saw on the table in the Birmingham courthouse eleven years ago was certainly very much a victim of violence. But what could be done about it? I discussed the incident at the time with other people at the Birmingham newspapers, and I recall what one experienced reporter told me:

"I don't know what good it would do to write about it," he said. "It's not necessarily that the newspaper approves of such things or wouldn't want to print it. But if they printed it, the sheriff's office would deny it. It would be your word against theirs. And how could you prove it?"

I was helpless — helpless in the face of violence.

Today, if the same incident occurred, I do not think I would be helpless. There would be people who would believe my story, people willing and ready to do something about it. For today, when violence occurs against the Negro people, it is national and international news. Everyone who has lived very much in the South knows that the only unusual things about the Emmett Till case were the publicity it got and the fact that the men accused of his murder were brought to trial at all; the only unusual thing about the murders of Negroes that have occurred in Mississippi since the Till case is that the spotlight of public opinion all over the country has been turned upon them. Lynchings have decreased through the years and have practically disappeared, but the murder of individual Negroes continues.

Such a spotlight of public opinion does not make Emmett Till or the others any less dead; nor would Andrew and Charlotte Wade have been any less dead if that dynamite had killed them, just because people were watching. And these things are not pleasant to think about. But, to me, the significant thing is that today perhaps for the first time in history those of us in the South and all over America who do not believe in violence — and that is the majority of the people anywhere — have the practical possibility of stopping the violence against the Negro people. We have that opportunity by virtue of the very fact that public opinion is focused on race relations and it is no longer possible for a white man to "keep the nigger in his place" by killing a black man under a cloak of darkness. Today we have the power to turn back violence; we cannot, therefore, in good conscience allow our dislike of violence to lead us into an attempt to put the brakes on the movement toward integration. To do so is not really to oppose violence; it is to surrender to it — to surrender before it ever strikes, and to let the mere threat of violence set the timetable for progress. A good police force can control a mob — in Tuscaloosa or Louisville or anywhere — and good police can find the perpetrators of crime. But, as we have seen in the Louisville case, the diligence of any police force is usually determined by the sentiment of the people in any given community, and people usually get exactly the kind of police action they want and demand. Andrew Wade's house did not have to be bombed — and it would not have been bombed if enough people concerned about "race relations" had demanded apprehension of the lawbreakers as soon as the cross was burned on Rone Court.

Race relations will never be "good" in America until we who are white and they who are colored can look at each other and talk to each other and trust each other as if color did not exist. And we do not know each other today. Recently, a Negro editor in one of America's larger cities, a man who moves on occasion in high places in the white world and to all appearances has scaled the wall as much as any Negro can, asked me to write a series of articles for him on how white people — the liberal ones as well as the conservative ones — really feel about segregation.

"I don't want to know what white people say when they are at brotherhood meetings with Negroes," he explained. "I want to know what they say when they talk among themselves."

No Negro knows — and no white person knows what the Negro feels and thinks and says when no white man is present. Some of us, who have partially broken the wall, may know more than others.

But how little any of us know came home to me that night during Carl's trial when I sat isolated in my white world and read the transcript of what Andrew Wade had said, at his lowest ebb — when I realized that, despite my own feeling that the attack of our enemies had hurled us into the same world and broken down the wall, there had come a time when he could not completely trust me.

I remember hearing a Negro NAACP leader from the Deep South discussing the Emmett Till case before a predominantly Negro audience.

"They will not stop us by murder and killing," she said. "They cannot stop our march toward freedom."

She did not identify the "they," but I knew she was not speaking only of the men who murdered Emmett Till. She talked for an hour and not once did she mention any white person in the South as her friend or her ally in what she saw as a fight for survival. When she spoke of "they," she meant all of us cursed with white skin. And the fact that some of us may feel differently, the fact that we may attend brotherhood meetings now and then, even the fact that we might actively oppose segregation and might in fact sell a house in a white neighborhood to a Negro does not completely exempt us from the terrible indictment placed upon us by our white skin.

I think of a conversation I had with a Negro friend in regard to the school flare-ups in Clinton, Tennessee. It was soon after an all-white jury in Knoxville had convicted those accused of causing the trouble, and many of us were momentarily feeling a little better about our race. I mentioned this conviction as an indication that things were changing in the South.

My friend shook his head.

"That was just because they attacked that white minister down there," he said. "When they do things to Negroes, nothing ever happens to them."

It was a comment that I heard from many Negroes in regard to the Clinton case.

I think of one day when Charlotte Wade and I were discussing incidents of violence in Alabama — the mob action against Autherine Lucy, the bombing of churches in Montgomery, the bombing of a Negro minister's home in Birmingham. I told her I was sure there were many white people in Alabama who did not approve of these things and who were trying to do something about it. She looked at me in honest amazement.

"I didn't know there were any white people down there who were on our side," she said.

"Oh yes," I insisted, "I'm sure of it."

"Where are they? What are they doing?" she asked, in a tone that told me she did not think I knew what I was talking about.

I groped in my mind for the answer. Some wistful longing to believe that there are some scraps of decency left in the white world made me wish passionately in that moment that I could point out to Charlotte Wade *something,* some little thing, that might convince her that all white people were not her enemy.

"Well, I know that some white church leaders in Alabama have spoken out against the violence — and there have been some others," I finally said lamely.

She shook her head again.

"And all the time, Autherine Lucy is out of the university and she might have been killed, and more Negroes go on getting killed all the time," she said. "It's not enough. What are these people you talk about doing to change things?"

What are they doing to change things? What are any of us doing? Charlotte Wade is right; it is not enough. Not enough by far to convince many of the Negro people that we are with them.

The Negro people in the South today, most of them, feel that they are standing alone at this hour in history. I feel that they are wrong. I do not think they are standing alone. I feel — I know — that the South has many white people who will go with them to the task of breaking down the wall, wherever that course leads. But the crucial thing, the horrifying thing, is that most Negroes do not know it. They at best are not sure of it. They are not sure they can depend on any of us.

It is a situation we inflicted upon ourselves when we built the wall — or when our ancestors built it; and never has it proved so true that the sins of the fathers *are* visited upon the third and fourth generations. We put a whole race of people away from us and behind a wall; no white man should be shocked if these people do not now accept at face value his statements about his desire ultimately to crumble the wall; he should not be outraged if the Negro people do not accept his counsel of an approach of moderation and gradualism as the wisest way. White humanity has not earned the trust of the black man.

I think that trust can be established across the wall. Not to believe this is to deny every possibility of brotherhood among men. But it is white men who built the wall, and it is they who must take the initiative if the trust is to be established. And the first step is for the white men who believe they hold good will in their hearts to give full consideration to the needs and desires of the Negro people when setting their criteria of what constitutes good race relations. That is not an easy task, for rare is the occasion when a Negro will tell a white man what he really thinks, and the things he may say at a so-called race relations meeting may be far indeed from what he really thinks. But no matter how difficult, that is the task we face.

Let us indulge in a moment of fear, if we must, as we realize how formidable is the job we face. Let us quail before a challenge that we may feel is too big. We may be forgiven for that if the indulgence is not too long. But let us not talk of "good race relations" until we can know and understand and accept the desires of the other partner in the relationship.

22

"Would You Do It Again?"

It is this factor of the "other partner in the relationship" that I have found I must return to whenever Carl and I have tried to answer the question so often put to us about the Wade case: "Would you do it again?"

Knowing all that we now know, if we could turn time backward to the spring of 1954 and if Andrew Wade again asked us to buy a house, would we again say "yes"? Knowing what it would mean to us and to our family, the threats of death and the abuse, the criminal charges, the possibility of years in prison and the long fight for freedom, would we do it again? Putting it on a somewhat broader plane, as have some who asked the question — knowing that it would be in many ways a futile move, knowing that the neighbors on Rone Court would not allow Andrew and his family to live there happily, knowing it meant the danger of death to Andrew and his wife and his child and his unborn child, would we do it again? Or knowing that the violence that would ensue might damage what they persist in calling "race relations" in Louisville, would we do it again?

I have thought of all these factors, I have thought of the personal ones — involving what happened to us and our family. And when I have thought of them, I have only been thankful that life is not arranged in such a way that we can foresee at the time of any action we take what the consequences of that action will be. Fortunately, we cannot see into the future. For that reason, we are able to do the things that seem right to us at the time they arise. Then, if bad results follow, we cope with them as they come — and from somewhere comes the strength we need. If it were not so, if we could have seen ahead on that day when Andrew first came to us in the spring of 1954, I can only hope that I would not have been so selfish as to have been deterred merely by the prospect of the resulting trouble that would come to us. I cannot know.

But as to the other aspects of the question, as to what we would have done if we could have foreseen the danger to Andrew and his family and the possible damage to so-called race relations, here I find that I must turn to the thinking of Andrew and Charlotte Wade for a decision.

If we had been granted the supernatural gift of foresight so that we could predict for a certainty all that would follow our sale of the house to the Wades, I think it would have been my duty, on the first day Andrew approached us, to inform him of these facts. But, if he then, knowing all that could happen, still wanted to proceed with his plans, I think we would have been duty-bound to go along.

I do not think Andrew himself knows what he would have done in those circumstances. He like us could not say for a certainty what his personal qualms might have been. The whole speculation is purely hypothetical, for none of us could know the future — nor will any man when he faces a similar decision. But the point that matters, the point that must be made, is that it was Andrew's and Charlotte's decision to make, and not Carl's and mine.

It was Andrew's and Charlotte's rights that had been violated. It was they who were being deprived of a house. If they could have foreseen the future and still had hopes that by taking the risks involved they could overcome the difficulties and the opposition, if they were willing to take the chance, it was not for us to counsel them against taking this risk. We are white; we are committed against the system of segregation; we are convinced that segregation thwarts our own lives as well as those of the Negro people. But it is the Negro people who are the direct victims. It is they who must say when the battle will be joined against it. If we agree with their objectives, as Carl and I do, then it is our responsibilty to help where we can when they ask. *But we cannot set the timetable.* And, had we counseled Andrew Wade that 1954 was not the time to try to move on to Rone Court, we would have been attempting to set the timetable.

By the same token, I think it would have been wrong for us to do what the prosecution accused us of doing — that is, to go to

Andrew and suggest to him that, since segregated housing was un-desirable, it would be a good idea for him to try to break the pattern and that we would buy a house and transfer it to him if he was willing to buy it. There, too, we would have been trying to set the timetable. But once he made the choice himself, the decision, by our lights, was out of our hands.

I have felt sometimes as I have looked back over the events that followed that perhaps, if I had it to do over again, I might proceed in a somewhat different manner. For example, I have always thought that it was partly the shock with which Rone and the others in Shively found out about Wade's move that resulted in their inflamed reaction.

This was brought home to me by a conversation with one of our own neighbors one night in the summer of 1954. He was a white man who had believed automatically in segregation all of his life. He had never examined his beliefs; he had simply followed them be-cause they were the things he had always heard; he had never run into anybody who thought differently, and adherence to segregation was an accepted and unquestioned part of his existence. He was hot-headed besides, and I have often thought that had he lived in Shively, had he known Rone and Rinehart, he might have been among the people who burned the cross at the Wade home. But — another indication of how fluid people's opinions on this subject are — he had, by the very osmosis that came with living close to us, taken a different position. He had not thought through his attitudes toward the Negro and decided they were wrong; he simply found himself suddenly on the other side. He knew us well and liked us; we had been good neighbors for a couple of years. When we were under attack because we had sold a house to a Negro, he identified himself with us. Gradually, as an inevitable corollary, he identified himself also with Andrew Wade; he began to tell me how he felt Wade has "as much right to that house as the next man" and how "after all, people aren't much different under the skin." He and his wife sat in our living room or in our yard many a night while Carl was away at work during those early weeks after the sale and they helped me answer the constant telephone calls. I remember listening to him arguing my viewpoint with the hostile voices on the other end of the line; I remember marveling as I watched and thought how very much he was like James I. Rone.

All this is why I knew I could learn something when he gave me his opinions as to the reasons for what happened on Rone Court.

"You just shocked those people out there so, Anne," he said. "If they could just have had a little warning. But they thought they had their neighborhood all set — all white. And suddenly here was this colored family. It was just such a shock that it got them all excited. They didn't have time to think."

I pondered these words and wondered how we might have eased the shock for them. It occurred to me that we need not have transferred the house to Andrew so quickly. Maybe it would have been better, instead of Andrew breaking the news to Rone abruptly when Rone asked him if he was moving in, if we had all gone to Rone and tried to let him know more tactfully, tried to win him to our point of view. Considering his later reactions, it probably would not have worked. Probably with any approach he would have reacted in the same panic. But you can't tell. By the time I tried to talk to him on the telephone about the situation, he was already in a state of panic, and there was no possibility of a reasonable discussion. The other way might have been worth a try.

Or, on the other hand, perhaps we should have gone to some white ministers in the area — before Andrew told Rone instead of afterward. Maybe we should have asked them to direct us to some people in the vicinity who might be friendly or at least not hostile to the idea of having a Negro family in the neighborhood. Then we could have gone to these people, told them of Wade's plan, explained his viewpoint, asked their cooperation. Maybe some of these white people would then have joined together to welcome the Wades into the neighborhood and this kind of thing might have quickly offset any mob that might be organized. As it was, the other side was able to grasp control of the situation before the people inclined to have good will had any opportunity to organize.

But even as I go over these speculations of hindsight, I find that I am again bound by the desires and wishes of the Wades. For we discussed once — before anything happened — the possibility of approaching Rone and breaking the news to him quietly.

It was on that Thursday, May 13, 1954, the day that Rone

ultimately found out from Andrew — and the trouble started. Andrew had stopped by our house early in the afternoon on his way to Rone Court.

"I've been thinking — " he said — "about how we ought to go about letting Rone know. Maybe I should go and talk to him and tell him I'm buying the house and try to get him on my side."

"That might be a good idea," I commented. "He may not object at all. If you want us to, Carl and I could go with you, and we'll all talk to him."

Andrew sat a moment, thinking it over. Finally he spoke again.

"No, you know I just talked myself out of that idea," he said. "If I go to Rone, I'm apologizing for moving into that neighborhood. And I'm not going to apologize to anyone for doing what is only my natural right. I'm not asking Rone or anyone else in the neighborhood to be my special friend — I haven't bought the neighborhood, all I've bought is one house. If they want to be my friends, my welcome mat is out to them, but I'm not going to try to force my friendship on them. And I will not apologize for moving into my own house."

"Whatever you want to do," I said, and Carl nodded his agreement.

Andrew gathered up some papers he had brought with him and walked out of our house on his way to Rone Court and the beginning of three years of hell. I watched him as he went down our front walk — his head held high, walking into the face of a hostile white world.

I thought often, as events unfolded, of his pride and his dignity in that moment. Somewhere there is a solution to the problems in human relations that beset our region and our nation. But no solution will long survive the tests of life or the challenges of the future if it writes off that pride or ignores that dignity.

Epilogue 1999

It is forty-four years now since the story recounted in this book occurred, and about forty-two years since I first wrote it down. I did the first draft during those hectic three years of our fighting back, usually writing from 4 to 6 A.M., before the children woke up, driven by some inner fire that compelled me to put it on paper. Sometimes I worked on the road, traveling. I recall the night I searched my unconscious to write the chapter "Back to the Crossroads," pounding away at my portable typewriter in a motel room, during the trip Carl and I took from Louisville to California to talk to people there about "the case."

So much has changed since those years, and yet so much has stayed the same. The basic issue that exploded in our lives in Louisville is, if anything, a more urgent one as we approach the twenty-first century than it was four decades ago. Certainly, for all of us whose own lives were embroiled in that clash of values and worlds, life was never the same again. For me personally, the events in Louisville in the 1950s became the point of no return in a spiritual, moral, and political journey that I had begun years earlier in Alabama.

For a time, Andrew Wade fought beside Carl and me as we carried the story across the nation in an effort to get the support that the storm of hysteria and fear in Kentucky precluded our winning in our home state. On several trips, after Carl's release from prison on bond in mid-1955, Andrew accompanied him to tell the story—the two of them seeking support both for Andrew's struggle to keep his house and Carl's battle against his fifteen-year sentence. Before long, however—and long before the charges against us all were finally dropped—Andrew withdrew from such activity and set about the long and tedious task of rebuilding his life as best he could. The electrical contracting business he ran with his father had been devastated. Boycotts by bankers blocked loans to his big customers, and fear kept some of his smaller customers away. Andrew had his wife and two children to support, and the future looked grim.

Over the years, Andrew eventually won that battle, although the Wade Electric Company never became the large and prosperous business it might have been if the events of 1954 had not happened. But Andrew was and is a skilled electrician. In the early 1990s, *The Courier-Journal* ran a long feature on the Wade Electric Company, one of a series of articles on local business enterprises, citing it as an example of a successful small business in the African American community. Not surprisingly, the article did not mention the events of the 1950s, but I felt an inner thrill as I read that story. To me, it was testimony to the indestructibility of the human spirit.

The house that the Wades bought after they finally sold the one on Rone Court—and new supporters in Chicago replaced the money they had put into their original down payment—was in the West End of Louisville, the older section they had rejected for the newly developed suburbs when they went house-hunting in 1954. It was in that house that they raised their two daughters, and Andrew and Charlotte still live there today. In those days, the West End still had that "checker-board" pattern—one block white, the next one African American, or "changing." It was a pattern promoted by real estate agents who methodically worked to "break" the blocks, one by one, making quick profits from frightened white people who bought new houses elsewhere and from African Americans desperate for places to live, who paid inflated prices for the houses being abandoned. It would not be until the late 1960s, and then only after a tremendous movement of marches, demonstrations, arrests, and political pressure, that Louisville (and later the state of Kentucky) would pass open-housing legislation that at least on paper opened up other areas in the city and its suburbs to people of color.

By then, however, the West End was predominantly African American, despite diligent efforts by some of us to keep it integrated. Today, a number of whites still live in this area; I do, and so do quite a few others. But if you ask most people in Louisville's mainly white (and wealthier) East End, they'll tell you the West End is all black. In 1988, a panel of religious leaders held a hearing on racial discrimination in Louisville and issued a report entitled "A Tale of Two Cities." Louisville, like many other urban centers in the country today, is still a sharply divided city, and not just in housing.

In the early 1960s, Andrew reemerged briefly as something of a leader in local civil rights activity, helping to form the Louisville chapter of the Congress of Racial Equality (CORE), which was responsible for the first sit-ins here challenging segregation in public accommodations. After that, however, he seemed to retire to the sidelines of the movement, although as the fear of reprisals wore off, many people went to him for advice and inspiration. I don't think his commitments ever changed. Just recently, he said to me: "After it became clear that we could never move back to that house, I had one hope—that what had happened to us would make things easier for others later. I think that has happened." And it surely has.

Gradually, Carl and I saw less and less of Andrew; our lives simply moved in the other direction as we became more involved in activism, much of it outside Louisville. But we always kept in intermittent touch, and I still see Andrew from time to time today. He comes whenever I have electrical work to be done, and usually, if he is not rushed, stays to talk awhile about news of the day. Rarely do the events of the 1950s come into the conversation, as everything that could be said was said long ago. But our common experiences from the past provide a continuing unspoken, if tenuous, bond between us. There are starting points for any conversation that do not exist with a casual acquaintance, or even a person one has known in a less intense context; there are assumptions that no longer need to be discussed.

As for Charlotte, after those events of the mid-1950s, I never tried to reestablish the fragile relationship that once barely started and was shattered so quickly. It would have been important to me to make a struggle to do so, even if I failed. But I felt that Charlotte did not need to have to cope with my desire for her friendship, in addition to the other problems and burdens that faced her. Her dream of a ranch-style house on Rone Court brought more trouble to her than fulfillment. And I assumed over the years that she would not want to talk with me. I literally did not speak with her for about forty years.

Then, just recently, as I was writing this epilogue, I decided to call her. I wanted her to read what I had written and tell me if she found anything I was saying inaccurate or offensive. At first when I identified myself and told her I'd like to stop by and see her, she was very cool. "What about?" she asked. I told her what I was doing. She arranged for me to get the manuscript to her, and I said I'd call her back after she had time to read it. For days I postponed doing so—literally cringing at the possibility of a hostile reaction. But when I finally called, she was very warm and friendly. She wanted me to change only one thing I had written—a line where I said that I assumed that Charlotte still thought all the trouble that came to her was Carl's and my fault. She asked me to omit that, and said: "I didn't blame you. We asked you to buy the house. You didn't ask us to do anything." A vast sense of relief swept over me. I realized that for years I had borne a strange burden of thinking otherwise. On the phone, she and I began to talk some about those long-ago events and agreed that we would get together soon and talk more. It was the best thing that had happened to me in a long time.

Over the decades, as our lives became busier and busier in other struggles, I totally lost touch with some of the other people who had been major players in the events of the 1950s. For example, I don't know what became of Ben Hudson, who felt that we had destroyed the future of his small real estate business. And after that summer of 1954, I never talked again with James Rone, who had sold us the house. It sometimes occurred to me that I should call him, but I never did. In the 1980s, when ABC television reporters and camera people came to town to do a documentary on the case (which they never aired), Rone declined to be interviewed. The reporters did talk with two of the men—including Rone's son, Buster—who confessed to the 1954 grand jury that they burned the cross at the Wade house. I later watched the tape of the interview. Buster's comments were similar to those he made to the grand jury three decades earlier: he didn't know who instigated the incident, but "at that time you had a lot of this being done in the South, the whole neighborhood was there. It was just something that happened." In 1991, I read the elder Rone's obituary in the newspaper, which did not mention the events of the 1950s. He had worked at a local manufacturing company for most of the intervening years; apparently he built some more houses, but never on the scale he had once envisioned for Rone Court.

A few years after all the furor, and after the attacks on us had given the street's name national publicity, someone changed the name of Rone Court to Clyde Drive. Andrew stopped by our house one day, chuckling, to tell us he had been out that way and had noticed that the residents had placed a United States flag at the entrance to the court. "I guess they want everybody to know they are not subversive," he said.

By the 1980s, the terrain in that area had changed totally. Where in 1954 there was more farmland than houses, subdivisions now abounded. When Andrew and I looked for the house to show it to the ABC crew, we both had a hard time finding and identifying it. We finally did, after asking many of the area's residents, none of whom had lived there in 1954 but some of whom had heard vaguely about a house bombing there long before. Although many African Americans have now moved into some parts of Shively, the Clyde Drive section remains mostly white. But Andrew had one rather joyful moment when he went to one door on the street and met an African American man living there. The man had heard of him and was delighted to meet him.

For our chief assailant in 1954, local prosecutor A. Scott Hamilton, there was tragedy. In 1959, he committed suicide. Carl and I were in New England at the time, vacationing and visiting friends. The phone rang, and it was one of our lawyers, C. Ewbank Tucker, calling from Louisville to tell us the news. My reaction was shock and, in a strange way, sorrow. Carl was not shocked. Just about a year before, he had predicted that Hamilton would kill himself.

He made that prediction while we were trying to get back the books that had been seized from our home and used in the trial. That was another battle in itself. We finally did get them all back—plus some supposedly "subversive" ones we had never owned but which we kept, figuring that we had earned them. The hundreds of books taken from our house were a strange mixture. There were some by Marx and Lenin, and socialists of varied types, some about the labor movement, some about Eugene Debs and other radical organizers—all of which might logically have been considered "subversive" in the atmosphere of 1954. But there were also novels by Tolstoy and Dostoevsky, dating from an earlier interest of mine in Russian literature. If it had a Russian name, the raiders took it. After they were all returned to us, Carl delighted in placing the most "dangerous" ones, marked Government's Exhibit No. ———, in the most prominent place in our living-room bookcases, which had by then grown to the ceiling, covering two entire walls. Thus anybody entering the front door had to see them. For years, Carl would give them to people as souvenirs, one by one, until most of them were gone.

But in 1957, most of the books were still in the Kentucky Court of Appeals, at the state capitol in Frankfort, where they had been sent with Carl's appeal. Efforts by lawyers to retrieve them failed, so finally Carl drove to Frankfort himself, walked in and interrupted a session of the court, and told the judges he wanted his books. They professed not to know they were still there and said, "Sure, take them," which Carl did. Then we found that numerous ones were still missing and subsequently learned that some of them were in Scott Hamilton's office. Carl called Hamilton, who told him to come down and get them. Carl borrowed a truck from a friend and went. Hamilton ended up helping him carry boxes to the truck. Carl described the scene to me when he returned home.

Carl had the last box of books in his arms, and Hamilton followed him across the large courtroom where the 1954 trial had taken place. Carl said it seemed rather eerie. It was late afternoon, almost dark in the big empty chamber. As they stopped at the door leading to the outside, Hamilton waved his arm slightly toward the courtroom behind them and said, "Well, Carl, I'm glad all that is over." Carl replied: "Well, I guess you know I'm glad." Then, Carl told me, Hamilton extended his hand and said: "I guess history will decide which one of us was right." Carl replied: "There's not a doubt in my mind about that." They shook hands, and Carl left.

After describing the scene to me, Carl said: "That man is going to commit suicide." "Oh, Carl," I responded, "don't be ridiculous." As much as I loved Carl, I sometimes felt, as did many of his friends and foes, that he had a tendency to exaggerate the drama of life.

But his instincts were accurate, as they so often were. There was no implication, as some would have liked to believe, that Hamilton eventually felt remorse for what he had done and took his own life. In fact, quite the opposite was true. Almost until the moment of his death, he continued to be obsessed with the rightness of his cause. Many people who agreed with him that we were at best very foolish, and at worst the personification of evil, began to turn against him. In the immediate aftermath of our case, he ran roughshod over the rights of too many people, casting a very wide net, subpoenaing all sorts of people to grand juries, threatening to do so with others. And even after that spurt of activity died down, he continued to talk endlessly about "the Braden case," long after most people in town wanted to put it all behind them. He did so irrelevantly on TV appearances during a campaign a few months before his suicide, in which he served as campaign manager for a gubernatorial candidate; the candidate lost Jefferson County, where Louisville is located, by a wider margin than any other losing candidate in recent memory. Hamilton's political stature declined sharply.

Most politically aware people in Louisville had long assumed that

Hamilton's ultimate ambition was to be governor of the state, and many of our friends thought he cynically used our case to further that ambition. I continued to think, and still do, that he believed everything he said about us. Thus, he assumed that people in Kentucky would appreciate the great service he had rendered the Commonwealth by destroying the evil Bradens—and would therefore reward him by making him governor.

But things went in the opposite direction, and I think he simply could not deal with defeat. His life, apparently, began to disintegrate. According to press reports, the precipitating incident for the suicide was a family argument, involving a minor difference with his daughter. His wife told police that he said, "I'll just end it all right now," picked up a revolver, and shot himself in the heart.

Subsequent events were kinder to other lawyers on Hamilton's 1954 staff. Lawrence Higgins, his top assistant, who delivered the final exhortation to the jury in Carl's trial—the man I never thought believed a word he was saying—went on to become a circuit judge. Until he retired a few years ago, I would see him occasionally when I visited the courthouse with some delegation, or observing a trial; he usually spoke stiffly. On the other hand, another assistant, Henry Sadlo, stopped being a prosecutor years ago and became a defense attorney. He never fails, when he sees me, to engage me in conversation and tell me how young he was in 1954 and how he really didn't understand what was going on.

Most of our defense attorneys carried on as advocates for social justice throughout their lives. C. Ewbank Tucker curtailed his law practice to become a bishop in the AME Zion Church, but he continued to wage war on racism until his death in the 1970s. He remained our friend, often visiting our home to engage in conversation about various struggles and to strategize. George Ambro continued to battle for underdogs as a defense lawyer, as did Harry McAlpin, although he later left Louisville and moved to Washington.

Louis Lusky had a hard time, professionally, in Louisville after he came into Carl's case to handle the appeal; his law practice had been in real estate, and in this arena he was ostracized. Even his long-time secretary quit during the appeal, saying that as a "good American" she could not in conscience type the brief in Carl's case. But life opened up in other ways for Louis. His real passion had always been civil liberties. After his work on our case brought him attention, he became involved in some aspects of the later Freedom Ride cases in Mississippi and handled other significant human rights cases. Ultimately, he was appointed a full professor at Columbia University Law School.

When we first met Lusky in 1954, I believe he thought we and our co-defendants were quite undesirable people, and I did not care for him at all. I remember the day I met him, the day soon after our indictment when he argued on behalf of the national ACLU for dismissal of the charges. Maintaining that the sedition law was too broad, he said: "If you have cockroaches in your house, you don't take a shotgun to get rid of them." When court recessed, I approached him and said: "You called me a cockroach. If that's the way you feel, I'd just as soon you stay out of this case." He denied that he had intended to insult us.

Over the next few years, I sat in his office in long conversations that went far beyond the legal questions at hand, and a strange but deep mutual respect developed between us. I came to feel I could trust him with my right arm, and I think he developed respect for us as people. He was also one of a rare breed, a lawyer who was a talented writer. The 330-page brief he wrote for the Court of Appeals in Carl's case remains a classic that is used as a reference in some law schools. It also reads, in spots, like a novel. Carl once said in jest that I did not need to write a book on the case, that Lusky had already written it.

But the lawyer to whom I had felt closest, Bob Zollinger—the one who had been a pillar of strength to me when I wanted to give up the fight after Carl's trial—changed sides in the social struggle. In my view, his life—like Hamilton's—became tragedy, in a different way.

For some years after the case was over, we stayed in touch. But in the early 1960s, he began telling me how "the people who persecuted you ten years ago are now the ones being persecuted." This was in 1964, no less. He was referring to restaurant owners who were being "persecuted" by African American (and white) youth sitting in at their business establishments. Then he gave me a book he said I should read. It turned out to be one of those pseudo-scientific treatises purporting to present new evidence that people of color are inherently inferior to whites. I was appalled.

After that, I lost any real contact with Zollinger. He became a prosecutor. It was painful to encounter him again, as he helped in the arrests of many of us in open-housing demonstrations in the late 1960s, and as he led the prosecution in a case against members of the Louisville Black Panther Party in the early 1970s.

I could explain this distressing turn of events only by remembering that Zollinger had never seemed much interested in the basic issues of segregation and racism that undergirded our case. His interest was pure "civil liberties"—the rights people in this country are supposed to have, and which were being mutilated in the attacks on us. In 1955, when his words helped bring me back to sanity at a low moment, that commitment gave him the strength to stay on an even keel when I wavered. But in the long run, in the United States of America, where racism is so basic to all that is wrong in our society, this commitment alone was not enough.

When Zollinger died of a heart attack in the late 1970s, I went to the funeral home because he had been so vital to a very important part of my life. As I went in, I saw his children, whom I had come to know well when they were small. His son, now also a lawyer, living in another state, said that people would be making comments in the basement of the funeral home. He asked if I would like to say something. My reply was immediate: "I certainly would."

It was one of those half-joyful wakes, with drinks and food and anecdotes. Bob would have loved that part of it. Finally someone called the assemblage to order, and various co-workers and friends shared memories. When it came my turn to speak, I said I wanted to talk about a part of Bob's life that no one else had mentioned, but which I thought was his shining hour. Then I recalled how, when the dead hand of fear and the storms of hysteria gripped the Louisville community, when most people we had known for years feared to speak to us, Zollinger had the courage to come to our defense and in the process to defend the rights supposedly guaranteed in the Bill of Rights. I said that I assumed those assembled also thought these rights were important. Most of the people there were establishment-types, people who would not agree with me on much. But when I finished speaking, they applauded.

And finally tragedy in yet another way beset the life of one other key person in the case, Alberta Ahearn, the star witness against Carl at his trial. I never saw Alberta again after that final day of Carl's trial when she testified. A number of times, as the years went on, I noticed she was still listed in the phone book at the same address where I had known her. I would tell myself that I really should go to see her—and tell her I bore her no ill will. But I never did.

Then, in April 1995, I noticed a headline on the front page of the morning paper. It said: "Woman's body found in search of house." For some reason, I read the story. It said the woman was named Alberta Ahearn, and the address was the one I knew. The article said neighbors reported they had not seen her for months; police had finally come to the house with a search warrant, and found her badly decomposed body on the kitchen floor. Her daughter, Charlene, who had lived with her, was in the house. The body had been covered with a blanket, police said, as if to "keep it warm." They said she had been dead for weeks, maybe months.

The article made no mention of the 1954 case, and I realized that no one at the newspaper, forty years later, would have known about it. I debated with myself whether to call and tell them. A part of me said there was no reason to stir all that up again. But I started my adult life as a newspaper reporter and developed what we then called a sharp "nose for news" that has never left me. My reporter's instincts prevailed, and I called the city editor. They of course put a reporter on the story. He worked on it a week and found virtually no sources of information. County officials had asked the newspaper to issue a call for next of kin. There seemed to be no relatives except a sister-in-law who apparently took over funeral home arrangements but declined to be interviewed. There were no close friends; neighbors knew her but rarely saw her. Her daughter had worked many years as a school library clerk, but co-workers there said they knew little about her. She had left her job in 1993; according to the press report, after her mother's body was found, she was taken to a hospital for a psychiatric examination.

A week later, the reporter wrote a very sensitive story, recounting Alberta's earlier fame and her later years as a recluse. He quoted me as saying: "I certainly don't have any bitter feelings toward her. Those were different times. There were such pressures on people to conform in the hysteria of the time. I don't know that anybody came through that period unscathed."

I thought I would go to the funeral but learned from the funeral home that there would be only a private burial. I felt I should try in some manner to communicate to whatever family there was. I wrote a letter addressed to the "Family of Alberta Ahearn" and sent it to the funeral home, asking that it be delivered, hoping that it perhaps would reach the daughter. In it I said that I believed, as years go by, everyone who has ever been a part of our lives is important to our being, no matter what the circumstances of the relationship. And so, I said, I profoundly regretted the fact that I had never found the time to seek her out in recent years. "I will always feel that maybe I could have been of some help to her. Maybe not, but I'll always wonder. Please accept this expression of my concern. If there is anything I can do for any of you in her family, especially Charlene, please let me know." I never received a reply.

Among those whose lives were profoundly changed by the 1950s case were surely our co-defendants. All of them, except Carl and me, left Louisville within a few years. Those who were employed lost their jobs and, with one exception, could not possibly find other employment here. The exception was Lewis Lubka. Lew was a skilled welder, and at that time welders were in demand. He had no trouble finding jobs, usually losing them when an employer found out who he was, but then he'd just get another one. He ultimately left Louisville anyway because he decided he wanted to become a city planner. He went back to school and pursued that career for a number of years, encountering the "Braden problem" again in the early 1960s. At that time, Carl was in prison again, this time for defying the House Un-American Activities Committee (HUAC), and Lew invited me to come to Augusta, Georgia, where he was then working, to speak at a community center on HUAC, the First Amendment, and the civil rights movement. That ended his career in Augusta, but he was a person of wide-ranging interests, endless vitality, and a way with people that enabled him never to meet a stranger. He ultimately went into teaching and in 1973 joined the faculty of North Dakota State University in Fargo, where he continued his work for social justice that inspired his students and took him all over the world.

I. O. Ford, who was very elderly when the Louisville case caught him in its net, moved to California to be near old friends soon after he was released from jail, and he died there a few years later. We kept in touch a bit, and I think he never regretted the Louisville ordeal. Al-though it brought him some suffering, it thrust him again into the midst of issues which had been central to his life and work in his earlier years.

Vernon Bown, the white truck driver who stayed with Charlotte during the days on Rone Court, also moved to California, where he was active in justice and peace movements all through the 1960s and 1970s. In the 1980s he moved back to Wisconsin, where his roots were, and continued to be active. I noticed when I recently reread this book for the first time in decades that in describing Vern I did not mention that he was a veteran of the Abraham Lincoln Brigade[1] who went to Spain to fight at the age of nineteen. I was rather amused and bewildered as I noted this omission. Was I unconsciously self-censoring as I wrote, be-cause such associations were things one did not much talk about in the 1950s? Or was it because, perhaps for the same reason, Vern hardly mentioned that aspect of his life when I knew him in that period? I really don't remember. But as one grows older, the important things in life tend to sift out. When Vern came back to Louisville for a visit in 1989, he spoke to a group of veterans of the social justice movements of the 1960s who were having a reunion here. He said there were two high points in his life—his experience in Spain in the 1930s and his part in the struggle in Louisville in the 1950s.

After the case was over, LaRue Spiker went on with her writing career. Before long, she moved to Maine and became a widely re-spected writer for a newspaper, through the years working as an activ-ist in social justice movements, especially on environmental issues.

The national office of the Women's International League for Peace and Freedom (WILPF) created a job for Louise Gilbert, when she could not get one in Louisville, and she moved to Philadelphia. There she be-came a leader in movements against war and racism. After a few years, when the Cold War began to thaw, she was able to get a job again in social work and pursued a productive career in this field, along with other activities. Upon retirement, she also moved to Maine.

Although for all seven of us life was always too busy to maintain regular contact, our communication was never really broken by any-thing but death. There remained a sense of kinship that nothing could destroy. I recall in the very early days of our fight-back, the noted law-yer Frank Donner, who was helping us, said to me: "One thing you have to watch for is divisions among the defendants. It so often happens. The tension is so great. People start blaming each other; they fall out among themselves, they become bitter at each other."

This never happened to us. We worked together as a team. We became very close, and this closeness stood the test of time. In 1991, the five of us who survived gathered in Maine for a reunion. I believe the people one shares intense struggle with, especially the people one goes to jail with, become the closest and most valued friends. I found this to be true in my life later—in other battles, with other people. But I think the closest and most lasting relationships of all were with those who shared with me this first real struggle of my life, forty-four years ago.

There was a brief time in the late 1950s when Carl and I also considered leaving Louisville. We had to find a way to pay the grocery bills, and it appeared impossible for us to get jobs in Louisville. We figured I had a better chance than Carl, the result probably of a male supremacist atmosphere that assumed the man was the greater villain. I too encountered closed doors, however, and as a result had some very low moments. I recall especially one job interview, with a young white minister who wanted to write a book and needed someone with my skills to help him. I had been sent to him by an employment agency; he said I was just the person he needed. But a few days later, he called to say it just would not work; he had talked to some people in his congregation, and they were outraged at the thought. I can remember vividly, even now, how depressed I felt. Of all the things that had happened to me, I thought, perhaps this was the worst. The possibility of prison was one thing—but from prison one could speak, one could even organize in prison. But here I was, at age thirty-two, still young, healthy, and possessing certain talents. And yet there was no way to use them, and at that moment it appeared there would never be. It was an experience, I later learned, that many victims of the witch hunts went through in the 1950s, and most of them in a much more severe and lasting way than Carl and I experienced.

Finally, in the fall of 1956, I did get a job, as a typist in the office of a small company. The owner was a founder and leader of the new Kentucky Civil Liberties Union that had been formed in the wake of our case. I had been sent there by an employment agency; there was an opening, and he could scarcely have refused to hire me, in view of his commitments. I have a passion for work that I've never been able to explain. I really enjoy working more than just about anything else in my life, so I have always worked very hard at whatever task presented itself. Thus, I worked at that little typing job far beyond the call of duty, often staying overtime without pay, not because I felt I had to do so to keep my job, but because it was my nature. I always figured the company got me for about half of what I was worth financially, a situation many employers enjoyed in those days when they brought themselves to hire talented people labeled "subversives."

With our essential needs taken care of, we turned to the more significant question of what we could do for the causes we believed in. Everything that had happened to us had only served to sharpen Carl's and my feelings that we had to give ourselves to the struggle against segregation. In particular we felt a burning need to win more white people to this crusade, because we knew so well, from our own experience, that this was a battle in the interests of white people, too. And yet the atmosphere in Louisville at that point was such that we could not have organized a meeting in a phone booth.

Between 1954 and 1957, we traveled all over the United States. Between the two of us, we crisscrossed the country several times, usually separately so one of us could stay with the children. We had done this traveling as a matter of survival; we had to raise money and organize protests. But in the course of that work, we made friends all across the land; we met people everywhere who were fighting back. The 1950s were never completely silent, and we met the people who never stopped struggling—against segregation, against war, against the repression of what inaccurately became known as the McCarthy period (U.S. Senator Joseph McCarthy, from Wisconsin, did not start it). Looking back on it years later, I now realize that we were truly among the luckiest victims of the attacks of those years. Our case was so unusual, it dramatized so graphically the distortions of justice brought on by the anti-Communist hysteria, that it became a vehicle people could use to mount counter-offensives. Thus we got tremendous support, and we were able to help organize what I call the "resistance movement" of the 1950s.

In the process, we learned a great deal about how to fight back against attack. We learned that one must use every attack as a platform from which to reach more people with the issues that brought on the attack in the first place. We did that, using the platform history had given us to call attention to the issue of segregated housing, and also to what segregation and racism were doing to the South, and to the nation, on every front. The lessons we learned in that period, the philosophy and the techniques of fighting back, proved very useful in many subsequent struggles on behalf of ourselves and others in the decades that followed.

But in those anxious moments of decision in the late 1950s, it appeared that we might have to take what we had learned to a place other than Louisville, perhaps other than the South. Friends we had made across the country were urging us to move to their locales. But as we pondered the possibility of moving elsewhere, something kept nagging me in the depths of my heart, warning me that it would not be right to leave. I had never lived anywhere except the South, and despite all my deep disagreement with its policies, I loved the South. The South, I knew, needed its dissenters in that hour. Could we really run away?

One day I wrote a letter to Aubrey Williams, in Montgomery, Alabama. Aubrey was one of the many great people we had met in the course of our travels, a white Alabaman, a generation older than me, who had early seen the light and had become a high official in Franklin Roosevelt's New Deal government. He had earned the fury of southern congressmen by his pro–civil rights positions and was driven out of Washington in the mid-1940s, at which point he moved back to Alabama, planning someday to run for governor. He would have made an excellent one, but that possibility was shot to smithereens when he publicly supported the 1954 Supreme Court decision against school segregation. By the time we met him, he was already a pariah to many people in that state.

I admired Aubrey very much, so I told him in my letter that many people were urging Carl and me to leave Louisville and the South, and I wanted his advice. I think I knew what his advice would be; in a sense, my letter was just a search for moral support. Sure enough, his answer came back quickly in the mail: "You have shed your blood in the streets of Louisville," he wrote. "The only way you should leave is in a coffin."

We had not shed any blood. Aubrey, like Carl, had a flair for the dramatic. But his answer was what I wanted to hear, and I think Carl did, too. We decided to stay. I had no idea what we could ever do in Louisville that would be constructive, but some way I felt that "they also serve who only stay."

My letter also set Aubrey in motion in another direction. He was president of the Southern Conference Educational Fund (SCEF), a small and beleaguered, but determined, organization of African American and white southerners dedicated to the task of ending segregation. It descended from an earlier organization, the Southern Conference for Human Welfare (SCHW), which had been formed in 1938, based on a vision of a new and democratic South that would be built jointly by black and white people. SCHW was a New Deal organization that came together originally around issues of economic justice, but it soon had to deal with the issue of racial justice, so it became a pioneering force for civil rights. It also came under vicious attack from politicians intent on keeping economic and political power in a few hands and thus became one of the first targets of the domestic Cold War attacks after World War II.

The continuation of SCEF was the handiwork of one man more than any other—Jim Dombrowski, another white southerner who in time became one of our closest friends and one of the most important mentors of my life. After SCHW went out of existence, Jim decided that none of the other problems the South faced, including its dire economic ones, would ever be solved until legal segregation and the oppression of African Americans ended. He decided there was a need for an interracial organization committed to that goal. He led the continuation of SCEF with that one-point program.[2]

Carl and I first came into mail contact with SCEF when we were involved in the campaign in Kentucky in the early 1950s to open our state's hospitals to Blacks. When we and the Wades got in trouble in 1954, Jim and SCEF immediately came to our support. And although we had never met him, Jim sent a personal check for a thousand dollars to help make Carl's bond. About a year later, we met in person when he arranged a meeting for us in New Orleans, where SCEF had its headquarters.

By 1957, SCEF and what it stood for were beset from every side, with the White Citizens Councils and other organized groups of segregationists growing rapidly. With Jim as SCEF's only staff, the organization desperately needed someone to help him. After he got my letter,

Aubrey—as we learned later—told Jim that Carl and I were the people SCEF needed. Discussions followed, and in the fall of 1957 we went to work as traveling staff for SCEF, at a joint salary of forty-two hundred dollars a year, as I recall; the organization had very little money. Our assignment, although we continued to live in Louisville, was to travel the South, seeking out support for the civil rights movement, especially in white communities.

Thus began another phase in our lives, which extended for almost the next two decades. Carl and I always felt that we were among the world's most fortunate people to be able to have at least some relationship to the great social upsurges that developed in the South in those years, and which changed our region, and the nation, forever. In addition to traveling and encouraging white resistance to segregation, I edited SCEF's monthly newsletter, *The Southern Patriot,* developing it into a tabloid paper that became the movement newspaper of that era and a major organizing tool; it is a unique reference source today.

It would take another book to recount those years we spent with SCEF. But it is relevant to the present book to note that, through all those years, we remained somewhat on the fringes of the civil rights movement. Our reputation as "subversives," the label bestowed on us during the Louisville case, followed us into the wider movement. That, combined with SCEF's own history as a "labeled" organization, made us and SCEF the target of constant new attacks. When HUAC went to Atlanta in 1958 and subpoenaed people active in the civil rights movement, Carl was among those called. He told the committee his beliefs and associations were "none of the business of this committee," legally a First Amendment challenge to the committee's authority. His statement provided the title of a pamphlet I wrote at the time. (Carl often said that he went to prison and I wrote the books and pamphlets about it.) Three years later, after appeals failed, Carl went to prison for ten months on a contempt of Congress conviction, along with Frank Wilkinson of California, who by then was organizing a national campaign to abolish HUAC. We handled that situation with our technique of using attacks as a platform, and SCEF mounted a campaign to inform people in the South about the relationships between civil rights and civil liberties and to explain to them how the use of such witchhunting committees as HUAC was weakening the civil rights movement. Ultimately, the SCEF work led to a coming together of civil rights forces in the South and civil liberties advocates across the country. In my opinion, it was because of the power of this coalition that HUAC was finally abolished in 1975.

Meantime, the attack on us and SCEF had continued, not only from the federal committees but also from multiple little southern state committees modeled after HUAC. There was FUAC in Florida, the Sovereignty Commission in Mississippi, along with others. In 1963, the Louisiana Un-American Activities Committee raided the SCEF office in New Orleans, arrested Jim Dombrowski and others, setting in motion a famous test case, which Jim and SCEF won in 1965.[3]

In 1966, Jim retired as director of SCEF, and its board asked Carl and me to take over this job jointly. We agreed, but we were still determined not to leave Louisville, so the organization moved its headquarters here. And, in 1967, Carl and I were charged with sedition a second time; it turned out that the law under which we had been indicted in 1954 was never really nullified, just declared inoperative on the basis that the federal government had preempted the field of sedition against the federal government with the Smith Act. Carl and I, however, were peripheral to the new sedition case, as it was mainly directed at young people on the SCEF staff (by then SCEF had grown mightily), whose work included organizing in the Kentucky mountains against the strip mining that was destroying the land and the people, and trying to build coalitions between oppressed white people in this area and the by-then burgeoning African American movement throughout the South.

Not surprisingly, the SCEF program upset the coal operators, and we were all jailed in Pike County in the Kentucky mountains, charged with conspiring to overthrow the governments of Kentucky and of that county. (Carl used to joke that he and I were probably the only two people in the country who had been charged twice with trying to overthrow the same state government—and that, since the government was still standing, this could prove we were a bit ineffective.) But it is testimony to the change in the atmosphere that had occurred as a result of the southern upsurge that, whereas in the 1950s it took us about three years to win a case against the state sedition law, in 1967 it took just about three weeks. Our lawyers got a three-judge federal court convened immediately to consider the validity of the law.

I'll never forget the day we walked into a large federal courtroom in Lexington, Kentucky, having been brought there from the Pike

County Jail for a hearing on the law. The courtroom was packed—not, as in 1954 Louisville, with hostile faces and a lynch-mob atmosphere, but with our friends. The student movement at the University of Kentucky had come out in force. The noted civil rights attorney William Kunstler was representing us and at one point put me on the stand to describe what SCEF was trying to do in the mountains. When the Pike County prosecutor cross-examined me, he seemed to swell up like a toad as he thundered the question that had struck terror into the hearts of so many people in the 1950s: "Mrs. Braden, are you now or have you ever been a Communist?" At that point, that entire courtroom burst into a roar of laughter, and one of the young people later told me: "I had heard of that question, but I didn't believe anyone really said it." I knew on that day that the 1950s were finally over. The judges retired for an hour and returned to declare the entire Kentucky sedition law unconstitutional.

But, although for a younger generation the 1950s may have been over, many people in the South did not seem to know it yet. The unrelenting attacks on us continued and frightened many people within the civil rights movement. As a result, Carl and I were often unwelcome in coalitions and campaigns. Through all those years, we fought for our right and for SCEF's right to be a part of the movement for civil rights. We did this not because we felt our contribution was indispensable but because we felt that the attacks on us represented a lethal weapon that opponents of justice were using to divide and weaken the entire movement.

And within the movement, we always had strong and brave allies who agreed with us on this danger. One was the Rev. Fred Shuttlesworth, who led the movement in Birmingham and in 1963 accepted the presidency of SCEF at one of the most dangerous times to associate with us. Another was Ella Baker, the unofficial "godmother" of the student movement of the 1960s. Among others who never feared association with us were Jim Forman, executive secretary of the Student Nonviolent Coordinating Committee (SNCC); Vincent Harding, activist and historian then living in Atlanta; and the Rev. Wyatt Tee Walker, in the early 1960s the director of Dr. Martin Luther King Jr.'s Southern Christian Leadership Conference (SCLC).

And Martin himself, despite tremendous pressure, always maintained a close relationship with us personally and with SCEF. For example, when the U.S. Supreme Court upheld Carl's conviction on the contempt of Congress charge, I visited Martin at his home in Atlanta and asked him to initiate a clemency petition as an organizing tool for protest. I suggested that, if he signed, others would also have the courage to do so. He said he would think about it. A few weeks later, as we sought to complete a list of petition initiators, I tried several times to reach him on the phone. Finally, one Saturday night, I decided he was not going to call me back. Then, on Sunday morning very early, the phone rang. It was Martin. "Anne," he said, "I've been praying about this thing all night. I want you to put my name on that petition."

This action—and other similar ones later—gave me an opportunity to know a side of Martin that I think many in the movement did not know. In those days, he was not the universally revered figure he later became; like any leader, he had detractors—people who said, for example, that he was only seeking glory for himself. I always knew better. There was absolutely no personal advantage for him in his unwavering support of us; it could only bring him trouble and criticism— which it did. I have told a number of his biographers about such incidents, but so far as I know none has written about them. I think even now, at this late time, they do not want to deal with the impact of the anti-Communist hysteria on the civil rights movement.

Martin's wife, Coretta, was also courageously supportive of us in those early years. In the early 1960s, when she was in Louisville to speak, she came to our house—I'm sure to the consternation of the group that had brought her here. She said she was thinking of us especially at that time. It was soon after the Kings had moved from Montgomery to Atlanta, and Martin had been falsely charged in a tax case by Alabama state agents determined to destroy him. Because they were in a different city, Coretta said, for the first time in their own movement life, they felt alone. In Montgomery they had always been surrounded by friends; in Atlanta, for a short time, the phone did not ring and they went through a brief period of feeling very isolated, fearing that people were believing the false charges. "I understand, I think," Coretta said, "what you all have been through, when even friends seem to desert you, and how lonely you must sometimes have been."

As the new student movement of the 1960s took shape with the formation of SNCC, some of the young people at first heeded the advice of elders who told them we and SCEF were dangerous. But that soon changed, partly because of the influence of Ella Baker, and through their own experience. As time passed, we developed very close working relationships with the people in SNCC and worked closely with the growing number of southern white youth who came into the movement for civil rights and (against our advice) eventually formed their own organization, the Southern Student Organizing Committee (SSOC). Although they too were warned by some elders to stay away from us, they never really did.

In the late 1960s, a new wave of repression hit the country, one that I think was worse than the repression of the 1950s, but which unfortunately was hardly noticed by many white activists because its main targets were the Black Panthers and other organizations of people of color. Our experience in how to fight back proved very valuable in that period, although tragically nothing that we or others did effectively stopped those attacks. This country today still lives with the bitter fruits of that counter-attack against the civil rights movement.

In 1973 SCEF, which had withstood so many attacks from without and had actually grown stronger after each one, was finally destroyed by dissension from within. I am now totally convinced that this dissension was encouraged by the government through its COINTELPRO operation.[4] The breakup of SCEF was one of the great traumas of my life, worse than the ordeal of the 1950s. I had spent sixteen years of my life building this organization, and I watched as it was destroyed in six months.

But by 1975, some of us who had found a rallying point in SCEF formed a new organization, the Southern Organizing Committee for Economic and Social Justice (SOC), to carry the vision of what we now call the Southern Conference Movement into a new age. It continues to grow today as a network of people across the South, working in their communities against racism, war, economic injustice, and environmental destruction. It is very consciously multiethnic, led by people of color but including whites as well as African Americans, Latinos/Latinas, Native Americans, and Asian Americans. From the SOC base, I took part in the continuing organizing of the 1970s (when the media were telling us there was no "movement" anymore), fighting the appalling resurgence of racism both overt and covert, the new military buildup, and the new struggles for economic justice in the South.

I continued my activism into the 1980s—among other endeavors, in the two Jesse Jackson presidential campaigns, into which I hurled myself heart and soul. There I experienced the thrill of seeing significant numbers of whites, including white working-class southerners, join this movement led by African Americans, because it held out hope of real answers to their real problems. It was the kind of movement I had envisioned for so long, seeming to be a dream come true, and I was able to work to help make it happen. And then in the 1990s, and down to the present time, I went on working with SOC, as it nurtured a new grassroots movement challenging the racism and class bias that characterize the toxic pollution of the South's air and water.

Carl died in 1975 at age sixty, of heart failure, and suddenly, as he would have wanted to die, in the midst of work. I was not at home, having left the evening before to drive to Alabama to help my mother, who was ill. The morning after I left, Carl apparently wrote letters related to a training program he had recently set up to help young people learn skills of communication and organizing. And he wrote an article for a progressive publication on the recent demise of HUAC. Then he apparently took a bath, went to lie down on our couch, and there he died.

Nobody had expected Carl to die; to his friends, and to me, he seemed made of iron. His departure was a devastating shock to many people, and most certainly to me. He had been my liberator from the prisons of my childhood. Through him I had found new worlds I never knew existed and had gone through the difficult process of changing my class allegiance. (I often said I married into the working class.) And he, I knew, had found important new perspectives on life through me, especially on the issue of race. Over the twenty-seven years we lived and worked together, our lives had become totally intertwined like the trunks of two trees grown together. We often disagreed, we were as different as daylight and dark, but our work and our lives had always been as a team.

In the weeks immediately after his death, I told myself I must sit down and figure out how one part of a two-person team could and would function alone. I must take time to decide, I said to myself, what I should do with "the rest of my life." Strange as it may seem, I never did. Too many struggles continued to rise on the horizon, too many people looked to me to do too many things. Somehow, the "rest of my life" just set its own course, and it still seems to be doing that as I look at the world from the vantage point of age seventy-four.

Carl and I had endured our share of personal tragedy and sorrow through the years, the worst being in 1964. That was the year our daughter Anita, one of the children to whom this book was dedicated, died. She had been the picture of health until 1963, when at age ten she was diagnosed as having a very rare heart and lung condition. Our many friends rallied around us, raising funds for us to take her to the Mayo Clinic, and other friends contacted people in other parts of the world to see if research anywhere had found a cure for the problem she had. None was found, and she died at age eleven. By then I had developed a philosophy of life that told me that what happens to a person is less important than what the person does with it, and that creative results can come from even the worst experience. The death of a child, I found, is the one thing that cannot fit into that philosophy. There is no way to explain it, and no way to find a creative result from it. There is only the relentless pain that never leaves one, ever.

In 1960, a few years before Anita fell ill, we had a third child; in a way, we saw her as the one who got delayed during the 1950s ordeal. We named her for Carl's mother, Elizabeth, and called her Beth. Sonia, my stepdaughter, was almost grown when the turmoil of the 1950s occurred and went on to live her own life and produce her own family. But all three of Carl's and my children lived their childhood under the shadow of the constant attacks on their parents, facing a world that must have seemed to them even more hostile than it did to us; sometimes it seemed that they could not turn on the TV set without seeing their parents depicted as villains. Sometimes they were penalized for who their parents were. For example, in high school our son Jim was rejected for membership in the National Honor Society—although his grades were excellent and he went on to become a Rhodes Scholar and win a full-tuition scholarship to Harvard Law School. We learned from people close to the process that the rejection was because he was the child of Carl and Anne Braden. We wanted to fight about that one, but Jim asked us not to, saying he would be embarrassed.

Also, as I look back, I realize that our household was one where there was almost constant tension, very little relaxation. People have often asked me whether I felt the kind of life we lived affected our children adversely. Of course it did, and I don't know how it could have been otherwise. A friend of mine said something some years back that stayed with me. "In the 1950s, there was a war, you know," she said. "It was a war of the U.S. government on its own people. And children of war, no matter what kind of war, bear scars."

For us, the war went on long after the 1950s. And I realize there were injuries and scars. I've had to tell myself over and over that part of life, part of growing up, is learning to cope with whatever difficulties present themselves, and that my children would work out their problems in their own ways. One always wonders if one could have done things differently to make it easier. And yet I have always come back to the knowledge that, in the time and place in which I found myself, I lived my life in the only way I could have lived it.

I also had to remind myself over and over of that same proposition in relation to my parents. The ongoing strain between us was a never-ending source of pain—for them and for me. The small channels of honest communication that began to open between us during the pressure of the 1950s case seemed to close again rather quickly. They were deeply hurt when Carl and I did not fade into a more "normal" life after the case ended. They were constantly and excruciatingly embarrassed whenever my name surfaced in the papers in Alabama in connection with some new attack. My mother wrote me once: "Just stay out of Alabama. You can have the rest of the country, but leave us Alabama."

And yet they loved me, and I loved them, very much. I knew even then—as I related in this book—that my dilemma was not unique. A great many southern families have been divided by this issue. Many people, finding themselves totally at odds with family, just broke off connections. I never did that. I went to see them; I sent the children, whom they adored, for visits with them, often meeting in Nashville for this purpose, when my parents no longer wanted to come to our house because our neighborhood had changed to almost all African American. This furtiveness must have sent very mixed messages to our children. The continuing strain of the relationship was an ordeal for us all. And yet I still believe that I was right to maintain the relationship, and I am glad that I took this course.

Both my parents lived to be quite old, my mother dying in 1985 at age eighty-eight, and my father in 1987 at ninety-two. By that time, they had moved to Virginia to be near the place to which my brother had retired. I made many trips to see them in their final years; parents, no matter what has gone before, desperately want to see their children as they grow older. Not surprisingly, relationships mellowed considerably with their age. My mother, despite the embarrassment my activities caused her in an earlier period, I think was always proud of me, down in her deepest self. She thought I was quite misguided, yes; but she was always sure I had the highest of motives.

My father was much more rigid in his allegiance to philosophies of racism. Out of consideration to them when they were living, I did not say this when I wrote this book, but it was he who made the comment I quote in chapter 3 that so traumatized me—about how "we have to have a good lynching every once in a while to keep the nigger in his place."

Long before he moved to Virginia, we had agreed we just would not discuss race or anything related to it anymore—although he continued to make a habit of sitting down at the breakfast table and saying, "Now we are not going to have an argument, but I just want to say one thing." At that point, of course, I was supposed to listen and remain silent, which I rarely did.

But some of the things I saw happen to my father in his very old age were almost unbelievable. I recall an occasion after my mother fell and broke her hip. Daddy almost had a heart attack when he saw the hospital bill. He did not have to pay any of it, because Medicare covered most of it, and he had supplemental insurance. But he said to me: "What did people do before there was Medicare?" I told him I didn't know, and then, although something told me I should keep quiet, added: "Now, Daddy, I don't want to start an argument, but I'd like to point out to you that Medicare is something the civil rights movement got for you." (Which it was, like all the humane legislation of the 1960s.) He thought a minute and then said, "I guess you're right."

A few years later, after my mother died, when my father was a very feeble ninety-one, he got on an airplane alone and came to Louisville. He came because he wanted to meet his three-year-old great granddaughter, my Beth's child, and circumstances prevented her from making the trip the other way. Beth's daughter is biracial, and my father knew that, but he came. He and the child, of course, loved each other, and that is not surprising. What is surprising is the fact that he came. He never met my daughter's second biracial child or her African American husband in person, but he later talked with him on the phone a few times. I can remember the night he telephoned me from Virginia and said, among other things; "I tried to call Beth; she wasn't home, but I talked with Henry. Had a very satisfactory conversation. At least, it seemed satisfactory to me. I hope it seemed that way to him."

I could hardly believe my ears. This man, with his rigid, violent views. Born in 1894, he had lived through almost a century of social change that had an impact on him personally in ways that most people of his station in life never encountered. It seemed almost like a miracle. Of course he had not changed his racist views; that would have been asking, I think, more than was possible. But he was a very kind man, and he loved his family more than anything in the world. Somehow, in the end, that made whatever they did almost all right.

It took Louisville longer to get over the events of the Wade/Braden situation of the 1950s than it did us. The fury against us persisted unabated at least until the early 1970s, and somewhat even after that. When Carl died in 1975, *The Courier-Journal* wrote an editorial about him, generally saying some of the favorable things one must say of the dead and noting that a community must be able to "tolerate" the kind of "zealot" he had been. But even then, the editors felt the necessity to say again, twenty years later, that his actions in 1954 concerning the Wade house had been no doing of the newspaper.

Through all those intervening years, we had always known that there were people in town whose blood pressure shot up when they heard the name "Braden." Although neither Carl nor I ever ran for public office, and never intended to, it seemed that there was never an election in which some candidate did not run against us. Carl used to say he could always tell when a candidate was losing, because at that point he or she began accusing the opponent of associating with us. Most often, the opponent was someone we had never met. When we moved the headquarters of SCEF to Louisville in the mid-1960s, the winning candidate for governor the next year ran on a platform that promised to run the Bradens and SCEF out of Kentucky.

We learned to live with these constant attacks, for we came to understand what it means to be a symbol. Most of the people who hated us so intensely had never met us, so we knew their hatred had nothing to do with us; rather it reflected a problem of their own, and a desperate need for a scapegoat for Louisville's and the nation's problems. I began to call the entire syndrome the "Braden sickness."

Its main practical effect on us was in the continuing erection of barriers to our organizing anything effective. Even so-called "white liberals" were reluctant to have their efforts associated with us, since they felt that our participation would be the "kiss of death." I recall conversations with a young white Presbyterian minister who moved to Louisville and immediately looked us up because some of our friends elsewhere had suggested that he do so. We were kindred spirits right away, and he professed a desire to work with us. By then it was the mid-1960s. I warned the new minister that he would soon find people who would tell him to stay away from us. "Oh, it can't be that bad," he said. It was only a few weeks later that this same minister came into the SCEF office, ashen-faced and looking as if he had seen a ghost. "I just couldn't believe it," he said. "I've lived in a number of places, and I've never seen anything like this." He had been in a meeting that day, some embryonic coalition effort around an issue of civil rights. Those attending, he said, instead of talking about the work at hand, had spent several hours discussing how they could ensure that the Bradens did not get involved. It was a coalition we had not even thought of trying to join. We were too busy at that point with SCEF work throughout the South.

I know many people across the country who during the 1950s were under attacks as vitriolic as those directed at us. And yet I too find it hard to think of an instance where this kind of animosity continued so long against the same people. The only way I've ever been able to explain it is by observing that, in most instances, the targets of attack either moved away or fell into inactivity. Witches are supposed at least to disappear. We didn't. We stayed, and we continued active.

I took a step toward defying the ostracism when in the early 1960s I suggested to an African American friend that we form an organization to try to keep the West End integrated. I had sat and watched in the late 1950s, feeling there was nothing I could personally do as real estate agents profited by scaring most of the white people out of one section of the West End. At that time, I visited various white ministers in the area, suggesting that they do what I could not. They all agreed the situation was deplorable, but they said it was a very hard issue— and they did nothing. In the early 1960s, when the real estate people started the same process in another part of the West End, I decided I would not sit by this time. My friend and I did indeed start the West End Community Council. It became quite viable—for several years projecting a message to West End whites that we welcomed Blacks as they moved into our neighborhoods and that we intended to stay and help build a truly interracial community. Ultimately, this effort failed—as have similar ones across the country—because the pressures were too great. Even we knew that each time we persuaded a white family to stay we were taking a house off the market that was needed by Blacks who had no other place to go. The West End Community Council eventually became an organization seeking to solve neighborhood problems and get attention to the area from City Hall, and it became the sparkplug for the citywide movement that finally passed an Open Housing law in the late 1960s.

At one point, however, there was a crisis when the West End Community Council obtained some of the early money from the federal anti-poverty program for its work. A congressman got upset about this and tried to get the funds cut off because of my connection with the organization. That resulted in a soul-searching session by the council board that lasted long after midnight as these people (all of whom were my good friends) tried to decide whether I should leave the organization to "protect" it. Finally, a Catholic nun, who had sat silent during most of the evening, said: "If you can put Anne Braden out because she's supposed to be a Communist, then you would put me out because I'm Catholic. I can't go along with this. If Anne leaves, I will leave." That settled the matter; the council fought for and retained its funds. The question never came up in that group again.

Finally, in the late 1960s, the fear of us seemed to us to be less pervasive because a new generation of social justice activists had arisen. These young people did not remember the 1950s, and if they had heard of the events then they figured that whatever we had been involved in must have conferred some wisdom upon us. They began to seek us out, and the SCEF headquarters became a center of the civil rights and anti-war activities of that period. Our own small house became something of a "Freedom House" for people traveling between North and South. Sometimes visitors stayed for weeks, and on many nights I had to count to determine whether there would be ten or fifteen people for supper.

But in 1975, after Carl's death, another crisis erupted in Louisville around the issue of racism, when a federal judge ordered cross-county busing to change the community's school desegregation program from the tokenism that had prevailed since the mid-1950s. It was the year after a similar crisis in Boston, and in Louisville, too, there arose a mass antibusing movement and mobs gathered in the street. Even then, some people told me to stay out of things to "protect" them, but I didn't. Indeed, public officials who opposed the busing program publicly cited my presence at hearings as the source of the problem. But a group of which I was a part organized an effective counter-movement in the white community, and over about two years the hysteria quieted, and busing seemed to become an accepted part of the scenery. Later developments undermined it, and today racism within the schools remains a critical problem on the local agenda. But at least, in distinction from twenty years before, by 1975 there were significant numbers of white people willing to act against at least the most violent forms of racism.

This change is what I think of when people ask me, as they often do, whether I think what happened in Louisville in the 1950s could happen again. What happened to the Wades surely could—if not in Louisville or Shively, certainly in other parts of Kentucky. In the 1980s, the ABC crew that visited Louisville filmed me telling the 1954 story to a predominantly white class of high school students in Shively. I asked these young people whether *they* thought it could happen again. Several embarrassed students told how African Americans had been driven from their neighborhoods by constant harassment. And it was not very many years ago that the house of an African American family was firebombed in the same general part of the county where Shively is located, although much farther from town. Although the family escaped injury, they felt they had to move.

The difference from 1954, however, was that on two days' notice some of us organized a mass delegation to the bombed home of that family, and over two hundred people came, many of them white. Ultimately a man was arrested for that incident and sent to prison. What happened to Carl and me in the 1950s probably could not happen now. One thing that provoked the attack on us was that so few white people were speaking out then, and we stood out like sore thumbs. Now, although the whites actively opposing racism are still tragically in the minority—and we need many, many more—the numbers are significant. And despite all the discouraging new manifestations of overt racism that we have seen in recent years, I believe those numbers are growing. That difference, I think, provides hope, in Louisville and in other places where I work today in the South, and where I visit in other parts of the nation.

Vestiges of the "Braden sickness" continued to plague me through most of the 1980s. For example, there were a number of times when some people refused to appear on a program if I was going to speak. In 1984, when I was elected a delegate for Jesse Jackson to the Democratic National Convention, state leaders of the Democratic Party apparently suffered severe shock and telephoned the Jackson caucus with some technicality about gender balance they said would preclude my serving. The caucus handled that by making me an alternate delegate instead. Thus I attended the convention in 1984 and became a delegate to the 1988 convention.

In the early 1990s, the "Braden sickness" seemed to play itself out. If there are still people around whose blood pressure climbs when they hear my name, I don't hear about them. My activities are no longer hampered because people fear to associate with me. In addition to my southern regional activities with the Southern Organizing Committee, I am today very active in social justice movements in Louisville. In fact, I have more demands on my time than I can possibly handle. For two semesters now, I have served as visiting professor at Northern Kentucky University, where I've taught a class on civil rights history in a building named for the former governor of the state who, during his 1960s campaign, vowed he'd run Carl and Anne Braden out of Kentucky.

In Louisville, I work mainly with the Kentucky Alliance against Racist and Political Repression, an organization that brings people of color and whites together for action against racism, and the local Rainbow Coalition. And, perhaps returning to my roots, I have become quite active in St. George's Episcopal Church, a small but very active predominantly African American church that runs a vital community center in the West End. I still live in the house Carl and I bought in 1952.

Recently, people suddenly began to give me awards. Someone said I had been transformed "from a pariah into a heroine." I have an idea that most of the people who give the awards have no notion what I ever did or did not do but figure anyone who has been around as long as I have must have done something. This development has all been a very disconcerting experience for me. I learned long ago how to handle attacks; I haven't yet quite learned how to handle awards. But I suppose it happens, if one lives long enough. Carl did not live long enough for it to happen to him.

As I look back now on those 1954 events, one thing that strikes me sharply is how different things seem from the vantage point of advancing age. When Carl was convicted and sentenced to fifteen years in prison, when I faced the prospect of a trial likely to bring the same results, I felt that the worst possible thing had happened to me, and that my life was over. Now, looking back, I see this set of events as the best thing that ever happened to me and in a real sense the beginning of my life. I often point this out in talking with young people. When bad things happen to you because of the things you stand for, I tell them, when you lose friends, or lose a job, or go to jail, take time to reflect on how all this may look when you are in your seventies, or even in your sixties.

For me the case in the 1950s opened up great new vistas. Through our fight-back in the immediately following years, we had the rare privilege of meeting people who were the salt of the country, those who were part of the resistance movement of that period, and we were able to help build that movement. From there, we were able to move into a role, however tenuous, in the great upsurges for justice in the 1960s.

Even more important for me personally was the fact that the case burned my bridges to a privileged past. There is a belief in many quarters that people like me can always "go back" when things get too rough. And I suppose for some this is true. But life made that decision for me. After this case, I could not have gone back if I had wanted to.

Another benefit that came to me, although it may seem a strange one, was that I had the humbling (or perhaps "leveling" is a better word) experience of rejection, of being part-pariah, even among people on "my side" of the social struggle. In social justice movements, especially in intense times, people are sometimes made into heroes and heroines, and paradoxically this can create all kinds of problems for them. Especially in the southern civil rights movement in the days in which I became active, this status was sometimes accorded white activists. I was never accorded that status; my subversive label precluded it. I think that saved me from some problems that some whites in the movement had later when the Black Power movement of the mid-1960s suggested to them that they weren't needed or wanted in organizations of African Americans, and that, although they had important roles to play in the struggle against racism, those roles were elsewhere. Lots of hurt feelings resulted as people felt rejected. It didn't bother me; I had been rejected too many times before. Thus, I (and others in a somewhat similar position) were able to look more objectively at the significance of the Black Power movement. We in SCEF, an interracial organization, strongly supported that movement. We saw it as a healthy development, a thrust forward for our region and the country, one that would ultimately increase rather than decrease the possibility of building strong, honest, and viable coalitions across the color line. I think history has proved us right in that analysis.

But even as I count the blessings that accrued to me as a result of the 1950s experience, I come face-to-face with what to me is the most profound lesson of the whole affair. Although the 1950s case turned out to be a very positive thing in my life (and I think in Carl's), it definitely did not have this effect in the life of the Wades. They survived, true, but they were never able to move back to that house, or any other like it, and many of their dreams were shattered.

When our fight-back first began, during that summer of 1954, before and after the bombing, the struggle around the house on Rone Court was known as the "Wade Case." After our indictment, people began calling it the "Wade-Braden Case." And that's what we always called it. But gradually over those years, and across the country, it became known as the "Braden Case." It is distressing to me, even now, to realize that, among many of the white people who poured out their support for us, it was apparently of more consequence that a white man had been unjustly sentenced to fifteen years in prison than that an African American family had been denied a house to live in.

We tried to resist this by always talking first and last about the house and the issue of segregation. I have wondered in recent years if there was something more we could have done to stop this gradual but decisive change in emphasis. I do not know.

This circumstance, however, leads me back almost to where I started this journey so long ago in Alabama, to the burning awareness of the depth of the evil that plagues our society, to a continuing burning knowledge that we must root it out.

In recent years, I have been asked to speak to varied audiences, both young and old, about the case in Louisville, its meaning for today and the ongoing struggle against racism. I have sometimes wearied of telling the story—and found myself embarrassed that I was being presented as some kind of expert on racism, not really because of what I had done but because of what some people had decided to do to me. I usually start with a disclaimer, telling my listeners to disabuse themselves of any idea that I am presenting myself as a white person who has totally escaped the monster of racism. I have been fighting this thing consciously for fifty years, but I know that even today I sometimes do and say things that are destructive because I still see the world through at least partly white eyes—and black eyes see the world very differently. Furthermore, even in the long years when I was the object of vicious attack, there were always certain advantages that came to me because I was white. There is a corruption that comes with such advantage that cramps the soul. And I think no white people in a society founded on racism ever totally free themselves from this prison.

But I always tell whites that they should not sit around feeling guilty about all this. Guilt is a debilitating emotion. The challenge to us as whites is to try to understand what racism is and what it has done, not just to us personally, but to the society we live in, and then to do something about it—about very specific manifestations of it in the here and now.

Finally, I have come to the conclusion that southern whites of my generation perhaps have something to say that the rest of this country needs to hear and heed. This is really why I wanted this book republished.

We who came to maturity when the South was totally segregated and ruled by terror had to turn ourselves inside out to deal with this question. Things were so stark in those days that there was no way to paper them over. Either we had to face them and turn our values and assumptions upside down—or end up with our souls and lives twisted and destroyed from within.

And I believe that what I and other white southerners went through in earlier times is a microcosm of what this entire nation must do. It must turn itself inside out, and turn its values, assumptions—*and* policies—upside down. So far the country has only picked around the edges of the problem.

Those of us involved in social struggle in the South during the second half of the twentieth century learned many things. In the 1940s and 1950s, I like many others, both African American and white, thought the problem was mainly one of our region. We learned that this was an illusion and that the same problem, although in different form, permeated the entire country. In those days, we talked about "segregation" as the problem. But our movement killed Jim Crow; that is, we did indeed destroy segregation enforced by law. Doing so was no small accomplishment, one achieved by the blood and sacrifice of many people. But we found that, even after that, the evil still existed. We learned to call it "racism," and later, more accurately, "white supremacy." We learned that the real problem was (and is) the assumption that everything should be run by white people for the benefit of whites, which is actually how I define racism. And we came to realize that the process of integration, even desegregation, often failed because African Americans on the one hand, and whites on the other, had very different concepts of the struggle against segregation. To African Americans, this struggle sought freedom, dignity, liberation; for many whites, it meant people of color being absorbed into "their" white world, which whites would still run.

And, as we began to understand all this better, we came to a deeper understanding of how this assumption—that everything should be run by whites and for their benefit—was the assumption on which this nation had been founded. We began to understand that it was this assumption that, from the beginning, corrupted the country's shining ideals of freedom and democracy. It was this assumption that enabled the European invaders to commit genocide against the Native Americans without ever realizing they had committed a crime. It was this assumption that justified the enslavement of Africans, the theft of land from Chicanos in the Southwest, and the confiscation of the labor of Asians who came and built our railroads.

Furthermore, we began to see that this assumption that white people should run everything for their own benefit has led the whites who run this particular country to assume that they should also run the world for their own benefit. Thus, the six-sevenths of the world's population who are non-white are considered expendable. This kind of thinking has led to national policies that have sought to dominate the world by military force while basic needs of all people at home are neglected. And it has led our national policy-makers to surrender decision-making powers to huge faceless global corporations that care nothing about people of any color.

When they realize all this, some people feel overwhelmed by the enormous nature of the evil and doubt that anything can be done about it. But we who grew up white southerners two and three generations ago learned something else the whole society needs to ponder. We found that when we turned ourselves inside out to face the truth, it was a painful process, but it was not destructive. Rather, it became a moment of rebirth—and opened up new creative vistas in our lives.

This too, I believe, is in microcosm what can happen to the whole society. We saw it begin to happen in a very tentative way as movements of African Americans shook the nation in the 1960s. But the process was cut short, as the nation as a whole drew back from commitment to racial justice and therefore from its moment of truth. I am convinced, however, that this awakening must happen again in a more far-reaching way, and that it can.

I came into social justice movements at the height of the repression of the Cold War period. The labor movement was being decimated by anti-Communist hysteria; the CIO's "Operation Dixie," which had set out to organize the South, lay shipwrecked on this division. Organizations seeking civil rights, peace, and justice had been crushed everywhere. People were being told that social change groups were subversive, and many stayed away. First Communists, and then many others, were fired from their jobs, careers were destroyed, many people went to jail, and some committed suicide. Most people became afraid to speak, to meet, to organize; the "Silent '50s" descended. And although I discovered in those years that there was always a resistance movement, many people did indeed fall into silence and inactivity; social problems festered that still plague us today.

But the one thing that could not be crushed was a burning desire of African Americans to be free. Suddenly, in the depth of this repression, and in what might have seemed the most unlikely place in the country, the capitol of the Confederacy, Montgomery, Alabama, a new movement arose. The long years of work by African Americans in Montgomery— mostly women,[5] and people like the Pullman porter and unionist E. D. Nixon—came to fruition on December 1, 1955, when Rosa Parks refused to move on that bus. That day was really the beginning of the end of the 1950s. From there, the movement began to ignite the South. When the student movement arose among young African Americans in 1960 the region was on fire, and the flames fanned out across the country. The movement of African Americans in the South, ultimately joined by an increasing number of white people, won victories that many would have said were impossible just a few years earlier, tearing down the walls of Jim Crow and establishing the universal right to vote, at least on paper. It also changed the atmosphere in the country, broke the pall of the 1950s, opened up everything in our society to question, and made it possible for all people seeking justice to make their voices heard. It brought longstanding struggles of Latinos and Native Americans to the nation's center stage. And it set in motion the mass antiwar movement of the 1960s, the new women's movement, new openings for workers to organize unions in the South—and later movements of other oppressed people seeking full rights: the disabled, lesbians and gays, environmentalists seeking to save our earth from destruction.

Bob Moses, the architect of the 1960s voting rights movement that shook the country from Mississippi, made a profound comment in that period. I quoted it in a pamphlet I wrote on HUAC and the civil rights movement in 1964, and it has stayed with me through the years. He said:

> The Negro seeks his own place within the existing institutional framework, but to accommodate him society will have to modify its institutions—and in many cases make far-reaching fundamental changes. . . . The struggle for jobs for Negroes forces questions about the ability of the economy to provide jobs for everyone within our present socio-economic structure; lack of legal counsel for Negroes brings into focus the general lack of legal counsel for the poor. . . . *The function of the white American is not so much to prepare the Negro for entrance into the larger society—but to prepare society for the changes it must make to include Negroes.*

Truly, as African Americans moved for freedom in the 1960s, it was as if the foundation stone of a building shifted, and the whole structure shook. That movement never achieved political power in that decade, but for a few shining years it was setting the agenda of the country. And the agenda was a humane one that held out the promise of a better life for everyone.

Some years ago, I did an oral history interview with the Rev. C. T. Vivian, who was one of Martin Luther King's top aides and who has long been a friend and co-worker of mine. C. T. put his analysis of the 1960s in theological terms, and I think it is valid. "You know it is really true," he said, "what it says in the Bible, that a person must repent of his sins before he can be saved. That's true of a nation, too. What really happened in the 1960s was that this nation as a whole took just the first step toward admitting it had been wrong on race. The result was an explosion of creativity that burst forth everywhere."

That is what happened. And people in power who felt threatened by these new upsurges became very frightened. They moved in many ways to stop the escalating movements. And they knew, perhaps better than some people working for social justice, that the root of their problem lay in the African American freedom movement, as well as in similar movements among Latinos and Native Americans. They acted to destroy those movements. During that intense period of repression, the late 1960s— ignored by too many white people at the time, and today ignored by many historians—Black Panthers were crushed and murdered all over the country; organizations were destroyed by COINTELPRO operations, and activists were framed on a wide assortment of contrived charges. I do not have first-hand knowledge of what happened elsewhere in the country, but I saw with my own eyes what was happening in the South. I was traveling the region then for *The Southern Patriot,* and one could visit hardly any community where the Black organizers (not necessarily the recognized spokespeople, but those doing the organizing) were not either in jail, on their way, or just out by dint of much local struggle. The attack was massive.

No people's movement is ever totally destroyed, and the seeds planted by this one lived on to take new root another day. But there is no doubt that the African American movement was blunted at a critical moment—just as it was launching major offensives for economic justice, the issue which remains today the unfinished business of the 1960s revolution.

Meantime, there was a tremendous propaganda assault on the minds of white people. More and more in the late 1960s, we began to read in the mainstream media about the "white backlash." Of course there was white resistance to change; there always had been. But actually by the late 1960s more and more whites were joining our movement. In fact, at the very time when the "white backlash" was receiving so much media attention, public opinion polls were showing that a greatly increased number of white people favored measures to ensure equal justice and opportunity (including affirmative action) for people of color.[6]

Soon white people were hearing—from the media, from academics, and later from the government itself—that what African Americans had gained had taken something away from them. The exact opposite was true. Everything Blacks had won had benefited most of the people in the country. Every piece of legislation that addressed injustice—no matter how inadequate those of us in the movement thought they all were at the time—benefited whites too, especially poor and working-class whites. For example, job programs were set up, and young unemployed whites got jobs too. Blacks demanded access to education, and scholarship programs opened college doors to masses of young whites, as well as African Americans.

But the dominant propaganda said otherwise, and soon whites were hearing they were victims of something called "reverse discrimination," the idea that Blacks had won "too much" and now it was whites who were discriminated against. I believe the most pernicious danger our country faces today is the widespread acceptance of this myth. And over the decade of the 1970s, as so many whites were led to feel threatened, a total reversal in the mood of the country occurred—from one that encouraged cooperative effort and the solving of social problems by collective efforts that would benefit everyone, to an atmosphere that encouraged each man and woman to turn inward and seek to solve problems for self alone, in private backyards, far from the arena of public issues.

Some civil rights advocates blame the administration of Ronald Reagan for the backward drive to reverse the gains of the 1960s. I think it worked the other way around. The attack on the African American movement that began in the late 1960s and the campaign for the minds of this nation's white people that permeated the 1970s created the base that put the Reagan administration in power and dictated that the 1980s would be a time when everyone would be encouraged to "get what you can for yourself alone."

New movements erupted in the 1980s, antiracist action to counter the growth of new hate groups, the mass movements formed in response to the two Jesse Jackson presidential campaigns, new stirrings of organizing within the labor movement. But as we moved into the 1990s, the visions of a new and just society that had fired the 1960s had been narrowed so far that even the most minor reforms—for example, the addition of more Head Start programs, important but a far cry from the needed massive overhaul and expansion of our educational system—seemed like great victories.

So we stand on the verge of the twenty-first century with a significant new black middle class produced by the decades of struggle—but with the great masses of African Americans living in poverty, with hopelessness destroying a generation of youth, and the poor being told they are the cause of their own problems. The truth is that this society has not yet done what Bob Moses said in 1964 it must do—make the changes necessary to make room for African Americans. According to every statistical table, people of color have only half as much of the good things of life as whites (things like housing, health care, jobs, educational opportunity, income) and twice or three times as much of the bad things (like infant mortality, slums, unemployment—*and* prison cells). In effect, it is as if our society has decided, although no one would ever say this and no legislative body would ever pass a law decreeing it, that a person of color is only 50 percent of a human being.

Because this society has never "made room" for African Americans, it is moving toward a situation in which it really does not have room for people of any color. The new global economy is being built on the cheap labor of people of color around the world, while fewer and fewer opportunities exist for masses of people of color *and* whites at home. Today, statistics tell us that 1 percent of American households own the same amount of wealth as the total owned by the 92 percent at the other end of the scale. Between 1979 and 1997, the poorest one-fifth of U.S. families saw their real income decline by 7 percent, while the income of the top 20 percent increased by 34 percent and the top 1 percent by 106 percent. The average corporate executive in this country now receives income 326 times that of the average factory worker's pay, and 728 times the annual income of a person working for the minimum wage. In other industrialized countries, this ratio of executive to factory worker is about 21 to 1; in this country in 1970, it was 41 to 1. "The rich get richer, and the poor get poorer" is a cliche, but it describes our society today, and there is really no other way to say it. This disparity has led to the collapse of many societies.[7]

A new massive thrust toward racial justice will not by itself solve all the problems that face us, but I am convinced that, unless such a thrust develops—one that is global in its outlook—the other problems will *not* be solved. As long as people of color can be written off as expendable, and therefore acceptable victims of the most extreme inequities, none of the basic injustices in our society will be addressed; they will only get worse.

Until a huge new crusade for racial justice develops, the white people who today are asking "What can I do"—and there are many of them—can help hasten that day by taking visible stands against specific manifestations of racism in their communities. In so doing, they create a break in what sometimes seems to be a solid wall of white resistance to justice—and often even a refusal to admit that a problem still exists. It helps to create a pole to which other whites can gravitate when the time comes that they realize they must act. We need to create in our communities what I call an "antiracist majority." Today we hear much talk about the need for "dialogue." That is all right, but dialogue alone, without visible action, will not move us toward real change.

Unfortunately, it is not likely that white people in significant numbers will take such action on their own initiative. They will do it as they began to do it in the 1960s when organized mass movements of people of color force them to face unpleasant truths. I have hope today because I see arising at the grassroots in myriad local communities new movements of people of color demanding justice—certainly in the South, which I know best, and I think in the rest of the country as well, not only among African Americans but among Native Americans, Latinos, and Asian Americans, with new bridges being built between these groups. And people are "thinking globally as they act locally."

Right now, there is no cohesive force bringing these localized movements together in a united crusade. Mass movements always come as the product of long years of mundane work by unsung heroes, but no one can predict when the upsurge will crystallize. No one could have predicted that it would happen in 1955 in Montgomery. We cannot predict today when it will happen again, and I am not at all sure I will live to see it. But as surely as I know that dawn will come tomorrow morning, I am convinced that it will happen. And when it does, a huge question will be how many white people will understand that this upsurge holds hope for their lives, too, and will therefore go through the personal metamorphosis that will be needed to join this new movement.

In the meantime, we do have control over the space we choose to occupy as the long struggle goes on. Sometimes people ask me how I've managed to stay active so long for the things I believe in. My first answer is that I don't understand how anyone can "drop out" as long as the need is there. Carl used to paraphrase the Bible and say, "When you put your hand to the plow, you cannot look back." I think that is true. But I've never felt that I was making any particular sacrifice; in all the movements in which I've been involved, I've gained much more, spiritually, than I was able to give. I've lived my life as I've wanted to live it, and it has been filled with a special kind of joy.

A long time ago, before the Louisville case, I met briefly one of the great African American leaders of an earlier generation, William L. Patterson, who in the late 1940s and 1950s headed the Civil Right Congress. I became peripherally involved in some of the work of CRC, and at one point I wrote to Patterson about this activity. For reasons I have never fathomed, this busy man took time to write me a long letter in reply—me, a young white woman from Alabama, not quite dry behind the ears, who must have seemed to him somewhat racist at the time.

One thing he said in that letter was exactly what I needed to hear at that moment, and it has a stayed with me all these years. "You don't have to be part of the world of the lynchers," he wrote, "or a part of those who deny justice. You do have a choice. You can join the other America."

He went on to say that this "other America" had always been here and has included whites as well as people of color—the people who fought *against* slavery, *against* oppression, *against* the inhumanity of people to their fellow human beings. This "other America," he pointed out, still existed, and it was open to me.

Since then, I've been a member of many organizations, but what I really felt I joined, and have never left, is that "other America." Everyone needs roots, a home. I had to separate myself from roots in the corrupt society I was born into; I found a new home in the "other America," in its current incarnation in the social justice movements of my time, and in the sense of connection to a past and future. More than anything else, this sense of home and this connection have given me the strength to keep going, feeling that in my small way I am a part of a long chain of humanity, a chain of struggle that stretches far into the past, long before I was here, and will go into the future, long after I'm gone.

I believe that in this society—shot through with injustice as it is—this "other America" is the only place where one can live a fulfilling life.

Louisville, Kentucky
February 1999

Notes

1. The Abraham Lincoln Brigade was the mobilization that took three thousand Americans to Spain in the 1930s to join the struggle against fascist overthrow of the elected government there. In the Cold War years, its veterans' organization was labeled a Communist front and vilified.

2. The story of Jim Dombrowski's life and work is told in a book by Frank T. Adams, *James A. Dombrowski: An American Heretic, 1897–1983* (University of Tennessee Press, 1992).

3. The case that SCEF won in a U.S. Supreme Court decision on April 25, 1965, was styled legally as *Dombrowski vs. Pfister* and became widely known among activists and lawyers alike as the "Dombrowski Case." In it, the court upheld a doctrine developed by the lawyer who represented SCEF, the noted civil rights attorney Arthur Kinoy. In lay language, this doctrine held that, when state criminal actions threaten to have a "chilling effect" on First Amendment rights, the federal courts have a duty to step in and stop an injustice before it happens. The decision was used in many cases involving civil rights activists in the 1960s, including our second sedition case in Kentucky, recounted in this epilogue. Subsequent Supreme Court decisions have gutted the 1965 decision.

(For more discussion of the Dombrowski case, see Adams, *James A. Dombrowski,* 276–78 and 332 note 22.)

4. COINTELPRO, or Counter-Intelligence Program, was the FBI campaign that sought to discredit and disrupt people's organizations it considered dangerous to the country. In the 1960s and early 1970s, it especially targeted civil rights and African American organizations. For more information on this program, see Ward Churchill and James Vander Wall, *COINTELPRO Papers: Documents from the FBI's Secret Wars against Dissent in the United States* (South End Press, 1990); Nelson Blackstock, *Cointelpro: The FBI's Secret War on Political Freedom* (Pathfinder Press, 1988); and Kenneth O'Reilly, *Racial Matters: The FBI's Secret File on Black America, 1960–1972* (Free Press, 1989).

5. For a first-hand account of the women who pioneered the civil rights movement in Montgomery and who were the heart and soul of the bus boycott, see Jo Ann Gibson Robinson, *The Montgomery Bus Boycott and the Women Who Started It* (University of Tennessee Press, 1987).

6. For a summary of what public opinion polls revealed in the late 1960s and one of the best analyses I have ever read of the 90-degree turn in the nation's policies between the mid-1960s and the early 1980s, see chapters 1 and 2 of *The Rainbow Challenge,* a book by Sheila Collins on the 1984 Jesse Jackson campaign (Monthly Review Press, 1986).

7. The statistics quoted here were provided by United for a Fair Economy in Boston and Campaign for America's Future, Washington, and come from U.S. Census reports and *Business Week.*

Date Due

JY 23			